"A Woman's Place Is in the Kitchen"

"A Woman's Place Is in the Kitchen"

The Evolution of Women Chefs

Ann Cooper

VNR Van Nostrand Reinhold
I(T)P® A Division of International Thomson Publishing Inc.

New York • Albany • Bonn • Boston • Detroit • London • Madrid • Melbourne
Mexico City • Paris • San Francisco • Singapore • Tokyo • Toronto

The women chefs whose photographs appear on the cover and on chapter openers in the text are identified on pages 313–314, which are an extension of this copyright page.

Chef Photo Credits   Jody Adams (p.53)—credit: Mr. Fran Collin. Judi Arnold (p.85)—credit: Charles R. Dean. Alison Awerbuch (p.115)—credit: Don Beatty Photo. Julia Child (p.53)—credit: Michael McLaughlin. Hilary DeMane (p.115)—credit: Frank Flavin. Raji Jallepalli (p. 53). Katy Keck (p.115)—credit: Carol Gillot Photography. Katy Keck (p.115)—credit: Robin X Photography. Shirley King (p.195)—credit: Becket Logan. Susan McCreight Lindeborg (p.27)—credit: Patricia Satterlee. Corinna Mozo (p.53)—credit: Andrew Ryan 1995. Traci Des Jardins (p.27)—credit: Frankie Fraukeney. Barbara Tropp (p.145)—credit: John Vaughan. Deborah Madison (p.53)—credit: Dominique Vobillon. Nora Pouillon (p.27)—credit: Gozen Koshida.

Library of Congress Cataloging-in-Publication Data

Cooper, Ann.
    A woman's place is in the kitchen : The evolution of women chefs/
  by Ann Cooper
        p.   cm.
    Includes bibliographical references and index.
    ISBN 0-442-02370-7
    1. Women cooks — United States —History. 2. Cookery — United States. 3. Women cooks — Biography. I. Title.
    TX649.A1C66   1997
    641.5'082—dc21   97–17963
                                                                CIP

http://www.vnr.com
product discounts • free email newsletters
software demos • online resources

email: info@vnr.com

A service of I(T)P®

To all the women throughout the ages who have cooked the food that has fed us all, thank you. To all the mothers, sisters, aunts, grandmothers, and cousins who taught us how to cook, thank you. And to all the women in the culinary field today and in the future: May you always cook with passion, have fire in your heart, and find a way to live your dreams.

Contents

Preface *xi*

Acknowledgments *xv*

The Scope and Methodology of the Book *xix*

CHAPTER ONE
The History of Women in the Kitchen: An Evolutionary Tale *1*

Women: In the Beginning *2*
Women in America: Reentering the Kitchen *7*
The Changing Role of Women from the Industrial Era Through the Early
    1900s *9*
The Beginnings of Cooking as a Profession *12*
Women and Their Cookbooks *13*
Women and Their Cooking Schools *20*
Women Working Their Way into the Professional Kitchen *22*
Women Making Their Mark in the Restaurant Business *25*

WOMEN IN THE CULINARY ARENA:
Fannie Merritt Farmer *15*
Ellen Swallow Richards *23*

CHAPTER TWO
The Passion of Women Chefs *27*

What Is a Chef? *28*
Driving Forces Behind Women's Desire to Become Chefs *33*
Becoming a Chef *39*
Being the Chef *41*

WOMEN IN THE CULINARY ARENA:
Edna Lewis   *34*
Madeleine Kamman   *43*

CHAPTER THREE
Women Chefs: Their Influences, Choices, and Sacrifices   *53*

Cultural Influences on Women and Their Food   *54*
The Art of Mentoring: Role Models of Women Chefs   *58*
The Influence of Education and Apprenticeship Programs   *64*
Making Decisions—Wading Through the Choices   *70*
Choosing to Make Personal Sacrifices   *81*
Sacrifices That Cost Women Their Marriages or Relationships   *83*

WOMEN IN THE CULINARY ARENA:
Alice Waters   *60*
Lydia Shire   *63*
Julia Child   *67*

CHAPTER FOUR
Challenges That Women Face in the Culinary Arena   *85*

Why Women Have Been Excluded   *86*
Women Confronting Discrimination   *90*
Substance Abuse in the Industry   *96*
Owning a Restaurant   *97*
Dealing with Health Issues   *100*
Being Older in a Young Kitchen   *103*
The Peter Principal at Work   *105*
Working in Remote Locations   *106*
The Power of the Press   *107*
Taking Risks   *110*
Setting Limits   *112*

WOMEN IN THE CULINARY ARENA:
Suzanne Bussiere   *102*
Leslie Revsin   *108*

CHAPTER FIVE
Work: Women's Roles in the Kitchen   *115*

Overview of Who's Working in the Industry   *116*
Women Working in the Kitchen   *116*

Owning and Operating a Food Business   *127*
Management and Work Styles of Women and Men   *137*
Women's and Men's Food Creations   *142*

WOMEN IN THE CULINARY ARENA:
Lidia Bastianich   *128*
Mary Sue Milliken and Susan Feniger   *132*

CHAPTER SIX
On Achieving Success: What It Means to Women in the Culinary
Arena   *145*

Defining Success and Knowing When You Have Arrived   *146*
Finding a Balance Between Success and Family   *159*
Finding the Balance Between Success and Personal Life   *162*

WOMEN IN THE CULINARY ARENA:
Barbara Tropp   *158*
Anne Rosenzweig   *164*

CHAPTER SEVEN
Women Chefs: Our Goals and Responsibilities   *169*

Goals for the Future   *170*
Women's Perspectives on Goals for the Workplace   *172*
What It Means to Be a Mentor   *177*
Using Organizations for Networking   *180*
Women and Their Involvement in Socially Responsible Causes   *185*

WOMEN IN THE CULINARY ARENA:
Barbara Sanders   *179*
Pat Thibodeau   *189*

CHAPTER EIGHT
Women and Their Future in the Culinary World   *195*

Future Trends   *196*
Changing the Arena   *205*
Advice for the Next Generation   *214*
How Can We Effect Change?   *219*

WOMEN IN THE CULINARY ARENA:
Pat Bartholomew   *204*
Tracy Cundiff   *207*

APPENDIX A
The Women Chefs' Biographies   *223*

APPENDIX B
Job Descriptions   *257*

APPENDIX C
Glossary   *261*

APPENDIX D
The Women Chefs' Recommended Reading List   *263*

APPENDIX E
A Sampling of Women Chefs and Their Restaurants Thoughout History   *269*

APPENDIX F
Survey Used in Research   *271*

APPENDIX G
Professional Organizations   *281*

Notes   *289*

Bibliography   *293*

Index   *303*

Identification of Women Chefs in Cover and Chapter-Opener Photographs   *313*

Preface

This book tells a story that needs to be told. In fact, it tells many stories of women in the culinary industry. It is about a number of women—chefs and cooks—who shared with me their passion for food, their struggles to be recognized and to get ahead, and their passion for their work. Their stories confirm something that I have believed deep in my heart for years, that indeed, "A woman's place *is* in the kitchen." I have wanted to tell this story for as long as I can remember, but I couldn't do it alone. With the help of the wonderful women throughout this book, the story has taken on a life of its own.

To understand my burning desire to tell this story I should begin with my own tale. It begins when I was seventeen years old. I decided to persue the life of a ski bum in Colorado. I hadn't graduated from high school, I had never had a job, and I had this sense that somehow, I would make it in the world. So, with my skis on my back and a couple hundred dollars in my pocket, I hitch-hiked out to Telluride, Colorado to find the snow and learn to ski. Arriving in town with no money, I started looking for work and talked my way into a position as an assistant breakfast cook at The Airport Bar and Grill. My culinary career was born.

From that assistant breakfast cook position, my life started to revolve around food, cooking, and restaurants. After two years and twice as many jobs, I started a baking company with a woman I met (another ski bum who went on to become a doctor), and we managed to make our living, for a number of years, by skiing all day and then baking until dawn. We taught ourselves everything; we bought books, gathered family recipes, and somehow, we just made it work. After a few years of baking and skiing, I eventually started to cook in the restaurants around town.

One day, five years later, I realized that there had to be life after skiing, so I decided to go to culinary school (no easy feat without a high school diploma). I talked to a number of people in the industry and was encouraged to apply to The Culinary Institute of America (CIA). The quest for a culinary education took me from GEDs to SATs, and finally to acceptance into that bastion of the culinary world. When I started at the CIA, I was one of five or six women in my class, and I had no female culinary instructors, let alone mentors or role models. One day as I was driving to school, it dawned on me that here I was, living forty-five minutes from school (as that was all I could afford), working full-time (I was paying for my education), and learning how to learn (since it was a skill I'd never acquired) all so that I could pursue a career in the kitchen. The irony was that for years I would go crazy if anyone spoke the dreaded words, "a woman's place is in the kitchen," and here I was, saving all my money, working day and night, giving up night after night of sleep, all so that I could find a place in the culinary world—in the kitchen. This was a place that I loved, that held all my passion, and one that would eventually become my life.

My career took me through many twists and turns. I eventually graduated with honors, having made my mark as an outspoken, hardworking, independent cook. I did my extended externship at the Royal Sonesta in New Orleans and was the only woman on the hot line, but I lived with a black woman who worked in the pantry and in whose home cooking was woman's work. I went on to take my first job as a cook with Holland America Cruise lines; I was one of the first women on their ships. I went from there to my first executive chef position at a restaurant in Colorado at age twenty-six. My next job took me to the Radisson Hotel, where I was the first female executive chef within the chain and the first female executive chef in the state of Virginia. After a two-year stint I went back to Colorado to become executive chef for the Telluride Ski Resort to become the town's first major event caterer, initially through the ski resort and eventually with my own company, and finally to achieve the dream of most young chefs—opening my own restaurant.

During most of my professional life, there were few other women. Often I would think about why one of the few traditionally women's arenas, one of the few traditionally women's roles, excluded women. Why were there only men in the kitchens, and why was being on the hot line and being a chef a male career? After a while, this was starting to obsess me, yet I didn't really know what to do with it. Finally, I decided to tell the story.

In 1990 I accepted an executive chef position with the Putney Inn in Putney, Vermont, a position I still hold as of this printing. I also joined a number of culinary organizations, and as I met more women there and spent more time in the industry, I found the story starting to come alive.

There's a place in the professional kitchen for women, and this is our story. The story is in three parts: the past, present, and future of women in the industry. The first part focuses on the history of women's roles in cooking and kitchens throughout the ages (chapter one); the second part speaks to what's in our hearts, the choices we've made, sacrifices that have been extolled, and the lives we've led and continue to lead (chapters two through six). The last part of this story focuses on the future of our industry and how we can make it an acceptable arena for women so that they can pursue their passion and love of food while balancing their lives outside of the kitchen (chapters seven and eight). This story is about the evolutionary cycle of women in the kitchen—where they started and how they worked their way back.

Ann Cooper

Executive Chef
The Putney Inn
Putney, Vermont

Acknowledgments

This book came into being with the help of so many different wonderful women and men that at times I have been truly overwhelmed by all the help, support, and time that the following people have given.

First and foremost, I want to thank Melissa Rosati, who was the first editor at VNR to hire me to write this book. Without her vision, this book never would have happened. Melissa, thank you for sharing my dream and supporting me through the good times and the bad.

"A Woman's Place Is in the Kitchen" owes its heart, soul, joy, laughter, and tears to all the women chefs and cooks who contributed their time, energy, and stories to this book. Over 130 women took time out of their busy schedules to be interviewed, then took more time to fill out paperwork and send pictures, recipes, ideas, and words of encouragement. From my heart, thank you; meeting all of you has been the best part of writing this book.

Over 1,000 women chefs and cooks took time to fill out a ten-page survey that has been likened to a college entrance exam. Thank you for your time, attention, and dedication; you have been an inspiration.

A number of the women I interviewed made the research for this book possible. First and foremost is Dr. Patricia Bartholomew, whose landmark research project on women chefs was the basis for many paths of thought that I traveled. Pat's thesis wasn't even published when I called and asked for a copy; she graciously gave of herself, her research, her ideas, and her friendship. Pat, thank you for your work, your ideas, and the beliefs you promote.

I have had the good fortune of meeting and working with some of the most dedicated educators and librarians imaginable. The research for my book could not have been done without the help of the following women and their institutions. They were there to answer questions, send information, and help find some bit of missing history; I can't imagine this process without them:

Barbara Haber, curator of the Schlessinger Library, Radcliffe College, Cambridge, MA; Gert Trani, Information Services, The Culinary Institute of America, Hyde Park, NY; and Jenny Hernenze and Sarah Koehl, "The Library Girls," New England Culinary Institute, Montpelier, VT.

Barbara Kuck and her staff at the Culinary Archives and Museum at Johnson and Wales University, Providence, RI, deserve a special thanks for all they gave. From the archives came most of the historical photographs in the book. Barbara and her staff did a number of photo shoots, sent us information, drove pictures to us when time was running out, and went all the way and beyond to help make this book be the best it could be.

A number of other institutions and organizations helped make the research for the book accurate and contemporary. The National Museum of Women in the Arts, Washington, DC; Melinda McIntosh, Reference Department, University Library, The University of Massachusetts, Amherst, MA; Mike Sutherland Ph.D., Statistical Consulting Department, University of Massachusetts, Amherst, MA; the office staff of the American Culinary Federation, St. Augustine, FL; the office staff of the National Restaurant Association, Washington, DC; Annie Copps, Program Manager, Chef's Collaborative 2000, Cambridge, MA; and Jerry Fernandez, Multi-Cultural Foodservice and Hospitality Alliance.

Numerous culinary schools and organizations helped make my database possible: Dell Hargis, Director of Alumni Affairs, The Culinary Institute of America in Hyde Park, NY; Albert Wutsch, President, IUP Academy of Culinary Arts, Punxutawney, PA; Ellen McShane, New England Culinary Institute, Montpelier, VT; Frankie Whitman, Women Chefs and Restaurateurs, San Francisco, CA; Chelsie Horn, Johnson and Wales University, Providence RI; Dorothy Hamilton, President, The French Culinary Institute, New York; and the American Culinary Federation, St. Augustine FL.

With all of the research that was conducted, including surveys, interviews, and phone calls, we produced over 10,000 typed pieces of paper. The surveys and interviews were transcribed, the information collated, and eventually through hard work, dedication, perseverance, and love, a book was produced with the help of some wonderful women.

Jill Overdorf, thank you for the many months of hard work, organization, patience, and fortitude—your skills really helped to shape this book. Your ideas, thoughts, and voice have had an impact on the success of this project.

Max Effenson Chuck was the editor who made a book out of 600 pages of words; I slept over at her house, her family took me in, we ate sushi and worked all night. Thank you for having the patience to try and teach me how to write and the perseverance to make me rewrite and rewrite and rewrite.

Denise LeClaire came to my rescue when I needed another person to help keep track of all the papers. Thank you for coming, and thank you for being there.

To KK, who on a moment's notice took a week out of her life to work 100 hours in six days to help make my words flow and communicate what they needed to say, thank you for your friendship and love.

Heather Freedman, Elizabeth Green, and the staff at VNR all gave time and energy to this project—especially Heather, who acquired carpal tunnel syndrome while typing madly for two months on 2,000 pages of transcriptions. Many thanks also to Mike Suh, VNR's designer extraordinaire, who transformed my vision into visual reality.

To Gary Holleman, I owe my undying gratitude for introducing me to Melissa, and for believing in my dream. Thanks for all of the support every time I thought I'd never be able to finish, and thank you for being there.

Randi Ziter and the kitchen staff at the Putney Inn gave me the time, support, food, and coffee to get through the last sixty days of working around the clock. To my staff: thank you for being the best kitchen crew a chef could ever hope for—Randi, thanks for being there and putting up with me—it's been a long few months.

The Scope and Methodology of the Book

The Historical Research

This book, especially chapter one, represents research gathered from the culinary archives and libraries at The Culinary Institute of America, Johnson and Wales Culinary Archives, Schlessinger Library, Willliamstown Library, The National Museum of Women and the Arts, the National Restaurant Association, and the American Culinary Federation. The research was done over a six-month period and is included in order to give the reader a brief history of women and food, and to put our struggle in a context. I do not profess to be a historian, nor do I want the reader to feel that this historical material does any more than provide a basis for what we know about women in the kitchen today and in our recent history. The bibliography and the recommended reading lists in the appendix should help those who want to find more in-depth studies on the subject of women and food. For those readers who are culinary historians, please forgive the brevity of the historical information—I realize how many of you spend a lifetime on this subject. I hope this section gives "food for thought" and a new basis from which to think of women and food.

The Women Chefs and Cooks Research

"A Woman's Place Is in the Kitchen" compiles survey analysis, historical and contemporary research, and interview transcription. A ten-page survey (Appendix F) was sent to 6,500 women chefs and cooks across the country. The analysis was based on 500 of the responses to these surveys. The database of women chefs and cooks who received the survey was comprised of the female members of a number of culinary organizations, including the American

Culinary Federation (ACF), Women Chefs and Restaurateurs (WCR), International Association of Culinary Professionals (IACP), American Institute of Wine and Food (AIWF), as well as the alumna of the following culinary schools: The Culinary Institute of America, Johnson and Wales University, New England Culinary Institute, IUP Academy of Culinary Arts, and The French Culinary Institute.

The survey results were compiled in two categories, first by quantifiable responses, which were put into a database with the help of Mike Sutherland and the University of Massachusetts Math Department. The second category was based on written responses: these descriptive responses are included throughout the book. The women surveyed come from various geographic locations, exhibit age, ethnic, and culinary diversity, and represent a broad spectrum of women in the industry.

The interview process took place over a six-month period. The interviews were conducted for the most part in person, with only a few conducted by phone. All of the interviews were tape recorded, transcribed, and then organized by category to be integrated into the various chapters. A typical interview took one and a half to two hours and produced twenty to thirty pages of transcriptions. Additionally, all of the women chefs and cooks interviewed were asked to provide biographies, pictures, recipes, and menus, all of which were collated for use in the book.

The women who participated in this project range in age from eighteen to eighty-four and hold a variety of positions from student, apprentice, and cook to executive chef, corporate chef, and chef-owner. The kitchens run the gamut from small, two-person restaurants to multi-unit corporations to large hotels and restaurants. The food is as diverse as the ethnic background of the women themselves and mirrors the ethnic diversity of our country. The one connection that all the women surveyed and interviewed share is their love and passion for food and kitchens. They all share the drive, passion, and love for preparing, serving, and sharing food.

I hope all of you reading this book already share that passion or find a little of your own as you read. Thank you for allowing me to share my story, their stories, and our passion for food, our work, and our industry with you.

"A Woman's Place Is in the Kitchen"

The History of
Women in the Kitchen

An Evolutionary Tale

Progress in civilization has been accompanied by progress in cookery.
—Fannie Merritt Farmer

"The role of fire in transforming food from raw to cooked [is] the mark of the emergence of humanity."[26]
—*Levi-Strauss*

The history of women in the kitchen and their relationship with food runs parallel to the story of the evolution of women, men, and the planet. I see this evolution as a circular one that began 10,000 years ago, when women's early influences on food supplies and preparation brought about the advent of family and community. Throughout history, women have provided food for the world's population; until very recently, however, they have been virtually excluded from professional kitchens. Today, women are emerging as a powerful force in the culinary arena, where they will continue to influence food, its preparation, and its presentation for future generations.

Women: In the Beginning

Woman cooking with young girl looking on. Fifth century B.C. Courtesy Museum of Fine Arts, Boston.

Since the beginning of time, women have been the tamers of fire, the inventors of most early cooking tools, and the creators of most elementary cooking techniques. Eating habits of prehistoric peoples lead us to believe that men, the hunters and warriors, ate meat, while women, by and large, were vegetarians. Hunting was man's domain; gathering and cultivating were woman's. As a result, the tools man invented—such as the club—were weapons, geared for the hunt, whereas woman's tools—such as the digging stick—were for feeding.

One of the issues that has plagued women in kitchens to this day is that men took up the profession as their own, excluding women on many levels. While women developed the techniques and the tools for cooking, it was the men who wielded the knife—the tool that was used to dominate and conquer. The corollary between knives as modern-day cooking tools and prehistoric man's use of tools as weapons has had a direct impact on women's inability to remain a force in kitchens throughout the ages. Alain Sailhac, Dean of Culinary Studies, French Culinary Institute, and formerly chef of The Plaza and Le Cirque, both in New York, tells of his memories growing up in his parents' French household. "When we [had] a chicken in the family, my father [would] cut the chicken. My mother [would] never cut the chicken. She did everything [else], but [she] never cut the chicken. When you have [men in the kitchen, they] will have the knife. When a man has a knife, a man has a weapon. This is really the beginning—the root of the problem. The man is the only one who has the weapon."

From Frederick Remington's "Texan Types and Contrasts," *Harper's New Monthly Magazine*, circa 1900.

This is indeed a problem against which women in the culinary field have battled for years. As our story unfolds, the struggle will bring us to contemporary times, where change is evolving, slowly.

Woman's Discovery of Fire

The story of women and cooking begins with the discovery of fire. The case can be made that fire was "invented" or discovered by women, who were the early "craftsmen." The carving of early wood tools generated friction, which created heat, sparks, and, finally, fire. With fire came new cooking techniques such as broiling, boiling, and roasting, as well as experimentation with new cooking ingredients. Women found these ingredients in nature.

Women Cultivating the Agricultural Community

Over the millennia, women discovered that if they planted the seeds of wild grasses, eventually, new grasses would grow. The planting and sowing of seeds and the bounty of the harvest that followed came to be recognized as a new food source. Over time, women began to understand nature's cycles and seasons, which brought about agriculture and an agrarian way of life. This new lifestyle replaced nomadic wandering, which had been necessary as hunting delivered the primary food supply. For the ensuing 10,000 years, humankind's

Open hearth cooking was not only time-consuming but hazardous for the women who did it, often setting fire to their cumbersome long skirts. In fact, fires were a leading cause of death to women, second only to childbirth.
—Mickey Rathburn–Daily Hampshire Gazette, *Northampton, MA*

In hunter-gatherer societies, women contributed four-fifths of the clan's food.

Native American women engaged in agriculture (circa 1780–1840). Courtesy of the Culinary Archives and Museum at Johnson and Wales University.

"The time is not far distant, when knowledge of the principles of diet will be an essential part of one's education. Then mankind will eat to live, will be able to do better mental and physical work, and disease will be less frequent."[1]

—Fannie Farmer

agriculture-based existence was the dominant culture worldwide, and its ramifications were far-reaching.

Dave Miller, in "Women, Food, and Technology," discusses the role of women's birthing cycles as it relates to present-day agricultural society. He describes how prehistoric women gave birth only in the spring because hunting yielded insufficient supplies of nutrients in the winter to allow for procreation. With the rise of an agrarian way of life and its more stable and diverse food supplies, woman's chemical makeup evolved. Eventually, children could be birthed year-round. According to Miller, "As chemically pre-set breeding with related social behavior changed, so did female/male relationships, resulting in longer-term relationships as the norm. For women, these changes meant the birth of children throughout the year, out of sync with the bounties of spring. The result, nurture technology—digging sticks, rock scrapers [and] rock cutters."[1]

Year-round breeding put new pressures on women to produce and provide nourishing food. The survival of the species, in fact, depended on it. We see this weighty responsibility for developing nurturing technologies in stories and myths that have been passed down through the ages. One such story—a creation story—tells of the Zuni Indian Tribe of the North American southwest: "Mother Earth poured water into a terrace-rimmed bowl, whipping it rapidly with her fingers. As the beaten foam rose to the rim, it covered the terraces as clouds cover mountains. She then blew on the foam and flake after flake it broke off, sending life-giving rain to fertilize the earth and nourish all the lives."[2]

The Miccosuke Indian Tribe of Florida and Alabama tells a story that depicts women as providers, and as central to the cycles of the seasons, of life, and of death: "A woman feeds her family a new and delicious food that they have not seen before. Her sons wonder where she is getting it, and they secretly follow her one day to find out. They discover that she is rubbing skin from her body and forming it into little balls. She sees them and tells them that since they have discovered her secret, they must kill her and bury her body in a nearby field. The next spring, corn stalks grow from her grave." Thus, we see in these stories the importance of nurture technology with its creativity and its life-giving force.[3]

As the agrarian lifestyle evolved and hunting declined in importance, primitive man had more leisure time. Women, on the other hand, worked harder than ever. June Stephenson, in her book, *Women's Roots, Status and Achievements in Western Civilization* writes: "Women invented work, for primitive man was only an idler.[4] Instead of living in a cave, bearing and burying children, and gathering such food and fuel as she could find, woman now had a primitive house to look after, essential crops to cultivate and care for, and most of the responsibility for husking and grinding the grain."

This new social structure gave birth to the family as we know it, where women juggle multiple roles as food providers, nurturers, and caregivers.

Women Cultivating Family Life

We have seen woman in her role as gatherer and cultivator of food. As time passed, women took on an increasing amount of responsibility. In the same way that she gathered, cultivated, and prepared food for her family, she cultivated the family bonds. She was the central figure in the family around whom all activities in the home revolved. Margaret Visser, a culinary chronologist, writes, "One definition of a family, which has different degrees of significance in different cultures, is 'those who eat together.' "[5] Levi-Strauss, the famous cultural historian, suggests that, "The role of fire in transforming food from raw to cooked [is] the mark of the emergence of humanity."[6] As historians have examined the history of the family, especially the role of women, it has become useful to know something about women's work. Barbara Wheaton, the noted culinary historian, discusses women's work in her book, *Savoring the Past*. "The

"The history of this hemisphere, is marked, whether we like it or not, whether we're comfortable with it or not and whether we choose to admit it or not, by slavery. The enslavement of Africans changed the food ways—people of African descent were in kitchens."
—Jessica Harris

170 B.C.: Rome's first professional cooks appear as bakers.

"Nothing in the whole range of domestic life more affects the health and happiness of the family than the quality of its daily bread."
—*Mary Johnson, director of the Boston Cooking School, in Mrs. Lincoln's* Boston Cook Book

preservation and preparation of food has made up a substantial part of most women's lives, and meals have been a focal point for the interplay of relationships within the family. Whatever a woman's cooking ability, her cookery flavored family life."[7]

This historical view reflects woman's inherent nature to nurture her family. This behavior has endured over time, as exemplified by Chef Katy Keck, chef-owner of New World Grill and Savoir Faire Foods in New York: "My beginning was an Easy-Bake Oven! I had my Easy-Bake Oven when I was about five years old. When my grandfather died, I stayed up—what to me seemed like all night—secretly baking in my room, to make this sympathy cake for my mother and grandmother when they came home from the funeral, because the funeral was in another town. I remember making a two-layer chocolate cake for my mother and an apple pie with a lattice top for my grandmother! But, I just remember always being in that whole woman's side of things: the nurturing, the food, the hospitality."

As Katy's story illustrates, it doesn't matter what tools are available or what ingredients are on hand, women always find a way to feed and nurture. In the relationship between food and family, women have made and continue to make an indelible imprint on society.

Women's Contributions to the Development of Food and Spirits

The relationship between women and food throughout history can be expanded to include drink as well. Women are said to have been some of the first hucksters and brewers [of beer];[8] and the first leavened bread is seen as an offshoot of the brewing process. As Maguelonne Toussaint-Samat surmises about the discovery of raised bread in the *History of Food*, "Dust perhaps on dirty hands, carrying with it minute fungi or yeasts, could have settled on the paste, which then fermented and swelled larger ... to the delight of the forgetful person who set it aside ... She may have cooked a little of the strange, swollen dough and found the result palatable."[9]

Women also may have been the first wine makers. As Reay Tannahill remarks with regard to the origin of wine in his book, *Food in History*, "A container of vinifera grapes was left neglected in a corner. The juice would run, and in the right conditions ferment and then settle; someone (a woman) had the courage to taste the result and found it congenial."[10] Tannahill suggests that the basis for this "picturesque tale" took place some time in the Neolithic era.

Women continued making their contributions to society and family life for many years, with their role as nurturer/provider being both acceptable and respectable. However, change was in store as attitudes and roles were reevaluated with the onset of the Christian calendar. A radical transition took place, which was to last until contemporary times.

Gleaming. From *The Illustrated London News,* Sept. 24, 1859.

Women's Fall from Grace

The beginning of the Christian calendar (A.D.) for many cultures saw the demise of worshipping multiple gods and goddesses and the rise of worshipping a single male figure. Where once women stood at the center of social structures, now there were men. According to Evelyn Reid in *Woman's Evolution: Matriarchal Clan to Patriarchal Family,* the transition from a matriarchal to a patriarchal society had to do, in part, with menstrual cycles. Previously seen as a life force, menstrual blood was now seen as "unclean." As a result, "unclean" women were segregated and prohibited from cooking for men. Suddenly the direct connection between women and food was being compromised by the male priest's newly acquired power. This male-based power structure stripped women of their role as provider and nurturer and seriously eroded their power in society.[11]

This transition from matriarchal to patriarchal society may explain the lack of historical data on women and food. At that time in history, women weren't encouraged to read or write, and hence, most history was being recorded by men—women were seen as slaves or chattel.

In general, wine was forbidden women, and historians report cases of husbands ... who killed their wives because they had gone to tipple secretly in the wine cellar.

—*Jean-François Revel in* Culture and Cuisine

Women in America: Reentering the Kitchen

The history of women and food continues in the United States during the early eighteenth century, when women were associated with every facet of food.

1071: A Greek princess introduces a two-pronged fork to Venice.

Cookbook frontispiece. Courtesy of the Culinary Museum at Johnson and Wales University.

Shaker women, colonial women, black southern slave women and the city gentry all made noteworthy contributions to America's culinary heritage.

In 1774, Mother Ann Lee, the founder of an offshoot of the English Quakers, which came to be known as the Shakers, brought her sect to New England. In this culture women did all the cooking, preserving, smoking, canning, farming, and gardening. Some culinary historians credit Shaker women with being the best cooks of their time.

During the same time period colonial women were seen as the main providers of food for their communities. Cooking and preparing food was a fundamental responsibility for all women, rich and poor. For example, each day, the women were responsible for baking bread and pies, cooking meats, cutting and drying apples, making cider, milking the cows, and making cream, butter, and cheese. Life was not easy for women of this era; in fact, cooking was quite dangerous. When scientist Count von Rumford invented the stove in 1800, it ended an era in which "cooking over an open fire competed with childbirth for the number one cause of women's death."[12]

Many black slave women made their mark on America's early culinary history. In Thomas Jefferson's White House (1800–1809), slave women worked in the kitchen. "Edith and Fanny helped prepare dishes considered novelties even by the standards of elite Washington society"[13] and helped promote Jefferson's recognition as "the greatest connoisseur of fine foods and wines" of all the presidents of his era.[14] In 1809 these two women took the skills they had developed working under Jefferson's French-trained chef, James Hennings, himself a black slave, and went to work for Jefferson at Monticello, his Virginia home. Another slave, Ursula, was purchased at his wife's request, her skills included "making pastry, bottling, salting, curing, and smoking meats ... she was paid $7 per month for these activities."[15]

Jessica Harris, a professor of English at Queens College and a culinary historian with a specialty in the foodways of Africa, believes that much of our culinary heritage stems from the African slave trade. According to Harris, "the tradition of hospitality is the bedrock on which much of African, African-American, and ... southern American hospitality is based! The size of the extended family in West Africa means that much of the cooking that is done on a daily basis is done by many [women's] hands, in a manner that parallels quite closely today's line in professional kitchens. The whole extended family, is such that 20, 30, 40 people may be there for dinner at a particular house and when feasts are held, this multi-generational, many-cook preparation is virtually transformed into a small catering business, capable of feeding hundreds of people at one time."[16]

Jessica explains why she views this type of meal preparation as the precursor to many forms of the foodservice industry today. "Coming out of this type of food preparation, it is not difficult to trace the progression from [woman as] home cook to [woman as] professional cook. In the years of the transatlantic slave trade, women would be transported to various parts of the New World. During the antebellum period in the United States, indeed up to and including much of the twentieth century, cities like Charleston, South Carolina; Savannah, Georgia; New Orleans, Louisiana; and even New York and Philadelphia in the north, rang with the cries of street hucksters that harked back to Africa. Whatever their [black women in food service] professional choices, from cook to executive chef, from coffee lady to catering business owner, they are all a part of the tradition of African-American women chefs, and they are all the culinary daughters of West Africa's marketwomen."

African-American women have had a place in the culinary history of America. From their roots in Africa to the hucksters of the south and the kitchens of mansions all over this country, they have provided the basis for much of what we think of as "comfort food" today.

Cover illustration for *La Cuisine Creole. A collection of culinary recipes. From leading chefs and noted Creole housewives, who have made New Orleans famous for its cuisine. Second Edition.* (New Orleans: F. F. Hansell & Bro., Ltd., 1885.)

The Changing Role of Women from the Industrial Era Through the Early 1900s

The development of manufacturing equipment at the end of the eighteenth century brought about unparalleled change in history and, likewise, in the roles of women and men. Prior to the Industrial Revolution, men's and women's work roles overlapped—most work was confined to the home, which enabled women to fulfill their role as the primary food provider and caretaker of their family, while participating in home-based manufacturing. But factories split the family unit: men left every day for the mines, mills, and workshops, and women remained at home with farm and family. These new distinctive roles gave birth to the title that would define the women's role for centuries to come: "homemaker."

In Linda Grant DePauw and Conover Hunt's *Remember the Ladies—Women in America 1750–1835*, we find the following reference, "The years between 1750–1815 witnessed the passing of a remarkable generation of

1393: In Europe, one pound of saffron would buy a plow horse; one pound of ginger would buy a sheep; two pounds of mace would buy a cow.

THE CHEMISTRY

OF

COOKING AND CLEANING

A MANUAL FOR HOUSEKEEPERS

BY

ELLEN H. RICHARDS

INSTRUCTOR IN CHEMISTRY, WOMAN'S LABORATORY,
MASSACHUSETTS INSTITUTE OF TECHNOLOGY,
BOSTON

BOSTON
ESTES & LAURIAT
301 — 305 WASHINGTON ST
1882

Cookbook title page.
Courtesy of the Culinary
Museum at Johnson and
Wales University.

women who were strong, self-reliant, employed in all occupations entered by men, although not in equal numbers, and active in political and military affairs. The conditions that enabled the U.S. to establish itself as an independent nation and permitted middle-class white men to achieve greater wealth and political power forced women into a more restricted role. Although the Founding Fathers never intended that slaves, servants, Indians, or women would share in the freedoms they demanded for themselves, the libertarian ideals they conceived remain a vital legacy."[17]

Women's roles changed rapidly in the late nineteenth and early twentieth centuries. During this time, there was a battle of the sexes that influenced much of the prevailing attitudes about women in the kitchen. In 1871, Charles Darwin wrote *The Descent of Man,* in which he states: "human progress occurs in the male struggle outside of the home and women are biologically and intellectually inferior to men."[18] With the publication of these writings, women were seen as deficient, and female pursuits, like cooking, seemingly lost value. To reassert their rights and push for equality, however, feminists had to turn their backs on that which historically had given them power—they launched a campaign to get women out of their kitchens and into that place where "human progress occurs."

Some women discovered that getting involved in the "male struggle outside of the home" didn't necessarily require rejecting the kitchen. That was the case with Ellen Swallow Richards, who in 1873, at the age of thirty-one, became the first woman graduate of the Massachusetts Institute of Technology (MIT). She is credited with being the founder and eventual president of the Home Economics Society and the Ecology movement; she also promoted the fledgling science of nutrition, pioneering school lunch programs and testing food products. In her book, *Sanitation in Daily Life,* published in 1907, she writes that, "It is crucial to secure and maintain a safe environment, promote and not diminish human development [and ensure] that everyone should acquire habits of belief in the importance of the environment. One of the most difficult lessons to learn is that our tolerance of evil conditions is not proof that the conditions are not evil."[19] These philosophies, almost a century old, express a set of beliefs that are reemerging in the forefront of society today.

"Kitchens of the Reform Club" (London), depicting female cooks in key positions. From *Portrait of a Chef: The life of Alexis Soyer, sometime chef to the Reform Club.*

Although women like Ellen Swallow Richards rose above the prevailing sentiment about the inferiority of women and women's work, many were confined by their "homemaker" status or were limited to menial labor. *Dirt and Domesticity: Construction of the Feminine,* from the Whitney Museum of American Arts, states: "Middle-class and working-class women were socially validated in relation to an idea of the home, and it was considered a social stigma for women to be in the workplace. Working-class women were closed out of factory, trade, and craft work through a variety of tactics, including laws barring women's employment, lack of training opportunities, and male-only membership in unions."[20] That left farm work or domestic servitude. In fact, as late as the dawn of the twentieth century, half of all working women were employed on farms or in the homes of the wealthy. So, while getting into the "job force" was new for women, their work was not—it still called upon the familiar duties of raising, producing, or providing food.

Another event during this era made its mark on the education of women and food. In 1893 the World's Colombian Exposition in Chicago featured the first "Woman's Building." This exposition culminated in the formation of the Woman's Congress, its offspring was the National Household Economics Association and the eventual founding of the General Federation of Women's Clubs. This premier event showcased the first electric kitchen

The London Worshipful Company of Bakers forbade bakers to employ women to "sett, season or carry any bread." A permissible activity for baker's wives and women servants was selling bread in the marketplace.
—Baking & Baking Off: Deskilling & the Changing Sex Makeup of Bakers

1532: Italian alchemist Maria de Cleofa introduces the double boiler to the French courts via Caterina de Medici's cooks. It is called the *bain-marie.*

"What is a Chef? …
"a chef is a man
capable of inventing
what has not yet been
eaten in the houses of
others."
—*Jean-François Revel*

ever exhibited, as well as a display by the U.S. Department of Agriculture with produce from around the world. One of the many offshoots of this event was the funding by Congress of the first investigation of nutritional content of products, from which the U.S. Bureau of Home Economics was founded.

In a 1904 edition of *The Successful Poultry Journal,* an editorial talked about the average poultry raiser: "The work is not onerous, but is rather one of detail, making it such that women are far better adapted to it than is a man. Her mother instinct, nurturing tenderness, care in feeding [and] love of cleanliness—all fit her in a pre-eminent degree to make a success of the work."[21] This description epitomizes the role of women in the work force at that time and their relegation to domestic duties.

Although a number of events took place during the course of the twentieth century that played a role in the continuing evolution of women in the home and in the workplace, the process of change was gradual. Every step that women took was a milestone, and many of these steps were met with challenges if not outright opposition. The next section of this chapter chronicles the development of the professional kitchen and the ostracism that women faced from the early days of the profession.

The Beginnings of Cooking as a Profession

One could say that wars were an offshoot of hunting, in that those who fought the wars used the tools of the hunt to control, protect, conquer, or to own. Because men were the ones who used the tools, it stands to reason that men were the ones who were fighting the wars. When armies traveled during the fourteenth and fifteenth centuries, they needed to be fed; hence, cooks were selected from the ranks. Each of these male cooks developed his craft based on what he had learned from his mother's kitchen. It was here, during wartime, that they claimed the profession as their own. When wars were in abeyance, the kings set up "war games" at the castles to keep the armies prepared for battle. The cooks from the armies followed the knights and became the first cooks to the kings.

Guilds first appeared in England in the eleventh century, and these associations were formed for cooks, bakers, caterers, and butchers to create a monopoly with the purpose of sustaining economic viability for their members. Admission was controlled and expensive. This type of organization systematically excluded women in a number of ways. No women in the armies meant no women in the kitchens and hence no women in the guilds. Entry into the guilds was either through father–son ascension or through the purchase of a position. But women, at that time, were under the strict control of either their fathers or their husbands and, by law, often were forbidden from owning property or from having control of their finances.

As men took over the professional culinary arena, they distanced their skills from those of their mothers and wives. In this vein, they established uniforms, structure, and hierarchy; by the 1820s, chefs began to wear white toques, a version of the black hats of Greek Orthodox priests and uniforms, based on those worn by soldiers in the Turkish Army.

Just as the guild system had connections to the army, so did Auguste Escoffier's brigade system. Escoffier, a French chef for whom the phrase "the King of Chefs and the Chef of Kings" was coined, has long been considered one of the greatest chefs of modern time. Escoffier spent much of his adult life in the military, and in 1898 he developed the brigade system at the Savoy Hotel in London in an effort to organize and control the efficiency of his large staff. It's no coincidence that this system resembles the military model with its hierarchies and autocratic structure. To this day, that model has acted as an obstacle to women both in kitchens and in management professions within the culinary field, as we will hear in later discussions on male and female management styles.

"I daresay, that every servant who can but read will be capable of making a tolerable good cook."
—Hannah Glasse

Women and Their Cookbooks

Women's connection with food is indelibly tied to their need to nourish, nurture, and provide for their families. That special desire is instilled from a very early age. The role of nurturer and provider has been passed on from mother to daughter, aunt to niece, cousin to kin. As more and more women were able to read and write, these skills were passed on through cookbooks. The majority of the cookbooks throughout the ages have been written by and for women, whose stories come to life in these books.

Women, although not the first writers of cookbooks, as a group have been the most prolific. In the early nineteenth century, educational reformers advocated mass elementary education in the form of common schools. Prior to that time, literacy for all but the wealthiest women was uncommon, and most recipes were passed down via verbal history. A number of trends surface when researching women and cookbooks. In some of the earliest of these books, there is a trend toward economy and frugality, management and organization, and a predilection for sweets. Recurring themes include a concern for the role of women, their duties, responsibilities, and rights, as well as finding ways to lighten women's workload and improve their lives.

British women authored many of the first cookbooks. One of the earliest, written in 1604 by Elinor Fettiplaces, was called the *Receipt Book,* which

1634: Women colonists in Baltimore, Maryland go to the beach at low tide and collect mussels and clams.

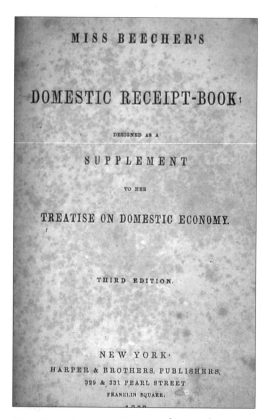

MISS BEECHER'S

DOMESTIC RECEIPT-BOOK:

DESIGNED AS A

SUPPLEMENT

TO HER

TREATISE ON DOMESTIC ECONOMY.

THIRD EDITION.

NEW YORK:
HARPER & BROTHERS, PUBLISHERS,
329 & 331 PEARL STREET
FRANKLIN SQUARE.

From Catherine Beecher's *Miss Beecher's Domestic Receipt-Book.* Courtesy of the Culinary Archives and Museum at Johnson and Wales University.

included 134 recipes. In 1742, Eliza Smith wrote *The Compleat Housewife, or Accomplish'd Gentlewoman's Companion,* published in Williamsburg, Virginia. This was believed to be the first cookbook published in Britain's American colony. Hannah Glasse's book, *The Art of Cookery made Plain and Easy,* written in 1747, was another of the original English manuals of cookery.

The first cookbook written by an American author for an American audience was Amelia Simmon's book, *American Cookery, or the Art of Dressing Viands, Fish, Poultry, and Vegetables, and the best Modes of Making Pastes, Puffs, Pies, Tarts, Puddings, Custards, and Preserves, and all Kinds of Cakes from the Imperial Plumb to Plain Cake Adapted to this Country and all Grades of Life.* This book, written in 1796 in Hartford, Connecticut, provided an early glimpse of American regional cuisine. Ms. Simmons provided the first instructions for some of the colonial specialties that appear on many New England menus today: Indian Pudding, Johnny-Cakes and Maple Syrup Pie. She is said to be the first to suggest serving cranberry sauce with roast turkey and using corncobs for smoking bacon. Ms. Simmons was the first person to publish recipes using a precursor of baking powder, called *pearlash,* which was a homemade ancestor of baking soda extracted from wood ashes, as a leavening ingredient for cakes. When the book was printed, signaling the birth of written American cuisine, complex French cuisine had already been flourishing for 150 years.

In 1824, the first true regional cookbook appeared: *The Virginia Housewife* by Mary Randolph, followed in 1828 by Eliza Leslie's *Directions for Cookery.* In 1833, Anna Dorn published her book, *The Newest or Great Universal Viennese Cookbook, a Guide to Cook for the Finest Tables in Ordinary Houses, Combining the Best of Taste and the Greatest Elegance, Taking Advantage of the Economic Possibilities to Make it Least Expense.* In this book, Ms. Dorn wrote, "Every year the number of new cookbooks increases, but in spite of them the progress made in this most useful of the arts is not ever overpowering. On the contrary, we must regretfully admit that nowadays people no longer prepare the fine and nourishing dishes that our mothers used to make. We place dishes on the table that are either too heavily spiced or plain dull, that are neither good for people's health nor economical."[22] These words, written over 150 years ago, can still be heard in professional kitchens today.

Women in the Culinary Arena: Fannie Merritt Farmer (1857–1915)

A permanently debilitating stroke at the age of thirteen did not deter Fannie Merritt Farmer from pursuing a lifetime of accomplishments: principal of the first incorporated cooking school in America, author of one of the best-selling cookbooks in history, and earning the moniker "the mother of level measure."

In 1889, Ms. Farmer graduated from the Boston Cooking School in Boston, Massachussetts at the age of thirty-two. She remained involved with her alma mater and rapidly attained the position of Assistant to the Director; in 1891, she was named Director of the school, and she maintained that position until her resignation when the school was sold to Simmons College in 1902. Fannie opened and oversaw her own school, "Miss Farmer's School of Cookery," where she taught "peasant girls who wish to become servants and millionaire's daughters who want to learn how to give orders." (Willan, p. 189)

Additionally, Ms. Farmer authored *The Boston Cooking-School Cookbook,* first published in 1896; her book has sold over four million copies. She was instrumental in advocating theories of nutrition and lectured frequently at the Harvard Medical School. One of her most important contributions to the culinary field was the suggestion of consistently using equal and level measures and uniform instructions while cooking.

Few cooks today are not impacted by Ms. Farmer's techniques and influence, whether it is the use of her still-popular publication or the careful measuring of ingredients. Culinarians can thank this stalwart woman for the implementation of standardized methods that enable chefs to share and exchange recipes effectively, easily, and consistently.

Catherine Beecher was 100 years ahead of her time in 1846, when she wrote *Miss Beecher's Domestic Receipt Book,* which helped promote her ideas on women and food. She believed that "Domestic science courses should be offered in all schools and that by receiving proper training for their profession, women would have more self-assurance and confidence and so be able to make more contributions to society."[23] Ms. Beecher's writing on home management added credibility to the work traditionally assigned to women. It launched a movement that viewed the household arts as a serious vocation. Ms. Beecher also pioneered scientific kitchen planning, suggesting specific preparation and clean-up areas as well as continuous work counters as opposed to numerous small tabletops.

During the late 1800s, two other culinary writing venues took shape, both of which have had a lasting effect on our written culinary heritage. The first of

In the eighteenth century ... women were productively employed in all of the occupations entered by men, since all occupations centered in the home.

—*1778,* Remember the Ladies, Women in America

1634: The women colonists are responsible for gathering wild greens and milking the goats. They barter with the Indians for venison and raccoon meat.

Cookbook frontispiece and title page from Isabella Beeton's *Mrs. Beeton's Everyday Cookery with about 2,500 Practical Recipes.* Courtesy of the Culinary Archives and Museum at Johnson and Wales University.

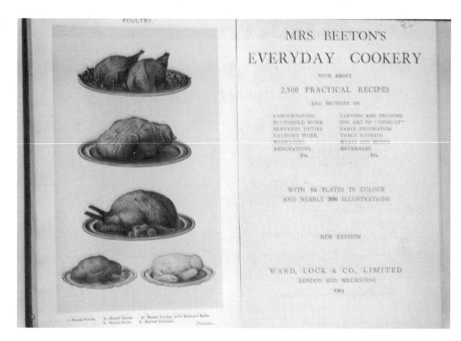

In 1936, "a mother and daughter managed to turn around a failed sandwich ... counter in New York's Grand Central Station ... the mother echoed the prevailing restaurant wisdom of the day, 'I would not have a man in the kitchen under any circumstances; I like to get a woman cook who has no experience except in a large family'."

—Paradox of Plenty

these legacies was the advent of cookbooks written to help support charitable causes. This phenomenon began with the end of the Civil War as a way of combating postwar poverty. To this day, women all over the country have sold cookbooks as a way to raise money for every imaginable cause. The second of these written culinary legacies is the woman's magazine or journal. The late 1800s saw the rise of such newsstand icons as *The Woman's Home Companion, The Ladies Home Journal,* and *Good Housekeeping.* These cornerstones of the homemaker's kitchen have flourished for almost 200 years and were the predecessors of the culinary print media we know today.

During the latter part of the nineteenth century and the early part of the twentieth century, there was a proliferation of cookbooks, many of which are still in print. In 1861, Isabella Beeton wrote *The Book of Household Management,* which was one of the most successful European cookbooks ever published. "Bella," who was twenty-five at the time of publication, provided product costs, cooking times, and ingredient quantities. Her philosophy was "All the indecisive terms expressed by a bit of this, some of that, a small piece of that and a handful of the other, shall never be made use of and that a uniform system of weights and measures should be adopted."[24] In 1896, Fannie Farmer's *Boston Cooking School Cookbook* championed these same ideas. In her book, she introduced and perpetuated level measurement by volume. Her beliefs have as much impact today as they did then. Ms. Farmer said, "Cookery is the art of preparing food for the nourishment of the body; progress in civilization has been accompanied by progress in cookery." Her book eventually sold over four million copies in twenty editions after the first order of 3,000.

The last of the authors from this era was Lizzie Black (Mrs. Simon Kander), who in 1901 published the *Settlement Cookbook*. This book was self-published by the women of the Settlement House with funds raised by volunteers. The Settlement House was started in Milwaukee at the turn of the century as a place to indoctrinate European immigrants into the American way of life. One of their projects was a cookbook to help the newly arrived better adjust to their new home. Through advertisements, this cookbook earned enough money over the course of eight years to pay for a new settlement house building.

In 1921, Betty Crocker's name was first used as the signature on replies to entries in a recipe contest held by Washburn Crosby, a forerunner of General Mills. Who among us didn't grow up thinking of Betty Crocker's image as an icon of women and food? *Betty Crocker's Cooking School of the Air* could be heard on radio broadcasts from 1924 to 1948, yet many failed to realize that she was a fictitious character suggested by the company in the hopes that her replies would carry more authority than those of a man. Betty Crocker's façade has undergone numerous changes to keep up with the times and the changing face of women in America. Her name and picture grace one of the best-known collections of cookbooks in the country, *The Betty Crocker Cookbooks*. In 1997, this collection totaled over fifty titles currently in print.

Cover of *American Cookery*, formerly *The Boston Cooking-School Magazine*. Courtesy of the Culinary Archives and Museum at Johnson and Wales University.

The first of the contempory cookbooks is Irma Rombauer's *Joy of Cooking*, which was first printed in 1931. This book, more than any other, saw American women through their first adventures in cooking. The next thirty years of women and cookbooks brought to light more sophisticated and regional food. Many of the women who tell their stories throughout this book, and certainly many of those who influenced generations of cooks and chefs, are listed in Appendix D.

For female cookbook authors, it seemed a natural progression to go from writing to teaching at cooking schools. Numerous cooking schools opened their doors originally as Home Economics instruction for women and

1736: The first Scottish cookbook, *Mrs. McLintock's Receipts for Cookery and Pastry-Work*, appears.

The Story of Betty Crocker

Since 1921, the Betty Crocker name has symbolized the General Mills continuing tradition of service to consumers. Although Betty was never a real person, her name and identity have become synonymous with helpfulness, trustworthiness, and quality. Betty Crocker has survived the decades by providing consumers with food information and food products that are contemporary without being faddish.

Betty Crocker has spent her entire life talking with consumers who cook. After all these years, people still relate to her. To her credit, she has worked hard to stay in touch with how changing lifestyles affect cooking and eating preferences.

The Betty Crocker Portraits

In celebration of the 15th anniversary of the Betty Crocker name in 1936, a portrait was commissioned from Neysa McMein, a prominent New York artist. In her rendition, McMein blended the features of several Home Service Department members into a motherly image, which remained the official likeness of Betty Crocker for nearly 20 years.

In 1955, six well-known artists, including Norman Rockwell, were invited to paint fresh interpretations of Betty Crocker. About 1,600 women from across the country evaluated the finished works. The one they chose, by illustrator Hilda Taylor, was a softer, smiling version of the original image.

In 1965 and again in 1968, the portrait was updated by Joe Bowler, noted magazine illustrator. Both Bowler versions were dramatic departures from the earlier two—Betty Crocker was changing with the times.

The fifth portrait, painted in 1972 by Minnesota artist Jerome Ryan, depicted a more businesslike Betty Crocker, symbolizing American women's newly significant role outside the home.

The 1980 version, however, has a softened image with more casual coiffure and clothing, allowing all women to identify more readily with her.

In 1986, New York artist Harriet Perchik portrayed Betty Crocker as a professional woman, approachable, friendly, competent, and as comfortable in the boardroom as in the dining room.

For her 75th anniversary in 1996, a nationwide search found 75 women of diverse backgrounds and ages who embody the characteristics of Betty Crocker. The characteristics that make up the spirit of Betty Crocker are: (1) enjoys cooking and baking; (2) is committed to family and friends; (3) is resourceful and creative in handling everyday tasks; and (4) is involved in her community. A computerized composite of the 75 women, along with the 1986 portrait of Betty, served as inspiration for the painting by internationally known artist John Stuart Ingle. The portrait was unveiled March 19, 1996, in New York City.

Courtesy of the Culinary Archives and Museum at Johnson and Wales University.

1936

1955

1965

1968

1972

1980

1986

1996

H. Patersen's "Seasoning Fricandeau of Veal." From *London Illustrated News,* July 18, 1873. Courtesy National Training School of Cookery, at South Kensington (London, England).

then—for a time—as cooking schools only for men. These schools eventually came full circle again and graduated women into the culinary arena.

Women and Their Cooking Schools

Cooking schools in the nineteenth century were an important part of women's education, but not necessarily as a means into professional kitchens. Women who attended culinary school during this period were there to learn how to oversee the kitchens in their own homes, or to work in the home of someone else.

The first of these schools, which opened in 1869, was Le Cordon Bleu, named after the blue ribbons made famous by King Henry III in the sixteenth century. He created L'Order des Chevaliers du Saint Espris, whose members were called "Cordon Bleu" after the blue ribbons that they wore as a sign of attaining the highest level of achievement. In the late nineteenth century, Marthe Distel founded a weekly publication called *La Cuisiniere Cordon Bleu,* which included recipes and cooking techniques. The publication was so well received that it eventually became a venue for free cooking classes. These informal classes became Le Cordon Bleu, and although originally a Parisian institution, it became international and by 1905 attracted students from as far away as Japan.

The Grand Diplome awarded by Le Cordon Bleu to its best pupils was the highest credential that a cook could have at that time. The school continues to this day to teach ladies "of a certain class" from all over the world to have a

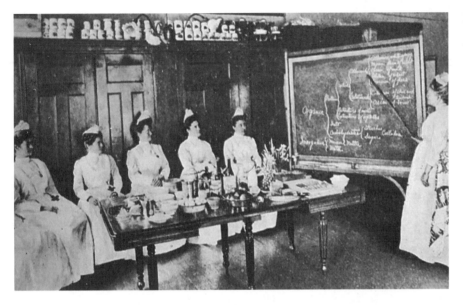

Fannie Farmer students. Courtesy if the Culinary Archives and Museum at Johnson and Wales University.

high level of culinary skill, as well as educating entry-level professionals and maintaining continuing education classes. One of these ladies, Julia Child, earned her toque in 1950, after which she taught generations of Americans "what French food was all about."

In 1884, Boston Cooking School opened under the direction of Mary Johnson, who taught many young, affluent, East-coast women their primary culinary skills. In 1891, Fannie Farmer became the director, a position she held until the school was sold to Simmons College in 1902. Ms. Farmer went on to open her own school, Miss Farmer's School of Cookery, also in Boston, which she ran until her death in 1915.

In 1942, Le Petite Cordon Bleu opened in New York City. Dione Lucas, a graduate of Le Cordon Bleu, ran the school with Rosemary Hume. During her career, Ms. Lucas was steward of the school, the author of many cookbooks, and in 1947, she became one of the first women with a cooking show on television, "To a Queen's Taste." This show, certainly one of the first to showcase instructional cooking, was the precursor to the TV Food Network almost fifty years later.

While others schools opened during this time, of major significance was the establishment of The Culinary Institute of America (CIA), founded in 1946 by Frances Roth and Katherine Angell in Hartford, Connecticut. The school was originally created for men coming home from the war with money from the GI bill to pay for their education. While American men were embarking on culinary

1742: The first American colonial cookbook, *The Compleat Housewife, or, Accomplish'd Gentlewoman's Companion*, is published by Eliza Smith.

training, French chefs, who had come to this country's kitchens during the height of *haute cuisine,* confronted a crackdown in immigration laws levied by the U.S. government. For the first time, their access to this country was curtailed. French chef André Soltner says that the CIA saved the culinary profession in America. He believed that the CIA would help to perpetuate the profession by teaching the young culinarians, who would eventually take the place of those French chefs no longer residing in this country. Chef Soltner may be accurate in his assessment of the CIA's success, but it wasn't until 1970—almost twenty-five years after its opening—that the first woman was enrolled in the culinary curriculum on a full-time basis.

In 1972, the CIA moved to Hyde Park, New York and at that time five percent of the students were women. One of the first women to graduate with a culinary degree was Lyde Buchtenkirch. When Lyde started school, she was offered a blue dress as a uniform; however, she insisted on and received chef whites. In 1996, fifty years after they had established the school, Frances Roth and Katherine Angell were inducted into the CIA Hall of Fame. At that time, twenty-four percent of the students were women, an increase of nineteen percent in twenty-four years.

Many other culinary schools, and their late twentieth-century offspring (TV cooking shows), have made their mark on the culinary world. The directors of some of these schools, most notably Julia Child, Anne Willan, and Madeleine Kamman, served as role models and mentors for many of the chefs featured throughout this book. Female chefs owe their roots in the culinary profession in large part to these women who paved the way. Today there are over 600 culinary schools and/or programs across America, with a total student population of over 60,000. These institutions number far too many to describe in these pages; however, ShawGuides publishes annually *The Guide to Cooking Schools,* where much of the information about culinary schools may be found.

Women Working Their Way into the Professional Kitchen

Throughout this chronology, we have outlined the hardship women have faced trying to get a toehold in the professional culinary world. By the end of the nineteenth century, women had made many inroads, but they faced many roadblocks as well. In 1890, Ellen Swallow Richards (the mother of Home Economics) and Mary Abel opened the New England Kitchen in Boston, an outlet where the working class could purchase hot nutritious meals. The response was less than enthusiastic. One woman from that era said, "I don't want to eat what's good for me. I'd rather eat what I'd rather."[25] With their

Women in the Culinary Arena: Ellen Swallow Richards

Ellen Swallow Richards was one of the initial advocates of the positive correlation between nutritious food and a sound environmental lifestyle. Both an academic and culinary pioneer, she was instrumental in promoting the fledgling sciences of Nutrition and Ecology, and she is credited as the founder of the Home Economics Association.

In 1873, Ms. Swallow was the first woman to graduate from the Massachusetts Institute of Technology (MIT) in Cambridge, Massachusetts. She was hired as an instructor in 1883 and established a "Women's Laboratory," which was utilized until women were accepted into the full undergraduate curriculum in 1887.

Throughout this period of her life, Ms. Richards increased her involvement with the public school system, and she was awarded a contract from the Boston high schools to provide a hot lunch for fifteen cents per student. In 1890, she opened The New England Kitchen with a colleague; their goal was to sell inexpensive, nourishing food in an attempt to change the eating habits of working-class Americans.

She melded both facets of her life by establishing a new branch of science that she called *oekologie*, a general understanding of nutrition, sanitation, and wholesome living. When the scientific community didn't embrace her new area of study, she touted it as *home science* in academic circles, and it evolved into the study we know today as *home economics*.

Ellen Swallow Richards, an early advocate of testing food products for adulteration, a pioneer of school-lunch programs, an MIT-educated chemist, and "the mother of home economics" is a brilliant example of women in America. Her determined, intelligent, and public-spirited endeavors still shine as ideals a century later.

strength and determination, these highly motivated women established the first school lunch program by delivering hot lunches to a local high school for fifteen cents each. They were eventually awarded a contract to supply all of the city's high schools with hot lunches.

Another determined woman who had earned her stripes cooking for the former prince of Wales, the German Kaiser Wilhelm and Lady Randolf Churchill was Rosa Lewis. Her accomplishments in the kitchen put her on equal footing with her male counterparts. In 1902, Ms. Lewis took over the Cavendish Hotel in London (just a few years after Escoffier took over The Carlton Hotel's kitchen, in the same city) and hired a cadre of young women cooks to run the kitchen. She and her staff of young women cooks ran the hotel's kitchen, and continued to cook for hostesses who entertained the king and other elite of that era. Ms. Lewis deserves her place in history as one of the first hotel executive chefs; although she was only afforded the title of cook, she was called "The Queen of Cooks & the Cook for Queens."

1765: The first French restaurant, Boulanger, opens and serves soup.

From Ellen H. Richards, *The Chemistry of Cooking and Cleaning: A Manual for Housekeepers.* Courtesy of the Culinary Archives and Museum at Johnson and Wales University.

"A 'historically male profession'—who do you think taught these men to cook? Their mothers, I would guess."
—Coral Elandt

The early twentieth century emerged with women showcasing their talent and entrepreneurial spirit in bakeries. Ninnie Lilla Baird, who lived in Fort Worth, Texas, baked bread each Monday for her neighbors, friends, and children. In 1908, this mother of eight, using her small wood-fired kitchen oven, started selling bread to her local community. Mrs. Baird's Bakeries eventually became one of the nation's largest family-owned wholesale bakeries. Another innovative woman of that time, Margaret Rudkin, established what was to become Pepperidge Farm Bread in 1937. Rudkin, who had never baked, was looking for additional income for her family after her husband suffered injuries as the result of a riding accident. She set up an oven in what used to be her husband's polo stable and began baking twenty-four loaves of bread per day; within a year, she was baking over 4,000 loaves per week. Pepperidge Farm eventually became synonymous with quality store-bought baked goods.

By the middle of the twentieth century, the role of women in the culinary world evolved professionally. In the early 1950s, Stouffer's hired only women in their food production plants because the company found them to be the most accurate in following recipes. Yet in 1961, Janet Leffler, head of the Hotel Department at New York City Technical College, when interviewed in *The New York World Telegram and Sun*, said, "A girl in the food field doesn't stand a chance beyond the salad department." To this day, female culinarians are still fighting the bias that keeps them from some of the top positions in the industry.

In 1971, the Random House Dictionary defined *chef* as "a cook, esp a male head cook," with no feminine terminology. But it wasn't only women who had trouble defining themselves as culinary professionals. In 1974, at the American Culinary Federation (ACF) national convention, Chef Louis Szathmáry, addressed the audience, and said, "Mr. President, distinguished head table, fellow domestics." His comment was directed at the fact that according to the U.S. Department of Labor's *Dictionary of Occupational Titles,* the job of chef was listed under domestics. The rationale for the designation had been that cooking was seen as a woman's role, with the knowledge base passed down through oral history, and hence not a profession in the eyes of men. This designation was finally changed in 1976 when the U.S. Department of Labor officially recognized chefs as professionals and designated them as such in their dictionary.

The 1990s are finally starting to witness a change for women in the culinary profession. Women are coming up through the ranks and are being counted on once they get to the top. In 1990, Lyde Buchtenkirch-Biscardi, who was already introduced as the first woman to graduate from the CIA with a culinary degree, became the first and, as of this writing, the only female Certified Master Chef in the world. In 1991, just one year later, the *New York* magazine ran the story "City Star Chefs," in which none of the chefs were women. In the next year, *Food Arts* magazine published "Woman Chefs: Role Models for the 90s," featuring ten successful women chefs. In 1992, women were again recognized when there was "A Salute to Women Chefs in America" at the James Beard Awards. At that event, Alice Waters, one of America's most recognized chefs, was awarded best chef and her restaurant, Chez Panisse, was honored as the best restaurant. Debra Ponzek, the only woman running a three-star restaurant in New York City at that time, was awarded Rising Star Chef of the Year.

As we head into the twenty-first century, women are back in the kitchen, but in a professional capacity. The evolution of women chefs comes full circle.

DIRECTIONS for CATERING, or the procuring the beſt VIANDS, FISH, &c.

How to chooſe Fleſh.

BEEF. The large ſtall fed ox beef is the beſt, it has a coarſe open grain, and oily ſmoothneſs ; dent it with your finger and it will immediately riſe again ; if old, it will be rough and ſpungy, and the dent remain.

Cow Beef is leſs boned, and generally more tender and juicy than the ox, in America, which is uſed to labor.

Of almoſt every ſpecies of Animals, Birds and Fiſhes, the female is the tendereſt, the richeſt flavour'd, and among poultry the ſooneſt fatened.

Mutton, grafs-fed, is good two or three years old.

Lamb, if under ſix months is rich, and no danger of impoſition ; it may be known by its ſize, in diſtinguiſhing either.

Veal, is ſoon loſt—great care therefore is neceſſary in purchaſing. Veal bro't to market in panniers, or in carriages, is to be prefered to that bro't in bags, and flouncing on a ſweaty horſe.

Pork, is known by its ſize, and whether properly fattened by its appearance.

To make the beſt Bacon.

To each ham put one ounce ſaltpetre, one pint bay ſalt, one pint molaſſes, ſhake together 6 or 8 weeks, or when a large quantity is together, baſte them with

From Amelia Simmons' *American Cookery.* Courtesy of the Culinary Archives and Museum at Johnson and Wales University.

Women Making Their Mark in the Restaurant Business

Women chefs, chef-owners, and restaurateurs have helped guide the industry for more than a century and have penetrated all aspects of the restaurant profession. National Restaurant Association (NRA) statistics from 1992 show

1789: Nine out of ten Americans are engaged in farming and food production.

"You don't just spend five years in the business and become a chef; you spend a career in the business and become a chef."
—Ana Sortun

that 128,000 women owned food and beverage establishments, with combined revenues of over 27 billion dollars, a figure that has risen more than ninety-five percent in the past decade. During that same time period, women-owned operations have increased in excess of forty percent, and the number of employees in women-owned businesses has risen almost eighty-two percent. Appendix E shows a sampling of women and their restaurants throughout modern history.

The 1994 NRA statistics show that sixty percent of foodservice workers are women, yet less than ten percent of executive chefs are women. Our story continues to unfold. The following chapters present stories and perspectives from women in the culinary arena. These stories show not only the evolution of women in the industry, but they tell how these women have persevered and overcome tremendous challenges to pursue their passion. These women have shown that indeed, without a doubt, a woman's place is in the kitchen.

The Passion of Women Chefs

Making Food Sing
—*Suzanne Bussiere*

"A chef is a leader and teacher of individuals who creates and then coordinates the production of food."

—Lisa Schroeder

Before we begin our discussion of women chefs, we need to clarify what the title *chef* really means. This chapter explores various definitions of the term and tries to ascertain why there have been so few women chefs. A variety of women discuss what it takes to become a chef, and they express the passion that led them to seek jobs in professional kitchens.

What Is a Chef?

In the French language, the word *chef* means "head" or "chief" and is a masculine term that actually is specific to men only. The closest feminine equivalent is *cuisinière*, which refers to a woman who prepares and cooks food. Whereas she may hold many of the same responsibilities as a chef, a cuisinière does not garner the respect and prestige that the male term connotes.

Both the American Culinary Federation (ACF) and The Culinary Institute of America (CIA) offer definitions for the term *chef*. In their certification manual, the ACF defines a *chef* as*:* "someone fully responsible for preparing, seasoning and cooking according to recipe ... supervises, coordinates and participates in activities of cooks ... estimates requirements, requisitions or purchases supplies." In *The New Professional Chef,* the CIA's primary textbook, a *chef* is described as "a lifelong student, a teacher, a craftsman, a leader and a manager. An open and inquiring mind, an appreciation of the dedication to quality and excellence and a sense of responsibility to self and the community are among the chef's cardinal virtues. The title is one that can only be earned through diligent practice and dedication."

Pat Bartholomew, chairwoman of the Department of Hospitality and Management at the New York City Technical College, wrote in her dissertation a genderless definition of chef: "The most highly skilled, trained and experienced kitchen worker [who is] responsible for all kitchen operations, including menu planning, purchasing, costing, and scheduling. The chef also trains the other kitchen workers ... [is] a first class cook, teacher, administrator [and] an expert in sanitation. [A chef has] a keen sense of taste and smell, an incredible palate with the ability by taste and smell, to know when something is coming out right or wrong. A chef must be a lover of good food, an artist or artisan who is always inventing and improving dishes."

Based on my own experience, the ascension to the position of chef was long and hard, but it was a journey during which knowledge was continuously acquired. I started my culinary career at seventeen and accepted my first chef position at twenty-six. During those intervening years, I went from prep cook to baker and from line cook to chef and manager. I apprenticed in a hotel, working all the stations in the kitchen, spent two years cooking in the kitchens of cruise ships, and somewhere in between, graduated from the CIA. My first position as executive chef was at a 200-seat restaurant, where I had responsibility for all the food and staff. I really thought I was a chef at twenty-six years old and thought I knew it all, but almost seventeen years later, I think I am evolving as a chef. While this was the process through which I progressed, every chef has a different story. I asked a number of chefs to tell me how they describe the role of a chef. The following are some of their responses.

In 1992, while presiding over the kitchen at Drew Nieporent's Montrachet, Debra Ponzek became the first female executive chef in New York City to receive three stars from the New York Times. Debra explains her perception of a chef's role in the kitchen: "You have to be into a lot of the management, seeing the big picture of the kitchen, how people work together, when they work together, scheduling, being able to solve conflicts, being able to make changes, to either eliminate conflicts, or to lessen them. [You have to be ready] to come up with more alternative solutions to problems."

Metzu (Gabriel) Dessine' par Desenne's "Une Cuisinière" depicts a woman peeling apples to be served with the rabbit she has by her side. (Engraver: J. B. L. Bassard.)

Edna Lewis' notion of "chef" came to her more as a revelation than as a conscious act. In 1948 at age thirty-one, Edna was running a kitchen in a New York City restaurant—unusual for a woman, but doubly uncommon because she is African-American. Edna remembers the first time she was called *chef:* "I tell you! I was on Lexington Avenue ... when I was at Café Nicholson. I was walking down the street, and someone said, 'You're the chef from Café Nicholson!' That was the first time I heard the chef bit! I never even thought of [it]. I just did the cooking." The 1996 Bureau of Labor Statistics Current Population Survey concludes that sixteen percent of cooks and chefs and ten percent of kitchen supervisors are African-American. It would be difficult to accurately assess how many black women chefs there were in 1948, but my guess is very few. Ms. Lewis paved the way for women into the professional kitchen, not only as one of the first women, but as a black woman as well.

"[A] chef is the chief running the kitchen. We use the term chef *very loosely (in America). A cook can be in the kitchen of a chef, but a cook is not the chef."*

—Julia Child

Regardless of how we define *chef*—"chief," "cook," or "manager"—chefs must be talented culinarians, craftspersons, and artists; they need to have vision and creativity; they need to be leaders and motivators, friends and bosses, number-crunchers and foragers; some even have to be TV personalities. Many chefs consider the art and/or the craft the most important aspect of their work.

1793: The French introduce the tall white toque to the British.

Chef's Work as an Art and a Craft

As chefs, what binds us all is food. It is our joy, our passion, and our craft—a craft that can become an art form. While individual chefs may view their work differently, in the end, it is a masterful presentation of food and flavor.

Gary Fine, Professor of Sociology at the University of Georgia, has researched human behavior in kitchens. His most recent work, written in 1996, is *Kitchens: The Culture of Restaurant Work,* which offers his perspective on this issue: "Some cooks speak of themselves as artists through their actions, making cooking a performance art. For some the criteria for quality labor are primarily in the product: the sight, feel, taste, or smell; for others they are in the performance; but for each the work has a style, a sense of form, an aesthetic."

When I asked individual chefs their perception of whether they practice a craft or an art form, I got a variety of responses, yet all of them replied with a unique guiding philosophy, revealing a personal approach to their work.

Anne Rosenzweig is renowned throughout the industry. She is chef-owner of both Arcadia and The Lobster Club in New York City. She opened Arcadia, her first restaurant, in 1987, and it has consistently been awarded three stars from the *New York Times* over the years. Her second restaurant, The Lobster Club, opened in 1995 and seems destined for similar success. Anne shares her thoughts on the idea of cooking as a craft versus art: "I think one can be artistic in one's craft, but it's still a craft. There's the component that food is social. … [F]ood, and music, and art—and all these other things—are closely woven together in the family fabric." While Anne feels strongly that cooking is a craft, she sees it as being central to the rhythms of our lives. This craft becomes a cultural entity that shapes our relationships and gives expression to women's historic role as nurturer and provider.

André Soltner began his career, like so many others of his era, as an apprentice in France, where he learned and honed his craft. André discusses the craft as a rigid, disciplined vocation, clearly distinctive from Anne's social perspective. André explains: "A big part is discipline. We are craftspeople. I said that a thousand times, we are craftspeople, we are not artists. We need a little talent, but we need the discipline of a craftsman … a chef, man or woman, has to love cooking. We cook with love."

Claire Stewart, an alumna of the CIA and The Rainbow Room in New York City, is currently executive chef of The Continental Club, also in New York. Claire grew up in a family full of artists. Like André Soltner, Claire believes that the technical precision required in cooking is something that is attributable to a craft: "I think [cooking is] a craft as well as an art … I have more respect for a craft than an art. A craft is really doing something very well and doing it continuously and [doing it] correctly. With a craft you are given parameters, wherein you're expected to perform. … It is a *science* and that is all there is to it. Maybe garnish is an art, [or] maybe I'm jealous—I am a craftsman and maybe I want to be an artist."

Eve Felder is a chef-instructor and an alumna of the CIA. Much of Eve's culinary perspective is based on her early experiences working at Chez Panisse with Alice Waters. Eve's philosophy is that the craft is the soul of the food. "I have internal and also external debates about art versus craft, and I believe food as art takes away the soul. I wonder if we're coming to a place now where we see the soul, and the heart in food, and [make] the connection. That's what women [see] in fact … it is not an intellectual decision, but more of an intuitive, organic [one]."

Regardless of whether cooking is viewed as a craft or an art, it must be executed with care and precision. The chef or cook is the medium through which this art or craft shines. Just as we have tried to distinguish cooking as an art or a craft, we will now look at the distinction between a cook and a chef in order to unearth the differences between these key roles in the kitchen.

Understanding the Distinction Between a Chef and a Cook

There is a distinction between being a chef and a cook; however, until people enter the culinary field, that distinction seems immaterial. To become a chef, one must climb the ranks of the kitchen, and being a cook is one of the key prerequisites. I spoke with many culinarians about how they viewed the distinction between being a cook and a chef—and it's not always black and white.

In *Kitchens: The Culture of Restaurant Work*, Gary Fine describes differences between the roles of cooks and chefs and the work they do: "Cooking is demanding work; it is experienced as hard labor. Like athletes, cooks must 'play' in pain. … Cooks are producers. They create products that can be beautiful and appealing to the senses. The cook may specialize in frying food, broiling steaks, or making salads; the chef should be able to do everything: keep a food budget, repair stoves, hire personnel, provide counseling, and know about food. A chef organizes the kitchen; while the cook focuses on limited tasks, the chef is responsible for a wide range of activities."

Many women in this book have become chef-owners through sheer will and perseverance, often times without formal training. Barbara Tropp, former chef-owner of China Moon Café, an Asian-influenced restaurant in San Francisco, is one of these women. After spending time in China, Japan, and two years in Taiwan, Barbara had formed her culinary philosophy and merged her passion for Tung-Sung-dynasty poetics with an equally consuming passion for food. Her decision to open a restaurant was driven more by passion than knowledge. Barbara explains: "You can be a great cook and a great cooking teacher … [but in a restaurant kitchen], you don't know beans from bazooka.

"You have to do it every day; that's the challenge. You can be the best chef in the world, but if you don't have this discipline of craftspeople, then you can't do it. No way."
—André Soltner

1793: The master, or head, chef continues to wear a short black cap in the kitchen.

*"[W]hen I look back
at my chefs, I think a
little bit about the
food they gave me. I
think about the peo-
ple that they were ...
the ones that I still to
this day think about,
admire, and respect
... they gave so much
of themselves."*

—*Tamara Murphy*

It is like being thrown into an Olympic pool after all you've ever done is swim in the bathtub—there's no correlation. You can't take your favorite recipe and do it times ten. This was a shock. I didn't earn the title "chef" until we were many, many years into it. I had a succession of fabulous sous chefs who ran the kitchen. I fed the vision; I was the palate. But they were chefs de cuisine."

Most chefs and chef-owners started as line cooks, and remember it fondly, although many line cooks are anxious to become chefs. Loretta Keller is chef-owner of San Francisco's Bizou, a small restaurant with French-influenced cuisine. Loretta spent much of her career at Jeremiah Tower's landmark San Francisco restaurant Stars, where she held both line cook and chef positions. Comparing those early influences to her experiences as chef of her own restaurant, Loretta describes the distinction between chef and cook: "A chef has some idea of everything. And a cook—it's great to be a cook—it's a luxury to be a cook. When you're a chef, you're caught up in everything. You're putting out fires—literally. You're hiring, firing, and dealing with all those employees, all of their idiosyncrasies, each one of their problems, each one of their needs. You have to inspire people, criticize people, instill discipline, order, and inspiration. Then, you have to make money [for your restaurant]!"

To be a great chef, you must be a good cook. Yet ironically, when cooks become chefs, other responsibilities overshadow cooking time. Emily Luchetti spent eight years as pastry chef of Stars in San Francisco, getting much of her training in the same restaurant as Loretta. She went on to open Star Bake, a bakery concept in San Francisco with Jeremiah Tower, and then to become a cookbook author and consultant. Emily started her career on the line, but eventually discovered her passion for baking pastry. Emily's view of the distinction between cooks and chefs is very similar to Loretta's: "I think every chef has to be a cook ... If you're a cook you can create good food. If you're a chef, whether it's in the kitchen or pastry, you have to know how to do a lot of different things. You have to know how to cook, ... how to manage, ... how to do eight million other things. Often a chef does know more about cooking, because he or she has more experience, ... they also often have a better palate, and are more creative." Emily points to an important issue that will be revisited later in this book—that good cooks do not necessarily make good chefs. She explains, "In our business, if you can cook well, they [want to] make you a chef. ... [But] that's not all that's required!

The distinction between chef and cook is important to understand. While a chef must know how to cook, a cook doesn't necessarily know how to be a chef, and making the leap to management is not right for everyone, especially early in their culinary careers. Becoming a chef takes years of experience and the ability to manage multiple priorities. People take different paths to achieve chef status, and the next section recounts those stories.

Driving Forces Behind Women's Desire to Become Chefs

The women in this book became chefs because of their love of creating and their deep connection to food. For many of them, it takes this kind of passion to persevere in an industry where men dominate the top positions. A quick look at the demographics of the industry are telling: According to the 1994 National Restaurant Association (NRA) *Foodservice Employee Profile*, a compilation of the *Current Population Survey*, the *Occupational Employment Statistics Survey* and the *Current Employment Statistics Survey*, women hold sixty percent of all foodservice positions, forty-three percent of all cooking positions, sixty-seven percent of all kitchen supervisor jobs, yet less than ten percent of executive chef positions. As these numbers suggest, it's an uphill battle for women trying to advance in the culinary field.

Such daunting barriers are rarely given a second's thought when career decisions are made. For most women in this book, their entry into the culinary arts felt like destiny; they were ineluctably drawn to the field. Some of the influences that took them there include early relationships with food in the context of family; an experience with food at a first job; or a chance encounter in life. Some women attribute their career choice to the need to nurture or to find expression for their innate knowledge of food. In this section, women tell their stories about why they became chefs.

Early Influence of Food and Family

For many chefs, their fates may have been set in childhood, when they formed their first attachments to food. Whether food evoked happy memories of family or provided comfort, it had a powerful impact that these chefs carried with them into adulthood.

Edna Lewis grew up in the small farm town of Freetown, Virginia, which was founded by her grandfather as a community for freed southern slaves. Edna learned the value and flavors of freshly grown food, lessons she carried forward into her career. According to Edna: "We had this little settlement, and it was all one big family. The housewives, they all *loved* to cook. They were really good cooks. Everybody was obsessed with food! Everybody's tasting, everybody's cooking … and in the wintertime, they'd exchange food. It really had great flavor." For Edna, those early life experiences shaped her destiny to become a chef.

Nora Pouillon, chef-owner of Restaurant Nora and Asia Nora in Washington DC, grew up in Europe, where her love affair with fresh, regional

"The chef is the organizer, the manager of the kitchen, and the restaurant's creative force. The cook, in contrast, is the line worker who prepares food on a routine, quotidian basis—a manual laborer."
—*Gary Fine*

1794: Paris has 500 public restaurants.

Women in the Culinary Arena: Edna Lewis

Edna Lewis grew up in the town her grandfather founded. Freetown, as the newly freed slaves called it, was her home and the origin of her culinary heritage. It has always been a struggle for women to find equality in the kitchen, but even more difficult for African-American women. I asked Edna what it was like to be one of the only women in the kitchens where she worked. Her response is that she never minded, no one ever gave her any trouble, and mostly the men were very respectful. She also says that she thought in some cases her age (older than her co-workers) helped to keep the men in line. Regardless, her presence must have somehow commanded the respect of her peers.

Edna went to Washington, DC as a teenager. Her first job was cooking at the Brazilian embassy; she was fifteen, and it was 1932. Her career took her from being the chef of Café Nicholson in New York City in 1948 at the age of thirty-one, to The Fearrington House and Middleton Place in Charleston and eventually back to New York City to become the chef of Aschkenasy's U.S. Steak House and then at Gage and Tollner in Brooklyn.

Ms. Lewis, long considered the foremost authority on southern cooking, has taken up the cause of organic and sustainable agriculture. With sixty-five years in the industry, Edna is in the process of writing her fourth book on southern cuisine. With her culinary partner Scott Peacock, she is organizing the Society for the Revival and Preservation of Southern Food and is very active in the Atlanta food community. As an expert on southern cooking, Edna offers this guiding principle of cooking: "You have to taste, and taste, and taste. Everything is creating; you develop your own flair, your own taste, and your own thoughts about it. ... The more you work in it, the more you become addicted to it!"

Along with a culinary career that has spanned more than six decades, Ms. Lewis has lectured on African culture at The American Museum of Natural History in New York City. She also has found time to raise a family of adopted Masai and Ethiopian children.

Women in the culinary field often discuss the difficulties they face in balancing work and their other responsibilities. Edna Lewis seems to have done it all, and continues to inspire those who have had the chance to experience her generosity of spirit, her dedication to her work, and her passion for food.

products got its start. Both of Nora's restaurants showcase her trademark style: creating with organic and seasonal local ingredients. She explains the influence of her upbringing on her culinary sensibilities: "I was born in Vienna in 1943 and I was very lucky, because my family [was] into healthy food and fresh vegetables, yogurt, and fresh fruit ... not the usual Viennese cuisine, ... in which everything is fried. They were really into healthy food. ... It gave me incentive to live in a certain way."

Since emigrating from Pula, Istria in 1958, Lidia Bastianich has earned the title of "First Lady" of Italian restaurants in the United States. Lidia is chef-owner of Felidia, Becco, and Frico, all restaurants in New York City, each with a different style and personality. Felidia, her first restaurant, is upscale, traditional Italian, Becco is more casual, and Frico is a bar/restaurant. Her family and their lifestyle in Italy fostered Lidia's connection to food. A childhood memory has been and continues to be an inspiration in her life: "My grandmother and grandfather had an inn in the house. Whatever she [her grandmother] cooked, that's what she served. My grandfather made wine and that's what they drank. They made all the food they ate and served, from growing their own wheat, to their own grapes, to potatoes, to their own olive oil … from hulling the beans and drying them, to milling the flour, to stomping grapes. They had ducks, pigs, and goats. We used goat milk for making cheese, for making sausage, for making prosciutto. I think that my understanding and passion for food came from there."

Madeleine Kamman has a similar story. She too grew up in a family involved in the hospitality field—her great aunt ran a small Michelin-starred hotel in the Loire Valley in France. "In a French family, if you were in a hotel family, you contributed. If you wanted to have lunch, you had to earn it. In this way I learned to french beans when I was nine years old. Then I started chopping everything … [also] I made cream puffs while standing on a box, a box for the apprentices when you're not high enough to get to the stove." Both Lidia and Madeleine had strong family/food ties that started them on their paths as passionate women chefs.

Food is so central to some families that the magic of familial bonds can be rekindled simply by cooking. In some ways it personifies the family who shares it. The mother/daughter food connection has been strong throughout history, and for Jody Adams, chef/co-owner of Rialto in Cambridge, Massachusetts, the connection is ingrained. Jody traces her passion for cooking to her childhood, where food played a key role in her family. "I grew up in a family that celebrated food; it was central to everything that was important. We sat down at the table every night, with candles and napkins. I think for my mother, it was symbolic of the strength of the family: to give, to take care—I wanted to do something that would make me feel that I was being good! If I was going to survive, I had to be happy—food [and cooking] had made me happy!"

For some women, their first connection to food came as a result of the influence of their families. Strong family ties bind their early memories of food in a way that carried into a future career. For other women, their first job, or a specific food experience at a job, helped steer their path toward the kitchen.

"My grandmother probably never cooked a meal for money, but the woman is absolutely in my heart a chef because she never put a plate out that wasn't her entire heart and soul. That's the difference to me between a cook and a chef."

—Toniann Beattie

1796: The *Veuve Clicquot* (Widow Clicquot), at age twenty, pioneers the process of "riddling" champagne.

The Influence of First Jobs

One of the requisites for surviving in the culinary field is working hard. Another is loving what you do. It's impossible to force the latter. That's why, for most women chefs, they know with their first kitchen job whether or not the food industry is their calling. Figures about employee tenure from the 1994 NRA *Foodservice Employee Profile* support this. The average tenure for a foodservice worker is 1.8 years; this compares to 4.5 years for workers in all other professions. Of the women who participated in my survey, about sixty-five percent said their first job was in the food and beverage industry; forty percent started as prep cooks or cooks, six percent as dishwashers, and fourteen percent worked in the front of the house. These figures indicate that first job experiences can have a profound impact on decisions to pursue a career in foodservice.

One woman who credits her career choice to her first job is Susan Weaver, executive chef at the Four Seasons Hotel, in New York City. Susan was the first female executive chef with a major Canadian hotel chain, and she later earned three stars for the New York City hotel. Here are her memories of her first kitchen job: "The first job that I ever enjoyed was washing dishes in a restaurant. It was not specifically the dishes, but the atmosphere, the ambiance, the craft around me. I thought that work was something you did to make money. This was a big discovery for me [that I could be happy at work]. That was my first job and I kept looking for other places that could give that to me."

The discipline required in Patricia Williams' first career, professional dance, prepared this Texas native for the rigors of the professional kitchen, a career that she has embraced with passion. Patricia is executive chef of the recently opened City Wine and Cigar Co., a Drew Nieporent project in New York City. Drew, owner of numerous restaurants both nationally and abroad, has worked with and promoted many women in his restaurants. Debra Ponzek, Traci Des Jardins and Patricia Williams are a few of his alumna. Patricia's latest venture features the food, wine, and flavors of cigar-producing regions and marries them with her own flair and style. Patricia explained her transition from professional dancer to culinarian: "I was about twenty-eight when I retired, which is middle-aged for a dancer. [Dancing was] the only thing [I'd] ever known. It [requires] tremendous discipline ... [I'd] done it for twelve hours a day [as long as I could] remember. I ended up on Barry Wine's doorstep, at Quilted Giraffe in New York City and said 'Can I have a job?' He said 'What can you do?' 'Well, not very much—I'm a fast learner, have good physical dexterity. I have a very good short-term memory and I'm cheap.' He hired me!" Patricia's passion for the kitchen was immediately apparent; her love for the "hot-line" and its choreography had its roots in her dancing career.

Anne Rosenzweig, like Patricia Williams, chose cooking as her second career. She had started in a much different field: "I was working as an anthropologist, as an ethnomusicologist, and lived in different parts of Africa, Nepal, and India. I always lived in remote places. The first thing people did was teach me to cook. They'd bring me food, show me how to cook, take me into the field, show me how to grow stuff. It started as an interest, and grew gradually to being a real passion. ...When I came back to New York City, I wanted to pursue that [food] interest and passion by working in a [professional] kitchen. I thought that would satisfy my curiosity, [I had this idea that in] professional kitchens, there were great secrets that weren't available to the average person. The very first day I was in a professional kitchen—[where] I started as an apprentice, working for free—that's exactly what happened. I was totally entranced. I thought this was the greatest thing—it was so rich with information. That was all I wanted to do and I've never looked back."

As Anne seemed to evolve into the culinary field, so too did Emily Luchetti. For Emily, her first job launched her lifetime career. "I was looking at the *New York Times* classified section and the top of the ad said, 'No Typing.' They wanted somebody interested in the culinary arts to work for a company near Wall Street, in their executive dining room. I'd always liked to cook. I think it was my enthusiasm, my excitement about food in general that got me the job. I didn't have any experience!" That excitement has stayed with her throughout her career.

First jobs and the excitement of the kitchen attract many women. For others, the attraction to food came from earlier influences—they "just knew" that food, cooking, and kitchens would be their life.

"I Just Knew"

At some time in all of our lives, we are struck by something that tells us the path we should take. For each individual, the timing of this revelation differs. Some know when they are children. Other people search for years. For me, it took a few jobs and starting my own business in the culinary field to know this is where I belonged.

My very first job was as an assistant breakfast cook in Telluride, Colorado. From there I graduated to baking breakfast pastries, cookies, and brownies in a deli. After a season of baking, another woman "ski bum" and I decided to try our hands at starting our own business, and we founded a baking company called Rising High Dough Rollers. From those first intense "all-nighters" spent rolling dough, I knew that I had found my home.

"There were two things that I wanted to be when I was a little girl. One was [to be] a doctor, the second was [to be] a chef."

—*Audrey Lennon*

1805: The Lewis and Clark expedition survives the winter because of the cooking skills of their guide's wife, a Shoshone teenager.

Claire Stewart knew at a much earlier age. She recalls a childhood experience that foretold her destiny: "When I was in third grade, we had to do a project called 'what I want to be when I grow up,' and we had to draw a picture. Children that age are drawing pictures of themselves in spaceships going to the moon and cowboys riding on horses, ballerinas, and everything very exciting. ... I drew a picture of myself cooking. The teacher said, 'But what do you want to be?' I said 'I don't know what that means! But this is what I want to be.' "

Many of us share a history of wanting to feed people from an early age. It's what Kathleen Kennedy wanted to do, too. Kathleen, presently an instructor at The California Culinary Academy, was a 1988 graduate of the CIA and an apprentice team member of the 1988 ACF/NRA Culinary Olympic Team. She shares a defining childhood memory: "The day that I said I wanted to be a chef was the day I got my Easy-Bake Oven. I turned a little powdered mix into a cake, and served [it] to my friends. ... I don't think I knew what 'chef' meant back then. ... But I knew [while] growing up that I had a talent to make people happy and to bring people into my home ... it's such a warm, loving, nurturing thing. I don't see how it couldn't have been women that started it!"

Kirsten Dixon is chef-owner of three lodges in the wilds of Alaska. In 1983, she and her husband began to assemble the first of these remote lodges, all built by hand from the ground up. All three properties, Riversong Lodge, Winterlake Lodge, and Redoubt Bay Lodge are accessible only by floatplane, and give even the most passionate chef enough challenges for a lifetime. Kirsten tells a story similar to Kathleen's, in that it reveals her connection to food from a very early age. "Even as a nine- or ten-year-old girl, I really liked to cook. I started out with little hamburger patties made with red wine. I'd go to the library and get *Gourmet*'s anthology of recipes. It didn't [really] mean anything to me—I couldn't even understand the words—[but] I really had a lot of energy for [cooking and food]."

For so many women, part of their lives, if not their sense of self, is wrapped up in the act of nurturing. Cooking can serve as an all-important expression of that instinct. Katy Keck describes how the role of nurturer started for her as a child: "Something had really upset my mother, she stormed off to her room, and slammed the door. This was not a common occurrence, but it was so upsetting to me, [that I had] to make things all better. I took a chocolate turtle candy, put it on a plate, rang the doorbell and ran away, so that she'd have to come out. I look back at that, and I think [how conditioned we are to make] things better with food."

The stories in this section reflect a deep-rooted love for a role that most of these women, then girls, couldn't even define. But what they recognized was the desire to comfort, nurture, and to entertain. Many of these are the same desires that have brought them to professional kitchens today.

Becoming a Chef

As with any profession, it takes years of labor, of paying your dues, and of climbing the ladder for a taste of success. The hard work and pressure associated with any craft can be intense, and the culinary world is no exception. Kitchen "proving grounds" are physically, emotionally, and intellectually strenuous, and trial periods can last up to ten years. A typical day in the kitchen can mean pulling a ten- to fifteen-hour shift in a hot (often 100°F), busy (feeding hundreds of people a day), stressful (everyone needs it now), and sometimes dangerous (wet floors, heavy pots, high flames, and boiling water) environment.

To be able to fulfill the standards of excellence that are expected of a chef, it takes most culinarians years of hard work and hands-on experience. The rungs on the ladder are many and may advance a young culinarian only from prep cook to the pantry or banquet prep. Frequently, cooks spend two to four years learning food production and line cooking, at which point they might progress to a lead line position for a few years. The next step up would be sous chef, then chef, and finally executive chef. Reaching the top position generally requires a minimum of ten years, suggest the ACF requirements. To put this in perspective, NRA and ACF job statistics show that certified executive chefs, working chefs, chefs de cuisine, and sous chefs make up only about twenty percent of the membership of the ACF. Likewise, the NRA tells us that only fifteen percent of all kitchen workers are supervisors or chefs. The rest are gaining skills and experience, working up to positions of higher responsibility. It's a long, strenuous climb to the top—one that takes years and one where less than ten percent of those who make it are women.

Mary Sue Milliken is co-chef/co-owner with Susan Feniger of Border Grill in Los Angeles. Mary Sue attended the culinary arts program at Washburne Trade School in Chicago and decided she wanted to work at the famous Le Perroquet. It was here that Mary Sue met Susan and launched a partnership that has spanned over fifteen years. The two related this story about Mary Sue's beginnings at Le Perroquet: "The chef wouldn't hire a woman in the kitchen. He said, 'I have a job as a hatcheck girl available.' I don't think I even reacted because I was so appalled. I remember crying in the car all the way back [home], and thinking, 'I just graduated chef's school! When I got home, I wrote an eloquent letter to Le Perroquet's chef; then the next week I wrote another one and then I started calling him, bugging him—I just kept calling and writing him letters. Finally, I called him up, [after] maybe six weeks of this barrage, and he says, 'Are you going to sue me, or something?' I said, 'No, I

"My inspiration ... was my mother, and my mother loves to cook—she was very good. ... In the industry we were a little bit brainwashed that it was a man's job, and it wasn't."
—André Soltner

1815: *Le Pâtissier royal parisien,* by Antonin Carême, is published in France.

"Look at what you have to do, seven days a week, all day long! No conductor of a symphony orchestra would conduct two symphonies a day, six days a week, year round! There's a season! The conductor of the orchestra is not playing every instrument. But they are supposed to understand how each instrument works, and they're supposed to bring the voices together in harmony, and have a vision. I think you can do that, but you can't do it day in, day out, and year-round! Which is what a chef has to do."

—*Judy Rodgers*

just want a job!' He said, 'I'm going to give you a job. Minimum wage. Come to work tomorrow morning—you can start peeling onions.' I said, 'Fine; great; I'll be there!' Shortly thereafter Susan got a job at the same restaurant, in part because of Mary Sue's performance, and the start of the friendship that would become the "Too Hot Tamales" TV Food Network show had begun.

Whether working for minimum wage or less, those determined to become a chef are willing to do whatever is necessary to achieve their goals. Amy Scherber enrolled in the New York Restaurant School and upon graduation, got her first job at Bouley in New York City, where she progressed through every station in the kitchen. It was here that Amy discovered her passion for bread. She went on to stagières in France, after which she returned to New York City and became the pastry chef at Mondrian before she opened Amy's Bread in 1992. Amy remembers working at Bouley without pay when she started so that she could learn. "Just trying out recipes and practicing, practicing ... it was a great chance because the ingredients were really good, and the support was there. I helped with pastry because they didn't have the pastry side. I got myself into making starters and learning about fermentation. Then, from the minute I got back from Europe, I knew that I wanted to start a bakery."

Kerry Heffernan is chef de cuisine of The Palace, a landmark in downtown San Francisco. Prior to becoming chef at this California legend, she was executive sous chef of Elka at the Miyako Hotel. Kerry describes her ascent to becoming a chef. "I always was a chef in my mind—always! When I was throwing pizzas at Marcello's Pizza on Castle Street, I was already a chef. When I got to the Ritz Carlton, I probably wouldn't have said that in front of other chefs, but I asked Franz Mitterer, (now the publisher of *Art Culinaire*), 'If my mom and my grandparents ask me what I do, what should I tell them.' He said, 'Tell them you're a chef!' I said, 'but I'm not the chef,' and he said, 'But you *are* going to *be* a chef.' I don't think that I ever thought I was anything else." For Kerry, the belief that she was always a chef helped empower her to overcome many of the obstacles to becoming a chef.

Traci Des Jardins' career has taken her from Montrachet with Debra Ponzek in 1986 to chef of Patina in San Francisco, California, at the age of twenty-three. Traci went on to become executive sous chef at Elka working with Elka Gilmore and then, with Drew Nieporent, opened Rubicon in 1994. Traci credits her early training with Joachim Splichal as having a tremendous impact on her beginnings in the culinary arena. "I guess I was fairly adept, given the fact that I didn't have any practical work experience. I remember one of the first days I was in the kitchen and I was watching him [the chef] doing some plates for a photo shoot, and I was so moved by what he was doing, it brought tears to my eyes. I really knew that it was what I wanted and I put everything I had into it. I said to myself, this is going to be tough, because he was a big screamer, he was in your face, and I said [to myself], you're going to have to be tough. I started out working sixteen-, seventeen-, eighteen-hour days. I was working for minimum wage and he immediately put me on split shift. I was living in and sleeping in my car between the split shifts. And that was the beginning."

No matter the path, all of these women succeeded in gaining a foothold in the culinary field. The next section explores what happens after women culiniarians have climbed the rungs—what it's like to be a chef.

"I come from many generations of bakers. I grew up in the back of a Mexican special-ty bakery and restau-rant. Creative stuff, it's in my blood."
—Silvana Salcido

Being the Chef

People often ask me what it is like to be a chef. For me, becoming a chef was the culmination of a dream, the attainment of my goals, the step that gave broader context to cooking. Most chefs come to this career because they love food; they love cooking. But as chef, the role changes dramatically. These "cooks" now need to learn management, accounting, people skills, budgeting, spreadsheet analysis, and so much more. The journey from the early influences to the climb up the career ladder culminates when they attain the position of chef. Each story that follows tells how these women chefs define and evolve with their new responsibilities.

Jody Adams describes what it was like for her to step up from cook to manager: "When you go from being a cook to being a manager, it's a huge leap. It's not natural! What drew me to restaurants is cooking and food—having hands-on everything, touching, tasting, and playing. As the chef of this big operation, I just don't have the opportunity to do that anymore. I had to step back, and let other people do that, [which] was really hard. It was learning the value of delegation, letting go."

Kerry Heffernan also reflects on her changing role as chef. "At this point, sixty percent of my job is human relations; forty percent is thinking of and executing menus. It's evolved into something other than what I imagined I would be as a chef. I can remember fantasizing, while peeling potatoes: someday when *I'm* the chef, *I'm* going to treat people so great and they're going to love me; it's going to be *great*."

In 1994, Debbie Gold and her husband, Michael, moved to Kansas City to begin the job as co-executive chefs at The American Restaurant. Debbie talks about her role as co-executive chef and the interesting challenge of balancing creativity and business: "I've seen chefs in different restaurants that feel that people come to the restaurant to see the chef. We're running a business; we need to make sure that the food will bring people in. They're not coming

1824: The first regional American cookbook, *The Virginia Housewife*, by Mary Randolph, is published.

"Take pride in what you do. ... Food is something that is a necessity, but it's also an art, and it's a passion. You have to be excited about some baby arugula that comes in, or saying, 'My god! I've never had a sauce like this!' And get up, stand up, and cheer: 'This is absolutely fantastic!' ... It's a way of life!"

—Deborah Huntley

to eat some exotic thing that Michael and I create. We have a really nice balance; this job of being [the] chef is very creative, but we also have to remember it's a business."

Before becoming curator and museum director of the Johnson and Wales Culinary Archives and Museum in Providence, Rhode Island in 1991, Barbara Kuck spent two decades as a cook and a chef. Barbara's culinary history is marked by her years of working at The Bakery, a Chicago institution, with Chef Louis Szathmáry. Barbara discusses her duties when she was working for Chef Louis, a man whose career spans most of the modern culinary history of this country. Barbara remembers: "I was responsible for training and making sure that everything was accurate. I had to come in every thirty minutes to taste the soup and the sauces, and make sure they didn't have too much wine or get too thick. I did all of the food ordering, the wine ordering, the equipment ordering; I planned the menus. I was [also] in charge of the catering: talking to the customer, working out the contracts, making sure everyone made what they were supposed to, scheduling, dealing with [all the] people." Barbara went on to say that she loved working with Chef Louis, who treated her with respect when few women were in kitchens and who remained her mentor throughout her career.

Being a chef, cooking, tasting, managing; the job takes many different forms in different kitchens. But what all these women share is the passion for the food and cooking, the subject of the next section.

Passion for Food

Passion for food is a driving force in the lives of female chefs. It permeates every aspect of their work, from motivation to creation. That passion is visceral and tangible, and it forms the basis for everything a chef does. The following stories give voice to this passion, which has brought these women to where they are today.

Sarah Langan, currently an instructor at the New England Culinary Institute in Vermont, spent much of her early culinary career in Hawaii, England, and France, where her love of fresh food flourished. She shares her intense and enthusiastic passion for this type of food with her students. "You should see the lettuce we're getting," she says. "I walk around like it's a bouquet of flowers. I make [the students] smell it, look at it, look at the color. This is *lettuce!* I get really excited about stuff like that." She will no doubt pass on this type of contagious excitement to her students.

Nancy Oakes has been tremendously successful in San Francisco. Her career as a chef-owner started in 1979, at the age of twenty-seven, when she opened her first restaurant, Pat O'Shea's Mad Hatter. Nine years later, Nancy opened L'Avenue next door and in 1993, she and her staff moved to

Women in the Culinary Arena: Madeleine Kamman

Madeleine Kamman is one of the most influential female culinarians of our time. She tells about her defining moment: "My story starts in 1940 when I was nine years old. We had to leave Paris because the Germans were coming. We took what I believed was the last train out of Paris. It took seventy hours to get to my aunt's place, only 130 kilometers away. What I remember most was when I walked in, [there] was the smell—delicious. It was dinnertime and it smelled absolutely fantastic in my aunt's home."

It was that smell and that feel that enveloped Madeleine and penetrated her entire being. From there, her culinary career unfolded. Madeleine came to America in 1960, and as she says, "I was made of 900 years of French blood. I started cooking up a storm to sublimate my homesickness." But, as much as Madeleine cooked for family and friends, she still felt that she needed something more.

In 1962, Madeleine launched her teaching career, starting at an adult education center, then eventually opening Madeleine Kamman's School of Traditional French Cuisine in 1964. In 1970, she opened The Modern Gourmet Cooking School, which evolved to include her restaurant Chez la Mère Madeleine in 1973. The Beringer Vineyard's School for American Chefs, founded in 1989, showcased Madeleine as an innovative and talented culinary instructor. The school's classes were taught in a small building behind the Beringer Vineyards in Napa Valley and for many years were a sought-after educational experience for chefs from across the country.

Ms. Kamman is a dedicated writer as well as an educator. Her books include:

Dinner Against the Clock
When French Women Cook
Dinner Against the Clock
In Madeleine's Kitchen
Larousse Light Cooking
Madeleine Cooks
The Making of a Cook
The New Making of a Cook
When French Women Cook
Madeleine Kamman's Savoie: The Land, People, and Food of the French Alps

After over fifty years of pursuing her passion, the young culinarian is wise to heed Ms. Kamman's advice, "Be patient, just work quietly and well so that your work shines and shows who you are. That's the best thing—don't worry about whatever anybody says." This philosophy has served her well throughout her monumental career; Madeleine's work certainly shines.

1828: Eliza Leslie publishes *Directions for Cookery*.

"[O]n good days in the kitchen, it's like a high. You just can work a million hours, and have so much energy; you're just running around, doing everything, producing everything, getting ahead, and you feel good about everything you did. Then there are those rare days when sometimes it becomes just a job."

—Kristina Neely

Boulevard. This latest venture has taken Nancy's food to new heights. Nancy describes her excitement about her work: "It's creative ... I get all caught up in what goes on the plate. When it comes to that I'm not particularly verbal; I can see what I want, but not always verbalize it. Some of my staff who have been with me a long time can read me and read what I want. One of my staff who's been with me for many years ... sometimes I think he knows my food better than I do—we don't even have to talk."

Raji Jallepalli has evolved her innovative and nationally acclaimed Indian-French fusion at Memphis' Restaurant Raji, where she has been chef-owner since 1989. One of Raji's role models was her father, who loved to eat great food, drink wonderful wine, and entertain. From those beginnings in India, her interest in food grew. "I always wanted to open a tiny restaurant like I saw in France, and I wanted the food to shine. I remember thinking in India that the food has so much to offer, but it could benefit from technique. I remember being in a French restaurant and thinking that the food is so beautiful, the flavors are great, the presentations are excellent, but it could really use a little bit of a lift, with spices and things like that." Raji married French techniques with her native Indian flavors and produced a new and exciting style of cooking.

Nancy Stark moved to New York City in 1995, after four years of being a chef-owner in Kansas City. She did a *stage* with chef pâtissier Jacques Torres, one of the most accomplished pastry chefs in the world, at Le Cirque in New York City. In 1995, Nancy assisted in the opening of Osteria del Circo, the latest venue for the owners of Le Cirque, and became assistant pastry chef. Nancy explains how she feels the joy of food: "I really like food. I like it as a material, as a medium. I love putting something together. It's right there, in that moment and [then] you get to do it again and do it a little bit better. There are those tiny increments of joy—the pastry cream ... totally smooth. [And then finally] you have one of those days when all of the food is perfect. I feel so happy when that happens."

Barbara Tropp discusses her deep connection with food and the mix of cultures that fostered that relationship: "Taiwan was such a relief! The ferocity of the passion behind eating, the total absorption of the culture of food. Take Jewish food culture, strip it of its neurosis, and you get the Taiwanese approach to food. It's all pleasure, there's not the food guilt of the Judeo-Christian culture. There were no good foods/bad foods. You ate everything! And it was considered unhealthy if you didn't eat everything! For me it was a joy to be in Chinese society, where there's not even a word for diet!" Given the opportunity to love food, guilt-free, for the first time in her life, Barabara seized the moment and, from that point on, made food her life.

Loretta Barrett Oden, a member of the Potawatomi Indian tribe, traveled the country talking and cooking with Native American women and comparing different regional cuisines. This journey helped form her food philosophy, which embraces healthy foods of Native American origin. Loretta found her way to Santa Fe, where in 1993 she opened the Corn Dance Café. There she serves her version of Native American fare. Says Loretta, "It's hard work, but it's such a passionate thing; food is from the heart of a woman. I think that there's so much love and personal attention that goes into the preparation of food for the nourishment of the people that you care about. If you have an unhappy chef, it shows in the food. If the chef absolutely loves what they do, the food is glorious. I don't care if it's a bowl of corn mush—your heart has to go into it, or the food just isn't what it needs to be."

The joy, love, and passion for food is what drives me and so many other women. The absolute ecstasy of the tastes, flavors, and feel is what motivates us through the long days, hot kitchens, and grueling pace. Although we relate to food with numerous sensations, flavor shines above all others, as the following stories attest.

Passion for Flavor

What is it about food that incites such passion? There is the look and feel; yet these mean nothing if there's no flavor. Flavor is the key to cooking. The highlighting and blending of flavors in an appealing way is the culinarian's biggest challenge and greatest joy. These days, there is some concern over the loss of flavor in foods, and the loss of appreciation of flavor. It seems that the purer the food supplies, the better the flavors; however, because of "technological advances" in producing, harvesting, and manufacturing, we are losing our "real" flavors. The taste of food has been adulterated in these processes—the "clock" has to be turned back to a time of purer more flavorful food.

Nora Pouillon describes first coming to understand the relationship between eating seasonally and flavor. "Each time I went to the supermarket I looked around and saw nothing [that] enticed me. Everything looks gorgeous and you have everything all year round; there's no season to look forward to—tomatoes, strawberries, bananas, or nuts—everything looks perfect, but when you bite into it, it doesn't have much flavor." Nora insists that flavor is key. This, as well as her belief in organics, is the driving force that keeps Nora pursuing her interest in foods from local farmland.

Cindy Pawlcyn found a perfect match for her passion for food in the Napa Valley, where she and her partners opened their first restaurant, Mustards Grill, in 1983. Cindy is now corporate chef for Real Restaurants and is partner in six of these restaurants, which range from California-style Mustards to a diner-with-an-attitude, and from Asian to barbeque. Cindy is concerned that people are losing their ability to really taste flavor. "I'm worried about the

"I don't really impose my ideas onto food; rather I look at the food and decide what best would complement its inherent qualities."
—*Eve Felder*

1836: New York's Park Hotel is opened by John Jacob Astor.

"I love touching, feeling, and listening to foods. I have a lot of memories about food in my childhood. I was eating something—always!"

—*Mika Iijima*

palate of our country, the degradation of tastes. People just don't have taste anymore. They're so sugared and greased out. If there's a palate, the demand is supplied, but if there's no demand, [that] is what I worry about."

Joyce Goldstein shares Cindy's and Nora's concern about the loss of the real flavors of food. "[So many young cooks] don't know what [authentic flavor] is! They're never going to go to Europe to eat the unpasteurized cheeses, because they're not going to earn enough as a line cook, at eight bucks an hour, to ever go. And by the time they get there, most of that [raw product] is going to be obsolete anyway. It's sad to say we were alive when this stuff was around, and we could taste it but they will not have that frame of reference! It's archaeology! We're dealing with food archaeology! How many craftspeople are left ... that are going to keep this culture alive?"

Edna Lewis is also concerned about food supplies and the loss of natural flavors: "There are a million chickens—so many that they have to give them antibiotics to keep them disease-free. They're too filled with medicine to have any taste. There are a lot of restaurants buying organic chickens now, organic beef, and [farmed] fish, just to get away from all the pollution."

Deborah Huntley, executive chef of The Harborview Inn on Martha's Vineyard, Massachusetts, offers another perspective. Deborah serves three meals a day to upward of 300 guests, most of whom visit from outside the area. Deborah says these tourists are paying much more attention to taste and flavor than ever before. "People are more daring and aggressive, and a lot more sensitive to what they're eating than they were ten years ago. The lighter cuisines, infused oils, reduction syrups, vinegars—they're all so much more popular. They're becoming more of an everyday thing."

Emily Luchetti talks about the different appreciation of flavor that chefs and pastry chefs have. "[Palate]—that's one thing that a lot of pastry chefs don't have—they don't use their palate. They don't know what a palate is. But with main course cooking, you [develop] a palate, much more than when you're a pastry chef. I took that palate [from cooking over to pastry] and I think that's one of the reasons that my desserts taste as good as they do. Flavor is the first thing!"

There is no single thing more important to food than its flavors. But flavor is only as good as the land on which foods grow. If the land is polluted or drained of nutrients then raw ingredients will suffer. The next section takes up the connection that so many chefs have with the land in their effort to provide the best, most nourishing, and most flavorful food possible.

Passion for the Land

The passion for food, its flavor, and wholesomeness has launched many chefs on a quest for safer, more flavorful food sources. As chefs have taken up this cause, many of their guests have followed. According to the 1997 NRA study, *Restaurant Industry Forecast Gets Inside Consumers' Heads,* fresh food is the number two reason underlying the choice of a restaurant. Buzzwords like "healthy," "regional," "seasonal," and "organic" are the criteria by which food is judged. The NRA's *Foodservice Industry 2000* lists two up-and-coming trends in the foodservice industry: guests' concerns about nutrition and the government's concerns for sanitation, food handling, and waste disposal. All these issues are tied to a safe food supply.

Many of the chefs in this book have a keen interest in protecting the land as a means of preserving our food, and from this desire, the Chefs Collaborative 2000 was born. Founded in 1993, the Chefs Collaborative is an impassioned group of chefs concerned with the future of our world's food sources. Chapter eight discusses this group at length.

Ana Sortun is executive chef of Casablanca in Cambridge, Massachusetts, where she gives her French training a Middle East twist to produce wonderfully flavorful casual fare. Ana promotes the chef/farmer connection, is an active member of Chefs Collaborative 2000, and expends tremendous energy promoting sustainable agriculture. One of Ana's personal projects has been the Fresh Sheet, a fax "alert" she sends to many area restaurants outlining where and from whom to procure the best local regional produce. Ana explains her involvement. "[This Fresh Sheet is] a very exciting thing. We have eighty chefs now in the city and it [serves as] a liaison between farmers and chefs. It tells what is out there locally, how you can get it and who you can call. We use it as a tool of encouragement [to help the chef/farmer connection]."

Alice Waters has made it her mission to promote sustainable, regional, and organic food supplies. For Alice, the chef/farmer connection is the basis for the food that she cooks and the lifestyle she promotes. "To develop honest relationships with the people who are growing or raising [food means] calling somebody up and communicating with them. What they can pick from their garden, and when they can bring it, and how important it is that we have not only the quality of the food, but the purity of the food as well ... that's what builds these friendships. We can buy things from people who really care about our nourishment. ... It's work to get so many people to start thinking about these things again. [But that's] the way that people have thought about food since the beginning of time."

For Eve Felder, her love of the land, tradition, and hard work is behind her love for food. Her passion for food and flavor became a passion for the land as well. "One of my greatest pleasures is to go to Debbie and Daryl Moser's Brittany Hollow Farm, in upstate New York, where they grow the most incredible fingerling potatoes—to talk about their potatoes, to [see them] love their potatoes and then to be able to turn my students on to their

"A cook is a person who understands how to balance his or her ... passion for food, with a curiosity about food, and great love and interest for food, with the practical application of taking all that, and integrating that into an economic framework that makes sense."

—Ferdinand Metz

1836: Delmonico's Restaurant in New York issues the first printed American menu.

"You know what makes something a comfort food? It's not necessarily mashed potatoes, it may be grilled clams. ... Those flavors just resonate, and they are connected to something from the past. ... The meals that you remember have a story to them."

—Jody Adams

potatoes—to support them and their hard work, [with] the dirt under their fingernails, and the blood, sweat, and tears they've put in so that I, as a cook, can then cook [their potatoes]. [If] you cook with heart and soul, it's going to be delicious because you care." Eve's passion for food and her belief in the necessity of quality farms and farmers can be seen in the wholesomeness of her food and the beliefs she shares with her students.

Loretta Barrett Oden's interest in her Native American culture fostered her belief in the relationship between people, food, and the land. During a journey that culminated in the opening of the Corn Dance Café, Loretta realized that it was time for the children on the reservation to learn about the land. She posed the question: "Why aren't [reservation] kids involved in planting and growing their own foods? I look at the heirloom beans, and the heirloom strains of corn, and [I try to] get these kids involved in the land. That's what this is all about—getting people back to the land. [After all], our farming methods work! [We need to] put the buffalo back on the tallgrass prairies. Put them back on [all that overgrazed] land, and the land springs back to life! There's a perfect synergy in nature. This land is our food! That's my passion; that's my wow!"

Eve Felder sees part of her role as a culinary instructor as that of teaching her students the responsibility of connecting to the land. "If I bring in tomatoes that [were] just picked then [I'm acting as a] role model for them; I'm showing them how you can work with farmers, which turns the students onto the farmers ... that's what it's all about."

Nora Pouillon, Odessa Piper, and Alice Waters are among the "mothers" of the movement toward organics. Nora tells the story of having to pick up her products before delivery was available. "I had to drive [to the farm] twice a week to pick up the vegetables. My car was full with all kinds of tomatoes and boxes. It was just a wonderful experience—so invigorating to see the food, to know the people who grew the food, to know about their life, to see them work. It was a wonderful family."

I'm often asked why buying seasonally is so important. I find that especially with students and young cooks, they want exotic food, food that's not readily available, most times not in season, and rarely flavorful. I have the flavor memory of warm ripe tomatoes, right from the garden; that is how I explain why it's important and what flavor really is.

Passion for the Job

Common threads for women who go into the culinary field are a passion for food and flavor and a respect for the land. But to succeed in the profession, it takes much more. It takes drive, motivation, and stamina. It takes loving what you do to compensate for the hard work, the long hours, the stress, and oftentimes the underappreciation.

Jamie Eisenberg is a chef-instructor and purchasing director at the New England Culinary Institute's Inn at Essex Campus in Vermont. In this capacity Jamie pursues her passion for food, and supports local, regional, sustainable food choices for the school through her buying for dozens of chefs. Through it all, Jamie loves her work. "We're all here for the same reason. It's because we love to cook. And we love to nurture other people. When I cook a good plate of food for somebody, it makes them feel good, and then that makes me feel good."

After working in France and England, Gale Gand came back to the U.S. and went to work at Charlie Trotter's in 1992. She opened her first restaurant, Trio, with her husband, Chef Rick Tramonto in 1993 and then opened Brasserie T in 1995 in a suburb of Chicago. Gale is enthusiastic about almost every aspect of being a chef: she loves food, she loves being in the kitchen, she loves her staff. "It's about the interaction," she says. "It's about touching the food. I get a lot out of my customers, feeding people, teaching my staff, and solving problems. I love discovering an area that needs development or an area to save money or an area [that] can give my staff better situations. We're [chefs] because it's a calling. In order to stay afloat, it takes a superwoman mentality. The trick is to be able to maintain that and not burn out. And not sacrifice the things that are important to you."

A native of Cambodia, Longteine de Monteiro never considered herself a chef or restaurateur, nor did she have any professional cooking experience. That all changed after the Khmer Rouge overthrew the Cambodian government in 1975, when Longteine and her family had to find a "safe haven" in France. After ten years in France, she and her husband went to Boston to join her youngest daughter; they opened The Elephant Walk in 1991 in Somerville, Massachusetts. Longteine found a home and a sense of belonging in her restaurant, which serves her native Cambodian fare. "(The restaurant) is my home. Even on my day off, I have to come in! At least I come here and spend a few hours or half a day, and after that I can leave. I think it's a passion, and also self-control. When I come to the restaurant, I see that everything is going right. Only then can I leave." And because of her dedication and passion for her job, she was able to open a second Elephant Walk in Brookline, Massachusetts in 1994.

Barbara Tropp's restaurant career started at Greens in San Francisco, which had been at its beginning the Zen Center (a San Francisco-based community whose members embraced a Buddhist lifestyle), with its alternative style of thought about work, food, and management. Barbara explains how the experience affected her career. "I was struck by what I saw there, because, mechanically and technically, it was a restaurant like all the others. But on a

"Cooking is about nurturing, and if you're bitchy and angry, you're not going to be able to nurture."
—*Zarela Martinez*

1838: French menus are printed daily at New York's Astor House.

philosophical and a spiritual plane, [which] was how I was still living a majority of my life, I found truthfulness there, and a fitting to my own needs that was profound. I begged Deborah [Madison] to let me come in and work for free, and at that point, the kitchen was just doing dinners on weekends. 'I'll stand in the corner and chop. I'll stay out of the way, and you can throw me anything you want to throw me. I have no desire to be at the stove, I'm just a meticulous chopper.' She agreed, after some hesitation. I was there for about two years, chopping in the corner." During Barbara's tenure as chef-owner of China Moon Café, she gave many young culinarians the same outlet for their passion that Deborah had given her.

Jody Adams was on a panel called "Successful Women under 35," when she discovered that not all people choose a career out of passion for the work. She said during the panel discussion: "You have to follow your heart, and you have to decide you're going to do whatever it is you need to do, regardless of how much money you're going to make." A response to her comment came from a woman on the panel who had a "career-changing" consulting company. She said, "You know, it's wonderful that you can do that, and I think it's great that all of you are able to do that, but many people cannot. They cannot find that, they don't know where their heart is." Jody's reaction was: "Well, that's a surprise!" Because her passion was so strong, she could not imagine that anyone would pursue a career without passion.

F. Bonvin's "La Cuisinière" depicts a woman in very professional attire with apron and hat preparing food in the kitchen. (Engraver: Daumont.)

Kerry Heffernan was inspired by her work at Elka with Elka Gilmore and Traci Des Jardins. She said of the experience: "The food was incredible. Traci Des Jardins was chef de cuisine; the food was just a phenomenon to me. I had always been a good, organized cook/chef, but I had never had the opportunity to do that kind of innovation with brains clicking into gear, and constantly in motion. I would sometimes be overwhelmed to the point where I wanted to cry. … Not because I was hurt or insulted, but just because I was blown away! I was just blown away at what they were able to accomplish."

Susan McCreight Lindeborg's career has taken her from Santa Fe, where she worked at the La Fonda Hotel and The Periscope to Odessa Piper's L'Etoile in Madison, Wisconsin, and finally in 1990 to the Morrison-Clark Inn in Washington, DC. She speaks of the incredible commitment she makes. "I'm a cook. I live it, I eat it, I can't imagine not cooking. I can't imagine not being in a kitchen. I can't imagine not being interested in food."

Noëlle Haddad apprenticed at Daniel's and Le Cirque, both prestigious New York City restaurants, and has cooked for the Swiss and Dutch embassies in addition to having been a private chef for numerous New York families. For Noëlle, her passion is fueled by the desire to please the people she feeds. "This goal gives me a way of expressing the art, having pride, expressing feelings. Maybe I'm not going to be paid anything, but I'm going to be plating things and making people feel [good]. [Suppose you] get the most depressed person in the world; you can give him an incredible plate of food; it doesn't have to be expensive. If you really feel the food and the plate and the warmth, you can make those ten or fifteen minutes that they're eating amazing. That person is going to forget about everything else that is troubling them in their world. We have the power to change their outlook for a few moments. I think that's so, so wonderful. ... We have the power to make people enjoy."

While Noëlle wants her customers to love her food, Suzanne Bussiere talks about the need to love your work. Both attitudes reflect the yin and yang of the industry—loving what you do and having other people love what you do. If the yin and the yang occur at the same time, then harmony results. Suzanne worked with Nancy Oakes, first at L'Avenue as sous chef, and now as executive sous chef at Boulevard. Suzanne has been deaf since birth, yet her communication skills are conveyed through the food she creates. "You have to love it. I do. You just have to love what you're doing, otherwise it won't come together. The food won't *sing*. There are no shortcuts. You have to have patience and take pride in what you do. It's a long, slow gentle simmer."

Women chefs have found their passion at different times and through different channels. Because this passion drives us, so many of us, it is sometimes difficult to realize that passion isn't something that everyone feels about their pursuits. This passion makes the hard work, the long hours, and the uphill battle endurable. Traci Des Jardins' story illustrates the love and passion that all these women exude: "It's a very small percentage of chefs that will [become a], really glamorous, high-profile chef—those are few and far between. There are hundreds of thousands of people working in professional kitchens who never get any kind of recognition. So if that's what you're going for, you're headed in the wrong direction. It has to be more organic than that; you have to have

"A chef is a mentor, a reader, a teacher ... the responsibility of a chef is to be teaching and training and mentoring. Cooks are designated to a position where they have to produce and keep up with that position, learn along the way, and look for new challenges. Most chefs don't have to look for new challenges!"
—*Kristina Neely*

1846: Philadelphia dairymaid Nancy Johnson devises a portable hand-cranked ice cream freezer.

a basic love for food. In a lot of ways [my career] chose me. ... It's a gift. It's something I haven't been able to walk away from because it grabbed onto me."

The chapters that follow uncover the influences that have shaped these women, the challenges they've faced, the work they do, and the success they have achieved. I hope you will find these women as inspiring as I do.

Women Chefs

Their Influences, Choices, and Sacrifices

Sacrificing lives to the kitchen god
—Hilary DeMane

"When I asked my father if I could be a chef, he said: 'Why (do) you want to be a chef? Men don't cook in our family, only the women cook."

—*Alain Sailhac*

"I was lucky when I started out; I found a chef (Richard Burns) who took me under his wing. I [had gone] around to a lot of kitchens— French kitchens— and no one would even answer the door. Richard took me on because I said I would work for free."

—*Anne Rosenzweig*

Women have been connected with food throughout history. We've seen their passion, the fire in their bellies and the fire in their hearts. In this chapter, women discuss the things that have influenced their lives, the choices they've faced, and sacrifices they've made in order to pursue their culinary careers.

Cultural Influences on Women and Their Food

America has been called a "melting pot." This blend of language and peoples has had a profound effect on politics and culture in this country, and its impact on the culinary world has been similarly far-reaching. In a kitchen, the passionate chef finds ways to bring cultures alive, to give expression to flavors, tastes, and techniques from stoves on the other side of the world. In this arena it's possible to reconnect with one's roots, and because of that, the culinary world draws women from a wide variety of ethnic backgrounds.

Based on the results of my survey of women in the culinary field, I found that over fourteen percent of the women chefs come from "ethnic" backgrounds; thirteen percent are bilingual, and of those, twenty-eight percent speak Spanish as their second language. The early influences of many of these women are starting to change the food in restaurants today. In fact, recent NRA studies note that ethnic-oriented cuisines from all over the world are among the industry's strongest new trends. The following is a look at how ethnic heritages have influenced women chefs, their work, and their worlds.

The American Influence

Cultural influences shape the lives and affect the choices of individuals all across America. For many women chefs, entry into the culinary field was driven by the need to reconnect with their ethnic heritage. A variety of cultures, including Native American, Italian, African-American, and Asian, have had a powerful and unique impact on the lives and careers of these women.

Food and family have tremendous impact on scores of women. Many of our initial food memories emanate from our mothers and grandmothers, or are perpetuated through our children. Loretta Barrett Oden's Native American heritage has a powerful influence on who she is today. "What I really remember, most fondly, are the women in the kitchen. We would go out and gather what we called possum grapes and sand plums; the aunts would all get together and cook, and see who could make the clearest jelly. They'd have competitions, and they'd enter their foods in the country and state fairs. It was just wonderful—the camaraderie, laughing, singing, and all of that in the kitchen! … These women were able to create, during times of plenty and times of famine, from the beginning of time. The women were the key to the survival of the people because they were the ones who were responsible for feeding and making food happen!"

Loretta describes how she was inspired to share her diverse culture with others by using food as her medium. "I left Oklahoma and embarked on this pilgrimage. A lightbulb just went off in my head; I thought: 'This is it, this is it, this is it!' The only thing I really know how to do is cook, and my background is [filled with the] diversity of the Native American tribes." So Loretta put her skills and knowledge to use as she realized, "I can use the food as a tool, to teach people about the enormous diversity of the Indian people, as well as the diversity of the indigenous [foods]. I'd go to one reservation, with an introduction from the previous reservation, and say, 'This is who I am, I want to know more, I want to cook with the women,' and that's what I did."

Cultural influences manifest themselves in a variety of ways. During the late 1960s and early 1970s, this country went through a revolution that forever changed our way of thinking. It altered our attitudes about sexual identity and our perceptions of the roles of women and men. It also changed how we viewed the land and the food we ate. We saw the advent of conscious vegetarianism and a new way of thinking about the shared lives of plants and animals on the planet. Like the Native American cultures, other Americans were also becoming increasingly committed to using ingredients from the land. Deborah Madison discusses her own evolution in dealing with food during that era: "In the seventies I was challenged by how to make vegetarian food that people who were not vegetarian felt at ease with. I think food has to have an element of real familiarity, and certainly recognizability, in order to be truly nourishing. It's important to try to develop a cuisine that [people] feel comfortable with! That [was] how I defined my job." Ultimately, the growth that she experienced during that time period, similar to the evolution that much of America was experiencing, had a lasting impact that has continued to influence her food choices and beliefs today.

The culinary world can thank the African-American culture for a large part of its history. But because much of the African-American contribution took place under the oppressive institution of slavery, many African-American culinarians still struggle with how to shed the negative connotations of being in the kitchen. Jessica Harris discusses the impact of slave history on African-Americans' relationship with the culinary world. "I think you would be hard-pressed to find any family that says, 'Oh no, don't be a doctor or a lawyer or a schoolteacher—go into food.' I think that attitude is intensified for people with a history of enslavement and a history of being unpaid, then underpaid, for doing the work that somebody else gets credit for. Even today, if you go into most kitchens, or many kitchens, and scratch the surface and see who's back there, you discover the person out front with the white hat and the name [isn't necessarily doing the work]."

"When I was first here, I just needed someone to be able to show me and to help me. Now it is my job as a chef to teach these people, to show these people, they have nobody to teach them. I like to give, I love to give, and I feel good. I am always like that in everything I do."
—*Guida Ponte*

1850: Mammy Pleasant sells her skills as a cook in San Francisco for $500/year.

*"The idea that you
would not eat meat
because of an emo-
tional connection
with an animal, to
them, was crazy. They
believed that a rock
and a carrot have the
same spirit as a cow,
and it became for me
a very interesting
first year there, in
embracing the
Chinese way of food,
and with a great sigh
of relief giving up
all of my Western
neurosis!"*

—Barbara Tropp

Edna Lewis, whose career in the kitchen spans sixty-five years, says, "I think [there are so few African-American cooks] because we have a history of being in the kitchen and [the young women] want to do something else. There were women cooks even after slavery in hotels and restaurants all through the south. But, when [women could go] to school, they all studied other professions." As these stories illustrate, many cultures within the United States have helped to put us on the culinary map and have influenced our food choices. The next section explores how cultural influences from other parts of the world affected the culinary beginnings of women who now pursue their passions here.

International Influences

From Europe to Asia, women have learned from and have been influenced by the cultures of their youth. Rick O'Connell's memories of growing up under the influence of her Italian grandmother resonate in her life today: "Ever since I was a little girl I wanted to be in the kitchen. Part of that was probably from [my upbringing in] an Italian family, where everything centered on food. My grandmother worked in the kitchen constantly. She made handmade pastas and I can remember shopping with her, going to the market and all the little specialty shops. There was one butcher my mother would go to and I can remember the conversations about the food, it became so much a part of my life."

The Irish culture has had an overwhelming impact on the culinary history of the United States, especially in the Northeast. Siobhan Carew, chef-owner of Pomodoro in Boston, describes it: "Ireland is not known for its food, but for its food quality. It's superb—[there are] very pure ingredients in Ireland; because people didn't have money, and they weren't sophisticated, the food was simple. ... We like to cook with certain foods in as natural a way as possible. The challenge is to keep food in a pure, simple state." Siobhan explained that when she arrived in this country, "the first things I really noticed were the dairy products—milk didn't taste like milk and butter didn't taste like butter." The lack of flavorful food influenced her choice to become a chef-owner: "I just wanted to work in places that had better quality food, and so it evolved into having my own place, and having really good quality food. I don't compromise myself when it comes to ingredients. I buy the best meats, all organic chicken, vegetables, game, and rabbit."

Barbara Tropp's exposure to the Asian philosophy of food is at the root of her culinary career. Barbara had spent many of her formative years living and studying in Asia. What she learned and experienced was inspirational: "I was amazed that eating began when you got up and didn't go away until you went to sleep. The old man who headed my Chinese family was a wonderful gourmand. He would knock on the door of my cottage at ten at night, and ask if I

Postcard of a French café. Courtesy of the Culinary Archives and Museum at Johnson and Wales University.

wanted to go downtown for spring rolls with him. Downtown was a world of street stalls that appeared at seven or eight at night and closed down around two or three in the morning. We'd just wander the streets with the bare light bulbs hanging from the street stalls and we'd eat—this from a child who was taught to never eat after eight at night." The contrast for Barbara was dramatic, coming from a society where dieting was a constant in life, in a country where eating disorders are abundant. Living, then, where eating was an integral part of life, and food was treasured, Barbara was drawn to the Asian way of looking at food. She carried that with her into her professional career.

Madeleine Kamman's early food memories are of her aunt's hotel and the food she learned to prepare in the kitchen when she was nine years old. But it wasn't until a number of years later that she really started to cook and think about the food she was preparing. "After my father died when I was seventeen, my mother went to work, and I became the cook in the family while I was going to school. It is very easy to cook an interesting meal while you are studying at the same time, going back and forth from my books to the stove. All the women in my family on both my mother and my father's side were great cooks." Madeleine's food experiences as a young wife in this country were very different. She thought the flavors so horrid that she was inspired to teach others to cook the foods of her childhood.

Raji Jallepalli's love for food and entertaining drew her toward a restaurant career as well. Raji talks about the conflict between her love of food and wanting

"I really think Madeleine helped me shape the way I thought about food and the way I studied food. You got a real sense of the pleasure of the table from her, and the passion that she had for the food, but also, she was a scientist. She would talk about the chemistry of food, and that was very fascinating to me."

—Anne Rosenzweig

1850: President Fillmore and his wife Abigail install the first White House cooking stove.

to work with it, and her native culture's mandate that according to the caste structure in India, cooking is considered below her station. A woman in a manual labor occupation is frowned upon. After emigrating from India, Raji pursued what she couldn't have in her native land: a culinary career. She explains: "I came [from] a very well-to-do family in India. My father was an icon—the biggest influence in my life. He had style, he [was] very well educated, [and he] loved food and wine. A lot of entertaining happened [in my household, but my mother] was an extremely private person. [She] shied away from the pomp and circumstance, so as a teenager I took it over." Raji goes on to say: "My Dad was deceased before I had the restaurant, but I never could have told him I was a cook—he knew I owned the restaurant, but not that I worked there. When my mom found out I was a cook, she hit the ceiling."

In China, as in India, cultural taboos dictate who should and should not work in the kitchen. Susanna Foo, who came to America from China, explains that in China, women are not welcome in the professional kitchen. This attitude toward women affected Susanna directly when her husband started to help his parents in their restaurant. While her husband and his family assumed that Susanna would help too, they expected her role to be that of a cashier or waitress, not a cook. She explains, "[In China, a woman may cook] in a kitchen for the family, but not [as a] professional. ... It seems unthinkable in that culture because [in a kitchen] a woman would have to lift the big wok and all the heavy [pots]. When I told my parents that I cooked in [a] kitchen, they didn't really like it—they were very upset and shocked." Susanna's cultural heritage hasn't prevented her from becoming an impassioned chef. In fact, she says she can't imagine not being in the kitchen, where she produces her creative brand of Asian cuisine based on the food memories of her childhood.

These stories reflect the background of some of the ethnic food served in restaurants throughout America. The 1996 NRA *Restaurant Operations Report* notes that thirty-seven percent of all American restaurants feature ethnic cuisine. These cultural influences contribute to women's histories and choices in professional kitchens. Their cultural roots, however, are just one of the many influences that have guided these women in their quests. For many women chefs, mentors are critical in helping them to find their way.

The Art of Mentoring: Role Models of Women Chefs

Most culinarians would not be where they are today without a mentor. Mentors help us formulate attitudes about food; they show us generosity of spirit; they give us confidence in our creative vision; and they teach us by example about the day-to-day professionalism required to succeed in the kitchen. This section explores the ways in which mentors have inspired the careers of women cooks and chefs.

Mentors Influencing Attitudes about Food

Most of us enter the culinary field because we already possess a passion for food. Food is also the medium through which we express our passion. As we have seen, it takes years of hard work to reach a level that allows us to make the most of that medium. If we're lucky, along the way, we'll find a mentor who wants to share that passion and help us to develop the skills we need to prepare the best possible food. Alice Waters, with her belief in organic, sustainable food choices, has mentored, influenced, and inspired many women chefs.

Eve Felder attributes her decision to go to culinary school to Alice's influence: "I had started hearing titters about this person [Alice Waters] who was doing garden-farm-to-restaurant. I was very interested in being mentored, and finding someone who could bring those things together for me. I decided I needed to go to The Culinary Institute of America and get training [first because] there was no way I could walk into her kitchen, even though I had been a chef." After graduating with honors from the CIA in 1988, Eve went to work at Chez Panisse, where she worked with Alice for seven years.

Deborah Madison is another chef whom Alice inspired: "I met Alice Waters [at Green Gulch Farm]. I was asked to show [her and pastry chef Lindsey Shere] around, and I just fell in love with them. I thought they were the most wonderful women!" At dinner the next night with Alice, Deborah describes the food as "exactly the way it should be. I can remember everything I ate. It was a thrill; we licked our plates clean. … I went back the next day, and talked to Alice and I actually [ended up working] in the restaurant. What a requited life, to get up at 5:00 a.m., go to meditation, take a bus to Berkeley, and work both the lunch and dinner shift at Chez Panisse."

Johanne Killeen, who herself has been role model to so many women, remembers an inspirational meal she had at Chez Panisse: "A meal I had in 1981 was definitely a turning point for me. The simplicity in Alice's food was so good, the quality so good, it was really like the food that I ate in Italy. It gave me the courage to focus more and more on the stuff that we really liked, the stuff that made sense to us, the stuff that we wanted to eat."

For other women, employees, employers, or peers serve as their mentors. Having an employee as a mentor sounds particularly unusual. It's assumed their expertise and instincts will be less honed than the chef's. Not for RoxSand Scocos, chef/co-owner of RoxSand in Arizona, which she opened in 1988. Before opening her Phoenix restaurant, however, she moved to Hawaii at the age of twenty-four. It was there she found one of her mentors, a chef she had hired to work in her kitchen. "The business was so large," she explains, "that I needed a lot of help. I had a chef working under me who was Moroccan, and I learned tons from him. Yet I was his boss, and worked in the kitchen side by

"I'd stay up late, I'd study and study and read. I knew that I was making this paste, which was a roux, but I didn't know it was a roux back then. I knew that I was doing the basics right, but I didn't know the terminology for it. That was hard, reading and sifting through the terminology, and not knowing."

—*Barbara Lynch*

1850: Women make up thirteen percent of America's paid labor force, with most of them employed in agriculture or as domestic servants.

Women in the Culinary Arena: Alice Waters

Alice Waters is one of the three women most often thought of as a mentor by the chefs and cooks surveyed and interviewed for this book. Alice came to the culinary world via a circuitous route. She began as a French Cultural Studies major at the University of California, Berkeley, and went on to study in London to become a Montessori school teacher. While in Europe, Alice had the good fortune of eating her way around France; she ended up falling in love with the food. That trip to France clearly influenced how Alice thought about food. Like many other chefs interviewed in this book, Alice's experiences with French food inspired her entry into the culinary field.

After returning from France, Alice started cooking for her friends, trying to recreate the food that she had come to love. Elizabeth David and Richard Olney (noted culinary writers) both inspired Alice with their love for food, and her culinary horizons started to broaden. Alice's travels in France, the inspiration of the communities and local food that she was exposed to, and her passion for fresh flavorful ingredients cultivated her belief in the importance of organic, regional, sustainable food choices.

In 1971, Alice opened Chez Panisse in Berkeley, California. Her intent was to serve great-tasting flavorful food to her friends. This landmark restaurant, which in 1996 celebrated its twenty-fifth anniversary, was one of the most influential restaurants for American chefs in the 1970s and 1980s.

Alice teaches young chefs and cooks to use the best seasonal, regional, and ecologically sound ingredients possible. In this vein, she has authored a number of books, including *The Chez Panisse Menu Book, Fanny at Chez Panisse,* and the *Chez Panisse Vegetable Book.* Alice continues to tour the country, educating people about the importance of guarding and protecting our food supplies.

"In this industry it takes a certain type of person, not necessarily a certain type of woman, to succeed. Being a chef demands a lot of work, a lot of physical work, and women need to look at the full picture and determine whether being a chef is really right for them."

—*Jody Adams*

side with him every day. When I wasn't in the kitchen, everyone would defer to him. He was probably one of the best chefs I've ever met. [His was the best] food I've ever tasted … he taught me fifty percent of what I know about cooking."

Tamara Murphy attributes some of her own ideas about food to a couple that she worked for in North Carolina at a little family-run Italian restaurant. "Roberto ran the front, Anna ran the back, and I just cooked. Anna was a mentor [for me] in the way she thought about food. … Food was not an intellectual thing for her; it wasn't artistic either … she cooked from her heart. It was just important for her to make things taste good and not do too much with them. That stuck with me; I think about that now."

For Susan McCreight Lindeborg, one of the most important lessons of her culinary career came from the owners of a restaurant in New Mexico. "Everything at The Periscope focused on the food—always the food, the food, the food. [The owners main concern was] 'Is the customer going to like it?' " This has been a guiding principle for Susan throughout her career.

A common thread in these stories about mentors is that their influence is often based on the food they serve. They believe foremost in quality, and they want to please their customers. The women who tell these stories carry these messages with them continuously throughout their careers.

Mentors as Teachers and Professional Advisors

An important part of the mentoring or teaching process is to bring out the best in those you are mentoring. Once students discover their own capabilities, they are well on their way. Another part of the mentoring process is to help students make decisions about their future. As exciting as this can be for those just embarking on their careers, it can also be overwhelming. Students often turn to their mentors as inspiration or as a source of advice. In many cases, mentors can help students develop expertise and reach a higher level within the profession. The following stories come from former students who were the beneficiaries of mentors who helped them develop the confidence and expertise they needed to cultivate their own culinary careers.

Traci Des Jardins' mentoring experience with Elka Gilmore went well beyond the exchanging of professional tips. It was a journey into the spirit of cooking, the act of creating. As Traci describes it: "Elka and I really meshed. I was in awe of her overall creativity, her visions of what she wanted to do and her willfulness. I was amazed by how forthcoming a woman would be with information, help, and support. I think if you are a creative cook, sometimes you guard that creative spirit. You don't necessarily want to give it away to someone that may not acknowledge it as a precious thing. So that support was really different for me. I was kind of broken down about what I had been doing and where I was going. Elka started to help me and give me the support I needed to believe in [my work] again. We embarked on this great adventure, discovering what we could do with my technical skills and her wild obtuse creativity and it was good." From that great food adventure, Traci went on to open Rubicon with Drew Nieporent in San Francisco and earned the James Beard 'Rising Star Chef of the Year' award in 1995.

Some mentoring relationships rise out of meetings; others require planning and initiative. Raji Jallepalli's first mentor came to her through the pages of a book. "I saw Jean-Louis Palladin's book, *Cooking with the Seasons,* and it just spoke to me. I called him and told him I did French-Indian Fusion and he was fascinated." When Palladin traveled to Memphis, he told her: "Raji, you are a talent waiting to be discovered. If you don't mind traveling three to four times a year I'll tell people about you." Shortly after he left, Raji started getting calls from all over the country. She explains, "I started wondering, 'how do I live up

> *"I found people were asking me all the time, 'So, where'd you go to school? Did you go to the CIA?' At first, I didn't mind, and I'd say, 'no, I'm self-taught.' After a while, it started to get to me. I decided that I was going to take care of that problem—I decided to go to Paris. I did that to legitimize myself in the world's eyes, not in my own."*
>
> —Gale Gand

1850: The United States has 2,017 bakeries, but more than ninety percent of the United States' bread is still baked at home.

"The French are very different in the kitchen—they're very serious. The concentration and the focus on certain skills are a lot different over there than they are here. I think that's what the environment is, a more military environment over there—it's very serious, and it's very harsh."

—*Ana Sortun*

to this man's expectations? I pushed and pushed myself not to embarrass him and then, I finally realized, I needed to be myself.' Then I relaxed and took stock of myself ... and everyone was very happy."

Corinna Mozo's choice of mentors was also very deliberate. This chef de cuisine at Chez Henri, knew when she graduated from Stratford Chefs School, in Ontario, Canada that she wanted to work for a woman, and Lydia Shire at BIBA in Boston was at the top of her list. "I knew that I wanted my first job to [be] working for a woman. [I decided] I was going to write to Lydia, because she was, in my eyes, at the top. It's all I could think about, [that] she was the one. So I wrote to her. When I didn't hear back, I decided to go to Portugal and then [the] day before I left, Lydia called and offered me a job [which I happily accepted]."

Sometimes circumstances, not just people, are our motivators. Phyllis Flaherty, who became a chef-instructor at the CIA, remembers the pressure of her own student days. "I was in Richard Czak's demo (a class where the chef does demonstrations in front of the students), with seventy-two guys and a couple of girls. [Just] to make sure he couldn't ask me something I didn't know, I'd go home and study half the night so I wouldn't be humiliated in front of all these guys."

Zarela Martinez, chef-owner of Zarela in New York City and creator of Signature Foods, credits her mentor, Lillian Hain, with helping to form her professional persona. "She taught me the most important lesson of my whole life. She said, 'You have to decide on an identity, so that once people get to know your food, they can walk into a party, taste something, and know that it's your food. And you have to decide [specifically] what you want to do. Do you want to be a mass-caterer, and make more money and have this set menu and not have a creative outlet, or [do you want to] make less money and do different things?" Zarela used this early lesson to help keep her restaurant and business on the forefront of the New York culinary scene with a style that's truly all her own.

Another career path is working for a major hotel chain. Sarah Stegner and Susan Weaver are both hotel executive chefs and learned within the kitchens of Four Seasons hotels. Sarah attributes much of her success to being treated fairly and being shown the ropes. "There were two people who really influenced my training and my career. One was Fernand Gutierrez, who is an executive chef and food and beverage director in Mexico City. He's very dynamic, a visionary, and I felt absolutely no discrimination within the field at the hotel. He was very fair, and it was clear that your promotions, your raises, all those things were based on how well you performed on the job—period." Her other mentor was Susan Weaver. She explains: "Susan Weaver was the chef-garde-manger at the time, and she kind of took me on as a project; she was a mentor to me. In this business, you really need to have somebody there

Women in the Culinary Arena: Lydia Shire

This talented woman graduated from the Cordon Bleu Cooking School at the age of twenty-two and has persevered professionally in the culinary world for three decades. Little did she know that she would be setting examples for numbers of young women who were watching her from the sidelines.

Lydia grew up in a small town outside of Boston and was the daughter of two artists. Her forays into the kitchen began at the age of eight, helping her father make foods like spaghetti aglio olio. Her parent's lessons about color, symmetry, and design laid a foundation for Lydia's cooking career and those tenets are evidenced in each of her intricate and well-composed plates.

After graduating from the Cordon Bleu, Lydia returned to Boston to cook at Maison Robert. She progressed through some of the best known of Cambridge and Boston's kitchens: the Harvest, the Copley Plaza Hotel, and the Parker House Hotel. She joined forces with Jasper White at Seasons Restaurant and succeeded him as executive chef in 1982. During this time, women like Susan Regis, Corinna Mozo, Jody Adams, and Sara Moulton were gaining from Lydia's knowledge. Each of these women passed through her kitchens and was mentored by their vivacious and gifted chef.

In 1986, Lydia was asked to manage the opening of the Four Seasons Hotel in Beverly Hills, California as executive chef; she was the first woman to achieve this position in a luxury hotel. Lydia remained on the West coast for two years before a yearning for her own restaurant initiated her return to New England. Lydia's premiere restaurant, BIBA, opened in 1989, and her second restaurant, Pignoli, opened in 1994.

In addition to mentoring young cooks and students, Lydia runs two restaurants and has raised four children. Her peers frequently acknowledge her as innovative and resourceful. Lydia's friendship with working partner Susan Regis has spanned two decades and exemplifies her sense of commitment and dedication to the good things in life.

who can see the whole picture from the other end, and keep you on track—Susan did that for me."

Pat Thibodeau was trained through the American Culinary Federation (ACF) apprenticeship program, and she entered the culinary world as a second career. Pat remembers how hard it was to move from the mentor who guided her into the field. "Major Jarmon, who works for Minor's Base Company, was the head of the apprenticeship [program] and was also teaching me. He took me as his personal student; I took him as my mentor and it stayed that way forever. He thought that we would [always be] together. When I veered into my own little niche he told me, 'I let you go.' He said, 'If I had ever kept you with

1851: A bottle of Mumm's champagne served in a silver bucket costs $2.00 in most of the better U.S. restaurants.

H. Patersen's "Morning in the Scullery." From *London Illustrated News*, July 18, 1873. Courtesy National Training School of Cookery, at South Kensington (London, England).

> *"Just because you get out of school, it does-n't mean that you know anything. There is a very big difference between practical informa-tion and theoretical information. You do get a lot of training in food, but it still isn't your food yet."*
>
> —Zarela Martinez

me you wouldn't have done what you were supposed to do.' That was really hard." But his job was done. Pat had been trained as a cook, with the base that enabled her to become a driving force behind the Chef and the Child Foundation (see chapter seven). Like the other students, her mentor helped her move to the next level, which is the goal of any student/mentor relationship.

Mentors push us to be the best that we can be, help us attain our goals, and help us set our standards as high as possible. Chapter seven discusses how to go about finding a mentor.

The Influence of Education and Apprenticeship Programs

For anyone considering entering the culinary field, one of the most critical decisions concerns training: does one attend a culinary school? Work as an apprentice? Or try and combine both of the experiences? The following sec-tions detail the challenges and successes, the joys and the tears that women cooks and chefs experienced during their early years of training. But first a brief description of the two most prominent training vehicles: apprenticeship pro-grams and culinary institutions.

Many foodservice companies offer training, but the ACF has the largest nationwide apprenticeship program. The ACF program has approximately 2,000 apprentices at over 100 locations. This three-year, structured learning environment combines hands-on work experience with a classroom education.

Students who complete the program are certified as cooks and ready to participate as a member of a kitchen team.

With over 600 culinary schools from which to choose, a culinary school candidate finds varying levels of academic and hands-on course work. Culinary institutions offer a wide variety of degrees and curricula, with program completion taking from three to twenty-one months. Graduates from these schools may have many varied levels of skill and, as with the apprentice graduates, need a number of years of practical experience to hone their craft. Chapter eight discusses educational opportunities at greater length.

Apprenticeship Experiences—The French Influence

Many established female culinarians acquired much of their formative training in France. In fact, for women who came into the field prior to the 1980s, working in France was a priority and a stepping stone to where they are today. This belief in the superiority of the French culinary training stems from the long history the French have with food. When Americans were penning their first cookbooks, the French already had over 150 years of documented culinary expertise.

Traci Des Jardins describes her path to France and her experiences there: "I thought about going to culinary school and applied, but didn't get accepted; at that time they were demanding practical restaurant experience." Traci explains that her aunt and uncle were frequent travelers to France, where they knew chefs at many three-star restaurants. This connection gave her access to kitchen jobs that were so elusive to many others in search of similar opportunities. Traci adds: "Initially the [kitchen staff] thought I was an anomaly, a bizarre creature from another land. They were fascinated by the idea of a young woman from California coming all the way to France to learn about cooking."

Gale Gand also spent time in France, working incredibly hard to get there. "I sent out twenty letters to the three-star Michelin restaurants, in French, requesting to be a stagière in their restaurant. My name is spelled G-A-L-E, which is the male spelling for Gail—which my mother did on purpose! Out of the twenty places I sent letters to, ten didn't respond, nine said 'no,' and one, from Troisgros, said yes. But it read: 'Dear Mr. Gand: We would be very excited to welcome you in our kitchen.' So I went! I showed up … knocked on the door, showed my letter, and they said, 'You're Mr. Gand? Just a minute please'—and they closed the door in my face! You could tell they were very nervous. They didn't know I was a woman! And they came back to the door, and said, 'Are you sure this [is your] letter?' And I said, 'Yes!' They said, 'Are you sure you're not an American journalist?' I said, 'No, I'm just a young woman

"Culinary school pushed me into positions and kitchens I never would have had the guts to pursue on my own. I gained a lot of personal and professional knowledge and strength that helped prepare me for life."
—Elaine Deal
Frauenhofer

1855: Boston's Parker House restaurant starts serving à la carte meals instead of the traditional single mealtime service.

Two female cooks cooking in empire dress (possibly French). Courtesy of the Culinary Archives and Museum at Johnson and Wales University.

who wants to learn how to cook.' I knew that it was going to be hard for them. Initially, they didn't want me there. I would look for the guy doing the shittiest job in the kitchen, I'd go up to him and say, 'Show me how you're doing that,' and then, 'You don't need to do it, [I'll] do this for you.' I would let them see me peeling potatoes for sixteen hours a day, not minding it, and being happy about it. When they found I was willing to do anything, they let down their guard and shared information.''

Katy Keck's ticket to France was winning a Marie Brizard recipe contest; the prize was apprenticeships in three French kitchens. For Katy, this was a far cry from her position on Wall Street. "I was in the Loire Valley, [with] weddings every week. Since those French love their canapés, we'd make 15,000 a week—[just] two of us. We worked a completely different schedule from the rest of the kitchen, from seven or eight in the morning, when the kitchen wasn't busy, until five at night. Then I'd stay on and work the dinner service. I had nothing else to do.'' Katy's experience gave her the basis from which to become chef-owner of New World Grill, a restaurant/catering company in New York City.

Ana Sortun, a young woman from Washington, got brutally tough treatment during her time in French kitchens. "It was like boot camp. They were very hard on people. They snapped their fingers at me and called me names I'd never heard before and I even spoke French. My real name was never used until I had earned [their] respect and proved to them [what] I was worth. Once they think you're a good investment, then they'll teach you, work with you, and treat you nicely. It took three or four months of fifteen-hour days—it was a pretty overwhelming experience. I was in the bathroom crying every day.''

Mary Sue Milliken and Susan Feniger have spent almost their entire culinary career together. They ended up in France at the same time, but in very different kitchens. Mary Sue describes her experience as one that gave her insight into women's food without the pretension of the tall hats and starched uniforms that male French chefs had made the standard. "Dominique Nahmias [was the chef], and her husband, Albert, ran the dining room. When I started working, I didn't even speak French—not a word. Dominique would come in the kitchen every night, around 8:00. She wore high, high heels, a beautiful,

Women in the Culinary Arena: Julia Child

Julia Child is the mother of the American culinary world. More than any other person, she has brought the culinary profession into the homes of people throughout the United States. In fact, Julia's name was cited more often in responses to my survey than any other as the reason women first thought of cooking as a career. She has truly touched the lives of many of the women in this book. Ms. Child earned her toque from Le Cordon Bleu in 1948 and just three years later, in 1951, founded L'Ecole des Trois in Paris with her culinary partners, Simone Beck and Louisette Bertholle.

Julia's love of food and her natural ability to teach took her from Paris to Boston, where, in 1963, her cooking series debuted on WGBH, the city's public television network. From media personality to author of a number of books, including *Mastering the Art of French Cooking, The French Chef Cookbook,* and *The Way to Cook,* Julia's career as a culinary educator and celebrity flourished. Julia has numerous newspaper and magazine articles to her credit, and has contributed over 2,000 books to the Schlesinger Library's Culinary Collection.

After enjoying over five decades in the culinary field, Julia is still active in it, not only on television, but with videos, CD ROMS, and numerous ongoing guest appearances on a variety of shows. The James Beard Foundation, Inc., and The American Institute of Wine and Food (AIWF), both of which she was instrumental in founding, are among the culinary associations that she helps to promote.

---

white, pouffy skirt, a low-cut V-neck T-shirt, and an apron. This was the chef—it was just amazing! She was a really good cook though. She could really put flavors together and had a vision for what she wanted."

For many of these women, the stress didn't stop even after the day in the kitchen was done. Emily Luchetti recalls: "I didn't get paid in France. They gave me a little room the size of a table. Every Saturday night, I'd go out and buy a bottle of wine for five francs. I'd fill my only cup—this big coffee mug—with wine, turn off all the lights and just sit in bed and drink! That was the high point of my week!" Kathleen Kennedy had a similar experience. "We were working from eight in the morning until midnight, with a two-hour break. I lived in a *chambre-abode,* which was smaller than a walk-in closet, and I couldn't even sit up in bed! I had no refrigerator, no heater, no bath, no tub. It was pretty bad! It made me really appreciate coming home."

It takes long hours and many years for culinarians to climb the ladder to become a chef. These stories further testify to the hard work and conditions that women chefs are willing to endure in order to get to where they are today.

"I was thirty-four years old when I graduated with another whole career behind me, and my experience was that education only presents a field in its broadest sense. The actual work experience is where you grow. I was well prepared to start in the industry."
—Mary Pat Kiernan

1856: Baking powder is introduced commercially for the first time in the United States.

"Becoming and being a successful chef requires certain sacrifices, regardless of gender. The major disparity found in this study was that women's sacrifices include families— husbands and/or children—while male chefs may have wives to assume responsibility for their families."

—Pat Bartholomew

"Being a good chef takes 110 percent and being a good mother takes another 110 percent. As of right now, I do not see how I can do that without one of the choices suffering. When the time comes, I will have to make a certain choice."

—Marlo Hix

Apprenticeship Experiences—The American Influence

In the last two decades, training opportunities in the United States have exploded, making stints in France less essential to a career in the culinary arts. Today's up-and-coming culinarians have over 100 ACF-sponsored apprenticeship programs to choose from. And more than 17,000 apprentices have been enrolled in the last two decades at such renowned "apprentice houses" as the Ritz Carlton in Atlanta, Disney World, Opryland, and The Cloister on Sea Island.[27] Many other large hotels and resorts have similar programs, while chefs from around the country are becoming increasingly willing to accept apprentices into their kitchens.

Kathleen Kennedy's experience was very different. While a student at the CIA, Kathleen was asked by a master chef to apprentice with the 1988 Culinary Olympic team. "I got on the Olympic team as an apprentice, even though [the majority of the team members] didn't know me. They whipped me into shape and I worked for eight months, went to Germany, and did the Olympics. I was the only woman in that group—I was with fourteen guys." The Olympic team went on to bring home "the gold" and Kathleen has become a chef, a culinary educator, and most recently a mom.

Whether in this country or abroad, the apprenticeship experiences that these women have shared illustrate the strength and determination needed to successfully find a place in the culinary arena.

Culinary School and Educational Influences

While some choose to learn by participating in apprenticeship programs, others choose to attend culinary school. Two very different paths, but they both allow students to get hands-on experience—one in a kitchen classroom and the other, on an actual restaurant line. Of the women surveyed for the book, eighty percent went to culinary school, and of those, seventy-five percent went to a two-year Associate of Occupational Studies (AOS) program. This section outlines culinary experience from the perspectives of students and former students.

Not all women know from the onset how or where they can acquire the skills and knowledge they need to get them to the next skill level. Nadsa Perry's story illustrates this point. She realized that she needed more culinary education than what she had garnered from her mother, Longteine de Monteiro, chef-owner of the Elephant Walk restaurants in Somerville and Boston, Massachusetts, but she was unclear which path to take. "I needed to learn more, and I thought [I] should go to school. I picked up the CIA textbook, *The Professional Chef,* and read it from cover to cover, but the 'stock' part was kind of weird, because [I thought], where am I going to practice making stock? … I found The Cambridge School of Culinary Arts; they had a ten-month program, part-time, three nights a week—perfect. I learned basic French cooking and baking. I got what I needed—how to make a mousse, a soufflé, or whatever. I didn't know how to do any of those things. It was helpful and it gave me more confidence."

For Noëlle Haddad, the influence of school and an internship at a restaurant kept her in this country rather than going back home to Chile as she had originally planned to do. "There was a six-month course at The French Culinary Institute in New York City and I applied. I was studying, working, and doing an internship in Daniel's, all at the same time. I was absorbing like a sponge, because I thought it was only going to be six months in New York and then I would have to go back to Chile. When the six months were over, I found a job [in a kitchen] and I stayed."

Many culinary graduates say they feel their education was difficult but was the best career decision they could have made. Claire Stewart agrees as she describes her experience at the CIA: "I think the CIA is like being in the military. When someone tells you to wear white socks, you wear them—you do what you are told. ... But it was one of the best decisions in my life." Claire speaks of the hard work and commitment required to make it through the program, but in the end, she feels: "The school definitely pumps you up and makes you think. It hardens you. When I graduated I could stand a chef screaming at me. It gives you a taste of what it is going to be like when you graduate."

Sharon Brooks-Moses, another CIA alumna, tells the story of how she got there and what kept her there. Her mother had seen an ad for a culinary school on a bus. Sharon followed up on that ad and applied for a scholarship, but was rejected. Later, however, she met Chef Natale from the CIA, who helped her get a job as a cook in a local hotel, but persistently encouraged her to go to the school. After applying to school, she realized that the tuition was prohibitive. But when Sharon was ultimately accepted to the CIA, she was offered an anonymous full scholarship (to this day she doesn't know where the money came from). She describes her immediate reaction to the CIA: "It was a culture shock! It was a no-nonsense atmosphere, that I appreciated. In terms of education, the CIA was the best experience I've had." On this point, Sharon agrees with Claire Stewart: "It really gives you the real-world base because people are going to treat you like that in the industry—you're going to have to be able to deal with it."

Melissa Kelly believes that in education, you get out of it what you put in. She used her education to develop the foundations for what has become a

"I suggest if anyone was planning a family, she take an extended leave of absence if possible and essentially put her career on hold. The demands of the job are so immense that to do your job well, it's just not realistic to handle both."

—*RoxSand Scocos*

"My job was my life ... I devoted 80 percent of my waking hours to how to work better with what I had and only 20 percent to my child. I have put my culinary career on hold so that I can raise my two children into decent people."

—*Michele A. Houghton*

1859: The American Strangers Line to London says, "It is not a recognized custom to take women into restaurants."

"My mother was such a great dynamic woman—I thought I had the best mother in the world and never complained that she didn't stay at home—I never would have thought of that."
—Lydia Shire

"My children encourage me to be a good student, and my being a good student encourages them to be good students. It has done us all a world of good. It's taken us from the conventional 'mommy knows everything' attitude, and it's put us, in certain places, on an equal footing."
—Toniann Beattie

successful career. Once at culinary school, in skills class, she explains, "the whole thing really forced me to work twice as hard and read twice as much. ... I worked really hard. I knew that this was what I wanted to do—I just got the most out of school [that I could]."

But going to culinary school isn't right for everyone. Some people know this and opt for other avenues into the field. Others end up finding out the hard way. In many ways Monique Barbeau felt going to school turned out to be the wrong choice. Whether it was the people with whom she surrounded herself, or just a bad experience overall, she describes her situation as follows: "[I] was just very disappointed in a lot of different areas. ... But I thought, 'I have to finish.' I thought I would [find] really disciplined students—people knowing what they wanted to do. But instead, here I was, with my peers, and all they wanted to do was drink beer and find a girl to date. It was just disappointing." While Monique's story is not typical of what we have heard from most culinary students, there are always situations or classes that just don't turn out as they should. Nevertheless, Monique went on to become a chef, today she is executive chef at Fuller's in Seattle.

Going to culinary school is a choice, just as becoming a cook or a chef is a choice. Many women chefs who chose to pursue their educational goals are content with their decisions. The next section looks at some other decisions women face as their careers begin to take shape.

Making Decisions—Wading Through the Choices

For most women, a culinary career involves trade-offs and tough decisions that most of their male counterparts don't have to face. For men, their choices focus on where to go to school and what to do in the field. For women, there are other variables, such as whether or not to have children and how to balance family and career. This issue is pressing for so many female culinarians that one of the highlights of the Women Chefs and Restaurateurs (WCR) 1995 convention was a session called "Mothering and Mentoring: The Dynamics of Parenting in the Restaurant Workplace." In the following section, many of the same women who spoke at that conference share their perspectives on these issues.

One of the survey questions I asked women chefs and cooks is: "What were the three predominant factors in choosing your current position?" The answers give us some insight into what drives these women and the choices that they make. Sixty percent of the respondents said that challenge was one of their reasons for choosing a job. Creativity was the second most common factor chosen; fifty-seven percent of the women made this choice. Advancement and location tied at thirty-two percent. Interestingly, salary was one of the least important issues, with only twenty-seven percent of the respondents choosing this as a key factor.

Choices with Regard to Family and Children

Women entering the culinary industry often find that they have difficult decisions to make. Do they opt to choose their career over having a family? Do they have a family and juggle between their career and family? Do they put off having a family until they are established in their career? These are just some of the options that women have to confront as they approach the culinary field.

My survey of women chefs and cooks gives insight into the career direction many women are pursuing and the choices they have made:

Survey Results versus the NRA *Foodservice Employee Profile* **and** *Foodservice Employment 2000**

	Survey Results (women)	Industry Standards (all foodservice workers)
Married	44%	31%
Single	37%	54%
Divorced	10%	14%
Women with Children	37%	50–60%
Executive Chefs with Children	43%	
Chef-Owners with Children	53%	
Chef-Instructors with Children	57%	

*The percents of the breakdown by position of women with children are of the total.

What I learned from my survey and the NRA studies is that many women chefs and cooks have found a way to have both career *and* family. What the statistics don't tell us is *how* they manage, and at what cost. The following stories tell of women who chose to forego having families, as well as those who chose to alter their careers so that they could make room for both.

Two of the women who decided not to have children share similar perspectives on their desire to pursue their careers. For these women, this wasn't a hard choice because having children wasn't a priority for them. For others, however, the decision has been a matter of timing and, for them, making time to do both.

Lyde Buchtenkirch-Biscardi, the first female certified master chef, chose not to have children—work was the priority for her and her husband. "I can't say that [having children] was high, high, high on my priority list. ... I don't have any regrets, certainly, especially now that I do have a little bit more freedom than I did in the early years of my career. I can travel, I can do what I want to do; I'm not financially strapped with college education." For Lyde,

"Chef Heywood told me when I was at the Culinary, 'Make sure whenever you decide to get married that you pick the right mate for the industry'—it does make a difference."
—Sharon Brooks-Moses

"I really learned in a very humbling way, through making a lot of mistakes and doing a lot of things wrong! I think that's how I got to this point! I'm very grateful for a lot of those battles and struggles, because they really taught me what I needed to do."
—Odessa Piper

1862: Iowa widow Annie Wittenmyer, in conjunction with the Sanitary Commission, is the first to devise a dietary feeding plan for soldiers too sick to eat standard rations.

this wasn't a story of sacrifice. In fact, it illustrates that her overriding goal was to pursue her culinary career, which has taken her to heights within the ACF that no other woman in the field has achieved to date.

Hilary DeMane chose the same path as Lyde. Her priority was also her career. "I never really wanted to have children and I knew that this career was more important to me than anything else. I married a man who had that same attitude. I think that, if you really want to be successful in our business, though, that's a choice you have to make. The culinary business has got to change. We've got to stop expecting people to give up their lives. And that's what we've been doing. Sacrifice your life to the kitchen god, and then you can be a success."

For Monique Barbeau, completely sacrificing her life to the kitchen god, as Hilary and Lyde have chosen to do, is not her ultimate desire. She agrees with both women that you can't be a mother and push your career to its highest heights. While she has chosen to put off having a family at this point in her career, she hopes her decision isn't irrevocable. "I think I'm so stimulated by what I do every day that I need to spend the time and get good. I want to have a family. I don't want to wake up when I'm fifty and not have one, and it's not going to happen unless I cultivate it like I cultivated this career. I could be a mom … but [I] don't think I could have this job and have a family."

Like Monique, Traci Des Jardins is another of the many young chefs who wants to incorporate a family into her life. When I spoke with Traci, she was getting ready to embark on a new restaurant, where she will be chef-owner. Yet Traci seemed adamant that her passions for her work not overshadow her desire to have a family. "I think that in some ways we have an advantage in the restaurant business, despite the long hours that we work. If you own your own business, you have more flexibility than somebody who works nine to five in a law office. I'm sure it will be really hard, but I'm not going to give it up, I'm not going to turn forty-five and not have had a child." To help her figure out how to make this work, she states, "It's a matter of finding role models who have done it: Mary Sue (Milliken) has a son and Nancy Silverton has three kids. It won't be easy, but nothing good ever is. There's no doubt in my mind that a family is what I want and I'm not going to give it up."

The women who chose their careers over having a family decided that you can't fully commit your entire being to both work and family at the same time. Those who have put off having a family also came to this realization. Women who choose to have families also acknowledge that you can't be in two places at once, or give one hundred percent to your career and your family simultaneously. Consequently, these women found that they either had to find alternatives within the field, or cut back on their responsibilities in the kitchen. Kathleen Kennedy chose an alternative that took her out of the kitchen, allowing for more flexibility. She became an instructor because she felt it gave her more options when she decided to have a child. When I interviewed Kathleen, she was still teaching, and almost eight months pregnant. She explained that working at the school gave her the option to teach in a kitchen or a classroom. "This has been really great; at California Culinary Academy (CCA), there's so much opportunity. I had been in the restaurant [of the school] for a year and a half, I became pregnant, and there's still someplace else for me to go [within the school]. And there's still someplace I can go back to [after I have the baby] and make a difference in the school." Kathleen's decision is working well for her, and is allowing her to look forward to her career in the industry while she also looks forward to building a family.

Gale Gand is another chef who was pregnant during the interview process, but she was exploring options different from Kathleen's. Gale wants to keep doing what she's doing; however, she knows that she can't do everything herself. She told me of how difficult it has been to make the decision to have a child because of her commitment to her profession: "I turned 39 this year. I put off [having children] as long as I possibly could. I think that whether I had been working for myself or somebody else, I probably still would have done it now, because it's my last chance. It's been a real dilemma; how [to] keep what I've got, or stay home and sacrifice everything—I've been just too scared to try." Gale's solution is to hire a full-time nanny; for the first time, she says, she feels as if she is going to have a "wife." She explains that she had been working over eighty hours a week alongside her husband, yet still she had been the one making sure that milk was in the refrigerator and there were clean socks in the drawer. She was looking forward to having someone do those things for her.

Debra Ponzek, like Kathleen Kennedy, chose to seek an alternative career path that would allow her to focus on her family. She left her position as executive chef at the three-star Montrachet in New York City and opened her own business, Aux Délices, Foods by Debra Ponzek, a gourmet deli and catering establishment in Greenwich, Connecticut. Debra explains why this career decision worked so well for her: "Owning your own business is easier to do than working for somebody else. I have the choice of bringing my baby to work. I can come and go as I want to; if I want to delegate work to somebody else, I can do that. There's a price to pay for all that, but it means you have the power to do it. I always [think], 'What's the worst that can happen?' The worst thing that can happen is I don't have this business; I won't lose my ability to cook; I'll always have my passion for food."

It took a second child for RoxSand Scocos to realize that her career and her family belong to two separate worlds. After her second child was born, she

"In the past year, I have just realized the importance of family and private time. No job is worth sacrificing personal well being."
—Anita L. Storch

"There is no overt prejudice against women in kitchens today, but I do think there is a sort of locker-room mentality that takes it's toll."
—Dorothy Cann Hamilton

1862: U.S. women take the place of men in factories, arsenals, bakeries, retail shops, and government offices throughout the Union and the Confederacy as military draft calls create labor shortages.

decided that she needed to give up some of the control in the kitchen so she could spend more time with her children. The day I interviewed RoxSand was the day her youngest daughter took her first steps. RoxSand had brought up her first daughter, Tatiana, in the restaurant. She explained why with the younger child, Theo, she's going to do things differently. "I couldn't do it, just couldn't bring up another child in the restaurant. Tatiana, our first child, *lived* here. I wore her in a front pack—I wore her to work, literally. She worked on me for nine months after she was born. I'll never forget when I brought Theo in: … I put her on my workbench, which is where I had always put Tatiana. The woman who was doing pastry was working and this huge rolling pin rolled right off the shelf and just missed Theo. She was barely a week old! That nearly killed her, nearly killed my baby. So I decided that was it. 'I hate this place, I'm outta here.' I ended up burying my anger and anxiety about that. I just buried and buried and buried." RoxSand now has her sous-chefs running the day-to-day operation, which allows her more time with her family. And while it took her a little while to figure out the right solution for her, she has succeeded in keeping both her restaurant and her family as priorities.

Just as it had taken RoxSand two tries to find the right balance for her and her family, Nora Pouillon also had two separate opportunities. The difference is that her second opportunity was with a second family. During her first marriage, she explains, she chose her career over her family. With Nora's second family, however, she made some different decisions. She explains that with her first family, one of her two children held her accountable for her choice when he was only nine years old: "Alexis came to me and [said], 'I wish you would never have started the (restaurant).' He said, 'I'm not upset that you left, that you and Daddy are separated, but that you started the restaurant. I'm very upset about that.' It was the beginning of the restaurant—I hardly saw them—I saw them maybe once a month or on weekends." Nora did things differently with her second family. "When I agreed to … [have] another child, it was with the understanding that her father would take care of her, share or take the majority of the work. It's very nice for me; I have this relationship where her father takes complete care of the everyday nitty-gritty things. I now play the male role where I come home and [say,] 'Hi.' The most difficult part of being a mother at home is that you spend all day with the children and you have to discipline and teach them. You are the bad guy, and then here comes the father [who] hasn't done a thing for them, and he's God. Well, now I feel a little bit able to play God." While this role reversal might not work for all the women in the field, it has worked well for Nora, her family, and her thriving career. Her youngest child visits the restaurant, so she sees her every day, yet her husband deals with the day-to-day issues that she is not available to address.

Jody Adams tries to balance her work and family and to make the hard choices that she thinks are best. Her family arrangement is similar to Nora's in that her husband handles most of the childcare issues while she is at work. She explains: "In the first five months, Ken [her husband] and I shared [childcare]. I would stay home until about one and then Ken would take over. The first night I went back to work, I remember coming home and Ken was sitting in the rocking chair with Oliver, and Oliver was screaming. [Ken said,] 'Here, take your son!' He was no longer ours, he was mine! ... And I nursed and I pumped. Eventually I gave up pumping, because I didn't have an electric pump, and the only privacy [in the restaurant] was a little tiny bathroom at the bottom of the stairs, where I had to sit with my knees against the door, hoping nobody would come in. I also had to think about what was on my hands—if I had garlic on my hands, would that contaminate the milk?" Jody made it through the early years; however, she still finds herself confronted with difficult situations. A recent conflict: "Yesterday after work, I went and picked up my son to take him to soccer and on the way home, he asked, 'Is it a family night?' Family night is the night that I'm at home. When I said 'no,' he burst into tears. I had to take him home and drop him off, and [when] I walked in, and the baby started crying—that's hard. We survive it. That's what our life has always been like."

The same can be said for Clara Craig, executive chef for Project Open Hand, an outreach program feeding thousands of housebound AIDS patients each day in San Francisco. She tells of how difficult it is to make the choices, then find the balance. "My kids tell me all the time, 'The only thing we regret about when we were younger is that you were not home enough.' What is that like to hear? It's like, 'Oh, God, did I screw up?' They look at me, when they see my face, and say, 'Well, you're a good mom—it's just, you were never there!'" She speaks of the important family events that she missed out on: "I was there, sometimes! I was there for graduation, but no Christmases—we'd have Christmas Eve at 9:00 or 10:00 at night. At the time, it seemed necessary to do, to have the stable home life they needed, take care of them, and make the job work. So those are two focuses I had at that point in time. I would say, 'We won't have Christmas today—we'll wait; mom's day off is two days from now, we'll do it two days later.'" Yet she acknowledges that Christmas two days later just wasn't the same. This was her choice, and while she admits that it wasn't easy, one has to persevere.

Lidia Bastianich comes from a family-oriented background heavily influenced by her heritage. Hers is the story of the choices she made so that she could integrate her family into her career. "The kids were always part of everything we did—they were never a hindrance to me. If we toughed it out, they toughed it out with us. And they are the better for it. I remember when we

"Even though I did not have the opportunity to go to cooking school, I would recommend it, as I would recommend any school in one's desired field. Then, I think it is imperative to put yourself in a professional environment that is equal to your dream."

—Rozanne Gold

1869: The Campbell Soup Company has its beginnings in a cannery opened in Camden, New Jersey.

"It's great to have someone who's passionate about the industry who can understand why you work twelve-hour days and sit around and read cookbooks and magazines on your day off. We talk about food; eat, sleep, and breathe it!"

—*Leslie Myers*

were building Felidia, we had sold the other restaurants and my husband got ill. My daughter was little; my son was delivering newspapers! The cash flow was tight. And that was my son's part to put food on the table. I mean, minimally, but I let him know he was part of that." The choices that Lidia made allowed her to mesh the two facets of her life that were most important to her. This unusual ability has served her and her family well over the years.

Anne Gingrass's choices were less difficult than they were for some of the other women because Anne worked in a restaurant that had already made adjustments for women and children in the workplace. She explains: "I worked days, David worked nights, or vice-versa. I worked half days, half nights, I had the baby and she came to work with me for the first year of her life. … She was upstairs in the accounting office for the whole day. She slept, the first six months. It was fine, but after a year we had to get a baby-sitter and we worked it out." She goes on to say: "I don't feel that I gave up a life—I feel that *this* is the life that I have. So Rebecca grows up in the restaurant—I don't mind as a mom. And she has a baby-sitter; she's always had a full-time baby-sitter. But that's *her* life and I don't think she's suffering!! She has a mom who loves her very much and she comes and visits me all the time and she has dinner here. I just think that it's a different way of life, but it's not *bad*. She does very well and I feel good about it."

Like Anne, Mary Sue Milliken's child also joined her in the kitchen for part of his early life. She talks about her son, her family, and the decisions she has made. "When Declan was born, I took a month off, and I took him to work for the first year. I'd tie him in a little sling and I'd go in the kitchen. I wouldn't work the hot line, but I might expedite, or help out. Then, there have been a few times that were a little bit crunched and I felt like I just couldn't spend enough time with him. But spending time with my son is a big priority for me. I'm home, cooking in my kitchen with him at least five nights a week. We eat there as family, we talk about our days, and we share. It's made me think about quality of life, time spent. The whole reason we as chefs do all this is because eating and sharing food is such an important part of everybody's daily life."

Madeleine Kamman's refrigerator is covered with the pictures of her children, grandchildren, and her husband. It's clear that like many of the other women I spoke with, she had the same tough choices to make regarding her work and her family. "Those woman who don't have children have a lot more possibilities to give of themselves. For me even, it was hard; any capital we had was for the children—for their education. That's an impediment. Just to have to think about them, that they exist is an impediment. If you look at women, there's so much more that we're supposed to do. We're responsible for the children; we're responsible for the house. Whether or not we work, it's all got to be done."

Toniann Beattie's story is a little different from the others we have heard. It is about a woman who had a difficult decision to make: should she take the leap into the culinary field and commit whatever time she needed in order to learn the craft, or work at an unfulfilling job just to support her family? She made her choice to pursue a culinary career well after her children were born. She explains that the inspiration for her decision was Karen Page and Andrew Dornenburg's book, *Becoming a Chef*. That book awakened something in her that told her she needed to go to culinary school and follow her heart. She explains her plight: "I'm the mother of two children and the noblest thing I ever did was to become a parent. Parenting is a very humbling experience, but not a selfish experience. Pursuing a culinary career is absolutely the first selfish decision I have ever made in my life." Toniann is finishing her culinary education and pursuing her dream, while still taking care of her children.

This section outlines some difficult choices that women make. In fact, even after decisions are made, many women still feel torn between their two great loves—their work and their family. Right now in the industry, very little is being done to lessen the burden of these decisions and to support the women who'd like to have both. This issue is considered further in chapter eight as we look toward the workplace of the future.

"I have worked at places where somebody has gotten pregnant. People said, 'OK, now we have to be careful'—the laws and regulations that go along with having someone pregnant are looked at as a handicap. I don't want someone to think of my being pregnant and starting a family as a handicap."
—*Debbie Gold*

Relationship Choices: Finding the Right Combination

Being involved with another human being is possibly the hardest thing we do in our lives. In this section, women who have lost relationships and other women who have found relationships in the course of pursuing careers in the culinary world tell their stories. All of them have found that maintaining relationships that revolve around their careers means making trade-offs. You'll hear about some women who have become involved with partners who work within the industry and who share their drive to succeed in the business. You'll also hear from women whose partners are in other lines of work, and they must contend with another set of challenges.

Johanne Killeen is one of the women whose spouse is in the same industry. She has found that her work in their restaurant is tied in a positive way to her partnership with her husband, George. "I would never do this by myself. I might work as a chef in somebody else's business, but I would never have my own restaurant by myself. I feel extremely lucky to be married to the person who works beside me because I think this is the kind of business where you really can't have a life. I marvel at people who can stay married where one person is in the restaurant business and the other person's not. It's so difficult and the pressures are so great." For Johanne and George, working toward a common goal is an important part of what makes their relationship succeed.

1871: Amanda Jones is awarded five patents for a vacuum process that she has developed for preserving food.

Like Johanne and George, Rozanne Gold and her husband have also been working as a team for many years. They too, find that their working partnership keeps their relationship strong. "I love working—a lot of women love working. I think there's nothing wrong with the hours, or keeping up with this business, and working as long as any man would, six to seven days a week. I know far more couples now who are both in this business. Maybe that's what it takes, or that's why it's working."

Kerry Heffernan and her partner also work in the same industry and find that sharing the passion for their work has been essential. "It helps a lot to be involved with someone who's in the business. I don't know *how* people get involved with people who aren't in the business—and how they stay together. I've worked six days a week for the last four weeks now, and it didn't occur to my partner to say, 'Why don't you spend more time with me?' It would never come up. Food is part of our lives—we do food."

Phyllis Flaherty reflects on the issues that women confront when dealing with relationships and work. These are issues she feels must be addressed regardless of whether or not you're involved with someone in the industry. She has been in both situations and compares the challenges that arise in each: "My first husband was a teacher; my second husband is a chef. I believe it's very difficult to be married, male or female—to someone that's not in this business. Being married to someone in the industry ... you both have a passion for the business. It's like artists—there is that passion. [A] problem I see, when you marry someone in the business ... is, that it can create jealousy and competition. That's a different kind of a problem."

Sharon Brooks-Moses remembers advice given to her by one of the chefs at the CIA. She begins by sharing insight she gives her students. "I tell them that this is not a nine to five job where you're going to clock in at nine and clock out at five o'clock. You have to redefine what you want your life to be and [determine how] those people who you feel are special to you are going to fit in it. Chef Heywood told me that when I was at the Culinary, 'Make sure whenever you decide to get married that you pick the right mate for the industry.' I was thinking to myself 'What difference does that make?' But it does make a difference, sometimes with my husband ... we'll go all weekend and I won't see his face."

For Gwen Kvavli Gulliksen, the differences between her career and her husband's haven't been a problem. They have found a way to spend time together and also give enough attention to their work. Gwen has made a priority of having meals with her husband to help keep her relationship healthy. "I've been married for eleven years; my husband's an artist, and he has a passion. We have oddball schedules that we work with, [but] I make sure that we eat together. Sometimes that means we don't eat until eleven o'clock at night, but we still sit down and eat together. We always do. I really need that."

These choices involve personal relationships and building family. These are just some of the issues that arise when women immerse themselves in the culinary field. Other choices concern their jobs and careers.

Making the Right Career Choices

For most of us, our job is what we do every day, or for many hours each week. It is important that we like what we're doing because our time and energy is invested in making it productive. For this reason, before committing to a job or a career path, it is necessary to explore options and really examine the consequences of your choice. In the following stories, you will hear from women who have made many right choices and others who have made some wrong choices for themselves. Many have tried their hands at several different jobs until they found what worked for them.

Many women believe that running their own restaurant will allow them a flexibility and control that was elusive to them when they worked for others. But some, such as Nancy Stark, discovered that there's more to ownership than simply gaining control of their lives. She explains why her decision to run a restaurant ultimately didn't work out for her. "When I had the restaurant, I'd lay awake in the night and cry, 'How am I going to make the payroll? How am I going to pay these people?' It's really scary." She chose to go back to work for someone else as an assistant pastry chef. "I don't have the heavy pressures, and to me that's worth the low pay; that's worth a lot of things! I never wake up in the middle of the night having a panic attack. My God, that used to happen a lot!" For Nancy, her negative experience running her own restaurant gave her a new appreciation for positions with less responsibility, where someone else is in charge.

Carol Levenherz's experience working for herself has been the opposite of Nancy's. Carol, who has owned and operated a catering company for over a decade, can't imagine working for anyone but herself. "I've never worked for anyone other than myself. I don't want to come home from work every day and be upset and angry about how I've been treated [by my employer]. It has just reinforced the fact that I have to work for myself. Work gives me a feeling of self-worth. I like making my own money, making my own decisions, and running my own company."

Like Carol, Raji Jallepalli wanted a business of her own. Her dream became a reality when she opened Restaurant Raji, where she was the owner and she hired a chef. Eventually, Raji realized she also wanted to be the chef. "I started the restaurant and hired the first chef. Then I was hiring and firing chefs every day because they would just want to get the job done. Nobody had the passion. It [was] not coming from their heart; they were not getting excited. I said, 'How

"You know, it's great to be able to eat well in restaurants, but to me, it's even greater to eat well at home. We're now generations away from producing girls and women who learn to cook!"
—*Deborah Madison*

"The question I ask is not what's it like to be a woman in this field, but what can we (as men and women) do so that these questions can be eliminated."
—*Kate Mortellaro*

1876: San Francisco's Palace Hotel opens on October 2.

can you not get excited—this is the most wonderful thing in the world.' It was at that point that I said, 'If I want to accomplish this, I'm going to have to be in the kitchen.' After a while of working in the kitchen, I realized that I had never been happier." Unlike Nancy, who didn't want all of the responsibility of running a restaurant, Raji thrived on every aspect of running her restaurant.

Kirsten Dixon has chosen the beauty and wilds of Alaska as her place of business. Kirsten's three lodges are accessible only by floatplane, and during the winter the plane might come only once or twice a month. She was in New York when she shared some of the trade-offs she endures operating businesses in such a remote land: "I love the aesthetic of our lives [in Alaska]. I love the natural beauty that surrounds us—the purity of the natural experience. But this morning I got up early [in New York City] and went down to Balducci's and almost started crying—to be able to go to stores like that every day and get fresh mozzarella made that morning. It would be wonderful to have more culinary resources than I do."

Some women decide to alleviate the pressure by getting out of the kitchen altogether. That was the case for both Pam Parseghian and Monica Velgos, who each took their passion for food and creativity with them into another medium. Pam reflects: "The reason I left cooking was because of burnt hands, tired legs, a little bit too much abuse from male co-workers, and just a general lack of interest in putting in that physically hard work. Cooking is so physically demanding. I knew I had to find something else to do in the industry." For Pam, becoming a food writer for *Nation's Restaurant News* (NRN) was her solution. Monica Velgos also became a food writer, most recently at *Food Arts*. She knew from the time that she graduated from The French Culinary Institute (FCI) that this was what she wanted to do. "I was very passionate about food and I needed to fit it in, in a way that was going to work with all of my interests. It took a while to do it with food publishing. Food publishing was a good blend, because then I could work with language every day and I could talk about food with people who wanted to talk about it with me all day."

Another chef turned writer is Emily Luchetti. During her career, she has had many culinary roles; her most recent decision was to leave her position as pastry chef and go out on her own to write and consult. She explains: "[Over] the last year I [have] just loved my freedom. I mean I love to work, but I love to get up, and go for a run, and if I don't start at 7:00, but I start at 7:45, it's no problem." There is the down side as well, she admits: "I miss a place where I can hang my shingle, and say, 'This is where you can come for my desserts, this is my creation. But I don't want to give up all my freedom. So I'm going to try [not] to have a business that's so hands-on, and try to be able to have [my] cake and eat it too."

For Clara Craig, the decision to leave her position as an executive chef in a hotel was a step she had to take to preserve her self-respect. She cites her lack of freedom and support as the reason behind her decision to leave her position. "I was executive chef, and they wouldn't get me a sous chef. They were trying to keep their bottom line. I told them I hadn't had a day off in thirty days!'" For Clara, the realization that the situation wasn't going to improve was the last straw. Even the salary of $60,000 to $80,000 a year wasn't enough of an incentive to hold her interest. She explains: "I don't want to spend twelve hours in the kitchen anymore." Clara may not be in a hotel anymore, but feeding thousands of AIDS patients every day at Project Open Hand in San Francisco is keeping her fulfilled and challenged.

Let's face it—making a career decision is difficult for most of us. Some of us even grapple with what we want for dinner, or how we want to spend our valuable time off. The choices that women make, in many cases, have dramatic effects on their daily lives and their futures. While some decisions may not be the best at the time, they all offer valuable lessons that help us see things more clearly the next time around.

"I would be in the library studying economics and I would be falling asleep, thinking, 'How am I going to do research in some bank?' I worked breakfast, lunch, and dinner in the cafeteria, and I really loved it, but I never thought that cooking school was something that I would consider."
—Susan Feniger

Choosing to Make Personal Sacrifices

Many of our choices are laden with sacrifice. The kitchen can be a very demanding place, a place that consumes all of our time. More than thirty-eight percent of the women chefs and cooks I surveyed work twelve hours per day or more, and more than forty percent work a minimum of six days per week. Long hours aside, these schedules are particularly taxing since these women often work weekends, holidays, and evenings. In this section, we hear from women about the sacrifices they had to make in order to pursue their passion.

Amy Scherber spends most of her time in one of her bakeries, and the hours she and her staff work precludes having time for a social life. "I work now, noon to midnight, five days a week, so I do have some weekend time off. When I go out for some function at seven or eight o'clock at night, there are all of these people out there, in the restaurants, on the street, going out dancing, to bars, and museums, and having fun. I don't know *anything* about all that—which makes my work a big sacrifice. If I change my schedule to work in the morning, then I don't see the people who are coming in to bake. I want to be involved with the baking experience. It's very important to me and those people need a lot of nurturing. They work all night and they don't get to see daylight very much—they sleep during the day. I feel like they're sacrificing so much, so I need to sacrifice and be with them, too."

Nancy Stark addresses many of the same issues as Amy. She too feels that she does not have a life outside of work. She talks about all the sacrifices that

1878: Cheribino Angelica, a railroad chef, asks his wife to make a more practical chef's coat, a precursor of our contemporary chef's coat.

she made to pursue her career. "I gave up my nice home and my dog and my cat and my car. Mostly, I've just given up my time. I don't have time to go out, just for fun. I always feel like I'm marshaling my energy—I can't go out, because I have to have my sleep. I can't have a glamorous life; I can't have nice clothes and painted fingernails—which I don't want anyway—but sometimes I think it'd be fun to be a little less macho."

Claire Stewart looks at what she has given up for her career. She is feeling the years pass, and thinking of all of the holidays she has missed, and her fleeting youth. She explains that until two years ago, missing holidays didn't bother her. However, along the way, her perspective has changed: "It has to do with family getting older and thinking that maybe they won't be here next Christmas." Like Nancy and Amy, she laments some of what she's missing. "It's the feeling of missing out; of never seeing the same movies that are being reviewed. You get too involved with your world. You know the right people, the right names, and you just ate at the right restaurant. You've got the look and you've got the burns. When someone invites you to a party, a wedding, a funeral or anything, you're not really sure if you are going to have that night off. Now my friends are having babies and my youth is gone because every time I went out, it was one o'clock in the morning."

Raji Jallepalli was married to a doctor from her native India, and she describes her sacrifices with her marriage, family, and career. "After my divorce I had to start from scratch—I really had the confidence that I could do it. Then one very busy Friday afternoon when I was pulling my hair out, I get a call from India and my mom is shouting at the top of her lungs saying that somebody from India had been to the States and told her I was divorced. I said, 'Mom I can't talk to you right now; I'm at the restaurant and I have to cook.' 'What do you mean you have to cook;' she still didn't know I cooked. There was a lot of crying. Finally she came to visit me and came to the restaurant and her heart bled watching how hard I worked. She said, 'Raji, find another doctor and get married.' I said to her, 'Mom, life is not about getting married to a doctor; first of all, marriage is just an option. You've got to understand there's something to be said for being happy with yourself, feeling a sense of accomplishment.' I didn't speak to her for quite some time and when we finally did she said, 'I've been thinking a lot about this and I think it takes a woman like you to make a difference.'"

Sacrifice for Longteine de Monteiro has a very different meaning than it has for most of us. She and her husband came from a very privileged background in Cambodia. Although Longteine and her husband own their restaurants, she still has trouble reconciling part of their responsibilities with her Old World upbringing. "The most difficult thing for me to see ... is my husband, waiting tables. That hurts me a lot. He never did this in his life. He used to sit down and people served him. Even a glass of water. He never did it." Today, this is a way of life for her whole family.

Sacrifices That Cost Women Their Marriages or Relationships

Women's choices are often difficult and impact the lives of their family. While for the most part, families remain intact, that doesn't always happen. Sometimes there are casualties when women can't strike the balance between family and work.

Gale Gand attributes her passion for her work as a factor behind the breakup of her first marriage. "You say to [your] husband, 'I'll be home at eight o'clock,' and at eight o'clock you call and say 'Party went up by 55; I have to stay another couple of hours.' We went through years of, 'When do you think you're going to be here? When do you think you're going to be home?' The first couple of years, you say, 'As soon as I can.' The second couple of years you say, 'When I'm ready!' The third couple of years you say, 'I'm not coming home, OK, I'm leaving you.'" Gale's second marriage is very different than her first. She and her husband are co-chefs/co-owners of Brasserie T in Chicago, and they have recently had their first child.

Susan Weaver's first marriage also did not fare well when it collided with her work. "It was difficult. He also worked in the industry; he worked nights and I worked days. I just spent far too much time at work, and if I wasn't at work, my mind was there. There was simply nothing left after the day. We both reached a point where we had to choose what we were going to do about it. The marriage failed. I have now learned to take control and to spend as much time on my personal life as I did building my professional life; it's sort of a balance."

While Cindy Salvato has never been married, she attributes the destruction of a couple of serious relationships to her work. "I've worked so many hours, twelve and fourteen hours a day. I've been engaged twice! … I just decided that I was going to marry my work. I decided to make my career really important. Now I think I'm in a place where I'd really like to have a relationship. Everybody should have that. It's really important."

Raji Jallepalli's story gives us a perspective on the additional burdens and sacrifice of different cultures. For Raji, the conflicts that arose because of her hours and commitment to her job, cost her a marriage. She explains: "My husband wasn't happy; I was spending too much time in the restaurant so he thought I was having an affair with somebody. I told him it was with food. He's a physician—he eats to live—but doesn't live to eat, so he doesn't understand how a person [can] be like this." There were also cultural issues Raji was dealing with that interfered with her marriage. As she explains it: "Cooks aren't respected in India. One day a group of doctors were having a party at my

"You know what it's like to put out hundreds of plates every single day! And to realize every single day that is what I do, how much I don't know, and how much there is to learn?"

—*Elizabeth Germain*

1880: *The Cordon Bleu was founded by Marthe Distel at Palais-Royal.*

restaurant. A food writer [had] come by and done a really great review and all the doctors were congratulating me about that. My husband said to them, 'Raji really doesn't cook anything; we have other people that work in the kitchen. She just looks after things—she's not a cook.' I spoke with my husband and he said, 'I worked very hard to get where I am today and I have a problem with you being a cook.' He said, 'Sell it, sell the damn thing, we don't need it, I just want you to be my wife and I want you to be at home. You don't really need to work.' I realized that there was a fundamental philosophy difference between us, so we got divorced."

This chapter reveals a lot about the demands of the culinary industry on people and, in particular, on women. While women have more choices today than they have ever had before, they come at a price. The passion that drives these women helps make their decisions easier, but the bottom line is what they are willing to "sacrifice to the kitchen gods." For most, the choice has been the degree of sacrifice they have had to make.

Challenges That Women Face in the Culinary Arena

"A thing in its time and a time for each thing."
—Madeleine Kamman

*"Things are chang-
ing more and more,
I can see. I feel as
though women deliv-
er a security to
employers; we are
smart, knowledge-
able, organized, and
determined. That is
what an employer is
looking for; women
can deliver all these
things."*
—*Darlene Gaudreau*

Women chefs and cooks have faced some daunting challenges in the culinary field. Aside from dealing with the sheer physical and emotional stresses inherent in the business, they also have faced sexism, double standards, and harassment. That these women persevere at all is a testament to their strength, determination, and passion for what they do. Some of the obstacles are exclusive to women's experiences; others plague just about everyone who works in the industry.

Why Women Have Been Excluded

As of February 1997, of the 2,134 certified executive chefs (currently active) practicing their craft in the United States, only 92 are women (see Appendix B for ACF certification levels). That represents only 4.3 percent, a far cry from what you'd expect to see in an industry where cooking was traditionally a woman's domain. Women's absence from the upper echelons of the culinary world is disturbing for many reasons: it discourages future generations of women from pursuing a culinary career; it shortchanges the health and vibrancy of the industry; it's at odds with our notions of a fair, just, and equal world. The following sections explore the dynamics behind why professional kitchens have been slow to welcome women and investigate how today's female chefs and cooks view the situation.

In *Patriarchal Attitudes: Women in Society,* Eva Figes quotes Margaret Mead in a way that I think exemplifies many of the challenges facing women chefs. "Men," she says, "may cook or weave or dress dolls or hunt hummingbirds, but if such activities are appropriate occupations for men, then society votes them as important. But when the same occupations are performed by women, they are regarded as less important."

Dr. Pat Bartholomew is one of the leading sources of information on women chefs. Her landmark dissertation on career success for women chefs, was the first in-depth study of contemporary women chefs who paved the way into professional kitchens. One of the questions she explores is why male cooks have found high prestige and why that same prestige has been denied women. One of the historians she cites is Stephan Mennell, who offers this explanation: "It's the inseparability of women and domestic cooking." Mennell says that when socially prestigious cuisine appeared, it had to be differentiated from ordinary cooking. The way to do that was through disciplined technique and male cooks—essentially a mimic of the military model. This new "court cuisine" reinforced the notion that what mothers, sisters, and wives did in the kitchen was ordinary, not professional cooking. In that way, male cooks and male cooks only came to be viewed as "instruments of refinement."[28]

Cooks and servers. Dover Publications, circa 1880s. Courtesy of the Culinary Archives and Museum at Johnson and Wales University.

The idea of gender bias isn't new, but what compounded the problem was the fact that when women were ready to come back into the workforce, at the onset of the radical 1960s, they clearly weren't wanted by many of the men currently in the workforce. Felice Schwartz and Jean Zimmerman in *Breaking with Tradition: Women and Work, the New Facts of Life,* take this thought one step further. "There were two parallel worlds occupied by men and women. There was the men's world, [which was] the paid workplace, and the women's world, [which was] dominated by home and family. Women entered the workforce [1965 ish] in an era when they weren't perceived to be needed … when men and many women thought they [the women] should be home tending the hearth and raising the children."

Pat Bartholomew and I spoke at length about the challenges women encounter on the road to a culinary career. "I found a lot of women are very, very shy—especially women who go into cooking. The reason they go into the back of the house, part of it, is there's an inherent shyness and they think, 'Oh I'm going to work with carrots. I don't have to talk to them.' " This is just one reason why Pat believes women have had such a hard time in this industry. She also believes they have had more to juggle in their lives than men. She explains, "I talked to all the culinary instructors—from the CIA, FCI, New York Restaurant School—the people who run those schools, everyone agrees that

1881: *What Mrs. Fisher Knows About Old Southern Cooking,* written by Abby Fisher, is the earliest known cookbook by an African-American.

"I believe certainly discrimination continues to exist, in all areas, not just culinary, but in every area for women. But I think that it is better than it was, certainly when I was looking at things back in the early 1980s."
—Dell Hargis

women are the smartest. They have the best GPAs overall, statistically. They are the most determined, the most focused, the most organized, [and] the most obsessed. [They are also] the most passionate ... [but] five years down the line they're gone. That woman in your class who you thought was 'going to set the bloody world on fire'—you can't find her. The basic bottom line is that women struggle to find some way to combine their careers with a life ... the major responsibilities of a family or a relationship seem to fall on the women still. If they're going to have that, they have to pick up all of that plus their job. ... They may be just smart enough to say, 'this is just crap, who needs all this stuff?' But it forces them out of some arenas where they might have had opportunities to do very well."

Discrimination in the workplace is not a new problem, nor is it unique to the culinary field. In 1986, the placement office of the CIA received a grant from the New York State Education Department to study the unique problems facing female graduates currently employed in the foodservice industry. The survey was conducted by Dell Hargis, the Director of Alumni Affairs; although it is unpublished and is now over a decade old, the survey results help to illustrate the challenges faced by many of the women in contemporary kitchens.

The study sheds some light on the challenges women graduates felt then and that women in the kitchens continue to confront today. Dell talked about the process of doing the study. "The results of what we finally printed in-house was simply something I knew to be true. Even though it was a small number (under 100 respondents), I was absolutely certain that, had we had the opportunity to expand it, it would have proven itself to be true. ... Discrimination was definitely an issue that at least eighty percent of the women had experienced in some fashion."

She explains that there was a preconceived notion that females were not physically able to do the work that needed to be done in a professional kitchen. Despite that attitude, however, she adds that there were women who loved their jobs, and whose employers said good things about them. Some employers went so far as to say, "hiring them was the greatest thing that has ever happened."

Here are some of the key findings:

- Women entering foodservice fields are not prepared for competition, team playing, negotiating, and assertiveness.

- All women reported some difficulty with the politics of competition. Findings indicate that the normal avenues of competition—hard work, quality performance, dedication, and conscientiousness—do not necessarily place them on an equal level with male counterparts.

- Negotiating proved difficult for most of the female graduates. Most felt it was directly related to their "female status," which made them feel as if employers viewed them as less capable and/or desirable.

- All women reported difficulty in negotiating salary, both at initial employment and subsequent increases, including promotions.

- When female graduates acted assertive, their superiors often viewed their behavior as aggressive. Assertiveness in men, however, [was seen] as maturity, having [his] feet on the ground, and knowing where he wants to go.

- Women, often smaller in stature, are believed less capable of performing necessary kitchen duties. Females also felt that chefs often related "smallness in stature" with an inability to "think big," "perform with excellence," and "carry their weight in the kitchen."

- Women are often placed in "support roles" rather than direct management or supervision. Men are perceived as "leaders," women are perceived as followers/supporters. Women graduates feel the "female support role" is generally encouraged by society at large, and also feel this incorrect concept in the foodservice industry is further strengthened by attitudes displayed at culinary training schools.

- Male supervisors/managers are threatened by females seeking upward growth and appear to deal superficially with women who have achieved positions at an equal level. This reaction is understood to mean: "She is not really capable of dealing with her role at this level."

- Blatant discrimination was reported by some female graduates at all levels in the foodservice industry. Use of the terms "girl," "cutie," and "sweetie" reflect a lack of respect and recognition of women as mature equals. These references are often coupled with flirtation, teasing, and on occasion, harassment.

- Every female indicated discrepancies in pay for the same or similar work.

A Newsweek poll in 1991 found 21 percent of women said they had endured sexual harassment; 42 percent said they knew someone who had been the object of harassment.
—Newsweek, October 21, 1991, p. 34

While this survey may be over a decade old, its conclusions are still relevant today. Women I spoke with voiced frustrations about gender-based discrimination and harassment. Forty-four percent of the women chefs and cooks I surveyed felt they had either been discriminated against or had suffered sexual harassment. Of those women, only thirty-seven percent reported the incidents to management but only fourteen percent of those cases had positive

1882: Japan's first cooking school opens for the instruction of women.

"Every time someone comes in and wants to speak to the owner, they would go to my husband. I have had salesmen who won't do business with me because I am female."

—*Laurene R. Reuter*

resolution. Half the women I spoke with said pay discrepancies were an issue, and the vast majority of the women felt that they needed to work longer and work harder to be compensated equitably with their male counterparts. While the industry has made a commitment to ensuring equality in the workplace, many women feel that they still have a long way to go.

Women Confronting Discrimination

Women have confronted discrimination since the beginning of time—it is nothing new. If you are a woman reading this book, no doubt you have your own stories to tell. The statistics in Appendix B tell part of the story.

The last two chapters have explored theories about why discrimination exists. In the following stories, which these women have to tell about themselves, we find out whether or not the theories ring true. While the theories and stories may offer some valuable insights, they don't really address why discriminatory attitudes continue to prevail.

Sexism

A clear picture of gender bias in the culinary world and elsewhere can be ascertained by having a look at industry job classifieds. Advertisements from the 1950s through the 1970s are particularly telling because they list positions by gender. In a *New York Times* dated 1956, the only cooking job openings for women were as housekeepers, which paid fifty to eighty dollars per week.

There were no female chef positions listed; however, an ad for a female dietitian reads: "ADA preferred for production in main kitchen. You will supervise twenty employees and have responsibility for full food production. Will also assist in preparing plans for new kitchen—must have experience in large institution." The ad reads like a chef's position, although the chef positions were only listed under the male category.

In 1966, the *New York Times* listed chef positions under the "male" category with salaries in the range of $225 per week. Under the "female" category, there was one chef position listed, and the salary was $80 per week. The practice of gender-based ads, with differing pay scales, continued until the mid-1970s. Today, pay parity may still be an issue, but when pay is gender-based, it is much less overt.

In *Breaking with Tradition: Women and Work, the New Facts of Life,* authors Felice Schwartz and Jean Zimmerman address ongoing gender bias: "Corporate leaders' preconception that women don't take risks and are not cut out for technical jobs leads them to shunt talented women away from line positions that are essential to running a business. Men who supervise women often are not comfortable giving them the candid performance evaluations, with constructive suggestions for growth they need, if they are to move up as rapidly and as far as their male colleagues." These are perpetual issues that women have faced in every field, and ones that are still faced every day by some women in the foodservice industry.

Some of the stories of discrimination begin even before women have been allowed to enter the kitchen. Sarah Langan describes the blatant discrimination she experienced during one of her first job searches. "I remember this job fair so well; I went up to this guy from The Plaza or the St. Regis, and he said, 'We want a lead saucier, but you're a woman.' I was shocked, and [asked], 'Why wouldn't you hire a woman?' He said, 'It's a very heavy job, and you wouldn't be able to lift the pots.' 'Do men lift them by themselves?' [I asked] 'Well, no.' I just walked away." This was not the only incident where Sarah confronted this type of gender bias. She tells another story of being in New York City in search of a job. She recalls: "All my friends, all the guy friends I had from CIA were ... at all the best restaurants. I went to visit them, and there were no women in the kitchen. I said, 'I want to work with you. I want to work where you're working.' They said, no, they'd never hire a woman in the kitchen, the only woman is the cashier, and she sits right there.' I got really kind of upset about that."

Cindy Salvato found that once she got into a kitchen, she seemed to be a non-entity. While Sarah's discrimination was blatant, Cindy's was subtler, yet equally frustrating. She remembers: "I was the pastry chef for two years and the chef wouldn't even talk to me. [There was] another woman chef who was in charge of all the production and working the line. She got the same treatment. We would sit in the locker room and [ask ourselves], 'What is going on here?' There was just no conversation, there was no [feedback]. No 'hey, that's a really nice dessert.' I knew that I was doing a good job, because people would say, 'Wow! That is so beautiful!' But, you have to hear it from your boss." Cindy never did. Her experience resembles my own. During the two years that I worked on cruise ships, the saucier never spoke to me—not once. His nonverbals told me all that I needed to know: he clearly believed women did not belong in the professional kitchen.

Phyllis Flaherty talks about feeling devalued by her employer's refusal to acknowledge her as a chef. "When General Foods offered me a job, they sent me a letter saying the title was, 'Senior Home Economist.' I explained that I was not a home economist (this was 1987) [and] that I was an executive chef. They then said the title would be 'Senior Chef for Technoculinary Development,' and I accepted the job. Six months down the road, at my first

"I once confronted a chef about wages—he was paying my male co-workers a dollar more an hour than me. He told me I came from a good family and I didn't need to make as much an hour as they did—I quit."
—*Brittany Wiederhold*

1883: The Boston Cooking School opens and becomes the first incorporated cooking school in America.

"I believe (some) men still think women should not be in the kitchen. Purveyors are sometimes the same way. They will automatically assume if there is a man standing next to me, he must be in charge. Gaining respect is the hardest challenge."

—*Holly Dion*

review, with a man who was a chef, I found out that on my paperwork, guess what the title is? Senior Home Economist ... they never did resolve it."

Fritz Sonnenschmidt, Dean of Students at CIA, remembers an incident involving discrimination against Lyde Buchtenkirch-Biscardi. "I remember years ago, some of the chefs came over (from France), and the conversation came to women chefs. A French chef said, 'a woman can't be a chef, because they can't get up at four in the morning, and they don't have any taste sensation like [men] have.' Mr. Metz, president of CIA said, 'OK, we fix this right,' and he asked all the French chefs to come up to [CIA, for a banquet]; Lyde was a chef [here] at that time. 'Lyde' doesn't sound like a woman's name, so on the menu, it says Lyde Buchtenkirch. The French chefs said: 'la grande cuisine, ah c'est si bon!'—and then Mr. Metz, said: 'Let me introduce the chef, *Miss* Lyde Buchtenkirch—silence for a moment—a big splash in the *Times!!!*"

Noëlle Haddad describes her experience with discrimination: "The sous chef I was working with yelled at me to 'run and get me some olives' and I'd go and run—like God is dying—to get [the olives] because I thought they were for a VIP. I brought them back and found that it was *he* who wanted to eat olives! Being a woman—a South American woman—didn't raise his opinion of me at all. I speak English and Spanish and French and I'm learning Italian; this sous chef barely spoke English, and he grew up *here*."

Stacy Radin is a pastry chef-instructor at the CIA and an alumna as well. She raises an issue we have heard time and again as historians attempt to explain why women have had such a hard time getting key positions in the kitchen—their stature. Stacy is petite, and as it turns out, her size has proven to be the basis of people's misconceptions of her as a chef. "When I walked in the door, [the pastry chef] stormed into that chef's office and said, 'this is what you got me?' The image [that] people have of a chef or a pastry chef does not fit my physique. The credibility, visually, which is very important ... isn't always there. I have been really successful in the field. I've had great opportunities, wonderful experiences, a lot of support, but I still think that the physical image really makes a difference."

Anne Gingrass discusses the frustration she experienced as a result of being a woman in a male-dominated kitchen, where not only were most of the line cooks men, but her boss and partner were as well. "At Postrio, it was terrible. I could not say anything because it was *so manly*. When the guys [were] cooking and thought that they were hot shit, tongs and everything [were] all [being] thrown around." Anne explains that she had trouble getting the cooks to respect her and consult her with their problems and questions; the cooks seemed to always gravitate toward her husband David or the owner, Wolfgang Puck. "Everybody would go to Wolfgang; then it was, 'Wolfgang said.' I was always the third person [behind David and Wolfgang]. I said to them, 'This does not work for me and what needs to happen is that all of the questions that need to be answered by me get directed to me.' "

Most of the cases of discrimination in these stories is based on archaic, sexist attitudes. These attitudes have been prevalent for decades, and it would be unrealistic to think that they will dissipate over the next few years. We can hope, however, that they will decrease as women continue to follow their passion and reach new heights in the industry. Also, as young men and women enter the field with more enlightened attitudes, things will change, but this is an evolutionary process that will take time.

Women Dealing with Harassment

Harassment is a gray area: it takes many forms, strikes people in different ways, and is largely situational. What does it really mean and how do we define it? Is it unwanted flirtation? Inappropriate language for a particular situation? Or is it physical advances? All of these definitions may apply. Hilary DeMane describes how a lot of women feel about harassment: "The whole issue of harassment is very cloudy, because first one must define it. There are so many definitions, and the law isn't clear. If [we] say that harassment is treatment or comments that make you uncomfortable, then the answer is yes [there is harassment in kitchens]. The atmosphere in most kitchens is harassing—the comments, language, swearing, and rudeness. Everyone always told me, from the time I was in school, that it was a part of working in kitchens. [But] why does it have to be a part? Why should it be a part? [Harassment] shouldn't be a part of [the kitchen]."

Loretta Keller agrees with Hilary's perspective that there is no room in the professional kitchen for rude, harassing language. "I get young men who come here specifically because I'm a woman! They don't want to work in a cowboy kitchen; they don't want to work in a macho kitchen! There's a real issue of professionalism. It's about the food! It's not about macho bantering. [That's] not productive. [The kitchen] really requires seriousness, and rigor, and passion."

For Susanna Foo, her Asian heritage did not prepare her for the "kitchen talk" she encountered from her own staff. She explains: "I was trying to hire an executive sous chef. He [was] always [telling] dirty jokes [in the kitchen], and I'm not used to [that]. I was kind of embarrassed … I [didn't] know what to do because it's not the way I grew up." That sous chef no longer works in Susanna's kitchen.

Susanna's dismissal of her sous chef is one way to deal with harassing language in the kitchen. Lyde Buchtenkirch-Biscardi found another way to deal with this problem. Fritz Sonnenschmidt recalls a situation where Lyde was

"Why can't I just be a good cook? Why do I have to have a gender? I love the kitchen and feel very confident with myself. But I don't want to continue to fight to work."
—Sandra Durrenberger

1886: A dishwasher patented by Josephine Cochrane is crude but effective. Hotels and restaurants will be Cochrane's best customers.

"It is not how good a worker you are, how talented a cook you are; it's really have you gone through the wars, and the battles? ... Where did you earn your stripes?"
—*Dorothy Hamilton*

being continually harassed by another chef who insisted on using sexist, condescending language, which she continually asked him to stop using. "In 1977 Lyde was participating in the Pan-American Olympics in New Orleans, and this fellow, [this] chef thought he was God's gift to earth. He said 'honey-babe' or something like that, to Lyde, and she said, 'My name is Chef, or Ms. Buchtenkirch.' And he came back again, said the same thing, and she said, 'I told you, my name is Chef, or Ms. Buchtenkirch.' Well, [when] he said it the third time, he got it right on the chin!"

Whether someone harasses by using inappropriate language or by inflicting an unwanted gesture on another person, the behavior is unacceptable. Jody Adams expresses how infuriated she was over a particular encounter with harassment. "I was leaning over to get something out of a reach-in, and a guy came up and swatted me on the butt. [He was] a peer, a cook. I stood up, and rage just soared through me. I turned around and said, 'What do you think you're doing?' He said, 'It's your fault. You tempted me. What could I do?' I was absolutely flabbergasted. I could not speak to him for the rest of the time we worked together. He didn't understand why. I think now I would get beyond something like that, but I was so shocked that somebody would think that was okay to do."

Kerry Heffernan has not found sexual harassment to be out of the ordinary in professional kitchens. In fact, she has had several experiences during her years in the industry. One in particular stands out in her mind. "I punched a guy out one day. I had a milk crate braced between a stainless steel counter and my hips. A waiter [who had] been working there for thirty years came up behind me, grabbed my butt, and picked me up off the ground! I screamed, 'Put me down! Put me down!' [When he did] I just turned around—BOOM!—punched him as hard as I could, knocked him down, and out. As he fell I looked up, and behind him was the executive chef. [I thought], 'I'm going to get fired.' [Instead] he just looked at me, looked at [the waiter] lying on the ground, and said, 'I didn't see anything!' and walked away. At that time, that was a gift. Nowadays, that guy would've been fired immediately for laying his hands on me. No one would *ever* be allowed to behave that way. But back then, [with] sexual harassment, there were no clear lines."

As Jody and Kerry reveal, these types of occurrences in the kitchen are tolerated to a much lesser degree today than they were ten to fifteen years ago; however, sexist behavior is still an issue. Fortunately, women are becoming more confident and able to deal with it than in the past. We look forward to a time, when this too can become part of our culinary history.

Women Dealing with Hazing

In some respects, hazing is an inherent part of working in the kitchen for both women and men. For women, however, this can be taken to an extreme as their stamina and fortitude are put to the test time and again. Many women speak of the pressure of trying to "be one of the guys."

Mary Sue Milliken reflects on her dogged determination in the face of blatant hazing; her insistence that there was no way she was ever going to give up and 'let them win' was a potent motivator. "I was a rounds person, for banquets, and [I] would [be told to] make sixty quarts of hollandaise by hand, [without using] the mixer. I thought my arm would come off, and I smiled through the whole thing, just whipping whipping whipping whipping [and] the whole time, never even *winced!* ... I literally thought that my arm was just going to *die*. I was practicing that Zen thing, where you separate your body and your mind. And [I kept telling myself], 'These guys are not going to get to me!'" What is the price we pay for that kind of abuse?

Another story of harassment which only makes us wonder what the motivation can be for such mistreatment, is Anne Rosenzweig's recollection of the cruel test of determination she endured at her first job: "They made me stand on milk crates to work at the stove because I was short. They would tell me that women didn't have enough stamina, concentration, or strength to work in a kitchen—they were constantly telling me that. In retrospect, it was like a fraternity hazing. They used to make me carry the stockpots, and in that kitchen, stockpots were huge; nobody carried them by themselves—they always shared them. But they made me do it. Once I got through enough of [that] stuff, I was sort of begrudgingly accepted."

Both Mary Sue and Anne's stories illustrate the macho influence that prevails in the industry, whether you are female or male. Another side of the issue facing women in the culinary field is masochism. As Claire Stewart explains: "I think that masochism is not cool. There is such a love of masochism (in this industry) it's obscene." Claire explains how one of her staff was bragging about the fourteen-hour day she had put in. Claire's feeling about this is: "It is a badge of honor and everybody has stories of how awful their chefs were and how, 'he yelled at me and how I got this cut and this scar and this burn.' They are horror stories! They are twisted and they are wrong, but we get off on it. From them, you get a certain camaraderie and a certain understanding. While we may try to keep our distance from this ultimately destructive orientation, I know that when I meet a chef, I always look at their hands and arms, looking for those 'war wounds,' looking to see if they are really 'working the line and part of the fraternity.'"

Discrimination, harassment, and hazing have been part of the initiation rites for too many women in the industry. Women who have endured mistreatment and ill will have persevered so that they could reach their goals, so they could express their passion for food. The fact that their stories are retold

"I never approached anything as a woman. I approached it as, this is what I want to do, and I am going to do it!"
—Lidia Bastianich

"The only place for [women] is in bed. Anyone who doesn't change his woman every week or so lacks imagination."
—Paul Bocuse, Newsweek, *1975*

1889: Aunt Jemima Pancake Flour is invented in St. Joseph, Missouri.

"[We] have drug and alcohol problems, and issues that have come up in [employee's] lives. A lot of chefs deal with this, because wine and alcohol is so directly linked with the business."
—*Kerry Heffernan*

in this book is testament to their determination to stay in the professional kitchen—where they belong.

Substance Abuse in the Industry

Substance abuse spans all socioeconomic groups, cultures, genders, and age groups and is no stranger to the culinary field. Some of the women interviewed are recovering alcoholics or have had painful bouts with other drugs. The most common factors underlying abuse in this industry seem to be stress, long and frantic hours on the job, and having cash tip-outs at the end of the night. Many look to drugs to tame the adrenaline-high after a night on the line. Others look for a "pick-up" to get back at it the next morning, and still others are just trying to perpetually keep up with the pace.

The U.S. Department of Health and Human Services published a report based on 1991-1993 survey figures. The report, *Drug Use Among U.S. Workers: Prevalence and Trends by Occupation and Industry Categories,* gives additional insights into these problems. Food preparation workers have the third highest rate of illicit drug use at over sixteen percent, and of those, over forty-three percent of users are women. The report specifies that food preparation workers rank fifth in heavy alcohol usage, with sixteen percent of the workers indicating this as a problem area—forty-five percent of those are women. The report suggests that there may be a correlation between drug and alcohol abuse and missed or skipped workdays. Although not conclusive, the findings show that among illicit drug users, those reporting skipping work in the previous thirty days total 18.5 percent, versus 7.5 percent of the non-drug users who reported skipping a day of work. The cost to the industry of this problem is staggering, and given the cost of labor and the shrinking labor pool, this is an area that must be addressed in the future.

Drug and alcohol abuse is a difficult topic to discuss, and many women did not want their experiences revealed in this book; however, two women who had the strength and courage to overcome their addictions were willing to share their stories. Pitita Lago explains: "I am recovering from alcohol and cocaine addiction, and I wonder if all the years I spent partying and doing drugs and drinking [has kept me from progressing in my career]. There are a lot of drugs and alcohol in the business. ... [Fortunately] I've been clean and sober for eight years. ... It never affected my work performance, or so I thought, but it was always there. I'm sure that has a lot to do with my not growing in my career as much as I should have or could have or would have."

Jamie Eisenberg also spoke about her experience with addiction. "I got a chance to create the menu, and found myself falling into a creative niche. ... At the same time, I was also falling into another scary niche—substance abuse. I got enmeshed in that world. I drank heavily and there were definitely drugs in the workplace. You go, go, go, you run the line, the lights are on, the curtains are open, the show is on. It's all this hype. Then when the last ticket goes out the window, you're still revving, but everything else is keying down. This industry's notorious for it! I stayed in that place, mentally and physically for many years, and then woke up one morning and said, what the heck am I doing? I'm not an artist, I'm not a chef. I was bereft—there was nothing there. I couldn't hold a relationship, I had very few friends outside of my drinking circle, and without my restaurant buddies, there was nothing left. I had cut all ties. I never saw my family—every holiday, I was in the kitchen!''

Drug and alcohol abuse is a sensitive subject; it is one that touches most of us in the industry in some way. In my experience, I have witnessed a number of chef-owners lose their businesses to drugs and alcohol. This type of abuse is so prevalent in our industry that at times it seems there's a nonchalance about it. Many large companies are starting to demand drug testing, and some are offering employee assistance programs that counsel those with addictions. But in the end, what we really need is a way to promote balance and healthy outlets, which will help alleviate some of these problems.

Owning a Restaurant

I know from experience that opening a restaurant can be the challenge of a lifetime. Opening your first restaurant, in particular, can be an overwhelming task. It requires not only a substantial financial investment, but an enormous commitment of time and energy as well. Openings are all-consuming. You literally work around the clock; your staff is generally under-trained; your costs are spiraling out of control and on top of that, you're probably under-capitalized. Statistics showing the failure rate of restaurants vary. I have seen reports that suggest that as many as ninety percent of all restaurants close within their first five years of operation due to financial insolvency. In 1996, NRA statistics show that 14,000 new foodservice facilities opened, and Dunn & Bradstreet reports 3,750 restaurant closings in that same year. Whatever the exact figures, industry analysts agree that opening restaurants is a highly risky business and the fact remains that many bankers consider loaning money to a new restaurant as one of the greatest risks that they might take. For women who have opened and operated restaurants, it's their passion, drive, and perseverance that gets them through this incredibly stressful time in their professional lives.

"For many years we said, 'It's too tough for a woman.' But physically, it's not too tough. I found that out by watching women; there is no difference. Physically they can do it."
—André Soltner

1890: The U.S. Women's Pure Food Vacuum Preserving Co., founded by Amanda Jones, uses her methods to preserve rice, tapioca pudding, and luncheon meats. Officers, employees, and stockholders are all women.

Amy Scherber shares the challenges of starting her bakeries in New York City. In particular, she remembers the isolation and stress she felt from having to make tremendous decisions on a daily basis. "I couldn't pay my help very much. I couldn't pay other people to come in. I didn't have a partner to do off-shifts. I never had a vacation or any time off. There was no one to share the risk with. I didn't have anyone to ask for help. I kept on thinking, 'How can I do it? How can I keep on doing this? What happens if I quit now; what will I lose? Who would I owe the most?' I had one breakdown where I went home from total exhaustion; I sat at my desk, took out a pad, scribbled some figures, and sobbed for four hours. 'What to do, what to do?' I had to go back to work and just keep on going." Amy's perseverance got her beyond those times. Her bakeries continue to produce high-quality breads for many of the restaurants in Manhattan.

Like Amy, Mary Sue Milliken and Susan Feniger had a less than smooth start to their business venture. They recall the "Opening from Hell." Susan remembers: "The night before we opened, Mary Sue and I both slept on the mats in front of the stoves—for about twenty minutes. We kept [messing] up the naan [Indian homestyle flatbread], it was three or four o'clock in the morning, and we're opening the next day." Not only were they inexperienced with making naan, they were moving from a kitchen that served eleven tables to one that served forty-five, with a brand new staff. They explain: "We really had worked independently of the rest of the chefs in the area—we were so insulated from everybody and everything. We didn't know what anybody else was doing in their restaurants! We didn't really know that having a staff in the kitchen for four days before you opened wasn't quite enough! We didn't know that having us as the only people who knew how to make the dishes was going to be a problem!" They learned the hard way.

Their story continues. "Opening night was a nightmare. It was horrible! We were so busy. It was August, in Los Angeles I think it was literally 112°F on the line. The fans didn't work. We had the tandoori oven going *full* heat; because we didn't know how to make the naan, we thought that we needed to make the oven as hot as possible! We're the only two on the line who knew the menu, and the waiters didn't know what they were doing. We just made the same food over and over again. Later on in the night, we're about to die and the manager was on the other side of the line, and we said, 'What should we do? There's all this food! Should we just throw it all way?' And he said, 'Yes, throw it all away! At the very end of that first night, we collapsed in a corner. We hadn't slept much in three or four days. We're completely raw. I don't even know how the brains were firing. We're saying, 'Well that was really screwed up!' We're sitting there, and we're sweating and crying and sweating! And Mary Sue said, 'Do you think everything we served was shit?' Susan wasn't sure at that point, but as she remembers, she said, 'Tomorrow, this is what we've got to do. We've got to get one more person who knows what they're doing! We've got to get the fans working!'" Would they have ever imagined, that night, that today they'd be running a successful restaurant? Maybe not, but they proved that through trial and error, talent and determination, their nightmare could be transformed into their dream.

Alison Barshak opened Striped Bass in Philadelphia in 1994 and remembers the problems and pressures she endured during that opening. "We needed a little bit of help, because it was evolving so fast. I tested recipes and menus, but when the menu changes, how do you catch up? How do you train the new people, [after] you fired everybody because the first staff didn't work? How do you go backwards while you're still moving forwards?" Alison took the lessons she learned during the opening of Striped Bass and used them as the basis for her latest venue, Venus and the Cowboy, which is projected to open in Philadelphia in 1997.

Odessa Piper, chef-owner of L'Etoile, grew up a child of the 1960s. The way she explains it, one day she just woke up and was a restaurant owner. "I didn't really think it through. I wasn't really qualified. But I basically woke up one morning, knocked up with a restaurant! We found ourselves deeply entrenched in problems. My partner said, 'Look, this is more than I can handle—I've got to leave.' By the first year, I was looking at about $80,000 worth of debt—it was a nightmare. I was very frightened, and at that point ..., I was 24 [and] didn't have any mentors. It was so intense, and there weren't people I could turn to!" Odessa eventually overcame the obstacles, and her restaurant, L'Etoile, celebrated its twenty-fifth birthday in 1996.

The restaurants in these stories started out as nightmarish experiences but can be chalked up to "growing pains." In all of these cases, the women were able to overcome their initial problems in due time. Barbara Tropp, however, was not as fortunate with her first venture into the food business: "We had all this publicity, nationwide, for a restaurant that turned out to be a mythological restaurant. We never opened on [the site advertised]. The landlord had decided he'd given us too good of a deal—it's called 'construction eviction.' He literally froze us out of the site." That was the first misfortune in her story; there were more to follow. "My partner had invested our partnership money in a bank that went belly-up in the great California bank scandals of the 1980s. We lost $300,000-plus, which to me, might as well have been $300 million. I retreated."

Barbara went back to teaching for a while, and then decided to try again. This time, she opened her restaurant, China Moon Café, in San Francisco, which brought on a new financial challenge. "Classic story—I was not in

"We have to prove our ability every day. We have a harder time being professionally respected as 'serious.'"
—*Hilary DeMane*

1893: Respectable New York women can now eat in the public rooms of restaurants without causing gossip.

charge of anything except the food side! My partner was in charge of the business side. Four years later, he left. Overnight, I had to take over the business side, of which I knew nothing. I had never even taken a look at the daily accounts. I had never paid rent. The restaurant paid my rent, and that's all I was concerned about. I was totally devoted to the power of the vision, and trying to make that happen." Barbara survived without her partner, and China Moon Café was a San Francisco landmark until she sold it in 1997.

Financing any new venture is a challenge. However, in the restaurant business, options are limited because the failure rate is so high and many banks are not willing to risk their capital. Nora Pouillon remembers finding the money for her first restaurant. "To get the money (for the restaurant), I had to ask my husband to refinance our house and ask for a home improvement loan. Steven and Thomas [my partners, had to] ask their parents, who had just paid off their thirty-year mortgage, to refinance their house. They got $100,000; that's how we started out with $150,000," Nora explained: "We found another $50,000 through friends, and then we went to a bank to ask for $25,000 ... I cannot tell you how many banks we had to go to to give us $25,000. Nobody wanted to give us money." However, Nora and her partners finally did put together enough money to finance the opening of their first restaurant, Restaurant Nora, which has flourished in Washington, DC for almost two decades.

Nora goes on to say that, once the restaurant was opened, she learned by doing. "It's overwhelming when you start. I never went to school—I had to learn it all myself. I had no idea how many people to hire, and since I didn't have much money, I tried to do it all by myself. I was the prep person in the evening and then I got ready for lunch for the next day. I could only afford two people, one that served the food and one that did the hot and the cold food. I ran around between the two ... expediting and ordering and hiring. ... I came to the conclusion, [eventually], that it couldn't work this way. I made enough money to pay my employees, but I couldn't make enough money to pay myself." Through trial and error, Nora eventually learned how to operate not one but two successful restaurants.

Dealing with Health Issues

The lack of health insurance and dealing with the potential of catastrophic illnesses are among the most serious challenges any of us face. The food service industry does not offer most of its employees the breadth of support needed in these areas. Yet, according to the recent NRA report *Business Culture's Impact on Restaurant Performance,* seventy percent of all companies surveyed agreed that operational profitability is positively impacted when health insurance and paid family leave are part of compensation packages. The following stories relate how health issues affect the lives of women, their families, and their careers in the culinary world.

For Lucie Costa, chef-owner of the Historic North Plank Road Tavern, the difficulty of running her own business was complicated by the fact that she had an extremely ill child and at the onset of his illness, she had no health insurance. She explains: "My second child [had been born] and I was working in the kitchen. He had an accident learning to walk, and fell. By the time he was in a hospital, his head injury had become so severe that he went into a coma. It was very traumatic." To make things worse, she explains, this happened while she and her husband were switching from one health insurance plan to another. Her son had injured himself during that two-week period, which meant that they had no coverage at the time. "When he got out of the hospital, I had a $40,000 debt. I don't have to tell you that for the next ten years all I did was pay money I owed! But I was so grateful my child was OK, and I spent a year following his injury in rehab trying to just soothe him and help him." Lucie and her husband have since closed their restaurant and Lucie is pursuing her career as an executive chef.

Hilary DeMane was working as executive sous chef and her husband, Tim, was the executive chef when Tim had an unexpected debilitating illness. Hilary took over running the operation while trying to juggle caring for her husband during an extended recuperation period. She remembers having to deal with the challenge of a union walk-out. "I was running the hotel, and then they went out on strike. Everybody, the whole staff walked off at 6:00 pm. We were just getting ready to open for dinner, and everybody walked off—the whole staff in the whole hotel, including the kitchen staff. We had a full house, dinner reservations for 375 people, and a banquet. I was amazingly calm, considering that my whole world was like falling to shit around me." Hilary put out a buffet for the dinner guests, got everyone fed, and proceeded to run the operation while the staff stayed out on strike for six more weeks. Tim recuperated, and they have gone on to become chef-instructors at Indiana University of Pennsylvania Academy of Culinary Arts.

While these stories address how women coped when there was illness in the family, the next stories present women who have been confronted with their own physical disabilities and illnesses. Suzanne Bussiere describes the challenges that she confronts every day as a hearing-impaired executive sous chef. "The challenge, really, is being alert, every single minute thinking about what's going on. There's just so much going on, and not everybody else is together. It's hard because I've expedited before, and they respect me and they do a great job. They know that they have to keep quiet more, they can't talk as much

"Not only historically, but continually, a foodservice professional is predominantly male. When the words 'waitress' and 'chef' come up, even I am guilty of a stereotypical image coming into my mind."
—H.J. Metzler

1893: Aunt Jemima Pancake mix is promoted at the Chicago Fair with demonstrations performed by former Kentucky slave Nancy Green, age fifty-nine.

Women in the Culinary Arena: Suzanne Bussiere

Being diagnosed as hearing-impaired at the age of four never thwarted Suzanne Bussiere in any of her ambitious pursuits. Suzanne wears two hearing aids, speaks, reads lips, and emphasizes to her staff the importance of communication. A Bay-area native, Suzanne earned a Bachelor of Arts degree from San Francisco State University in 1975. Her original intention was to become a physical education teacher. However, food and cooking had always been a passionate avocation, so much so that at twenty-six, she went to study at Le Cordon Bleu de Paris under Richard Grausman and enrolled in wine and cheese courses in San Francisco to satisfy her yearning to learn about food.

Suzanne graduated from California Culinary Academy in 1980 at the age of twenty-seven and found her first job in San Rafael, under the tutelage of a conscientious chef-owner in a very small kitchen at Maurice et Charles Bistro. After two years, she was ready to take on a bigger challenge, and she ended up at Campton Place under Chef Bradley Ogden. Suzanne was responsible for creating and maintaining the acclaimed breakfast menu of Campton Place from 1983 to 1989. In 1990, Suzanne helped Anne and David Gingrass open Postrio with Wolfgang Puck. In her capacity as line cook, she created specials and participated in menu development and the training of new personnel.

Suzanne joined Nancy Oakes' staff in 1991 as sous chef at L'Avenue. Nancy then asked Suzanne to join the opening crew of Boulevard in 1993 as sous chef and saucier, and she has been the executive sous chef since 1995.

Suzanne acknowledges that being hearing-impaired can be difficult, but she makes sure that her staff members are aware of her challenge. Additionally, the socialization of the public has changed dramatically in the past twenty years. She shows all of the dishwashers her hearing aids and explains her limitations to them. She discusses the need for quiet during service and the common kitchen courtesy of alerting one to a staff member "behind," all practices that are inherent to any kitchen. Suzanne was recently highlighted in a magazine for hearing-impaired children called, *Hip.* Her advice to future hard-of-hearing chefs? "If a hearing-impaired kid wants to be a chef, I say—*go for it!*" Suzanne certainly *went for it,* and her career exemplifies the determination and fortitude of women in the kitchen.

when I'm on the line because I can't hear. But in the kitchen, everybody knows [that I'm hearing-impaired], and they're always touching me or they just yell louder. Even all of the dishwashers. I show them all my hearing aids. If the battery goes dead, I just replace it right on the line. I wouldn't have been able to do that twenty years ago. I was so ashamed to be wearing a hearing aid. High school, grammar school, and a little bit in college; it wasn't until maybe I was about thirty that I began to accept it."

Pat Thibodeau's mission in life is to eradicate childhood hunger. Even in the face of cancer, she never wavered from her goals. "This [food reclamation and the Chef and the Child Foundation] is way more important to me than anything else. [Cancer] was a catalyst too, because I decided that I had to do whatever I had to do in three years. I wanted to get it all done, just in case. ... I had very aggressive cancer, and they did very aggressive treatment. I have had a lot of side effects from it that really caused me a lot of problems, but if I hadn't done [the treatment], I probably would have died. I never had the time to worry about it. ... Just leave me alone and let me produce something! I really never looked back. The only time I would be morbid would be if I had a day off to ponder my own mortality. You don't want to ponder your own mortality. So now I'm over that, and I figure, I'm too mean to die!" Pat is well and continues her work with the Chef and the Child Foundation and as an advocate of hunger relief.

Barbara Tropp has spent over two years fighting cancer. Her battle changed the way that she ran her restaurant and eventually prompted her decision to sell it. Barbara shared these thoughts: "It's very humbling and in some ways a wonderful experience to discover that you can leave your business for two and a half years and it's run better than ever. The bowls are still lined up the way they should be lined up, everything is spotlessly clean, the cooks are still being trained to cut every water chestnut cube the same way. The vision has been powerful enough, so that anybody who's worked for me even for a short time gets it! And they carry it. In some ways, it's a little bit like those cartoons with angels—people look down and they see that they're better thought of in their afterlife then they were in their life. You become a little bit of a bigger person when you're out of the scene than you were when you were there! Your myth is more powerful than your reality!" For me, Barbara is an inspiration. Even during the time she was going through her chemotherapy treatments, she took the time to talk to me, share her stories, and her passion for women working in the industry.

The women throughout this book continue to reveal that they are strong, capable, and determined to succeed. The stories in the following section show that even under the most adverse circumstances, they are able to rise above their obstacles and win the respect and admiration of those around them.

"[I]t has been estimated that at the current rate of change it would take between 75-100 years to achieve complete occupational integration in the workforce."
—The American Woman 1990-91, A Status Report

Being Older in a Young Kitchen

Women increasingly populate the professional kitchen, but by and large, they are young women who are resilient and energetic enough to slough off the physical stresses of the job. For career-changer Toniann Beattie, entering the culinary field at an older age is a formidable challenge. "The coldest harshest

1894: Auguste Escoffier creates the Pêche Melba to honor the Australian Grande Cantrice Mme. Nellie Melba. He also slices white bread as thinly as possible, toasts it, and calls it "Melba Toast."

"(Women) have an edge; we are naturally accustomed to handling numerous tasks within a time frame."

—*Gilda Ann Doganiero*

reality is, I'm going to spend the next couple of years making very little money, working long hours. Physical reality: am I limited because I'm forty years old? Are my legs going to ache? Is my back going to hurt a little sooner than a twenty-one-year-olds' does? … It probably will. I think the coldest harshest reality is: *my age could stop me*. People are going to say 'You're forty, you're too old.' Am I afraid of that? Only if they make that judgment without meeting me and they say it's too late, this isn't a trainable person, this isn't a person we want … my age could be a detriment. I am hell bent on not allowing it to be."

A number of the women I spoke with have been in the industry for decades and are getting ready to retire. This too has its own particular challenges. Barbara Sanders, who has recently retired from a long career as a culinary educator, talks about aging in the industry. "It's very disappointing to turn fifty-five and realize that your energy level is not keeping up with your head. That's discouraging. So you start saying, 'what's really important, where can I put my energy and still be a nice human being?'" How did Barbara know when to retire? "I was realizing about three or four years ago that my energy level was decreasing; therefore my patience level was going down, and the generation [gap] between the kids and myself was getting wider and wider. They say that you will know it when the time comes. You could probably stay on till you're seventy-five, if there's no one trying to nudge you out of the situation! I just knew it was time."

Madeleine Kamman's feelings are similar to Barbara's in that she too is willing to step aside for the younger generation entering the industry. "[If] there's one thing I object to, [it] is obstructing the profession for the young people coming behind. That is absolutely a horror as far as I'm concerned. You have done the thing you know; [now] finish doing it quietly at home. Retire with grace when you're at the height of your power—and don't push your luck. You will find that those who've had a very publicized life will have troubles accepting this. There's a time and a place for everything; in French we say 'A thing in it's time and a time for each thing."

Rick O'Connell also talks freely about how it feels to age in this industry. After spending decades in the kitchen, she now manages multiple food and beverage operations in San Francisco, but as she explains, this isn't getting any easier as she gets older. "I really don't work in the kitchen now. I'm sixty-three and my hands can't lift the pots. I work with my chefs on taste and composition; creating menus and making sure they are reflective of what I sell to the customer. [Just because] I can't stand on my feet all day anymore doesn't mean I can't still be involved in this business. I know that there will be something else out there." Rick is starting to feel ready to enjoy new experiences. "I'd like to do some more traveling; it's not over for me at sixty-three; I feel like I have some good years left … *The road never ends*."

As an industry, one of the challenges that we face is keeping our aging population of cooks and chefs meaningfully integrated. The nation is aging with a healthier more physically fit population, who in many cases are capable, motivated, and creative workers. It is up to us to figure out how we can make the best use of their years of experience and wisdom.

The Peter Principle at Work

The Peter Principle states that we tend to promote people above their abilities and often without sufficient training. Sometimes we fall subject to this by working for someone who hasn't yet learned how to manage a staff. Others may find that they are operating under the Peter Principal themselves, being placed in a position for which they feel under-qualified. The following stories reveal why and how this happens in the culinary industry and how different women deal with their individual situations.

Sarah Stegner distinguishes between being a cook and a chef, and how being a cook doesn't necessarily prepare you for the next step: "One of the key difficulties in a kitchen for a cook is that you spend six nights a week generally, twelve to fourteen hours a day, working in an environment with a handful of people dealing with food. [If you're a chef], you need to know management, payroll, how to order, and all the other things that go into the business that they don't tell you along the way! You get a promotion based on how quickly you can set your station, how great you can make a soup taste, how efficient you are at organizing the pickup of a plate, or if you have a great flair with food. [But then] you get into the position (of chef), and you have to learn how to write a menu and how to deal with eight other people working for you." She explains that juggling these responsibilities is important, but of equal importance is keeping your eye on the food. She says: "If you take your eye off of the food, you lose the credibility of being a chef. You have to remember your training … that you have a talent for the food—a talent that you've paid dearly for over the years."

Susan Spicer's career path is similar to many other women who climb the ladder to chef sooner than anticipated. She explains how she felt when she took her first chef position: "The restaurant was a fairly classical, fancy French restaurant. They decided that [in their new venue] they wanted to go with a more bistro-style, smaller restaurant, and my chef recommended me for that position. I'd only been cooking for three years, and I told him I thought he was nuts. … I had worked the line, and at that point I was the sous chef in the daytime; I felt pretty insecure about taking a chef position. I managed to arrange a stagière for myself at a hotel in Paris for the summer. I came back,

"People always seem so shocked to see me when I step out of the kitchen. They usually say, 'oh, we were expecting a man.' Is that a compliment? People expect great cooking to only be a man's domain."
—*Karyn Anastasio*

1896: *Dainty Desserts* is a booklet compiled by entrepreneur Rose Knox containing recipes she developed using Knox Gelatin.

worked on a menu, [and when we opened] I thought everybody I hired knew more than I did. [I did] a lot of hiding and crying in the office."

Like Sarah and Susan, Melissa Kelly also achieved chef status early in her career, and also found the task a formidable and intimidating challenge. "I think I was twenty-four. I didn't have that much experience. It was pretty scary thinking of all the things I probably didn't know. I was sure they would come up, as soon as I started working there [The Beekman Arms]. Larry Forgione brought me up [to the inn] and didn't tell the staff who I was. He showed me around; I was really excited, and I had a million ideas. I kept a logbook and wrote everything down. It was a very different kitchen from the kitchens I had been in. They didn't have ingredients I was used to cooking with on the line. They had a steam table with lots of food in it, and I was used to having a steam table full of ice, with raw ingredients, and starting from scratch. Then Larry had a meeting and announced to everyone that I was going to be the chef and that I was taking over the whole crew. One by one [the staff] ended up drop-ping off, either on their own, or getting fired. It was really difficult. We trans-formed the restaurant from one style, a prime rib-steak house, to cooking—real cooking, and tasting, and making sauces, and making stocks." Melissa pro-ceeded to bring the quality and reputation of The Beekman Arms up to new heights before going on to become chef of The Old Chatham Shepherding Company Inn in upstate New York.

In many cases, people put in positions beyond their abilities don't really adapt—they just may not be up to the job. In these stories, however, that is not the case. These women were young and inexperienced when they rose to their positions as chefs, because they were talented and determined, however, they learned what they had to do; in each case, they evolved into the position over time.

Working in Remote Locations

The location of a restaurant can make or break its success. You can have a great restaurant, but if it's in a terrible location and you haven't gotten the word out, it will be doomed to failure. You need to make sure to bring your restaurant into the public eye. Depending on where you are located, operating your restaurant can be an inspiration, but at other times a challenge. To quote Conrad Hilton, the three keys to success are: "location, location, location."

In Telluride, Colorado, I managed a restaurant at the top of the ski area, almost 12,000 feet above sea level. The views were spectacular, an inspiration, but there was no running water, and access was by snowmobile or snow-cat only. But this experience pales next to Kirsten Dixon's tales from Alaska. When Kirsten and her young family moved to the wilds of Alaska in 1983 and started construction of Riversong Lodge, her challenges were unique and varied. She admits: "I didn't really know how to cook at all and was a little frustrated because I was in a remote environment. There were no peers to call upon, no grandmothers in my community to help me understand how to cook or even take care of babies." Kirsten's first step was to get a cookbook, but none that she found impressed her. She took her next big step—a trip to Paris and Le Cordon Bleu. The final challenge for Kirsten in her quest to feed her guests was to figure out how to get the food to her lodge's remote location, forty miles outside of Anchorage. "We have to be very flexible because everything arrives by plane and sometimes you just don't get it. In the summer I have planes that come out every day. In the winter it may be three weeks between airplanes. It costs me $350 per delivery for a plane to go from Anchorage to Winter Lake, and that plane can hold maybe 1,200 pounds. If I go into town and bring a planeload back, that's like a $700 shopping trip. I have to be very selective."

In both of these cases, choices were made with the realization that neither of us were taking the easy route to sell our food; however, we figured out how to make it work, which was an accomplishment in itself. Whenever you choose a more remote location for a restaurant, it requires extra effort, but for those whose hearts only sing when in tune with nature, the effort is well worth it.

The Power of the Press

This book covers the challenges that women face in the culinary arena from many angles, from discrimination, sexism, and harassment to grueling hours, financial struggles, and physical adversity. Another topic, however, also causes many in the industry a high degree of stress—the role of the press. The role of the media is a very powerful force in the culinary field. Get a good review, you've got it made. Get a bad review, you're in trouble. Women, in the minority of high-profile chefs, in many cases were seen as "good press" when they first began to emerge as a force in the culinary field. This situation pushed a number of women into celebrity status and numerous others out of the business. The following stories are from women who have had experience with the media and what happened as a result.

Leslie Revsin was one of the first women in New York City to feel the pressures of media coverage. "The newspapers and the media can catapult you to fame; they can give you tremendous appreciation and tremendous value; but they can also cut you to ribbons. I think the feedback was hard—reviews I took to my *marrow*. And they were ninety-nine percent positive, but of course the only one that I paid attention to was the negative one, and it was a vicious one,

"I have always found that being a woman in a historically male profession has given me power. When faced with it initially, I was challenged to rise above it or to always finish second."
—Kate Mortellaro

1898: Escoffier develops the brigade system at the Savoy.

Women in the Culinary Arena: Leslie Revsin

Leslie is cited by Madeleine Kamman, in *Becoming a Chef,* as "one of the first three 'visible' women chefs in the United States." The other two? Alice Waters and Madeleine, herself. This incredible triumvirate of culinarians became role models for countless numbers of women who are passionate about food.

Leslie's memories of food and restaurants in her native Chicago are fond, but they laid dormant for many years. She curbed her culinary yearnings until after graduation from Macalester College in St. Paul, Minnesota. Shortly thereafter, at a dinner party of a close friend, Leslie found her passion for food rekindled and realized she had to journey down that path. In 1968, Leslie, her husband, and infant daughter moved to Brooklyn Heights, where Leslie enrolled at New York Technical College. There she earned her Hotel and Restaurant Management degree and made in-roads into the professional kitchen via an introduction to Chef Arno Schmidt. In 1972, at age twenty-eight, Leslie started her first job as "kitchen man" at the Waldorf Astoria Hotel. Within nine months, she progressed to poissonnière and was internationally acclaimed as the first female chef of the hotel.

Leslie left the Waldorf Astoria in 1976 and worked at other restaurants in New York City. In 1977, she opened Restaurant Leslie in Greenwich Village. As chef-owner at her nine-table bistro, restaurant critic Gael Greene called Leslie a "glorious innovator." Leslie was executive chef at an array of New York City restaurants after her bistro closed, including The Bridge Café, One Fifth Avenue, and Argenteuil. In 1985, she was named one of thirteen "Master Chefs of New York" and starred in a half-hour PBS segment. In 1992, Leslie chose to leave New York City and joined The Inn at Pound Ridge as executive chef. During the same period, she became the national spokesperson for Driscoll Strawberries, where she was instrumental in recipe development and product recognition.

Today, Leslie is an accomplished author and consultant involved with culinary television productions and active on the Educational Policy Committee of the Culinary Institute of America. Leslie acknowledges that being a pioneer has been a challenge she has had to confront many times in her career. This has led to some difficult working circumstances. However, she confesses that it is a matter of having the courage to know oneself and to know when to question a situation and when to persevere. Because of Leslie's endurance and resolution, she made the trail to the kitchen a little smoother for the women who follow her. Her passionate pursuit of excellence, despite the odds, created a model for culinarians, both women and men, to strive to achieve.

a personal one ... It took me twenty years to recover from that! Chefs have to be callous, and not as much of a delicate flower as I am."

While painful for Leslie, the courage she exhibited defending her vision against caustic attacks in the press was an inspiration to those who would follow. According to Pat Bartholomew, "Leslie's typical of some of the real pioneers ... who stuck their heads out. People who are the first to stick their heads out get killed. You get creamed—she got creamed. She got held to higher standards than anyone on the planet forever. ... I don't think she ever got the credit for sticking her head out there first, for being that person who took the shots for everybody else. She opened those doors. Without her there wouldn't have been a lot of doors opened."

Nancy Oakes offers another perspective regarding the press. In the last few years, Nancy has had the good fortune of some great press, much of which has put her in the public eye. For her it's dealing with notoriety and the false sense of intimacy those who read about you develop toward you. "I can't think of anything else I'd rather do [than be a chef-owner], but it's hard sometimes being recognized. Someone came in the other night and said, "'Hi, you don't know me but I love you'; it's really weird. Feeding people is so personal. The only thing that comes close to it is sex—being as personal as what we do. If you really stop and think about it, it's a tough job; they come in as strangers, they've only been fed by their primary caretaker and suddenly they're turning themselves over to you. It's a weird business."

Some chefs share the concern that when the media gets involved, the focus shifts away from the aspects of the food that are most important. Joyce Goldstein bemoans all the misplaced hype that press has foisted on the culinary world. "Tastiness does not get press, but a swordfish chop gets press! It's a marketing bonanza! The fact that it's now a prestigious, glamorous career, with press kits, press agents, and travel junkets has changed the way the game is played! And it's a tragedy—but it's also wonderful! It's wonderful for business; it keeps excitement in the field. But it's also a tragedy, because it's taken all the emphasis off food, quality, and taste. It's style and not substance. ... The press wants *new!* If everybody wants new, you're going to get new all the time. [But] new can't always be good. New is [only] around for a minute."

Anne Rosenzweig also believes that the press has fueled a view of food that isn't necessarily based in reality. "The press has created a monster among the dining public. They're always looking for something new, something exciting. People go into restaurants and say, 'There's nothing here that titillates me.' You [can] go to restaurants and see plates that are very titillating, but they taste like nothing and what's the point of that? I mean it's fun to be titillating, for a few moments. But the whole point of going out to eat, I think, is twofold: to enjoy something in your mouth and to have a satisfying dining experience. To feel comfortable, welcome, and to feel taken care of—all that is part of what it means to go out to eat. If it doesn't taste good, what's the point? There is this pull, both ways, [you have to decide], are you going to do food for the press, ... or are you going to be true [with] how you feel about food, how you like to cook food, what you like to do?" This is a question that everyone in the industry needs to consider.

"It was really a hard transition to go from school, thinking your life is big and grand, to working very hard. My first paycheck for two weeks was $180—it was a killer."
—*Susan Regis*

1900: Half of all working women are farmhands or domestic servants.

"Working in a kitchen forces me to shed my womanhood at the door. In order to compete in the current environment, I have to be as tough, as crass, as fast as the men around me. I feel showing any signs of femininity will be perceived as a weakness."
—*Joung Sohn*

"Perhaps coming from a role as a mother, where being a woman is necessary, I am less worried about the possible barriers. I do not need to be better than a man to feel successful; I only need to meet my own goals."
—*Cherie Twohy*

Rozanne Gold is afraid that the dual pressures of appeasing the press and staying true to a vision are undermining camaraderie among chefs. "I worry about the chefs who lose sight of the love of what they're doing and their passion. I think there is an explosion of creativity and talent, and I think there is an implosion of competition—people stepping on each other's faces. When you used to be a chef, you were a *chef;* that's what you did and there was a society of chefs! They were pretty supportive of each other, and there was a comradeship. Today, you're a chef, you do TV, you do radio, you write books; everyone's stepping on each other's toes, and it really is a scramble for attention."

Indeed the recent celebrity status of the industry as a whole has changed the way we do things, and as Rozanne points out, the competition is fierce. With not only the increase of media attention but also the increase in media venues, those of us in the industry need to keep our priorities in check.

Taking Risks

Many social chroniclers suggest that the most stressful times in our lives revolve around moving, changing jobs, and changing relationships. Each individual milestone is difficult enough; however, there are times when these three converge. All of these situations involve taking some kind of risk to get to the next level and women haven't always been taught the skills involved in risk taking.

One of the opportunities for learning in our industry is a *stagière,* a French term loosely interpreted as an apprenticeship where you work for free. Nancy Stark tells of first coming to New York and finding that type of position at Le Cirque. "I just wanted to come [to New York]. I went around knocking on doors, all the places I'd been reading about in magazines for years and thought would be cool. That was one of the scariest days of my life. I was completely lost in New York; [I had] this talk with myself, 'You are going in there, and asking for a job!' I was so scared." By the second day, she said, it was getting a little easier. It was on that day that she went into Le Cirque. "Jacques Torres said, 'What can I do for you?' And I said, 'Give me a job!' and he said, 'Well we don't have a job, but we have this thing we call stagiaire.' I said, 'Really? You'd let me come here and work?' I came home to Kansas City, Missouri and sold my car, I pretty much took my life savings in hand and came back."

Susan Weaver's journey took her to France in 1981. As risky as Nancy's adventure seemed, Susan was in a foreign country with no contacts, no job, and no prospects. Susan explains how she was badgering the chefs, calling and stopping by on a regular basis to try and get in the kitchen. "I was knocking on doors, offering to work for free, hitting the pavement every day. I called this chef every day and I went there once a week until he let me come into his kitchen [to work]." Prior to being allowed into the kitchen, Susan had this experience: "There were times when he would call me, one time he said, 'OK, you can come on Monday.' I was so excited, [but] when I got there, he told me he was all set [and didn't really need any help]. I can remember walking down the street in absolute hysteria … my toolbox in my hand, crying in the subway." A far cry from the woman who as executive chef for the Four Seasons oversees a restaurant that was just awarded its third star.

Of the many women who have faced risks and overcome numerous obstacles to rise to all degrees of success, few of us can imagine escaping a country ravaged by war. Longteine de Monteiro left Cambodia, where her husband had been the ambassador to Taiwan, when it fell and the Khmer Rouge came into power. For most of us, the closest we get to such grief and destruction is watching CNN from the comfort of our homes; for Longteine and her family, this was what they faced until they went to France to start a new life. Longteine had been a talented cook for many years, and after immigrating to France, she and her sister decided to try and open a restaurant. "I had all my savings with me, but it wasn't really enough to open [a restaurant], and we really wanted that. Finally we came up with a small restaurant with fifty seats, and I was [the] line cook. I cooked by myself." Longteine cooked lunch and dinner in that restaurant for ten years prior to immigrating to this country and eventually opening her restaurant The Elephant Walk in Somerville, Massachusetts.

In contrast to Longteine, who was forced to leave her home, I voluntarily picked up and left everything I had behind me in order to follow my passion for cooking. I left Telluride for the Culinary Institute in Hyde Park, with no family support, no money, no place to live, and nothing much in my life except my passion for food, my drive to succeed, and my car, which I lived in while looking for an apartment. Claire Stewart's journey was very similar to mine, and her destination was the same. Claire considers this one of the greatest risks she has taken in her life. She explains: "I moved from California to Hyde Park, New York, solo. I knew no one in New York. I had only money for the first semester's tuition. I hate to tell you what it was like; I worked every weekend and at night. I used to pay my tuition on Thursday at the bursar's office. It was hard."

Claire's story continues after the CIA. She describes her move to New York City: "I had no money. As I was driving into Manhattan, the gearshift on my car came out in my hand; every penny I had went to a repair shop. I parked in Pelham and took the train into the city and spent the night in Grand Central Station. I picked up one of each paper; I had no idea which one to buy. I decided the only thing I could do was to be a live-in maid somewhere. So I looked for live-in ads. I answered an ad for a housekeeper and the woman said, 'Are you responding to the live-in chef's position?' It turns out she had another ad out for a cook. I went for the interview. I ended up with my own little pad on

"We are good employees; neat, organized, creative, enduring, reliable, sensitive—all the 'ingredients' needed to be a skilled chef!"
—Linda A. Schloo-Yazujian

1901: *The Settlement Cookbook* by Lizzie Black is published.

Park Avenue. I worked like an absolute dog for her. I'd work twelve hours at the Rainbow Room; then I'd come home and work hours and hours for her. It was awful, but the bottom line is I had a good, healthy, clean, safe place to sleep in New York City."

Sharon Brooks-Moses also gave up the life she had been living to follow her passion. Once she made her decision to move to the culinary field, there was no turning back. "I saw this ad on a metro (actually my mother saw the ad) about a culinary arts program in DC, and it was a day before the deadline. I called and was told 'tomorrow it closes, and you need all of these things.' One of the things [was that] I had to be unemployed. ... I wasn't unemployed, so I had to quit my job. ... I went in and told my boss ... I'm giving you two weeks notice as of today, but I have to show that I'm unemployed as of today. So I quit my job, not knowing whether I was going to get in the program or not." Sharon didn't get accepted into that program but eventually graduated from the CIA and went on to become a culinary educator and role model for other women in the industry.

Some women take their chances when they are young and broke. Judi Arnold, however, defies that characterization. Judi left her marriage of twenty-six years and started a business making upscale hors d'oeuvres. She explains: "I remember people saying to me, 'You can't start a business and leave a marriage at the same time,' but I did. [They] sort of went together ... It was the most difficult thing I ever did, but I couldn't do one without the other and it enabled me to be independent. I couldn't be a caretaker anymore. I had to take care of myself. ... I took control of my life and I had my own business, which was like my child. My life kind of (transformed) into something I created for myself. Rather than a baby, I created a *business*." Judi goes on to explain how she started that business. "My partner and I read 10,000 cookbooks, we read histories, and we came up with our own kind of gourmet pizza before they existed. We just started producing them in my apartment. We took that risk; we just made that leap. We had no capital. Neither one of us had any money to speak of." Judi's company, DuFour Pastry Kitchen, is successfully selling its wares to restaurants all over the country.

Women who have taken risks and come out on top have succeeded because of their sheer will and passion. But after investing everything they have into their work, where do they draw the line? How do they set limits that will allow them to move on with other aspects of their lives when their work is done? The next section turns to these questions.

Setting Limits

Setting limits, saying no, putting parameters on your work world. All these things make sense for physical health, for mental health, for balance. But for women cooks and chefs, it can be virtually impossible to do. The pace in the business world is frenetic; the pressure is always acute; their own passion for their craft is all-consuming. Where to draw the line? I know I haven't always been able to do it and that I'm not the only one who has trouble with balance. It seems to be an inherent problem with women in this industry. We will hear from a number of women who are adamant about the need to set limits and others who haven't quite figured out how. One woman even claims that she's genetically incapable of saying "no."

Barbara Tropp says it's extremely difficult to set limits, but necessary. And in the end, it's turned into a gratifying, learning experience. "The running of my restaurant has really been a story of me being torn away from the stoves. I've never, in my own mode of correctness, found anyone to run the business that I could trust. I think I'm such a hands-on, all-over-everything personality that I don't make much room for somebody else! I take up too much of the oxygen here!" Because of her illness, Barbara learned to set limits, and found that she had accomplished her mission; she could now sit back knowing that her work was being done and her vision was being carried out.

Tamara Murphy describes the problems she had learning to let go of things. "That was tough," she explains. "I really learned when we opened up the café downstairs; it took so much from me. I realized that I'd have to figure out something because I couldn't touch all these plates. I was leaving the kitchen, there were lots of positive comments when I was gone, and that really felt good. The kitchen needs to be as good when I'm not here as when I'm here—it's there now. I just let go … it's only food."

Ana Sortun speaks of the intensity of the job and the necessity of being able to take a break. She says: "Burnout is a big issue for everybody in this business. I get counterproductive when I work too much. [When] you're on a working binge, you can't see anymore; you forget where you parked your car; you can't think anymore, you just can't. I think it's really important to know when to stop—just stopping for a couple days, really stopping. It means allowing yourself to be out of the restaurant for a week, if you have to. You have to figure out how to do it. It's a stage everyone goes through in their career."

Cindy Pawlcyn, corporate chef of Real Restaurants, at one point had over a dozen restaurants under her control. I asked Cindy how she kept from burning out when she had that responsibility scattered from California to Asia. She told me: "You can only do so much. I [was] spread too thin when I was involved in all of them. [It felt like] I wasn't getting anything accomplished. You feel so attached and it's probably the hardest thing—letting go, saying goodbye to things. Because you just put so much of yourself into it."

"In China … they don't respect [a] chef, it's like the second worst profession. I was thinking any profession is the same as long as you have a drive and you want to do the best, and that's what is driving me."
—Susanna Foo

1902: Rosa Lewis and her husband acquire the lease on the Cavendish Hotel.

"There's a wall that you hit when you realize that you're not going to make it in terms of the quality you want to put out and the constraints of either labor or cost, or both. I guess when you are so passionate about something and you want it to be perfect and then you can't because of other constraints, that's hellacious."
—*Laureen Gauthier*

When Susan McCreight Lindeborg found herself asking: "Why am I doing this? Why am I here? I could've done more at school!' But no, [I] had to cook!" she realized that she needed a break, a sabbatical, some time and space. "I [had] come to the point where I had to stop and do something else, or just forget cooking. [So] I left and took a sabbatical. I had a lot of things planned to do. My major mistake was that I didn't leave town and I answered my telephone. I have a genetic inability to say no! I worked harder in the first six months of my "sabbatical" than I ever had worked in a kitchen, doing a hundred different things."

Jamie Eisenberg learned the importance of setting limits when someone else's tragedy reminded her how tenuous our existence really is. "Until about a year ago, I wasn't really good at giving things up. I wanted to pull all the strings, and make it happen. [Then] one of our chefs lost her partner in a car crash. They had been together for eight years and they had finally decided to get married. There was nobody else around to tell her. I was trying to run my class, and all of a sudden we had a huge crisis. I had to go get her out of the kitchen, take her into an office, and give her this news. It was intense to watch somebody go through that kind of pain. It changed my life—that moment changed my life. I stopped everything, and I said it isn't worth it. It can be over in a fraction of a second; that's how short life can be."

Mary Sue Milliken and Susan Feniger have had a number of restaurants and even a number of different careers within their field. As they continue to broaden the scope of their careers, letting go has become essential. Mary Sue initially had a hard time with this, but she explains that it is getting easier. "It's so much easier because I feel like [with my staff], 'It's your turn! Fine, make your mistakes, so something isn't perfect! That's how you learn!' I just have a much easier time of letting them go on with [their work]. [Now] I'm working less hours, and working smarter. That comes with age, I think."

The desire for everything to be perfect makes it hard for a chef to step back. Anne Gingrass acknowledges this: "I don't really worry [anymore]; there's nothing that I can do if I'm not here. The best we can do is have people we've known for a long time, who will try to do it the way that you would like it to be done. When I'm here there are things that go wrong just as badly as when I'm not. You can't catch everything, and I know that everything can't be perfect and people's expectations of things are not always going to be met. This is not always fun—and you have to tell yourself that everyone is not going to be happy and *believe it*. I try and not go away too much, but again, I've worked really hard to get to this point, and I think that I have to start to enjoy."

Setting limits is key to achieving success in the culinary world. But like other challenges in the kitchen, it takes time, experience, knowledge, and courage to confront. Once some of these issues are dealt with, however, the chances for success increase dramatically. Next, our journey will take us to a discussion of women's roles in the kitchen, the venue in which success can be achieved.

CHAPTER FIVE

Work

Women's Roles in the Kitchen

"We do it for love, we do it for money. But honestly, I believe we do it because we have to, for our soul's content."
—Hilary DeMane

"I think tomorrow if I'm going to be a chef again, if I have a woman in the kitchen I will be very happy. I will put thirty percent women in the kitchen. Women are very precise, they are more responsible, they arrive in advance, [and] they [are] going to be more prepared [and] generally better."
—*Alain Sailhac*

According to the 1994 NRA study, *The Foodservice Employee Profile,* women account for sixty percent of all foodservice workers, yet only a small percentage (eight to ten percent) are in higher positions such as executive chef. However, women-owned foodservice operations have increased over forty percent in the past decade to 128,000, which represents over one-third of all eating and drinking establishments. The revenues of those businesses have grown ninety-five percent to over $27 million in the same time period, which bodes well for the future of women in the foodservice industry.

Overview of Who's Working in the Industry

Historically, women have always had a strong presence in the kitchen, but never in the upper echelons of the professional kitchen. As the twenty first century begins, we see more significant shifts in the industry's culture, work, and gender representation as women bring their perspective into the workplace. This chapter outlines the stories of some women who are making noteworthy impacts on the culinary landscape.

Women Working in the Kitchen

Culinary schools and professional kitchens are no longer the male-dominated cloisters they once were. Culinary school enrollments of the 1970s and the early 1980s were generally only five to ten percent women; today's average is about thirty-five percent. These increases are now having rippling effects in professional kitchens, where the number of female food preparation supervisors has risen from six to thirty-four percent in the past decade.[29] The Women Chefs and Restaurateurs (WCR) organization is now almost 2,000 strong. It's clear that women are becoming more viable professionals. But what are they doing day to day and how do they feel about their roles?

Jody Adams describes what it's like to work in the kitchen, addressing some of the misconceptions many have upon entering the business. "We're workhorses. You have to like getting your hands dirty, and you have to like stress! I've had a number of people come through my kitchen—really bright people. They like to cook, their parents sent them to cooking school, and suddenly they find themselves in a restaurant scheduled to work Christmas Eve and Saturday nights. I've seen people physically break down over the course of two months. They don't know what's happening to them, or why it's happening. But it's because they just physically cannot handle the stress. They could be great cooks, they could be hard workers, but they can't do stress."

To better understand the types of responsibilities and everyday tasks that await women in the kitchen, we'll look at several different job descriptions.

Chef-Owners

A chef-owner wears many hats. These women oversee the entire restaurant staff, look after food production, quality, and consistency, and keep an eye on the financial end of the business. The women chefs I spoke with said that on average, they spend sixty to eighty percent of their time hands-on in the kitchen.

Johanne Killeen describes how she and her husband George divide the duties that make up their workday at their restaurant, Al Forno, in Providence, Rhode Island. "There are things that I've had to do because George doesn't have an interest in them and vice-versa. He is mechanically inclined, so I don't have to worry about fixing the stove, plumbing, or the heating—he does all that. I'm better at figures and I'm better at business. I'll sell that duck breast for $25.95—God knows what he would have sold it for—so those concerns fall into my lap. I am a pastry chef in a sense, but it was something that came to me by default. That's how it works—whoever has the time, whoever has the inclination does it."

For the chefs who become owners, they see a culmination of the dream of most chefs and cooks. However, the reality can be very different than the dream: long hours, sleepless nights, becoming self-educated in the arts of plugged toilets, clogged garbage disposals, grease traps, and crashed hard drives. Joyce Goldstein sums it up: "If you do not have lots of stamina, a single-mindedness of purpose, and the ability to make decisions under pressure, choose another career."

Executive Chef

I have held the position of executive chef in various operations for the past sixteen years. During that time, I have overseen kitchens in freestanding restaurants, hotels, inns, at major catering events, and as a corporate chef for multiple locations. In each of the venues my responsibilities were different, but in every case, I had responsibility for the entire food operation. That meant looking after food procurement, food quality, staffing, guest satisfaction, and in most cases, budgetary feasibility.

The American Culinary Federation (ACF) certifies chefs and cooks through their educational arm, the American Culinary Federation Educational Institute (ACFEI). As of 1997, there were 2,134 certified executive chefs; about ninety-two of those or 4.3 percent, were women. You do not need to be certified to be an executive chef, but studies have shown that female executive chefs represent approximately ten percent of the total of all executive chefs.

One of the most exciting, the most stressful, the most wonderful, and the most overwhelming times in a chef's life is a restaurant opening. Melissa Kelly

"Not all kitchens are accessible to women, and I think it'll be a long, long time before they are, because I think there is still a bastion of males from traditional European kitchens who will prevail for some time. It's a pretty tough barrier to break completely."
—Susan Regis

1905: Any law limiting hours of work in the bakery to sixty per week is unconstitutional, rules the Supreme Court.

*"After working in
the restaurant for so
long, you really need
some fresh air, trees,
and flowers to kind
of relax you. In the
morning I usually
have a cup of coffee
and walk around
before I come to work,
or read the newspa-
per."*
—Susanna Foo

remembers the opening, last year, of The Old Chatham Shepherding Company Inn, where she is executive chef. "We got this place up and running, and I wasn't sure that it would be successful. I thought, if the restaurant could just hold its own, if I could just have a chance to work in this kind of environment ... that would be enough for me. The inn is small enough so that I can do the food that I like to do. We raise animals, milk sheep, and I make sheep's milk ice cream. We have a greenhouse, gardens, and are finishing a smokehouse. I am enthralled with that part of the operation, being that connected to the food. We make everything from scratch and we change the menu every day, so it's a lot of work. It's been a long, hard year, but a very fulfilling one."

Chef

The distinction between an executive chef position and a chef position is that a chef usually has more hands-on work in the kitchen and the executive chef usually has more managerial duties and fiscal responsibilities. Generally, executive chefs are found in large and often multi-unit properties with sous chefs and/or chefs de cuisine handling more of the hands-on duties.

Loretta Keller recalls her days as chef at Star's: "If it taught me one thing, it was tremendous organization. The restaurant had daily-changing menus, and the chefs had to write menus every night at the end of the shift, making sure to use whatever product was left over. I learned to do a lot of things with a small amount of stuff. We were grossing $1.3 or 1.4 million, with forty-eight seats, two people in the kitchen, one dishwasher—you know, two cooks and a prep cook. We were open seven days a week, breakfast, lunch, and dinner. I worked about thirteen hours a day, five days a week."

Dorothy Hamilton describes her thoughts on the duties of a chef: "It means the head person running the kitchen, putting together the team, and being responsible for menus; choosing the purveyors of products, putting together the organizational plans, and making sure the team works. The motivator. The trainer. It's pretty much the managing director of the back of hell!"

But even though the chef is the head person and in charge, often the chef is accountable to a supervisor as well. Leslie Revsin discusses the fact that while the chef may run the kitchen, she is still accountable to the manager or owner: "The chef calls the shots, but if the chef doesn't own the restaurant, you're under tremendous pressure to satisfy the owner. Those are the kinds of pressures that I remember to this day. ... The chef becomes responsible for all the problems in a restaurant, even when a chef does not own the restaurant." In my opinion it comes down to compromise; the owners may have their priorities set on the bottom line, but the chef may have hers set on quality and creativity. Often these two discordant sets of priorities result in the type of conflict Leslie mentions.

A chef is the "chief," the person who motivates, teaches the craft, has the artist's vision, and commands respect to keep the team on an organized yet flexible path toward the goal of feeding the guests a high-quality, flavorful, nourishing product.

Sous Chef

"Sous" is French for "under" so it follows that sous chef is the second to the chef in command. A sous chef must be able to work all of the stations in the kitchen and supervise all the cooks staffing those stations. In many kitchens, the sous chef, not the chef, runs the day-to-day operations, overseeing the hot-line, food production, and staffing. The best sous chefs are always one step ahead of the chefs and often know the chef's food and style as well as the chef does. Eight percent of the women I surveyed were sous chefs, and they reported that sixty to eighty percent of their time was spent "hands-on."

Deena Chafetz worked for me as a sous chef before taking her first chef's position. Here's what she says about being a great sous chef: "I want to be the best sous chef in the world. My demand for quality and consistency is huge and my commitment is to be able in the shortest amount of time possible, to get completely inside my chef's head, so that everything that I do to food is exactly what they would do to food. And when I can do that, I know that I am doing my job."

Suzanne Bussiere describes her position as sous chef at Boulevard: "I just tell the staff, I'm a cook. I don't need a title, I'm not one of those types of [sous chefs]. I just like to do my job and that's it. I have a title (executive sous chef), authority, and responsibility, and I have to perform managerial skills. I tell people what to do and what not to do in a nice way, an effective way. They respect *me* and my talent—they listen to me and ask me questions. But I never really think about it, and I don't talk about it. It's something I just do."

From a chef's point of view, a sous chef can be the most important person in the kitchen. They are your eyes and ears to the staff, they need to know your food as well as you do, and they need to run the kitchen in your absence. Being a sous chef also can be one of the hardest positions in the kitchen—you run the kitchen, you are responsible for its operation, but you're not the chef, who in many cases gets most of the credit and acclaim.

Line Cook

Line cooks are food production people. They work many stations: broilers, pantries or banquets, sauté or sauciers, or garde-mangers (cold kitchens). They work the kitchen's line; they make the chef's abstract food concept tangible. Because of that, being "on the line" means being under fire. In a busy

"You have to do what you want to do; you have to be happy at what you're doing because these are long hours! The hours that you spend working in your life are your life."
—*Corinna Mozo*

1908: Ellen Swallow Richards founds the American Home Economics Association.

Mrs. Marshall spinning sugar. Courtesy of the Culinary Archives and Museum at Johnson and Wales University.

restaurant, a line cook might cook and plate a meal a minute for hours on end.

Jill Overdorf, formerly a line cook at Osteria del Circo in New York City, shares her thoughts about being on the line: "Ten minutes on the line during a Saturday night rush is like ten minutes on stage in front of three hundred people or ten minutes of bump skiing the steeps in deep fresh powder. It takes intense concentration, a fluid synchronization, an awareness of the potential for failure, and drive for success. To put it into physical perspective, imagine yourself in a two-foot by three-foot space that reaches a temperature of up to 140°F. You can't leave that zone for up to four hours. You are responsible for producing 200 to 500 entrees in the next 360-minute period. You are expected to maintain a production rate of about a meal a minute. And you do this five to six nights a week. Those are the pressures of the line. There is nothing like the feeling of a line that works well together; conversely, there are few feelings as disheartening as a team out of sync."

Though a line cook takes most of the heat in the kitchen, the excitement can be an intense high. Jody Adams talks about her exhilarating stint as line cook: "Through my work as a line cook, I discovered I really loved working in a restaurant. Being part of a team, being in a situation where you had to coordinate a number of things at various times to get everything right. Before you know it you're using your entire body, your stomach and your elbows—I loved that part of it. The relationship with the group of people that you're working with is physical; you're moving around and touching them. On a good night, when things go well, there is nothing like being a line cook. I was fast, good, accurate, and learned how to be clean. A sign of efficiency: when you are really good you are not even thinking at all—it's just all-intuitive."

Like Jody, Patricia Williams loved the stress and the rush of the line. "Service—the time when food is actually being served in the restaurant—was just great for me. Some people say 'I hate service,' but I would look forward to it. I loved service, to hear the calls of the food being ordered—the adrenaline pumps just like it does on stage, and time passes so quickly. You're just doing something you totally love doing. You're in Zen at that point."

Almost every successful chef started on the line. It is the initiation process that helps to develop stamina, coordination, memory, timing, the ability to function under stress, and the ability to replicate flavors and cooking techniques while under immense pressure. For many cooks it's one of the highlights of their career, for others the memories bring to mind "cold-sweats," but for all it's one of the rites of passage in the culinary career.

Pastry Chef-Cook

Pastry chefs and cooks comprise forty-three percent of the book's survey respondents, the majority of whom felt that they spent seventy to eighty percent of their time "hands-on." Interestingly, this is one area where there's equal gender representation in the culinary schools: female enrollment in pastry arts courses at schools around the country is anywhere from fifty to seventy-five percent. The speculation about pastry's popularity among women is that it is perceived (seemingly erroneously) as offering more flexibility and less pressure than the main kitchen.

A pastry chef or pastry cook is responsible for all baked goods, pastries, and in some cases plated desserts (individual desserts). For Hilary DeMane—a pastry chef for over fifteen years—the making of desserts is where art meets science. She shares what it's like: "A slew of adjectives string me to the heart of the pastry chef. I can't speak for all, yet the score I know share so many traits: patient, practical, perfectionists with amazing artistic talents, razor-sharp food scientists with manic organizational skills and mathematical minds. Most are fearless risk-takers willing to stretch and hone their skills with outrageous requests for gingerbread metropoli, pulled sugar menageries, sculpted chocolate birds, replicas of the Titanic: virtually any dream begging for sweet form."

Hilary says: "Pastry chefs spend their professional lives under intense pressure, part of it generated by the high-production jobs we fill. We are organizers, teachers, artists, and mentors to mostly untrained staff, conducting a symphony of breakfast buffets, hearth-baked breads, pastry carts, wedding cakes, petits four, trendy towering desserts, and requests for Michelangelo's David in chocolate. We do it for love, we do it for money. But honestly, I believe we do it because we have to, for our soul's content."

The whole approach to food can be very different, depending on whether you're a line or a pastry cook. Laureen Gauthier describes some of

Frank Leslie's Illustrated Newspaper (New York, New York, April 3, 1880) shows "Massachusetts—Serving the Viands to Gentlemen Guests, at [Fannie Farmer's] The Young Ladies' Cooking School of Boston." From a sketch by Joseph Becker.

1914: The first National Mother's Day is proclaimed by President Wilson. The second Sunday in May will become the biggest business day of the year for U.S. restaurants and florists.

"Oh God, if you have a passion, follow it! Just do, forget about the toughness, forget about the hard work and the hard labor. If you have a passion for cooking, if you're cooking from your soul, and you want to present it, I say do it!"
—*Barbara Lynch*

those differences: "Baking and pastry are different, but both of them are different from line work in the sense that you can't throw the salt in at the end. That concept right there sets it apart. There's much more measuring and more organization that needs to be there for pastry work. I can get frozen chicken and serve it for lunch. I can't put out a wedding cake tomorrow if I don't know about it [in advance]. A lot of people get their kicks off of being on the line—they thrive on the heat, the excitement, and the stress. Baking and pastry is a different world! It requires more attention to detail, and projects take longer. Yes, in a kitchen it takes a long time to make stocks and sauces, but it doesn't take very long to put a plate together. A cake takes a long time to put together. And it takes a lot of persistence."

Other Culinary Roles

There are a number of other careers within the culinary arena, including caterer, food writer, culinary educator, and personal chef. Of the survey respondents for the book, food writers and personal chefs made up one percent each; three percent were caterers; and eight percent were culinary educators. Catering companies contribute only three percent of the total revenues of all food-and-beverage establishments but are projected to have a compound annual growth between 1994 and 1997 of over 5.2 percent, compared with a 4.5 percent rate for full-service restaurants.[30] Although I wasn't able to ascertain the gender breakdown in the catering industry, based on my research, more and more women are seeing catering as a growth industry that allows for more flexible work schedules than other culinary venues.

Catering spans requests for small, intimate dinner parties in someone's home to preparing food for tens of thousands. Alison Awerbuch is executive chef of Abigail Kirsch Culinary Productions in Tarrytown, New York, an exclusive catering company that operates three properties and also accommodates the private functions of a discerning clientele. Alison discusses her work and comments on her staff: "One of the reasons I have more women working for me is that catering is very creative and detail-oriented, and organizational skills are a real necessity. I find that more women versus men, in catering, are organized and detailed and they look at every little piece of the whole picture. Their human resources and management skills tend to be more innate than a man's, so that's one of the reasons women have finally succeeded in the kitchen." Alison provides the following example: "When we do recipe development, I'll create ideas and write out the basics, but the chefs in my kitchen help to create the actual recipe. It's like pulling teeth to get one of the male chefs to write down what they're doing—write down the method, and measure accurately. A woman, in the same period of time, gets the same recipe done, but gives it back to me in a usable form."

Cooking school, at a girls' normal school. Dover publications, circa 1880s. Courtesy of the Culinary Archives and Museum at Johnson and Wales University.

As each woman in this section describes the various positions in the kitchen, one thing is clear—that each person plays a significant role in producing the food that is delivered to the customer. While there is a definite hierarchy within the kitchen, based on the military model as described in chapter one, the most successful kitchens are ones in which everyone works together to produce the best possible food. The women whose perspectives we hear in this section clearly demonstrate their respect for each and every role in the kitchen. This attitude is most likely the reason that these women enjoy such high measures of success.

"Some people are scientists, and some people are artists; and that's not to denigrate either side of that coin, but some people like to weigh and some people like to pinch."
—*Jessica Harris*

Women Chefs as Teachers

In the past ten years, the number of culinary schools has grown from sixty to 600; student enrollment has increased from 6,000 to 60,000; and the average student body is comprised of thirty-five percent women. This figure has risen from an average of fewer than ten percent in the 1970s and early 1980s. However, the percentage of female instructors has not kept pace with the increase in female students. Ninety-four percent of the survey respondents said that only one in about eight (fifteen percent) of their instructors were female and that, of those, half were teaching nonculinary courses.

1914: Marjorie Merriweather Post, age twenty-seven, inherits the Postum Cereal Company and develops it into General Foods Corporation.

Students at Fannie
Farmer's cooking school.
Courtesy of the Culinary
Archives and Museum at
Johnson and Wales
University.

*"A good chef is anx-
ious to teach and
share knowledge.
There are a few out
there who are awful,
but generally, chefs
are very generous
people. They will
teach you if you want
to learn."*

—*Julia Child*

Taking a step back in time, we find Fannie Farmer, Ellen Swallow Richards, and others passing their knowledge on to up-and-coming chefs and cooks in the industry. Fast forward to the last quarter of the twentieth century, where women such as Madeleine Kamman, Anne Willan, and Julia Child are among the most respected in the industry. Many women beyond the walls of the classroom make major contributions to the culinary field, yet women are still far from having equal representation as culinary instructors.

Learning never stops. With 600 schools developing course material for 60,000 students, culinary teachers are in increasingly high demand. That means more and more opportunities for women to share their passion for food in a classroom setting. Whether in a formal classroom setting or teaching on-the-job in a restaurant kitchen, scores of women are passing on their knowledge and skills to others.

Chefs Teaching on the Job   Most chefs acknowledge the teaching of young culinarians as a part of their profession. This is one of the facets of the job from which they derive great satisfaction. Chefs are perpetual teachers and their staffs are their perpetual students.

Debbie Gold is one chef who has worked teaching into her career: "I've always been good at teaching people things—that's an important part of being a chef. You need to be willing to teach people. Keeping your recipes a secret and not telling anybody what you do, or only telling them part of the recipe—that's a thing of the past. I don't want to be a teacher in a school, but I like teaching people in the kitchen and in the atmosphere that I have in the kitchen."

Kristina Neely, who works on the line, shares her perspective of the chef-as-on-the-job-teacher: "A chef is a mentor, a reader, a teacher. … The responsibility of a chef is to be teaching and training. A cook is constantly learning, still working her way up to being that teacher. Then you come to a point where you can take that next position because you can answer more questions, you can teach more, learn along the way, and look for new challenges. Most chefs don't have to *look* for new challenges!"

Teaching in the Classroom A position as chef-instructor allows teachers to roll up their sleeves and do the work of the kitchen without the pressure of the customer on the other end, and without some of the rigid work schedules. The path toward a teaching career varies from chef to chef, but they all share a passion for their craft, a passion to teach, and the passion to motivate young culinarians.

Cindy Salvato's work as an instructor goes beyond lessons about food. "I like to teach my students about being honest, having integrity, working really hard, and all those other unwritten rules in our profession—things that you do and don't do. I also like to instill excitement. When blood orange season comes in, I tell my students, 'Wow, we're going to have a real treat today. Wait till you see this!' I'll have all these oranges lined up in a row, and I'll point out a clementine or a navel and cut them open. Then when I cut open the blood orange, their eyes pop out of their heads! I try to teach them that they should develop the desire to learn."

Both Leslie Myers, chef-instructor at New England Culinary Institute, and Mary Cech, chef-instructor at The Culinary Institute of America at Greystone, feel teaching is the most challenging work they have done. Leslie explains the difficulties inherent in teaching many different students with many different abilities: "I've become a lot more patient in the last four years. I'm teaching to fourteen different levels, so I always ask myself, 'How would I want to be taught if I was a student; what would I want to learn, and what wouldn't I care about?'"

Mary Cech goes on to say: "Teaching is the most difficult thing I've ever done. Every day is a new day; every week is a new student, every class

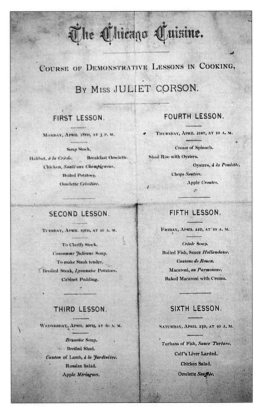

From Chicago Cuisine Cooking School, 1880. Courtesy of the Culinary Archives and Museum at Johnson and Wales University.

1920: Women are granted suffrage in an amendment to the American Constitution.

is different. You're on stage. You have to be 'on' all the time. You have to be incredibly organized. And you have to like psychology! Half of teaching is psychology; the other half is organization. If you can master those two, and you have skills, you'll succeed."

Jamie Eisenberg feels that communication is one of the most challenging aspects of teaching. "Teaching culinary arts is challenging not only in the sense that we have a lifetime of technical and professional experience to pass along in a matter of weeks, but how does one teach another how to communicate in such a short amount of time? No matter how well we perform in the kitchen, I believe it is more important to be able to speak up and voice our concerns, questions, and ideas to each other and to be able to listen to our own inner voice. Not only is it important to pass along information, but also to tell stories, give counsel and encourage students to live each day just for the joy of it; to help them understand the importance of giving back some of what they have gained through their own education to their future customers and co-workers with love and nurturing through their own cooking and styles."

Hilary DeMane's talent for teaching has inspired many young culinarians. "It's harder than any job I've ever had. It is so challenging, so frustrating, and so rewarding. It requires just as much time, if not more time, than any job I've ever done. But it's incredibly important—who's going to take our place in the industry? I try and impart some of the passion of what I do—the love of the food—and when you see somebody get that, it's so satisfying. When I see my students learn and excel, and when I see them actually go out and make it somewhere, it's so exciting." Hilary goes on to say that teaching also allows her to continue to work at her craft while she's teaching. "It gives me opportunities that I wouldn't necessarily get. During my school year, I get to do every aspect of my job, from pie dough to puff pastry to pulled sugar. It's very nice for me because, in a regular operation, if I'm executive pastry chef, so much of my time is spent overseeing, making sure it gets done. I don't get to actually do all of the different tasks that make up a pastry chef's day. When I teach, however, I get to do ninety-nine percent of them."

While Madeleine Kamman's view on teaching and her teaching style are quite different from most of the women I spoke with, she has fostered the careers and talents of many culinarians throughout her career. She explains: "When I teach someone, I do something other people don't do—I touch the personality. I find out if the person has a style, and I encourage that person in that style. Sometimes I'm not very popular in this, because sometimes this is not what they want to do. But I know that what they want to do is not what they need me to teach them, so I've got to gently force them and sometimes not that gently. The spark—it comes on very fast; you start explaining and they start doing. The first try is quite good, the second try is almost perfect, and the third try is right there. You have to look for it, and of course I've learned to look for it. Teaching professionally really opened my eyes, and I realized the responsibility of helping students reach where they were going."

Owning and Operating a Food Business

The dream of most chefs is to own a restaurant. As we saw in chapter four, this dream can start as a nightmare; ownership often turns out to be a bigger responsibility than anticipated. However, many women in those stories learned by doing and have ended up with very successful operations. As was also revealed earlier in this chapter, the percentage of woman-owned food-service operations has increased dramatically over the past decade. The draw? Perhaps being the boss, in charge, having creative license, being able to serve the food you want to serve and enjoying independence and freedom. More and more women are turning that dream into reality and overcoming hurdles to find a way to achieve those goals without fighting so many of the battles inherent in the traditional hierarchical kitchen structure.

Lidia Bastianich owns and operates three well-known restaurants in New York City: Felidia, with upscale Italian fare; the more casual Becco; and Frico, a bar/restaurant. Lidia is also marketing a specialty food line and has recently started a cuisine-oriented travel company with her daughter. I asked her to share a typical day with me. "Every day is different. But in general, I come in to Felidia about 10:30, unless I have a meeting scheduled. Along the way, I stop at the ethnic market if there's a specialty item we need. I'll go up and check my office, see what the activities are. I touch base with my son, who manages Frico and Becco to see what he's doing. I come down at about 11:00 or 11:30; I sit down with the chef, and we program the menu. Once all the products have come in, we taste, we do recipes, and decide the dishes. Then lunch happens. At about 1:30 or 2:00, planning continues and if I want to implement anything, then I find the time. I'll go down to the kitchen in my whites, go to the pastry chef or the chef, and work with them. Then I'll check all the reservations, see if there's anything special, any big parties, any menus or wine requests. I'll then talk to the manager. Now it's 2:30, 3:00, or 4:00, and time go over to the West Side to Becco or Frico." When Lidia goes to the other restaurants, she goes through a similar scenario of meetings. Then it's back to Felidia for dinner service. "So, by 7:30 p.m., I am back here, where I stay until 10:00 or 11:00, and take care of my customers. Maybe around ten, I'll go upstairs and finish up any paperwork or whatever, and then 11:00 or 11:30, I'll

"The reason to (cook) is because it's the only thing that's going to make you happy—you need to have that kind of drive to survive it. If that's your decision, I want to give you everything I can to follow through with it, because as a teacher, that's my job."
—Amy Handler

"There is a price to be paid for not knowing how to cook professionally. On the flip side, my creativity was never stifled by having a formal education, where I might think, 'Oh my God I can't do that.'"
—Raji Jallepalli

1921: General Mills uses the name "Betty Crocker" as a signature.

Women in the Culinary Arena: Lidia Bastianich

America is often referred to as "the land of opportunity;" that is the perception of many people who move here from other countries. In the U.S., there is an appreciation for diversity and an incredible potential for growth and success. Lidia Bastianich was born on the peninsula of Istria and moved to the United States with her family in 1958 after World War II to escape communist rule. Lidia and her family settled in Astoria, New York, and to help out financially, Lidia found a job as a salesgirl at the age of fourteen. That job parlayed into a cooking position, and Lidia was able to reconnect—through food—with her childhood memories of her grandparents' inn.

Lidia met Felice Bastianich when she was sixteen, and they married three years later. They opened their first restaurant, Buonavia, in New York in 1973, when Lidia was twenty-four. Their second restaurant opened seven years later in Fresh Meadows, New York. Both restaurants were sold in 1981 when Lidia and Felice opened their first Manhattan restaurant, Felidia. The 'First Lady' of Italian restaurants was beginning to make her mark.

The achievements of Felidia included: visibility for Italian food, an avenue for Lidia to showcase her talents as author, chef, and businesswoman; and an opportunity for the Bastianich family to maintain an internal nucleus of support and camaraderie. All of these positive aspects encouraged Lidia to increase her restaurant domain, and eleven years later she and her son, Joseph, opened Becco. Subsequently, in 1995, Frico began as a casual eatery in the theater district. Felidia has been listed in the *Zagat Survey* as one of the 'Top 50 Food' rankings and 'Top Italian' overall, and the restaurant consistently receives three-star reviews from *The New York Times*.

By maintaining strong family support in the restaurants, Lidia was able to extend her prowess into other facets of the culinary world. In 1994, she initiated a food catalog, *Il Cibo Di Lidia,* to share the importance of quality Italian products with her friends and guests. In 1995, she and her daughter, Tanya, launched an international travel company that focuses on cultural and gastronomic excursions; *Esperienze Italiane* specializes in regional trips to Italy.

Lidia has been a guest chef with Julia Child on the PBS series "Julia Child's Cooking with Master Chefs." In addition to her family and business commitments, Lidia finds time to participate in extensive community service projects. In 1994, she founded Good Samaritan Hospital to adopt and aid victims of the Bosnian war. She is also a member of the advisory board of UNICEF and has been responsible for organizing fund drives and charity events. The most important commitment in her life is her constant pledge to family and personal time. Lidia's life is an example of what can be attained with passion, dedication, and vision.

leave." A schedule like this—day in and day out—requires strength, stamina, and motivation.

Cindy Salvato owns and operates a small business called The Dowry Cookie Company. She explains the product: "The cookie is similar to the Italian one called *cantuccini,* which means "little brick." We also have a line of

Italian Renaissance cookies." Cindy emphasizes the commitment and dedication it takes, but also explains that her love for the business drives her to get her work done. "I really love my business. I work really long days. I'll get up and work from seven in the morning until one in the morning, with just maybe a little bit of time to chill in between. But even then—because my office is my living room and my dining room—work is always on my mind. I love it and wouldn't change it for the world."

Cindy offers some advice to anyone thinking of starting a business: "Be really clear on what you want to do. Make sure your concept is fresh, it's new, it's ironclad, and people will love it. Do a little market research, get your demographics down, go to some food shows. If it's a food thing, then get yourself one customer. Get one customer at a time. Do a really good job with that customer and get another. Never owe anybody any money. Start small and work your way up. And surround yourself with people who know what they're doing—really smart people."

Joyce Goldstein, owner and chef of the renowned Square One in San Francisco, talks about some of the responsibilities of owning your own restaurant. Like Cindy, Joyce offers advice to those who might want to pursue ownership. "Financial savvy, budgets, and balance sheets are what it's all about. In this business, money rears its ugly head right from the inception, and it never goes away. Avoid fads. Study your market. Hire people whose palates you trust and who think about food the way you do. Cost your menu items, don't guess about the right price. If you are not driven, and do not breathe, eat, and sleep pressure, don't enter this field."

Barbara Tropp's time spent living in Asia as a young woman had a lasting impact and influenced her decision to purchase her restaurant, China Moon Café. She speaks first of her initial attraction to the space that became her restaurant. "I saw this little place and it was magic. It clearly had been designed by Chinese. Everything was an octagon, which is good luck in Chinese. There were mirrors outside, which are always put outside Chinese establishments to deflect bad spirits. It was hideously filthy—roaches would dance in conga lines on the counter at night. There were fluorescent lights and strings hung from them—there was fuzz on the strings from the grease. To a neurotic Jewess, trained to clean the bottom of every pot three times, this was both a nightmare and a challenge. And it turned out, it was for sale."

Barbara goes on to explain how she got the restaurant staffed and operational. "We opened in 1986 and sat only fifty people. I had gotten no sleep and I was so fried from tasting that my mouth erupted in sores. I was sleep-deprived, so I was a maniac." Barbara credits much of her restaurant's

"After opening a first restaurant you learn how to pace yourself and make time for things that are important to you. I think the next step is making your business manageable and not letting it take you away with it. That's counter-productive."
—Diane Forley

1922: Eugenie Brazier of Lyon's restaurant, *La Mère Brazier,* is the one and only woman to be awarded three stars by the Michelin guide.

*"I'm lucky in the
sense that this is how
I like to live! I like to
live at full throttle. I
don't sleep very
much, and every day
is always very differ-
ent. It's certainly not
a dull life, by any
stretch of the imagi-
nation. I don't use
the word balance
anymore. I've given
up on balance!"*
—Anne Rosenzweig

success to her staff. "My scheme in hiring people was that everybody had to have significant restaurant experience, because I had none. I hired primarily from a refugee agency, because—between myself, my pastry chef, and my sous chefs—I had four people who spoke one dialect or another of Chinese. I had the blessings of an extraordinary staff, because I didn't know what I was doing. In old Jersey terms, I didn't know "my ass from my elbow" in restaurant work. I hadn't a clue. I had my vision, and it's my vision that sustained me. But I learned on the job, starting from day one."

When Susanna Foo and her husband opened their restaurant, Susanna Foo's Chinese Cuisine, in 1987, they had limited experience, developed from helping her in-laws operate their restaurant. "My husband said he would rather have his own business than work for another company. We didn't have any experience in restaurants. We thought that the business just entailed managing—standing in the front and greeting the customer, hiring a chef, a cook, and everyone else. We were wrong. It's totally different. And it's very shocking when you find out that customers are not coming to your door and they're complaining the food is not very good." Susanna told me that as a chef-owner she now does much of the cooking, making everything from scratch, and does much of the marketing as well. She works ten- to twelve-hour days, six days a week, making sure that her food is top quality and that her customers keep coming back.

When you own a restaurant, as most owners will tell you, you need to be prepared for anything. You may need to replace staff, make changes to accommodate new zoning laws, or replace equipment. Lucie Costa is owner and operator of the Historic North Plank Road Tavern in Newburgh, New York. She tells a story about one item that needed replacing, a fact that she just couldn't bear to face until it was absolutely necessary. "My old stove on which I cooked the whole time I had the restaurant was so damaged, I could not do anything with it. For no reason, in the middle of the busiest night with the dining room packed, the thermostat would go down to zero—we would say that the spirit of the ghost was in the oven! I was the only one that had the magic touch to make that oven work, but it got to the point that all the parts needed to be fixed and we could not find replacements. So we bought a new stove. I cried when my old stove left the kitchen—we'd had so many conversations, heart-to-heart conversations; I'd spent all my cooking career with that stove. It was almost like a companion. And when that stove went into the parking lot, and I said 'bye-bye,' I realized I had to get out of the kitchen, because I was losing my marbles."

When Katy Keck opened her restaurant, the New World Grill, in New York City, she joined the ranks of the other women whose stories we've been hearing. This was the point at which she started to realize how much she didn't know. She speaks of the huge investment and the importance of understanding the many different aspects of running a business: "Having the financial under-standing of what items cost and what their potential benefits are is really help-ful. It took me well over two years to realize that it's not just about food. You get into the restaurant business because you like food. But, at least in a small restaurant, where you wear a lot of hats, food is only one thing. You also have to deal with emergency room procedures when somebody cuts themselves! You have to be able to rewire a hard drive when the computer goes down! There are all these things that I never really thought about—marketing, finance, and legal issues."

Katy describes other responsibilities she took on as owner of her business. "I was also acting as the executive chef, spending time on the line, teaching the kitchen staff, and doing recipe development. Another thing that I did, which goes back to my background, was write a recipe book for each of the menus. I felt I had to keep up with the day-to-day things so that I could make progress on more proactive, procedural-type projects, like writing newsletters and mar-keting."

Elizabeth Terry opened her restaurant, Elizabeth on 37th, in Savannah, Georgia in 1981, with nothing more than a little business sense. "My hus-band and I thought we were smart cookies. The first two years, we worked about fifteen hours a day—it nearly killed us. But we were very organized and very anal. … It took about two years for it to get real organized and real smoothly run." Elizabeth emphasizes the challenges of reconciling the dual personality inherent in the business: "A lot of people are under the miscon-ception that the restaurant business is strictly a hospitality business, when in fact it's a small manufacturing business, too. Everything that comes into our kitchen gets changed. It's not sold in its original package—everything must be washed, chopped, and reassembled. That's the exciting and challenging part of the restaurant business. There are two very different things going on: the manufacturing part that's sort of physical and rough with shirtsleeves rolled up; and then there's the hospitality part that's very genteel, flowers-and-candlelight in the front of the house. For an owner and for a chef, it's important that both of those be going along the same track togeth-er so that the train can run!"

Every owner and chef-owner has her own way of doing things; there's really no right or wrong way. Raji Jallepalli takes a very hands-on approach and actually closes her restaurant when she can't be there. "I have a small restaurant," she says. "I define my own style, I earn my living, and I earn my acclaim with every single plate that goes out. I get dirty every day and cook every night, so if I can't be there, I'm not going to be open." This ideal, her

"When you stop hav-ing fun, it's time to change jobs. We're not making nuclear bombs here or saving the world; we're cook-ing, and it's food, we eat it every day. Have fun with it, do a good job, and enjoy it, but put things in perspective."
—*Debra Ponzek*

1931: U.S. women take in boarders, do sewing, laundry, and dressmaking, and set up parlor grocery stores to supplement their husbands' incomes as the economic depression deepens.

Women in the Culinary Arena: Mary Sue Milliken and Susan Feniger

Virtually inseparable almost twenty years into their culinary careers, these dynamic women both grew up in the Midwest. For their primary culinary training, Susan went to the CIA and Mary Sue attended the Washburne Trade School in Chicago. Their paths first crossed at Le Perroquet, the famed Chicago restaurant. Mary Sue was hired into the formerly all-male kitchen after being offered the position of coatcheck girl, and Susan was hired with respect for Mary Sue's success.

Independently, they traveled to France; Mary Sue worked in Paris at Restaurant d'Olympe and Susan worked in L'Oasis on the French Riviera (see chapter three). Susan was the first to return to California, and together they cooked in the cramped quarters of the original City Café starting in 1981. This led to the opening of CITY restaurant in 1985. In 1988, Mary Sue and Susan received the 'Chef of the Year' award from the California Restaurant Writers Association—the first time the honor was ever shared!

In 1990, Mary Sue and Susan opened the Border Grill, named one of the best restaurants in America by *Gourmet* magazine. Their "Too Hot Tamales," a TV Food Network cooking show, premiered in 1995 to national acclaim. In 1997, they were nominated for James Beard awards in two separate categories: 'Southwest Regional Chef of the Year,' and for their radio talk show.

Mary Sue and Susan are active members in Chef's Collaborative 2000 and Women Chefs and Restaurateurs. They are staunch supporters of the Scleroderma Research Foundation, for which they have spearheaded a dinner/comedy event since 1987. In addition to their civic, professional, and personal responsibilities, they continue to find new venues to display their talents. They have written three cookbooks and plan to open more restaurants and establish a product line of sauces and spices. The honest spirit of these two women epitomizes the positive aspects of achievement and hard work. May we all be able to work for two decades with a good friend who shares our vision, drive, and passion.

talent, and passion for food has brought her and her restaurant to national acclaim.

Anne Rosenzweig owns and operates two restaurants in New York City—Arcadia which she opened in 1985, and The Lobster Club which she opened ten years later. Anne discusses the distinction between being an owner and being a chef: "Chefs," she says, "are in charge of the kitchen, but not necessarily the budget. Being a business owner is a completely different career, and culinary school doesn't always set you up to do that. Bank loans, for starters, are extremely difficult to get. Banks are not that happy lending to women, and they loathe lending to restaurants, because the failure rate is the highest of any businesses around. Just having that information alone makes you sound like a businesswoman, which you need to do when trying to get a loan. All the odds are stacked against you—they don't really care how good a cook you are; they only want to know what kind of a businesswoman you are."

So many issues go along with owning a restaurant. While many of these women confess to not knowing much about how to make their dreams of restaurant ownership work, they learned on the job. Some decided that they felt more comfortable taking on multiple roles to ensure quality and control of the kitchen; others hired staff in whom they put their trust. For others, they revised and revamped their vision according to the budgets and "the numbers," and learned more about the business aspects so that they could make everything work according to a financially sound and reasonable plan. For most of these women, getting this all to work smoothly took time, but in the end, the result was financially viable restaurants.

Working with the Staff—Fostering a Team

As an executive chef, I spend at least half my time managing my staff, which, during peak season, numbers about thirty. For thirty people with wide-ranging personalities, temperaments, and backgrounds, I am motivator, trainer, scheduler, evaluator, supporter, nurturer, listener—and sometimes even banker. The larger the staff, the greater the time spent in these capacities. For most chefs, staff management is a gratifying, frustrating, and necessary part of their job. In this section, we'll hear what it takes for women chefs to create a healthy, harmonious, vibrant, and productive kitchen crew.

In the process of managing staff, many women chefs find themselves assuming the role of mother. Maureen Pothier, chef of the former Bluepoint Oyster Bar and Restaurant during its many years of operation, was a "mother figure" for her staff but believes it had a positive influence on the overall kitchen dynamics. "I have had to handle spats between this employee and that employee without causing World War III. I have also advised on decisions about which doctors to see and what to do about various boyfriends." Maureen thinks employees benefit from having a woman in this capacity because, "Women are calm, they're rational, they take time to listen, and they're understanding. I recently had a call from one of my dishwashers about a personal issue. He called because he knew that I'd listen to what he was saying and I'd give him the benefit of my experience. He's happy with that—he feels comfortable with that."

Anne Gingrass, co-chef/co-owner of Hawthorne Lane, in San Francisco, finds that accessibility, more than anything else, is the key to managing a kitchen's many different types of people. "I sit down every day at two o'clock, have some lunch, gather my thoughts and if there's anything I need to taste, it happens then. If there's anything I need to know about from staff, it also

"Women really communicate—they really talk to each other. We run a business differently. The thing is, we need to learn to run it another way; we tend to run it like a family, and that's not always the best way."
—Nancy Oakes

1931: The *Joy of Cooking* by Irma Rombauer is first published.

"There's a need that women feel, like being a mother; you feel like you're pushing [staff] along and teaching them. The only thing that I feel really badly about is if somebody leaves and they didn't learn what they were supposed to learn—I feel like I failed."
—Anne Gingrass

happens then. I let them know when I'm available. If somebody comes and says, 'What should I do about this or that' then I say, 'Let's figure out if it's an immediate problem or determine if it's something that can wait until we can talk about it at our staff meetings,' which we have every other Saturday." Anne felt this regimented accessibility has helped her communicate with and manage her staff more effectively.

To address the always-pressing and often-vexing issue of staff productivity, Kerry Heffernan uses a menu manual. Menu manuals generally contain pictures, recipes, and specifications for all menu items, and are designed to help the staff serve a consistent product. According to Kerry: "Staff want you to tell them what you want and to show them what you want. Menu manuals do that. They help people know what is being required of them. I just recently changed the room service menu. It took four weeks; we made and photographed every single item. We put together a table of contents, scanned the photographs into the computer, and then printed them onto the recipes. We have this whole, incredible book! I know people need it, read it, and use it, because the kitchen copy is already mangled."

Once a chef has trained her staff and the kitchen is running efficiently, there will always be one or more staff members whose talent really stands out. How do you help them excel? According to Jody Adams: "You need people who are progressing all the time. You need sous chefs who are always one step ahead of you. You need people excited about food and willing to work hard, hot, long hours. But when they're ready, when you've taught them all you can, you have to let them go on to be the best they can be and not hold them back, just because it might make your life a little easier."

Jody also addresses one of the most persistent and pernicious issues in managing kitchens: dealing with the differences between the back and front of the house. Jody says it's critical that we knock down that "wall of animosity," that barrier to healthy communication between kitchen and dining room staff. Says Jody of her restaurant, "We physically got rid of the wall between the front and the back of the house. There is no wall—there's no door. You can walk from the front to the back of the house. The feeling is that, since whatever's going on in the kitchen is going to affect the floor and ultimately the customer anyway, we need to deal with it right up front. The success of this restaurant is based not just on me and not just on the food. It's based on the ambiance, the service, the greeting when people walk through the door, the way they're handled on the phone—it's everything. And if there's a mistake made with the customer, it's everybody's mistake."

Traci Des Jardins feels strongly that in order to have a well-run operation with motivated staff, you have to have a good relationship between the front and back of the house. "I deal with the staffing in the front of the house and I have a strong relationship with everybody who works here. I think my biggest source of pride is that I feel like we've really managed to create an environment here where the staff is really happy. I think it reflects in the dining ... the people who come here to eat don't feel the palpable stress emanating from the wait staff because they've just gone back in the kitchen and the chef has thrown a plate at them, screamed at them and called them dirt, stupid, and foolish. I put a lot of energy into managing people and in figuring out how to motivate them and make them care about what they're doing ... and it is so much better."

A chef is a manager and a people person, and unless she nurtures the talents of her staff, she will end up trying to do everything herself and she will fail. But what does it mean to nurture and develop staff? Many things, but among the most important is delegation; the next section takes a closer look at this issue.

Delegating Responsibility

One of the key issues that many women identify as a difficult and stressful part of working with staff is delegating responsibilities. For many women who have worked hard and long to accomplish great things, it can be difficult to pass responsibility on to others. What if staff make a mistake? What if less-than-perfect food goes out the door? What if everyone does fine without me? What if ideas get better without me? The act of delegating brings with it a whole host of demons. But for chefs who recognize its importance to the growth and health of the restaurant, the rewards can be immeasurable.

Laureen Gauthier, chef-instructor at New England Culinary Institute, describes her struggles with delegation and the incremental steps she took. "Delegating is tough to learn. It takes a lot of trying to do it yourself and then realizing it's not going to work. I think that I probably learned to delegate because I couldn't do it myself, so it had to be delegated. I started delegating, just by saying to kitchen staff, 'This is what we need to accomplish; what part of it do you want to do?' Then, after time, I began to feel comfortable saying, 'This is what we need to do; it makes sense for you to do this.' I think that's how I learned to delegate."

For Judy Rodgers, chef of Zuni, in San Francisco, delegating never really has been a problem. The trick, for her, is knowing when it works and when it doesn't. She explains her strategy: "I've always tried to delegate. But if I delegate and it isn't done well, I take it right back, because I have a reputation to protect." To those whose mantra is "delegate, delegate, delegate," she says, "That's great, but you can't delegate to somebody if they do the work badly. Sometimes there's too much at stake."

Sarah Stegner has adopted a gradual approach to delegating. "People may be hesitant to delegate, but in a kitchen, unless it's a twenty-four-seat

"I think a sign of success [is knowing] how to let people go and do things themselves. Let them develop systems and manage staff the way they want, then they will come and talk about it. I'm not micromanaging."
—Jody Adams

1932: The average U.S. weekly wage falls to $17.00, down from $28.00 in 1929, and women generally are paid below the average. Breadlines form in many cities.

restaurant, you can't do it all yourself. You have to delegate; you're forced to delegate; you have no choice but to delegate. The question is, can you delegate and still maintain control? That comes from experience. When you talk about delegating, you're not going to turn your kitchen over to somebody. You're merely saying to your staff: 'You make the food, but then make sure I taste it.' You do that twenty times and finally ten times in a row, the person doesn't have to remake it because the person made it the way you want. At that point, you say, 'OK that's fine, you're in charge of it now'!''

One of my management beliefs is that the best managers always strive to replace themselves. The more we train, empower, and delegate, the more time we have to advance ourselves, which in turn will help us advance our staff. Emily Luchetti shares her thoughts on that subject: "My guiding principle is that I try to make it so people don't need me. If they don't need me, I don't take that as a threatening thing; it means I can go do something else. I can create something else for myself. If someone else takes over the cakes—great, fabulous. I have no problem with that. You have to train people really well and impart your vision. You can't just show them the technique. For the first couple years of being a chef, I was much more anal and picky. Once I started getting recognition, it probably got worse. Then I was afraid that someone would mess it up. But after a while, you risk leaving for a half a day, then for a whole day, and you start to realize, everything's OK."

Delegation is a management skill that all successful chefs learn during their career. It's not always easy to learn and it can at times be difficult to accomplish, but to be successful and to continue to grow in your career, it's a skill that must be acquired.

The Customer

The customer is the basis of all we do as chefs and cooks. They are the people who we try to please, who we want to make happy, and who we want to see returning to our restaurants. If we lose sight of that focus, we lose our business, and even our enthusiasm for food may wane as a result—our passion for food will have no outlet.

Many women in this book stress the importance of interacting with the customer. One predominant reason is to gain feedback. Kerry Heffernan says: "The customer is the reason we do what we do. Everybody's always talking in the kitchen about respect and communication, but the fact is, the respect and communication has to be for the customer first and always. You need people to tell you, 'Wow, this is the greatest dinner,' or 'Thank you so much for making this event special.' That's one of the greatest things about being a chef—getting people to say: 'Wow! That was the best salmon I've ever tasted!' Their experience was exceptional, because you took care of them."

Sometimes all-out devotion to taking care of the customer can have serious costs. Johanne Killeen explains: "I can understand wanting to eat healthy; I understand having diet restrictions and I can certainly understand having allergies. But Americans are going off the deep end with the 'having it my way' stage that they seem to be in. They look at a menu and want it without this and this and with this and this added." Johanne goes on to explain that she feels that the guest often doesn't understand the problems that these kinds of requests can cause for the kitchen. "An unusual request is like pushing the gearshift into reverse when you're going ninety miles an hour. Your mind snaps. People probably don't understand how much choreography and how much concentration it takes to do food to order. The annoying part is when the customer wants to completely rearrange a dish when there's a perfectly logical choice somewhere else on the menu."

Customers—without them we would have no businesses, no restaurants, and in most cases no jobs. They are part of our reason for creating; we nurture them and feed them and, like family, they can be frustrating, joyous, and can give us our gratification and a host of challenges. But whatever the relationship, they are at the core of most of our careers.

"Learn to love yourself more than your job, and then you can put that love into it. You have to deal with yourself first, work on yourself. Make yourself better, to make your job better, to make your work better; it's a daily thing. Take time for you, it will show in your food."
—*Kristina Neely*

Management and Work Styles of Women and Men

Much has been written in recent years about the change of management style in the workplace. As more and more women find their place in upper management, a new "management style" is coming into play. This section discusses what that style is, how women perceive themselves as managers, and the differences between the management styles of women and men.

The Foundation for Future Leadership conducted a study of over 6,000 women and men, and revealed that "corporate women outperform men in twenty-eight of thirty-one categories," say researchers Janet Irwin and Michael Perrault. Irwin goes on to state: "We have seen the successful executive of the future and she is a woman. This report indicates that women are stronger than men overall in both interpersonal and managerial skills." The study examined the performance differences between women and men, finding that women outperformed men in "the challenging areas of meeting deadlines, high productivity, and generating new ideas. ... Women are considered better performers in both right and left brain skill areas." Irwin and Perrault summarize their findings by saying, "Women managers and leaders have been successful by drawing upon what is unique to their experience as women. Women have learned to manage effectively without relying on the control of resources and

1932: Birdseye Frosted Foods go on sale across the U.S. as General Foods expands distribution. Only a few retail grocers have freezer cases for displaying frozen foods.

power to motivate others. Possibly because they've seldom had access to such power, women have developed alternative ways to achieve success. The data further support that women should not be discriminated against as they, in fact, have the edge in terms of their effectiveness."

Women's unique management savvy is also a focus of Patricia Aburdene and John Naisbitt's book *Megatrends for Women.* They write: "Women and the information society, … which celebrates brain over brawn, are a partnership made in heaven. … [There is a] change under way from the command-and-control leadership style of men to what some observers have described as the facilitating, orchestrating, leadership style of women. … The organizing principle of business has shifted from management to leadership, opening the doors to women."

The NRA *Foodservice Employee Profile* offers a snapshot of typical foodservice managers: They are women (sixty-seven percent) under 35, and they are usually working in a large company (revenues of $5 million per year). The larger the company, the more women employed in salaried (usually supervisory) positions (forty percent), and conversely, the smaller the company, the more women employed as hourly workers (sixty-seven percent). As we look forward to the twenty-first century, we see an increased number of women graduating from culinary schools, coupled with the increase in women-owned businesses. This trend may very well start diminishing the inequities that have dominated kitchens throughout history.

In 1993, the NRA published *Women in Foodservice,* which discusses women in management within the foodservice industry. It says: "More than one industry leader has pointed out that women may actually have an advantage in the hospitality industry because they traditionally have held roles that involve nurturing—an important concept for hospitality and customer service. In fact, leaders say nurturing is one of the many areas in which women may serve as role models." This quality has been demonstrated time and again throughout this book as we hear the stories in which women discuss how they interact with their staff and co-workers.

This new leadership style—or "Women's Leadership Style," as it has been formally dubbed—is defined in *Megatrends for Women* as: "valuing and using empowerment, motivating, valuing creativity, inviting people to speak out, being flexible, supporting pay for performance, encouraging a mutual contract for results, incorporating holistic views, initiating systemic solutions, and facilitating change." Aburdene and Naisbitt go on to say: "Many of the attributes for which women's leadership is praised are rooted in women's socialized roles. The traditional female value of caring for others—balanced with sufficient objectivity—is the basis of the management skill of supporting and encouraging people and bringing out their best. Women leaders are better at balancing than their male counterparts. The first reason is obviously intense family responsibility, but it does not stop there. Women do not identify exclusively with their careers as most men traditionally have. Female leaders take time out for recreation—attending plays and movies, looking at and collecting art, reading literature, gardening." They lead and share what could be considered a more balanced lifestyle.

Nora Pouillon addresses how difficult it is for women to succeed in a "male" management model. "Boys learn sports and math; girls do home economics, cooking, sewing, painting, or music and dance. And as adults, they're not encouraged to do the more competitive or ambitious jobs." She goes on to explain that the roles many women of her generation learned have been hard to overcome but now women are finally becoming leaders. "Women are fine at being leaders. They know they have to do it all, but they know they are not superwomen. They just do the best they can."

Learning how to manage and how to find a comfortable management style is often a formidable challenge. It's not always intuitive; it takes a conscious effort, and mimicking another's style doesn't necessarily guarantee good results. Corinna Mozo describes her struggles trying to find her stride. "I didn't know it, but I started out using two styles: Paul O'Connell's and Lydia Shire's. I was being hard on the kitchen, the line hated me, and I lost a few cooks. I realized that I was using two styles at once and it wasn't going to work! Now, on a Saturday night when a plate comes out to me and it's a little bit messy, or not quite the way I would have wanted it, I can clean it up and swallow my criticism. I know all the flavors are there, I know it's perfectly presentable, I know that if the red chard isn't exactly the way I would like it, we can fix it and it will be a little better next time."

Susan Spicer, like Corinna, has been learning how to manage as she goes. She describes her management odyssey, which has incorporated elements of "the nurturer" and "the coach" and several things in between. "I was in charge of the day crew and I had to fire a dishwasher, which of course wrecked me for four days. I was the mother hen; my management style was gathering all my little chicks around me to create a support team. It was all very much my family. I depended on everybody and if anybody left the nest, if anybody decided they wanted to move on, I took it very personally. I've also considered myself somewhat of a coach, giving staff feedback, guiding them and talking to them [throughout the process]."

Tamara Murphy, former executive chef of Campagne in Seattle, has found that allowing her staff to work four long days per week has been a positive influence. "The days can get to be long for them. We're open until midnight and—especially in the summertime—we stay pretty busy all the way through,

"As we convey a work standard example, for having integrity in what we do, producing great products and doing the wonderful things that we do, we also have to teach people to have balance."
—*Traci Des Jardins*

1933: The Baby Ruth candy bar is introduced, and women and girls are sought to wrap the candies. Women on straight wages could earn 31 cents/hour, while men could earn 45 cents/hour.

so it's a ten-hour day. They work four shifts and have three days off. They all work in this beautiful place, and they all love to hike and camp. They need to be able to go and enjoy themselves. And I get so much more from them because they're happy."

Tamara talks about what works for her: "I give people a lot of freedom; I like to teach people, show them where I'm going with things, and then I let them take it. I try to find out my staff's weaknesses and strengths and then match them up accordingly." In matching people up, Tamara has observed that women seem to be better team players. "I think women are better at taking care of each other. I see this over and over again in their *mise-en-place* and their setup. This is a terrible, terrible generalization, but you put a guy on a station, and the next day there's nothing left—nothing's prepped! You put a woman at a station, and they'll take care of each other. When they're prepping, they're prepping for the person coming up next on the shift."

Lucie Costa reflects on the differences in work habits between women and men and how that affects her management style. Her approach is very different than what we just heard from Tamara. Her perspective is: "Women have different work methods than guys. We're more soft-spoken, and we don't give commands as a guy would. We get the job done in our own way. It's unfortunate that, as managers, we have to draw on our testosterone level just to prove ourselves—just so that the guys can connect themselves to us. You almost have to do that to get accepted; sometimes you have to try to be like one of the boys."

Finding a management style that works can be a long process of growth and change. Susan McCreight Lindeborg shares her journey. "Women manage differently than men. A classic way for women to handle things in the kitchen is to internalize and then make somebody pay for it later instead of yelling. I decided a number of years ago that was what I was doing, and it was eating me alive. So then I started yelling—well, not really yelling—but raising my voice, and saying, 'NO. YOU WILL NOT DO THAT.' There's a lot of pressure in kitchens; it's really hot, really hard, your language gets very short and very direct." When Susan realized her technique wasn't the end-all-be-all for managing people, she tried something different. "I tried saying, 'Have you thought of—', 'Did you realize—', 'Have you taken responsibility for—?' Women are socialized and trained from day one, to please, to do things right—it's very hard to overcome that."

The issue of tailoring one's management styles to connect with one's employees can get tricky, especially for women chefs trying to reach their male kitchen staff. Many report that the authoritative model just doesn't work. Direct and forceful delivery is often not accepted from a woman. As a result, women chefs have the additional challenge of finding more creative ways to communicate.

Traci Des Jardins "grew up" in many kitchens with a male-oriented management style. She decided hers would be very different. She describes what works for the atmosphere she has created in her restaurant. "Because of my experiences with bad managers and bad environments in restaurants, one of my top priorities was to create an environment for my staff that was really positive. I've been in management for seven years now and I've given a lot of thought about how to do it best—how to get the best out of each person who works for me. I have a strong relationship with everybody who works here and I think that's my biggest source of pride. The staff is really happy. They walk through the door every day and feel like they're contributing something; they're learning something and they're participating in making this a good restaurant.

Traci goes on to say: "I put a lot of energy into managing people and into figuring out how to motivate them, make them care about what they're doing. Everyone who works in my kitchen is concerned with doing the best they can possibly do. They're motivated. And it's not out of fear, intimidation, humiliation, or any of those so-called management practices. I grew up with that in kitchens, but I don't abide by it anymore. I try to educate, teach, and promote caring so that each individual feels like they're contributing something. That's my greatest source of pride in this restaurant—what we've been able to achieve together."

Both Hilary DeMane and I had early kitchen experiences on cruise ships working under European chefs. In some ways, our experiences were similar to Traci's in that the men who were our managers used fear, intimidation, and humiliation as the means for motivating staff. Hilary describes how her management style has evolved into something quite different from the styles of her early managers. "When I was in charge the big difference was that I communicated a lot more with my staff." She explains that her method of communication is always clear and calm, nurturing and firm, as opposed to the screaming or shouting to which she had been subjected. "I didn't take any crap from anybody, and I didn't allow anybody any liberty to take advantage of my good nature—my good nature only goes so far. I was constantly telling my staff that they had done a good job, that they were progressing, that they were learning, or that I was pleased. I thanked them for their work. I actually brought this up to one male Swiss chef; I was so upset with him at one point that I said, 'Never, never once have you ever said 'thank you' for anything. I know I get paid, I'm not expecting you to grovel, but never once have you ever said, 'Good job! Thank you! That was a hard day today! Never!' And it was completely beyond his comprehension. I don't think he knew what I was talking about.'"

"Try to be able to answer the question: 'What is it you *want?—out of your life, your restaurant experience, your cooking—whatever it is, stick to it. Stick to your guns. I mean, who else is going to say it for you?"*
—Deborah Huntley

"There is a balance in life; if you have caviar every day, eventually it's not going to be as good as if you just have it occasionally. But you don't have to go through hard times of eating carrots for twenty years before you can enjoy foie gras; that's not the point of life!"
—Ariane Daguin

1933: The Toll House chocolate chip cookie is introduced by Ruth Wakefield, innkeeper of the Toll House Inn in Whitman, Massachusetts.

"Be confident, and passionate in what you know; allow yourself to know what you know, and be open to learn. You are bringing something very unique to somebody; if you are in a situation that is not conducive to your growth or to your contributing as well as you can contribute, then don't do it; its not good for you."

—Eve Felder

In the past few years more and more books have been published equating good management practices to the Zen philosophy. Annie Somerville was trained in the Zen culture, and she explains her feeling on it: "[The] practice of Zen is effectively to realize that things are constantly changing. You can't control nature. People are going to do what they're going to do. Cataclysmic events are going to happen in the world, and you have to be flexible. A big part of Zen practice is understanding that conflicts will constantly arise. The way we run the kitchen is very much influenced by the way we learned to work at the Zen Centre. We have consideration for people. There are a lot of very unfair practices that go on in a kitchen hierarchy, and there's a very dark side to most restaurants. It's important for chefs to be willing to do anything that needs to be done. The first thing I do when I walk in the door is pick up cigarette butts out in front; it's just as easy for me to do as it is to tell another person to do it! People who have to work very, very long hours should not end up leaving in a disgruntled way, feeling unrewarded, unappreciated. So we try to do things differently."

Sarah Stegner believes that, whatever management style a chef chooses, it needs to be grounded in professionalism. "Whenever you're faced with a stressful situation or problem that needs resolution, if you fall back on professionalism and respect, you'll be right on target. It's a very tough business. Not everybody is the same; not all staff responds to the same approach. There is a time when it's important to be very human with people, and to ask them why they're having difficulties. ... People should feel comfortable in a kitchen. You don't want them terrified of the chef, you want them comfortable so they can do their best work."

Two different gender-based management styles have started to merge—the traditional dictatorial model and the nurturing mother model. The traditional model is often attributed to the males, while the nurturing model is attributed to women; however, not everyone is comfortable with just one style or the other. Some try a little of both. For now, the ideal model hasn't been devised. We are left wondering what the outcome will be. Hopefully, the best of both.

Women's and Men's Food Creations

Many women believe that there is a difference between the way women and men manage, but what about the food they cook? Is there a gender-based difference at play there, too? This is a question I asked many of the women I spoke with and I got some very interesting answers.

Jean-François Revel, in his book *Culture and Cuisine*, written in 1982, relates this story: "Why should the desire to disconcert and dazzle so tirelessly [be] stigmatized ... be necessarily detestable? Is this not one of the forms of hospitality in a civilization in which the art of entertaining is not confined to the art of providing nourishment but rather extends to the art of distracting, amusing, surprising?" Revel goes on to describe a scene from ancient Greek and Roman times, in which a boar is brought to a banquet table for the guests. "Once at the table, the belly is cut open, out fly birds (caught by the bird sellers on hand for the occasion), acorns abound, and from baskets hanging on the tusks come dates." One can draw parallels to some of the "presentation and spectacle" that we see in food today and to some of the stories we hear in this chapter.

Loretta Keller describes a review of her restaurant that gets at the issue: "The opening paragraph of the review was something like 'Food mavens will tell you that they can always recognize when there's a woman in the kitchen and when there's a man in the kitchen. Men's cooking is slick and women's has soul.' I think that's true. Men have a tendency to overwork food; it tends to be more cerebral, more manipulated. Women's food is often more spontaneous, maybe simpler. There's definitely a style of male cooking that's very architecturally designed and cerebral. For me eating is not a cerebral activity. It's something to nourish, which should be satisfying. Food is for people to eat, to enjoy, and to feel sustenance."

Anne Rosenzweig adds these ideas to the discussion: "Women's cooking is more honest, it's more down to earth, it's more concerned with flavors. This isn't always true, but in general it is very true. I think food has evolved such that women are mainly concerned with taste and flavor and men are concerned with look and architecture. That's a big difference."

Emily Luchetti agrees: "Most of the architectural stuff is done by men—that's just a fact. They seem to have this flamboyant need to express themselves. They can't put out a humble little piece of cake and feel comfortable with it. It's just not enough. It's not a big enough statement. I just like it to taste good."

Lidia Bastianich suggests that women have a gentler approach to food. She explains: "When I cook, there's actually something, a feeling, I put in there. I just sense it. I don't know whether every woman has that; I think that there is in women a gentler approach to food preparation."

From Susan Regis's perspective, the differences between men and women's food can be seen in the light of their different approaches and techniques. Her belief is that men tend to work with food mechanically and women work with it viscerally. "In some ways, women are more thoughtful in the process of cooking; men want to know and want to jump; they want to dissect and attack. There's softness to a woman's approach. If you go to Italy, women are coming

"Do what you love. Don't be afraid. Don't put up with things you think are wrong; be true to yourself. Give others the benefit of the doubt. Never perceive yourself as a victim, or others will see you that way also."
—Ameila Rappaport

1936: The Supreme Court rules on June 1 that a New York minimum wage law for women passed in 1933 is unconstitutional.

*"Know yourself. Be
true to yourself. You
are a person before
you are anything
else. If you have that
instilled inside of
you, and you focus in
on what your goal is,
then your gender,
your race, or any-
thing else won't mat-
ter. Go in with an
open mind, and open
heart, but with deter-
mination."*
—*Sharon Waynes*

from a place where food started with the family; women want to embrace that. Some of the best cooking in the world is grounded there. It is about the hearth, home, family, and it is about warmth, softness—and it is all about love."

The sensibility of food is an issue that Diane Forley considers when looking at the differences between how men and women work with food. "I find that women bring a different sort of sensibility to cooking. People often have said that the chef is a woman, that they could tell when it's a woman's menu or that a woman is cooking. And that's not a political statement; it's a social statement. That's just the way it is. I have seen in my kitchen that women's attitudes and approach to food is different than men's. They look at different details. I also think that there is a male and female side to both men and women. And men who have more of a female side to them also have that sensibility."

Women and men have been living and working together throughout the ages and yet there seems to be a clear distinction, in many of the stories that we've read, between women's and men's management and food styles. What we have heard not only exemplifies the hard work and dedication it takes to succeed in the foodservice industry, but also some ideas on how to better manage the people working in it. Perhaps if there were a way for these two styles to complement each other so that the diversity could be a strength rather than a point of contention or competition, there would be a new attitude in the kitchen based on mutual respect for people and food. One of my greatest hopes is that this book can start that dialogue in motion, and with it the avenue toward future success of the industry.

On Achieving Success

*What It Means to Women in
the Culinary Arena*

*"Put your fingers in your ears
and listen to your heart."*
—Nancy Oakes

The Palmer House kitchen, 1880. Courtesy of the Culinary Archives and Museum at Johnson and Wales University.

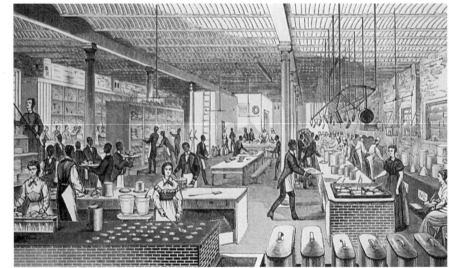

"I feel that success is utilizing my unique talents, being paid enough to enable me to enjoy my family and friends, and being mindful of continually striving to improve my spiritual, mental, and physical capabilities to the fullest. I am exceedingly blessed beyond my wildest expectations. ... I am most certainly successful."
—*Clara Craig*

Success. If you were to look it up in Webster's dictionary, you'd come away thinking it was all about money, fame, and fortune: "*the attainment of wealth, favor, or eminence.*" In reality, "success" is subjective—it means different things to different people. It can mean "straight As" for a student; it can mean summiting for a mountaineer; it can mean red tomatoes in August for a gardener. In general, it means fulfilling a particular internally set goal. This chapter asks what it means to be a successful woman chef—how you get there and what it's like when you arrive.

Defining Success and Knowing When You Have Arrived

While researching her doctoral thesis on women chefs, Pat Bartholomew discovered that women cooks and chefs are at odds with the traditional business community on matters of success. These women don't view success as securing management positions, receiving high wages, or winning power and fame. Instead, women in professional kitchens say they're successful when they achieve goals or are recognized by others, or they can contribute to their community.

When I think of success, I think about finding happiness, sharing, teaching, expressing passion, and giving back. Attaining money, power, and prestige are all peripheral; they may represent a job well done, but they are far from the focus of my life's work. My perception of success is shared by almost all of the women I spoke with while writing this book.

Giving Back to Others

One of the first issues raised in this book was: "Why be a chef?" One of the most common answers: "Because it's all about feeding people, nurturing people, because I can give back." Without being able to make that contribution, many of these women cooks and chefs would not have felt successful in their careers.

Madeleine Kamman has had a long and varied career and commands unmitigated respect from the industry. She shares the following about success: "It is essential not to confuse being a success with being successful. I am not a success and never strived to be one, because I would have had to compromise too many of my standards. Being successful for me meant first and foremost trying to steer away from mediocrity in my work. I was most successful, even if that does not necessarily mean that I never had a fight with myself on that major subject. It meant understanding my chosen work in such depth that I was most of the time able to communicate its techniques, intricacies and beauty to younger professionals. Triggering their enthusiasm and if I was especially lucky, transforming that enthusiasm into a lifetime passion. It meant being able to remain available as a companion, mother, grandmother, and friend to all members of my family and extended family in spite of a work schedule that was more often than not, short of brutal. It meant to be able to practice my art (read art as a synonym to technique, which it is) in as articulate a manner as I was able to, and, equally well in my teaching, on my restaurant plates, in my writings and in television work. It has never meant making a lot of money ever, because it is more important for me to be remembered for what I was able to do for others than for the amount I was able to put in my bank account. I have done, seen and had everything I always wished and generally much more than most of the numerous multi-millionaires who have crossed my life-path, and I have the satisfaction of making it entirely possible for myself or receiving it only from those who truly loved me. And last but not least, as I reach a semi-venerable age, it means leaving the field open to the younger generations that are coming up and are working hard to find their own ways and styles of expression, rather than stand in the way of their search and efforts."

Among Madeleine's many outstanding qualities, not only has she been able to pass on her knowledge, skill, and passion, but she also has the grace and dignity to let go and let others step up to the proverbial plate.

Katy Keck suggests that in our society, there is often all too little attention paid to qualitative issues like integrity, morality, and compassion. Our society tends to emphasize success in quantitative terms: financial success, public visibility, image, and often size of endeavor. Katy considers that success for her "will always be a work in progress. It does not make nearly as much noise as a

"I think most people who are successful do what they love—I think you drive yourself. I don't even think you know you're doing it!"
—Joyce Goldstein

1937: Margaret Rudkin bakes the first loaves of Pepperidge Farm breads.

New York Times review. It's treating people fairly, supporting the people who fill your life, whether on the job or in personal relationships, and setting and maintaining high standards of integrity, which you don't compromise. As both my parents taught by example, it's 'paying rent on the space you occupy'; giving something back to a world in need. Success is not about your personal achievements at any one point in your career, but about how you live your life over all its years. Can you make a difference?"

Cindy Salvato sees her success juxtaposed with the success of the students who have gained under her tutelage. "I define my success simply by the success of my students. Teaching is an occupation that calls on you to be successful. The art of teaching stretches beyond the paycheck. Over the past seven years, I have had the opportunity to mentor young men and women as they venture down the fun and often difficult road to a career in the kitchen. I have been a part of their highs and their lows and I am proud of them all. Am I successful? You bet I am! God has given me the best job and the strength to endure all the challenges."

Like other women in this section, Sarah Langan defines success in terms of giving back to the next generation. "I do consider myself successful when it comes to my professional life, in that I wanted to teach at a level where I would make a difference in my student's culinary futures—teaching not only techniques and procedures, but also the importance of professionalism, the continual striving for knowledge, and the giving back of oneself to the community. After teaching for just over five years, I have begun to see the difference I have made."

Gloria Ciccarone-Nehls, executive chef of the Huntington Hotel, in San Francisco, since 1981, attributes her success to her passion for her work: "I am very lucky to be able to consider myself successful at this point in my life. Success and happiness are close companions!" She finds the immediate gratification that she receives to be a great asset, but in the end: "The important thing is that you do what you do, and you do it well, and you don't give up at it. You absolutely must love it! You may not know that you love it; that's the hard part. You're not going to know that until you've really worked hard and you're falling apart and you're tired all the time, and then you go back the next day, start it all over again, and you still love it!"

For women in the culinary field, success is an ongoing quest to evolve—to learn more, give more, and all the while, to enjoy what they do. Success is not about money. That much is clear. Nor is success about competition. Success is just about being the best that you can be and helping others achieve that same goal for themselves.

Reaching Their Goals

Many women find that success starts with establishing goals for themselves. But once they have attained their goals, their work isn't done; they reestablish their priorities and set new goals. As many of them state, setting and reaching their goals is an ongoing process that keeps them motivated and striving to be the best that they can be. Finding a sense of balance is a goal that many women set as a primary objective, and most of them feel that they have been successful overall. In this section, we hear from several women and their views on balancing success.

Kathleen Kennedy explains success as a balancing act between her professional and personal life. "I define success as achieving personal, professional, and spiritual goals while being of service and giving back to the community. I feel I have been successful because I have continuously set and accomplished career and individual ambitions. Attending the CIA, working in Europe and at four-star establishments in the U.S., becoming an executive chef and cooking instructor have all been dreams that became reality." But as Kathleen points out, she must continue to define and reach new goals. "Getting published, food styling, and being a spokesperson are my latest incarnations. In my mind, career success without balance is unrewarding. At times in my career, work was the most important part of my existence." Yet as Kathleen states, goals continue to evolve over time. "Now that I am happily married and expecting a baby any day, I feel much more fulfilled. I strive to stay centered and balanced and I feel that I have more to give back when I can do that."

Setting and achieving professional and personal goals is also a means to success for Joyce Goldstein. "To me, success is earning the respect of your peers and accomplishing your goals. Some of my goals have been to be a good teacher/mentor to my students and staff, and to educate the dining public by broadening their culinary horizons. I still have more goals I want to accomplish. But that is what keeps me going. On the personal side, success is also having raised three wonderful children and having supported myself all these many years."

Along the same line of thought, Alison Awerbuch finds that reaching her goals, finding balance in her life, and sharing with others are key factors in achieving success. "For me, success is having the ability to define what is important, setting the goals to achieve what is important, and doing everything it takes to get there. As time goes on, goals and priorities change, and I find myself once again reaching to attain those new goals. I am lucky to consider myself successful in the fact that I have attained many goals I have set out to accomplish. These goals are reflected not only in professional life, but in my personal life as well, and include being very involved in helping others."

Tracy Cundiff, a culinary student, has a full and successful career to look forward to. Her ideas on success are particularly insightful considering her

"If you want to be successful, you have to work very hard, and you always have to keep up with what your goal is."
—*Susanna Foo*

1942: Dione Lucas and Rosemary Hume open Le Petit Cordon Bleu in New York City.

"The definition of success is elusive to me as I often measure my success in relation to others. I feel that I have accomplished the goals I set out; however, having 'been a success' at achieving those, I now look to the next level of success to conquer."
—RoxSand Scocos

age—eighteen—and her limited years of experience. "Success is achieving all your goals, dreams, and ambitions in life that make you happy. It is finding the one thing that you love to do in life. Am I successful? Yes I am. So far I have achieved and will continue to achieve all of my goals, dreams, and ambitions. I am fortunate enough to have found what I truly love to do. I love to cook. I could not imagine my life being complete without it. No matter where I go or where I end up in life I will always cook. That is what makes me successful."

Amy Scherber also equates success with achieving her goals: "If you set a major goal for your career that you achieve and that you enjoy doing in the process, you have been successful. If you find some measure of fame in the process, that is even better." Amy says money is seldom a motivation or goal of success. "I think that becoming wealthy in the process is not a great measure of success. It is not an important factor to me in defining success, and in this business, it is not that likely anyway! Yes, I think I am successful."

Rozanne Gold is part of a professional foodservice team that includes her husband. Together they have been involved with some of the most prestigious restaurant openings in New York City. Rozanne believes that success is achieved through goals and hard work. "Success is a state of mind and being successful comes slowly, only after years of dedicated hard work. It's the grand accumulation of many steps and mis-steps along a road sometimes traveled only by oneself. I feel successful when I'm in the process of being creative or being the first at something. I feel successful when I take risks. I feel successful when I help others achieve their goals. If defined by dollars, which I've also come to appreciate (only recently) as a more earthly measure, then I've also achieved success by making lots of money doing things I love."

Many of these women feel that being goal-oriented helped them achieve success. Once they reached a goal, they then set another to achieve. Achieving and maintaining success, then, is an ongoing process.

Sometimes Success Seems So Elusive

If anyone were to view both Deborah Madison's and Susan McCreight Lindeborg's careers from the outside, they would probably define each as being successful. However, according to both women, success can be ephemeral. At times, it can be elusive.

Deborah Madison, who for many years had been the chef at Greens, is now writing. She explains: "There are some days, lots of days, where I think 'Am I really doing enough? Am I accomplishing enough?' If you write, you have a feeling of being isolated and cut off. It's different from going to a job, or putting food on your restaurant table, where you feel you're really connecting to people. To me that's very important. So I might answer that question yes and no."

Susan McCreight Lindeborg equates her success with her work, her vision, and the food she creates. "For me, success as a cook comes when I like what I have created and other people like it, too—, whether it is making the entire restaurant as I envision it, getting an evening's service of food smoothly out of the kitchen, introducing a new menu, inventing a single menu item, preparing food with my own hands, showing a new technique to a young cook, doing a demonstration, teaching a class, or writing an article. Am I successful? Not as often as I would like. Many times I am not satisfied with the results of my work—that is failure. Sometimes I create something *I* think is truly wonderful—and no one notices. That, too, is failure. But success does come along every so often. When it does, I feel like singing opera or doing a little dance."

Success has touched every one of the women cooks and chefs with whom I spoke. Whether it's personal or professional, quantitative or qualitative, every one of them has achieved some measure of success.

How Success Is Achieved

The motivation for success is different in the culinary world when compared to other major industry segments. Monetary rewards, perks, and benefits rarely enter into the picture. Could the path to success be that much different as well? If the corporate world rewards hard work and demonstrated ability with promotions and raises, how are these same accomplishments rewarded in the culinary arena? The following stories and thoughts on the subject attempt to answer that question in light of the many different definitions of the word success.

In Pat Bartholomew's dissertation, she gives this formula for a woman chef's success: "[It takes] hard work, persistence, perseverance, and commitment to career and a clear sense of the direction they want to pursue." She also feels that to achieve success, the person must be, "self-reliant, aggressive, self-confident, autonomous, and unconventional." According to Pat, the following characteristics are also very important: "passion, patience, determination, risk-taking, aesthetic ability, good hands, hard work, serendipity, political skills, ability to get things done and the ability to get along." These characteristics typify women's strength and resilience in stories throughout this book.

Susan McCreight Lindeborg believes that to get ahead, and ultimately to find success, you must be assertive and attentive. She says that those in the kitchen who maintain success are those "who are aware of everything that goes on around them." She gives this example: "Maybe they're working the sauté station, yet they know exactly what's going on at the grill, and they

"[Success is] doing what you want to do in the way that you would like to do it, and having it accepted as you hope it might be.
Fortunately for me, I have been successful; and I am grateful for that because I love my work."
—*Julia Child*

1942: *How to Cook a Wolf* by M. F. K. Fisher is published.

"[To succeed] you've got to be passionate and an extrovert. ... I think that people who are good at this business are dramatic and full, full, full of energy. It helps if your partner is someone who knows this is important, and celebrates that particular quality."
—Elizabeth Terry

could walk over and do the full station if they had to. They know where everything is in the dry goods and in the walk-in; they know where it came from. People like that are the ones who *really* succeed."

Toniann Beattie speaks from experience when she says that to succeed, you need passion and you must be willing to go for it. "If you want something, you have to go after it. There was that point where I had to be practical and think, 'What will this do to my children?' But if my children realize that it's not too late for me to go after a dream, then it's never too late for them to go after a dream. They have a new respect for themselves because they see me with a new respect for myself. I think that you teach your children by example; that's a gift in it's own right—to be able to give children the outlook that it's never too late to start. I'm sure that there are a million people in the same set of circumstances. Hopefully somebody somewhere will feel the same way I did—that it's all worth chucking what hasn't worked for a dream that will set you on fire."

Clara Craig's love for the business shines through in her discussion of how success is achieved: "You have to love it to do it. Don't do it if you don't feel that it's what you want to do. Don't go for the money or the fame; go for what's in your heart." She explains that once you've made the decision to pursue your career, you must persevere. "Don't step off that stage if you know it's yours—it's not for the faint-hearted. I've had kids who came here, and I said to them after two weeks: 'You know what? I suggest you find another career—this is really not for you. You need to look at what you really want to do.' I'd much rather tell them that now, because I'm a loving and kind person when it comes to people's foibles."

Sometimes our lessons come from unexpected sources and take us on unexpected journeys. Katy Keck tells of a letter her mother wrote almost twenty years ago in which she advised taking time to smell the flowers. This letter gave her a sense of balance that has allowed her to grow and succeed. Katy explains: "She recognized, even though I was only a teenager at the time, I had that type-A, overdrive personality. Her lessons about balance and success are ones that most people don't get early on. To have somebody share those lessons with you is so important." That letter helped her pull herself away from a position on Wall Street to pursue her passion. She recalls: "I was in France and my father, who had paid for my MBA said, 'You've been over there for *how long?* You're not coming back till *when?'* I was somewhere on the coast of Spain, on a balcony, many glasses of wine later, and just wrote him this long letter about how my mother had told me to take time to smell the flowers. I said, 'This is what it's all about; it's doing something you enjoy.' How many people end up waiting for their gold watch and their fiftieth anniversary party and they've done jobs that they hate? Thank God I won't ever be there."

According to Leslie Revsin, success depends upon being true to yourself and trusting your instincts. "You must always listen to your inner voice. This voice is your guiding light." She also advises that it's important to make your-self visible. To do this, she suggests: "You've got to get out of the kitchen. You must meet people; you must thrust yourself into people's eyes, into their vision. It's all about having people see you and know you as a person too."

Nancy Oakes' advice for achieving success is based largely on how you deal with others: "People skills are the most important. Even if you're the greatest cook in the world, if you don't have good people skills, you're not going to go anywhere. You have to develop an ability to talk to your customers and to be somewhat likable. Your value in the community can be judged by what people are saying behind your back—things that you do really stick to you. What peo-ple say behind your back is your total worth. Try not to get sidetracked; try and stay focused; put your fingers in your ears and listen to your heart."

Each of these women offers her perspectives on what it takes to achieve success. There is a common thread through all of these stories—self-reliance, persistence, patience, perseverance, and passion. Many express that some if not all of these qualities, as well as having the ability to get along with others, whether kitchen staff or customers, are the fundamentals for success. As Toniann Beattie suggests, "just go for it." The following stories share how being recognized for their accomplishments can play an important role in iden-tifying women's success.

Loving What You Do and Being Recognized by Your Peers

We've heard that a prerequisite to being successful is loving what you do. But another component of success is being recognized for what you do. One of the reasons many women give for becoming a chef is the instant gratification that comes from sharing food that is appreciated. In the next stories we hear how recognition for a job well done affects women's feelings of success.

For Debbie Gold, recognition is a central part of feeling successful, and success is multifaceted. "One part of feeling successful is the public recognition of what I do. Guests come in and enjoy the food and dining experience. Along with that comes recognition from local and national press, such as good reviews in the paper and articles. I feel fortunate that my peers and food professionals recognize my hard work and talent. Another part is more of an internal feeling it brings to me. I enjoy my job and I actually get paid for what I love to do! There is also the gratification of creating a menu and or dish that guests truly enjoy—there is immediate response to what I do. Like a good stage play, I know when I have succeeded."

Judi Arnold's company, DuFour Pastry Kitchen, produces high-quality appetizers and savory pastry products. Her ability to manufacture and sell a quality product that consumers enjoy is one gauge of her success. "It's *not* the

"I feel successful when I see traces of the big goals that I'm dedicated to mani-festing within the little joys of each day."
—*Odessa Piper*

1942: Thirteen million women are in the United States work force.

"[To succeed you need] strength, self-esteem, determination, and stamina … you need to be a rebel sometimes."
—*Raji Jallepalli*

money. It's having created a product that is as fun as we can make it be. It's a really wonderful-quality product we've created and that we've brought to the public. We're acknowledged for it, people like it, they buy more of it—that's success. We make it work, we have great employees, we make our company work and that is success too—that we actually have a functioning company."

For Kerry Heffernan, success is a state of mind, a way of feeling about yourself and your work. "For me, at this point in my life, success [is] feeling successful—it's just as simple as that. I feel good about the work that I do. Even if I have a lousy day and some hateful interaction happens at work—say, the devil himself has totally infiltrated the body of the general manager—it's OK. I still know that what I'm really trying to do is good work that makes people feel good. That's the only thing that I can do for me."

For Janis Wertz, "success is in the mind of the beholder. There are days in which I finally hang a painting on a wall and that means success. On the other hand, there are days when I begin to feel that most of the faculty accepts my leadership—this, too, is success." She qualifies her definition: "Success is also defined by feedback and accepting what people are saying for purposes of continuous improvement. Finally, success is embraced by relationships and knowing who you can turn to during the tough times, and knowing who accepts you just as you are. In the context of cherished relationships, good feedback, acceptance by others, and an occasional accomplishment, I feel truly blessed with success."

Hilary DeMane's success as an educator is punctuated by the fact that she was awarded The Senate Award for Educator of the Year in 1996, an honor never before bestowed on a culinary educator. Hilary defines success as "a combination of personal as well as professional achievement and satisfaction. I have found the delicate balance between private and professional lives, and realize how it is possible to live both happily. I love my work passionately; there has never been a day I woke up and said, 'I wish I did something else for a living.' After twenty-four years, that has to mean I made some right choices along the way."

Both Deborah Huntley and Leslie Revsin talk about having fun and being happy as part of a successful and fulfilling life. Leslie had this to share: "I'm learning that it's OK to have fun—it's probably the answer to everything! When you're working with the people that you should be working with, it's so easy. Even when it's hard work, it's not like work. These are all revelations to me now." Deborah Huntley continues along these lines: "The most important thing is that you're happy with what you're doing. Don't kid yourself that it's a lot of glory, you'll have to make some sacrifices. If you indeed love it and love what you are doing with food and people, it can be very rewarding."

At a very young age, Traci Des Jardins has enjoyed a phenomenal amount of acclaim. She talks about her own experiences and how she has done so much so quickly. "You have got to be ready to work really hard; there is no way around it. It is a very demanding occupation and it's all-consuming. It really grabs onto you. I think it's because it's fulfilling in lots of different ways. It's constantly evolving; there's always something new to learn and some new experience to have. It's so multifaceted … it satisfies a lot of curiosity and you can use a lot of different skills. It takes a lot of energy and it's a very small percentage of chefs that will make it to that really glamorous, high-profile chef—they are few and far between." Traci also believes that "you have to have a basic love for food. I feel in a lot of ways it chose me. I think I'm talented; it's a gift and it's been something I haven't been able to walk away from because it grabbed onto me. I would say to people coming up through the ranks, 'be careful what you wish for.'"

To be careful what you wish for is certainly sage advice regarding success. With the attainment of success comes the challenges, which are portrayed in many of the following stories.

> *"True success is the ability to be in tune with your deepest self and then give of yourself in your work as a result. Nothing can compare to the pleasure of being able to do just that."*
> —Leslie Revsin

The Challenges That Accompany Success

While it is clearly a challenge to achieve success, it is also a challenge to deal with it constructively once you have attained it—to be able to redefine and reassess goals; to never stop growing. Success for many women chefs translates into some very concrete challenges, such as what to do when your level of business dramatically increases; how to maintain customer expectations; how to meet or exceed media expectations; and how to consistently live up to your own expectations.

Nancy Oakes discusses what happens when you and your restaurant "arrive." "The restaurant has become 'the family,' and therefore tremendous expectations have been attached to us. There is no central family as such any more—no central caregiver. People look to us to fulfill that need and some of it is idealistic. That's true particularly for women. People like to know who's feeding them. If you consider the amount of trust it takes for someone to walk in and put something into their body from someone they know nothing about—it's an act of faith. It's a very personal act that you do. We are like very high-paid prostitutes; we provide a service where people pay us to give them something that they place in their body—a very high act of faith." Nancy warns about the recent mass appeal of the industry. "In the last few years, you really can tell that too many people have been attracted to the industry because of the celebrities. [They're] attracted in a very unhealthy and unrealistic way. They have to realize it's repetitive, it's not romantic. You're more likely to be cleaning out the grease trap than squishing fresh herbs between your fingers."

1942: *Organic Gardening and Farming* begins publication by J. I. Rodale.

Barbara Tropp plays down the celebrity aspect of the job. For her, the only real advantage to being successful is being able to be heard. "When people say, 'What's it like to be a famous restaurateur?' I always laugh at that and say, 'First of all, you're famous to like a thimble-full of people in a small community.' The real glory is that you have the ability to have your voice heard and have the things that are important to you be heard. That's the only thing that's worthwhile."

That moment when true celebrity status is achieved—when the media is knocking down your door—isn't always what it's cracked up to be. Traci Des Jardins was awarded Rising Star Chef by the James Beard Foundation, Inc., in 1995, an award that is only available to those younger than thirty. This turned out to be an incredibly stressful experience. "I had it in my head that I wanted to win [it]. I'm sort of bashful to admit that it was a goal of mine. I wanted to be in a position by the time I was twenty-eight or twenty-nine where I might be able to achieve it. But winning the award was a lot of pressure. It was wonderful in a lot of ways; but to some extent, I was unprepared for what happened as a result of the award. It put me into a position of seeing huge media exposure. A few weeks after I won, CNN came and did a five-minute profile on me—CNN Headline News running around the world is pretty big media exposure. It has been hard to handle. I don't think anything really prepares a chef for that. Most of us who've gotten into this business haven't been coached on how to be good managers, or how to handle success, or how to handle failure. There isn't really any support system. There are no guides to tell us how to conduct our lives. If we are lucky, we connect with other people in the business and form intimate enough relationships that can give us support and guidance. I was fortunate enough to have that with Elka [Gilmore, mentor and friend]. [She] helped me along and supported me."

Another chef who has received an onslaught of exposure is Barbara Lynch, who was chosen in 1996 as one of *Food and Wine* magazine's top ten chefs of the year. She tells how she has dealt with the sudden glut of media exposure. "The press that I've gained from the award has been challenging! I'm almost suffocated. But I just love food. I love cooking it, I love creating it, and I love the intensity. But I don't like the pressure of the press or the celebrity aspect of it. I never wanted it and I still don't think I want it."

Debra Ponzek has seen many sides of success. Her achievements include being the first female chef to receive three stars in New York City as executive chef of the renowned Montrachet, and then finding success in a gourmet food and catering store. Debra describes the challenge of keeping up with the three-star reputation. "I cook very simply. Our approach was always to cook from simple products and put a twist on them, but make sure the ingredients are recognizable. When you've had public recognition, you feel a responsibility to cook consistently well. That's the thing about having three stars, or four stars, or whatever you have—every night, you must cook really well. Whether you're tired or you're not tired and whoever your clientele, you want to make it special."

Jody Adams uses the press to her advantage. She allows that the key is to keeping it in perspective so that the value outweighs the cost. Jody points to one of the grande dames of cuisine for whom the media has always been kind: "Look at somebody like Julia Child. I think when she started, the media migrated to her because she loved to cook and she loved French food. TV was fun and it was a way of getting a message across. It's clear how much she respects promotion. At first it can be uncomfortable, and you feel self-conscious. But you have to move to a place where you're respecting promotion—respecting it for what it is. People can take it too seriously; they can get caught on a wave that takes them—swish!—out of the kitchen and out of the restaurant. Eventually, that spotlight is going to be gone, and you *have* to be able to get back into your kitchen."

The challenges of success: keeping true to passion and craft, managing and motivating staff, operating a financially viable operation, balancing career and family, and many times juggling the media and press. One of the challenges that rides on the coattails of success is time management: how to balance a vibrant and all-consuming career with the need to reach out to family and friends and find occasional serenity. We'll take up the topic of balance next.

Balancing the Rest of Your Life

We've read about success—what it means, how to achieve it, and some of the pitfalls surrounding it. The final section of this chapter deals with the issues involved in balancing success with the other factors in life. Being successful in this industry requires remarkably hard work, a passion for your craft, and a deep appreciation of food. Achieving any measure of success means you've invested an enormous amount of time and energy. How do you temper your commitment to your work with other facets of life? Some women in this section tell how they have achieved this balance; others admit that striking a balance remains one of their ultimate—yet elusive—goals.

Jamie Eisenberg posits her beliefs: "To have a feeling of being successful, I would need to combine a sense of balance between good mental health, an overall sense of serenity, and the ability to be motivated toward personal and professional goals. Having a good view of where I have been and where I want to go next is vital to achieving a sense of success. I do feel

"Success to me means the ability to do freely and passionately what I love the most; to maintain a balanced life; to raise my sons to be happy productive members of society; and to always work toward attaining my goals."
—Carol Levenherz

1943: American women cultivate "Victory Gardens" in backyards and communal plots, as vegetables become scarce, especially in California.

Women in the Culinary Arena: Barbara Tropp

Barbara's early academic career in Chinese poetry was the catalyst for her passion and interest in Chinese cooking. She was a scholar at Columbia, Yale, and Princeton Universities, and spent two years at the University of Taiwan as a graduate student. Barbara enjoyed the culture of her adopted land: the language, the people, and their attitude toward food. Sharing food, in particular, became a means for communicating. Barbara moved to the West coast and settled in San Francisco in 1978.

The burgeoning food world of the Bay area was wide open at this time, and in 1985, Barbara started her restaurant, China Moon Café. She has written two books, *The Modern Art of Chinese Cooking* and *China Moon Cookbook*. The latter won the Julia Child Award for Best International Cookbook. Additionally, Barbara has supported other women in the restaurant industry—business owners and students, chefs and cooks—by helping found Women Chefs and Restaurateurs (WCR).

Barbara calls the founding of WCR "a mission." She felt that it was important for women nationwide to feel the unique strength of support that the culinarians in San Francisco felt, both professionally and personally. In 1993, Barbara met with eight other influential women and developed a mission statement and a skeletal structure for what would be the largest organization dedicated to educating, supporting, and empowering women chefs and restaurateurs. Through her vision, as founder and past president, she has been able to promote the equitable advancement of women in the restaurant industry into the twenty-first century.

as if I am successful, as I have been working toward a higher level of spiritual values for many years. Without that there can be no mental balance in my life. I feel I have much to contribute as a teacher and mentor, especially for women aspiring to be chefs. I also have much to learn about this industry and how to survive with success."

Barbara Tropp was diagnosed with cancer during the latter part of her career as chef-owner of China Moon Café. It has given her a unique perspective on what's important and what makes her feel successful, an ever-changing concept when one's future is uncertain. "When you're dying, you don't think about your business; you don't think about anything—you only think about the people you love. When you're at the end of the road, that's all that counts. But the people relationships here at China Moon Café have always been the most important to me. If you're a person who believes in a vision, then that's what fires your life. There are many ways in which I failed here. But the one way that I succeeded is that the vision has been powerful enough so that anybody who has worked for me even for a short period of time, gets it! And they carry it with them."

Finding a Balance Between Success and Family

The challenge of balancing career and family is one of the most important issues faced by the women I spoke with. This issue is so prevalent throughout the industry that we will take it up again in chapter eight. The next few stories give some insight into how some have found that balance.

Lidia Bastianich has spent her entire career working with her husband and both of her children. She describes how, for her, balance comes with creating her own space. Her ability to work with and be married to her business partner over many decades gives her credibility when she discusses what works for her in terms of balancing her work and family. She says: "There are certain things you need, your physical space is one. My husband and I come in with two different cars. We don't always eat lunch together; I might leave with my son, or with my friends, or eat by myself. You need the spaces because you're together so much."

Melissa Kelly also works with her partner. In fact, the local newspaper thought their relationship so unique that it did an article on them. Melissa shares her thoughts on balance and working with her boyfriend as her employee. "Balance is a goal—it's always a goal. I like to do a lot of other things besides cooking, but I don't find that it's that easy to do. My house is always in a shambles. I come to work between seven and nine o'clock, and then I get home at midnight. There's not much time. The *Albany Times-Union* just did a story on my boyfriend and me ... working in a restaurant together. In it, we discussed how we never see each other. I work about 100 hours a week; he works about 70 hours a week, and our one day off together is our only shared time. But I dedicated this portion of my life to my career. After another year here, I think things will settle in, where I won't feel so attached, and I won't feel that I have to be here for every single thing. It's just how I work; and hopefully, eventually, I'll feel a little more comfortable taking some time off."

Mary Sue Milliken discusses how bringing a child into the world has helped her achieve more of a balance between work and the rest of her life. She feels that she's working better and smarter to satisfy the time requirements of all parts of her life. "I had Declan in 1990; he's six years old. I've found that you can get just as much done in eight hours as you can in twelve if you're really focused. You have to be organized and focused. I used to use the restaurant as part of my social life, and a lot of cooks do. It's very common. People are drawn into the profession because they come from dysfunctional homes and it's very easy to make your eight-hour day last twelve hours because you're getting

"When I'm home, I'm home. When I'm at work, I'm at work. If you call that balance!"
—*Sara Moulton*

1943: Forty percent of all U.S. vegetables are produced in nearly 20 million "Victory Gardens."

"Success is not what you accomplish but rather how the accomplishments make you a better human being. Don't give up family life and personal rela- tionships for career. You don't have to! Balance and patience are the keys."
—Pam Price

emotional needs satisfied on the job. I don't see that as all bad, necessarily. But I do think that, as an owner, when you're not punching a clock, you can abuse it even more. I think that it's so important to be balanced."

Even though it took a while, Jody Adams found a balance between work and family. She attributes her ability to do this to the support of her husband, who cares for their children and home while she is at work. "I've had support and understanding from the people I've worked with and for. Then I have this balance at home, of somebody who understands the business, understands my need to be involved in it, and really loves food. That's one of the things that brought us together." But the work part is only one side of the balancing act. Jody also talks about her need to be with her family. "Somebody said some-thing about leisure, and I said, 'I don't do leisure.' Leisure is not something that I know how to do very well. Being at home, cooking a meal, playing soc-cer—leisure for me is being with my family. That's what leisure is."

Toniann Beattie has raised and supported her family and—in the midst of all this—she entered the culinary field. Balance for her is easy, she says, because she loves what she does. "I have more balance in my life than I've ever had. I don't have a personal life. But that doesn't bother me, because I didn't have one before. What I do have now is a passion that has been unleashed from my dreams, and that's carried itself into everything I do. That's balance. I am focused on the things that benefit me right now, that are going to benefit my family in the long term—I have more harmony in my life than I've ever known. If I could give everybody a little shot of what's inside of me, this world would be a better place."

Dina Altieri discusses the ways her partner helps her find balance in life. "I have somebody who's really, really calming for me and that's where I'm the happiest. Most chefs are workaholics. We work and we work and we work. I used to do that and I think in the last year, I've found my balance. I have down time, quiet time, reading time, and spare time."

Deborah Huntley has spent much of her career on a path that has taken her through many facets of the industry. It's this time spent in so many seg-ments of the industry that has helped her find a balance between her profes-sional and personal life. "I don't think that there's anything that I really want to do differently. I've balanced my career out very nicely between restaurants, hotels, catering, and markets. I've had a broad sense of everything in the indus-try." In relation to her life outside the industry, she says: "I always try to man-age to make the school plays. It's important that family is at the forefront. It needs to be. I get so excited about food, so excited about what I do, and at the same time, I try to balance, and make time for my daughter, the health club, and other important things."

Corinna Mozo acknowledges the struggle to find the balance between being a successful chef and being a successful life partner. She admits: "I don't think I've quite arrived. I definitely concentrated more on work this year. I was just very apologetic to my husband! 'Honey, it'll just be a few more months!' It's a matter of trusting the people you have working for you. Being able to take *two* full days off; not getting there at ten every morning if I closed up at one the morning before. I think you have to work at least fifty hours a week to get the job done. When you ask questions like this, 'can you manage career and home?' the answer is, 'I have to.' This is a huge part of my life—my husband and everything else is another huge part of my life. They're both equally as important."

For many successful women in the culinary world, a meaningful long-term relationship comes late in life. They just didn't have the time early on. Barbara Tropp shares with us the change that it created in her life. "I met and married an extraordinary man five years ago. I could never have opened a restaurant as a married woman! My God! But I've learned. When my husband came onto the scene, not only was I expected to, but I *wanted* to be home a couple of hours before he went to sleep, never mind a day or two a week! I didn't know how to take a day off. I salute the people who know how to do that. I'm an over-attached person; if the world is one part velcro, then I'm the other part!"

Nora Pouillon is starting to find some balance in her life, even as she takes on more than she had been doing. When I went to visit Nora at her restaurant, I met her daughter, just back from school, who had stopped in for a visit. Nora was on the phone discussing her upcoming book tour. The chef of one of her restaurants was on another phone and she was getting ready for a speaking engagement. For so many chefs, life's a juggling act, but with the help of a good sous chef and the ability to integrate her family into her career, she is finding balance. Nora told me: "The last three years I have been very lucky; I found a chef who really understood what I wanted to do. He has been very good—really into it. He's bright, he understands organics, he understands the kind of food I want to do." Nora went on to say that working with him has given her more freedom, and she has been able to see her family more.

Kathleen Kennedy has been striving to balance her success as an instructor and consultant with her new responsibilities of being a wife and mother. "As an executive chef, I was never able to find any balance, which is why I'm teaching and consulting now." She explains the increased flexibility that her work provides: "That's why I really like the idea of doing smaller projects and being able to pick and choose what you can do. But still, it's back and forth, sometimes I'm balanced, sometimes I'm not." Kathleen goes on to relate a story about when she worked for Charlie Trotter, whose Chicago restaurant has become one of the best known in the country. She recalls that Charlie used to say, "You shouldn't have a telephone, you shouldn't go out to bars at night,

"Instead of looking at balance, I look at 'work hard/play hard; that's my motto. It's a challenge. You do work hard, and you just have to learn how to say, 'OK, now it's time to turn that off and go and play hard.'"

—*Laureen Gauthier*

1943: *The Gastronomical Me* by M. F. K. Fisher is published.

"I feel that I am suc-
cessful, I'm proud of
everything I have
done in my life, and
proud of the way that
I have lived it. And
with each day, I wake
up happy knowing
what I have to do
that day, and I am
open to whatever life
wants to surprise me
with."
—*Noëlle Haddad*

you shouldn't have a life outside of staying home and reading cookbooks!" She doesn't agree. "I have to have balance. I've made choices now, and the choice is if I don't have anything inside, I have nothing to give back."

While finding a balance is difficult for women in this industry, some have been able to find a way to put their priorities in place without feeling that either their work or their families suffered. This balance, however, takes a long time to achieve and for those entering the industry, be forewarned. Some women felt that they needed to wait until later in their lives to become involved in relationships; other women waited until later in their lives to start their culinary careers. There isn't a right or a wrong way to find a balance. These are individual choices each woman has to make for herself.

Finding the Balance Between Success and Personal Life

Some women choose to throw themselves into their work and make that their central focus at some point in their lives. Most of us have done that at one time or another. However, there are other points when we feel that there needs to be more. We need some free time, some space, we need to have fun, see friends, have relationships, travel, listen to music, read books—anything—as long as it is outside of the kitchen. We need a break from the intensity. If we don't have families to go home to or significant others—some outside force that gives us license to tear ourselves away—it is sometimes harder to give ourselves permission to have a life. In this section, we'll hear from women who are confronted with this issue.

Sharon Brooks-Moses raises an issue that has vexed me and most other chefs—finding the time to exercise. When working in an industry as stressful and as physically draining as foodservice, it's doubly important to integrate exercise into one's regimen. Sharon states: "I always tell my students to have a workout plan. Whether it's walking, aerobics, or something, because this is a highly stressful business. Find a way to get rid of the stress before you develop things like cancer or diabetes."

Dorothy Hamilton, president of The French Culinary Institute, talks about what she had to do to achieve balance as a professional with an all-consuming career. "I resigned from all my boards, and I just cut out volunteer work. I now have an almost-normal life. The challenge of balancing one's personal life in this crazy business is probably the biggest challenge that we have—how to be a woman, a happy woman, with a balanced life in a profession that demands only the best, and demands everything from you. But it's one of those professions, that once you're in, you can't leave—it's almost an addiction."

Part of the persona of the chef gets wrapped up in logging marathon hours and exhibiting superhuman endurance. According to Emily Luchetti, it just doesn't need to be that way. She says there's this thinking that, "If you're not there, then you're not doing your job. The number of hours you are in the kitchen becomes a measure of what you deliver, what you produce. That's ridiculous, even comical. I've seen chefs just standing around with their arms crossed, not working for two hours. Why not work really hard while you're there and then leave. Go home for two hours, rent a movie, go for a bike ride, something! I believe in working hard, but at the same time, you have to have a life."

Mary Cech believes you need to separate your personal and professional life, but that it's up to the individual to find what works best. "I try to really separate my professional and personal life, and that makes a big difference—a *huge* difference. You have to have that separation. My personal time is my personal time; it regenerates me. No one's going to change anything for you; it's up to you. I need balance in my life, because I'm forty years old, and it's time!" Mary talks about the hold the culinary field has on people. "It's an addiction. You have a day off, and you don't know what to do—you're *not* balanced! There's a time, there's a place to make peace with yourself. Otherwise, burnout kicks in. It's a huge problem in our field. We are striving to be human beings, to balance our lives and make it work for us."

Cindy Salvato discusses the particular challenges that face food establishment owners who are seeking balance. "The hard part of being an entrepreneur is that you just don't know where one thing begins and another ends. Last year, when I was baking full-time, and teaching full-time, I took every Tuesday off. I would go out to dinner, sleep, or just watch a movie. Sunday mornings are always great—I have church, I hang out, relax, laugh, and then come home and do a little work for school." Cindy says that now that she has her own business, it's harder to take the time and find the balance. Especially for owners of small businesses, there's always just one more thing to do.

Susan Feniger says she needs "alone time" to help her achieve balance. "I need time when I feel like I don't have any commitments. I have a very difficult time committing to anything on my days off or on vacations. I start to feel overwhelmed when I have too many social commitments. I get overwhelmed when I don't have enough time to myself. I get up at six in the morning, go to the ocean, take a walk. It's amazingly relaxing to me. There's a different freedom there that gives me this whole sense of peacefulness."

One of the issues that surfaced continually in my discussions with women chefs and cooks was having an identity outside of being a chef. I know from my own experience that it can be difficult to find a balance between the persona of the chef and the person beneath. Susan Regis shares her thoughts: "Being a

"Success is knowing that I have reached my goals while keeping an open mind; to keep learning, seeing, and hearing what's happening, being able to teach and guide other cooks. I feel that I am successful."

—Suzanne Bussiere

1944: Less than one-fourth of Americans have "good" diets, according to a nutrition study begun in 1941.

Women in the Culinary Arena: Anne Rosenzweig

Like an ancient bronze that has hidden highlights, the rich patina of success is often subtle and needs to be sought out in the people who most seem to embody it in their lives. Success manifests itself in different ways: a strong marriage; sharp business acumen; a concern and an interest in one's community. Apparent in a healthy family that generates good will or in an ability to pursue a personal passion without risking the loss of everything else in one's life, achievement has many different measures. Anne Rosenzweig has accomplished all of these things in her culinary endeavors.

Anne's academic training in anthropology at Columbia University belies her passion for food, which became evident while she was participating in fieldwork in India, Africa, and Nepal. When she returned to New York, Anne wanted to prove her theory that there was a magical and secret world in the professional kitchen and she volunteered to apprentice for no pay. In professional kitchens, Anne found more than secrets—she found passion for a lifestyle that was fast, challenging, and rewarding. After a year of apprenticing, Anne moved to Vanessa in Greenwich Village in 1981, where she honed her skills and progressed to head chef. She was a freelance consultant and opened Arcadia, her first restaurant, in 1985 as chef and co-owner.

Anne accepted the additional responsibility of the "21" Club in 1987, and until 1991, she was responsible for restructuring the kitchen facilities, menus, and special wine and food programs. In 1993, Anne was selected to serve on the Kitchen Cabinet, a panel of three chefs who advise the President and First Lady on menus and American food. In 1995, she opened her second New York restaurant, The Lobster Club.

Anne's dedication to her community and to philanthropic events is commendable. In 1994, she was one of four chefs who participated in a venture to Israel called Women Chefs for Peace. She was instrumental in creating the Fresh Start Program, which works with inmates at Riker's Island correctional facility. She is also a founding member of the Women Chefs and Restaurateurs (WCR) in addition to being a national board member of Mothers and Others.

Despite Anne's multifaceted commitments, she has found the time to incorporate a family into her life. Her husband and her daughter Lily are both important components of Anne's overall sense of success.

chef does take up a lot of who you are. I have to have a life—one that's mine and not the restaurant's. I think on your deathbed, you don't say, 'Oh God, I wish I could make one more bowl of risotto for a customer;' you say, 'I wish I had time to enjoy my family.'"

Judi Arnold wants to be able to let go, turn off, and enjoy time outside of her business. "Work does consume me—it is my passion, my life. However, I am able to turn it off. I am able to go home. I love to read books and I can just totally get into whatever I'm reading or whatever my life is outside of work. I think that's my saving grace."

When Pat Bartholomew and I spoke about success and balance, she had these insights to share: "The largest single issue is how to balance life and career. There are people who do it; clearly, it can be done. Anne Rosenzweig has done it, Alice Waters has done it, but they are unique. There are a growing number of female executive chefs in hotels who can do it: Susan Weaver, Pat Williams. But many women don't have children. If they're married, they're married without children. There's something wrong with this picture. Why do women have to make that choice? Men don't have to. Perhaps the bigger issue is that the industry is so time-consumptive. It is incredibly demanding in that way. If you ever sat down and figured out what you earned per hour, you'd be so disgusted with your job."

There are no easy answers to Pat's question, "Why don't men have to make this choice?" For now, they don't and women do, so we need to be able to figure out how. We have seen some women who are able to find the balance. The first step is recognizing the need for a life outside the kitchen. This realization, plus the ability to do something about it makes them more content at and outside of work.

Balancing Success and Priorities on the Job

So far, we have heard from women who try to find the balance between their chef lives and their personal lives. For other women, however, their life is their work. For them, the challenge is to learn to balance their work priorities so that they have outlets within the culinary field.

Loretta Keller, chef-owner of Bizou, loves what she does and equates her balance and happiness in life to how she balances her priorities at work. "I have balance in that I really like what I do. I just do too much of it. I really love my work. There are difficult parts, tedious parts, and there are trying parts. But the big picture is the cooking, and I really enjoy it. I find sanctuary in the cooking. When I find that the balance is lost—when I'm going crazy because of too much promotional work, or administrative details, or dealing with people and problems—I'll write myself in on the cooking schedule a lot more. I find refuge in cooking. It is instantly rejuvenating and inspiring."

Like Loretta Keller, Sarah Stegner finds it's the kitchen that restores her balance. "I do a lot of cooking—it's a good release. You need to mix that into your day. There are times when you need to peel a bag of shallots or make the soup yourself. That creativity for me is a good outlet. I've found a nice balance where I have those things. I have enough time planned in my day where I am cooking. That *is* my outlet—that is my driving force."

Raji Jallepalli talks about balancing the happiness in her life and her work. Raji describes her busy schedule: "I work a lot. I come and go all day long since

"I'm happy when I have lots of little successes in a given day and try to savor each of them ... a dish, a happy client, a cook who shows improvement. If I focused on success, I'd probably get discouraged ... too many ongoing, ever-demanding restaurant traumas to imagine that."
—*Judy Rodgers*

1945: Mme. Elisabeth Brassard reopens L'Ecole de Cordon Bleu in Paris.

"We get all caught up, and it's only food; it's meant to nourish and nurture and promote life. There's a contradiction in what we do to ourselves—the exquisite torture of creating."

—*Traci Des Jardins*

we're only open for dinner. I do business in the morning; in the early afternoon I go home and take a nap and a shower and then I feel very refreshed. When I come back to work, I avoid business at all costs because I feel like that will influence my food. Any other business has to wait until the next morning. I owe that to my guest. I work hard, I play hard, I'm single, and I don't have any small children at home; this schedule gives me so much zest for life. I read a book that said happiness isn't something that's around the corner or over the curb; it's not something out there—it's here and now. [That's] the way I feel about it. My goal is to keep improving on what I have. I probably won't die wealthy, but if wealth is measured on happiness, I'm probably the wealthiest woman in the world. I'm very very happy."

As a chef, you're constantly bombarded with questions: "What do you think? What do you want? How do you want it to taste? How do you want the menu to look? What items do you want to order today? Who do you want to hire?" Everything is coming at you—it can deplete your inner resources.

Sarah Stegner speaks about the need to buffer the inner spirit so that there's something left to give to your work. "I pick and choose carefully what I want to put my energies toward. I don't say yes to everything—I say yes to the things that I think are important to the restaurant, important to me. You have to be smart and remember, if you are burned out and exhausted, you're never going to give 100 percent. To come to a restaurant or business and say, 'I'm going to give it my all, you have to have something to give.'"

We've now heard from numerous women about the importance of balance. They've told us how they have managed to find a way to balance their careers and family; they've shown us that while they are completely committed to their work, they also need to have a life that is separate from work in order to feel "in balance." Finally, we heard from those whose work is their lives, and their quest for balance lies in learning how to prioritize their responsibilities so that they'll have the time to do what they love most—cook. These women have found ways to strike a comfortable balance. However, what we haven't heard about is, "What happens when balance can't be achieved?" Some answers to that question are in the following stories.

When Balance Cannot Be Achieved

Not all women cooks and chefs are able to find balance in their lives. For some, work becomes an obsession from which they aren't able to extricate themselves. The passion, the obsession become the addiction—the rush of service, the instant gratification of providing the guests with great meals, the creativity, nurturing, and food, all feed the passion. All the while these chefs and cooks are coping with the stress, staff, family, purveyors, budgets, and managing their restaurant's needs. While some can accept this as their way of life, others want desperately to find a way to strike some balance.

This is a problem for Joyce Goldstein. She considers herself obsessed with food and cooking. "There is something about food and the business that is so addictive, you can't let it go! It's with you all the time. Between the cooking, the cookbooks, the kitchen equipment, the researching, the traveling to learn—it takes over your life and all of a sudden you haven't been with friends in six months. I feel guilty going to buy a pair of shoes because I'm wasting time! Yes, I'm out of balance. I don't know how to teach balance. I am not a balanced person." This isn't the way Joyce wants her life to be. "My personal goal would be to have a balanced life. The impossible dream! To work four to five days a week, like a normal person, and have two days where I don't feel guilty if I go to a movie or hang out with a friend. I would have time to find a friend—to make friends! I'd like to have time to read a book and not feel guilty. I'd like to have time to travel, actually learn what it is to relax and not think that I should be looking at every food product that's crossing my path while I'm there! I'd like to have time to go out on a date and let people know that I was available. I'd like to see if I could lead a balanced life!"

Rick O'Connell has been in this industry more years than most of us. Her children have grown and she now has grandchildren as well. Nonetheless, she says she's no closer to the attainment of balance than much younger members of the profession. Rick explains: "Balance—I'm having a little trouble with that now. I think that's partly the kind of person I am. Balance is something I've never quite understood and sometimes I'm distressed with how I live my life. I can't do things half-measure. I'm totally immersed in what I do. I guess I just don't understand balance, and I have less guilt about it than I used to."

Monique Barbeau also describes herself as obsessed with her work. Like Joyce and others, she believes this is one of the hazards of the business. "Sometimes, in this business, we can't enjoy life enough. Only when you get sick, or something happens in your family, do you ask, 'Well what's it all about?' Can I wake up when I'm sixty and be happy with all the things that I did, besides making food? I don't know. I think if I died tomorrow, I would regret a few things. I would regret not spending enough time with my sisters and brothers, and not spending time with my boyfriend. I want to be able to be happy, to have balance in my life, but this job is overwhelming."

As Monique, Joyce, and others have lamented, the workaholic chef's lifestyle becomes a habit and a badge of honor. It takes confidence, self-awareness, and motivation to be able to find some kind of a balance. Alison Awerbuch acknowledges this problem: "When I first started out at the CIA, I devoted 150 percent of my energy to work, and I loved every bit of it, so it was never even an issue with me. That's what I wanted to do. And after a period of

"My personal goal is serenity. To just be able to walk into an environment, make right decisions, and feel at peace with them. [To have] mental balance and to be able to have fun—that's it."
—*Jamie Eisenberg*

1945: U.S. women lose their jobs as men return from the war and reclaim the positions they left when they joined the service.

*"I've seen talented
young women leave
the industry because
they just don't see any
way to be both a ded-
icated employee and
a good mother.
Women have a lot to
offer the industry,
but we just need a
little help."*
—Cathy Bean

time, it's all I knew how to do. There just never seemed to be enough hours in the day. Up until about two years ago, I would probably work an average of eighty to ninety hours per week. I took an awful lot of work home—I'd be doing my administrative work at night at home. I never really thought about my personal life. I probably didn't meet many new people in my life who were outside of the business. I didn't have time for that. I'm single, I haven't been married, I haven't really been involved in a relationship in quite some time. For awhile, I chalked that up to the amount I was working and the lack of time I was devoting to my personal life." Alison says that she's really trying to find balance, that she really wants to have a life, and that she thinks that she's final-ly at the point in her career when she can have one.

From Noëlle Haddad's perspective, balance is all about having a life that includes others. This section closes with her thoughts because they are senti-ments that I believe are at the heart and soul of the issue of balance: "There are a lot of people who are workaholics; and maybe they are happy, but I don't think a stable person can have just one focus in life. Everybody was made to be diverse and have life filled with love, work, joy, and sorrow. You need to have feelings to share. While cooking is one of the careers that lets you give the most, it's not the same; you need feedback. You can't just give and give and give. Everyone needs to receive at some point. Maybe you're going to get a great review of your restaurant, but there's nobody there to hug you when you need it, or somebody *you* can hug. You need more stability than just being great in a job. You get home, and what do you have there? Emptiness. I used to feel guilty about being lazy after I worked a thirteen-hour day!! Then I real-ized it's not about being lazy, it's just normal to have a little time for yourself. It's normal to have a minute to sit down and think about nothing. It's healthy to have a minute to clear your mind; everyone needs it."

These stories help define the meaning of success for many women chefs by discussing the means to success, the unanticipated challenges that success can bring, and the need for balancing that success with the rest of one's life. Once success is attained and some semblance of balance is maintained, then there may be time for goals for the future. The next chapter discusses the goals and responsibilities that successful women chefs share for the future.

CHAPTER SEVEN

Women Chefs

Our Goals and Responsibilities

"If you're passionate about food, you have to be able to share it."
—Siobhan Carew

We have heard the reasons why women enter the culinary profession, the choices they make, challenges they encounter along the way, and how they perceive
success. In this chapter, women describe their goals and responsibilities based
on their experiences. They also discuss ways in which they can serve as mentors, and the role of culinary organizations where women can find mentors.
Finally, we hear about ways in which women have used their craft to benefit the
greater good of their communities.

Goals for the Future

Throughout this book, we've seen that women are just beginning to enter the
upper echelons of the industry. One of the goals for kitchens of the future
needs to be parity in position and pay at the highest ranks. But this is just the
beginning. The last two chapters show that women have some very difficult
choices to make in order to be able to continue in the industry. At times, it
comes down to choosing between work and family or relationships. Why
should this be the case? Why is it that women are the ones having to do the
majority of the juggling in order to make room for the many aspects of their
lives? This chapter suggests ways in which the industry needs to change in
order to accommodate the growing number of women in kitchens, and it
examines what has been done thus far. In addition, this chapter looks at ways
in which women have risen above and beyond their responsibilities in the
kitchen in order to lend their talents to their communities.

The foodservice industry needs to become more family-friendly. This
means that it needs to be able to provide more options that allow women to
be able to choose to maintain their careers while they raise a family. The NRA
Compensation for Salaried Personnel in Foodservice studies the benefits given to
salaried employees. The findings of this 1995 report represent over 12,000
foodservice facilities with more than 26,000 salaried workers. It shows that
eighty percent of full-service establishments offer insurance; approximately half
of those employers share the cost with the employee. According to this study,
the smaller the company, the less likely it is to provide insurance. Most companies provide minimal family benefits.

In 1995, another NRA study, *Business Culture's Impact on Restaurant
Performance,* found the results shown in the accompanying table. This study
highlights benefits to salaried employees, yet the majority of those in the
foodservice industry are hourly employees. Very few if any companies offer
benefits of any kind to hourly employees. Among benefits, both sick days
and most maternity leave are unpaid. Essentially what this means is that if
you are sick or take time off to have a baby, you won't lose your job, but
neither will you be paid for your time. Bottom line here: our industry has a

long way to go before it can be considered family-friendly, let alone employee-friendly.

1995 NRA Business Culture's Impact on Restaurant Performance	
Benefits Offered to Salaried Employees	Percentage of Companies offering Benefits
Job-sharing	14%
Compressed work weeks	21%
Dependent care	6%
Paid maternity leave	26%
Unpaid maternity leave (usually 6 weeks)	84%
Unpaid sick leave	78%
Flexible scheduling	77%
Pension Plans	9%
401K	17%

"I think that women make good managers because we think about other people more than men think about other people. Being a manager has a lot to do with ... putting yourself in [a staff member's] position, imagining their intentions, goals, and their reason for doing things."
—*Loretta Keller*

While the majority of foodservice companies are not as progressive as other industries regarding "family orientation," some role models can be held up as examples of where we need to go in the future. In 1996, Milton Moskowitz and Carol Townsend published their tenth anniversary edition study, *The 100 Best Companies for Working Mothers.* Although this study was not exclusive to the foodservice industry, the results included a few food-oriented companies. This study is important as it shows how companies outside the food industry have made tremendous strides over the past ten years in their effort to accommodate working mothers and women in the workplace. Over seventy-five percent of the companies on the list offer childcare, and many are beginning to offer before- and after-school care, summer programs, and holiday care.

The study found that the following foodservice companies offer ways in which to accommodate women and families: Ben & Jerry's, Marriott International, Sara Lee Corporation, and Wegman's Food Markets. The following is a synopsis of these companies' plans, showing how they are working toward becoming more family-oriented and offering more equality for women.

Ben & Jerry's is a premium ice cream manufacturer in Vermont. Women comprise up to forty-one percent of the work force at Ben & Jerry's and hold forty-seven percent of the highest paid jobs. They have on-site daycare, paid maternity and paternity leave, adoption aid, flextime, compressed workweeks,

1946: The Culinary Institute of America opens in Hartford, Connecticut for men returning from the war to find vocational training.

"When women have the chance to perform, they frequently do better than men. They're able to focus more directly, stick with it; in spite of being discouraged on a particular project, they can work until they drop! I think women simply just have not had the chance to really prove that over the years."
—*Dell Hargis*

part-time benefits, profit sharing, and fully paid health insurance. At Sara Lee Corporation, a working mother is employed as chief financial officer. This multinational food and service products company has limited child care and sick days, but it is one of the few large corporations to tie manager bonuses to their success in advancing women. Wegman's Food Markets also have many family-oriented programs similar to these, but they have a few unique situations as well. They are in the process of setting up a system in which employees can opt for four-day workweeks, schedules that dovetail with school hours, and even four-hour days mixed in with eight-hour days.

Marriott International has a number of foodservice divisions within its multinational holdings. Among the benefits they offer are childcare facilities at their corporate offices and at a number of their other locations. They also have after-school programs, paid sick-child days, paid childbirth leave, adoption aid, job-sharing, flextime, part-time benefits, and elder care. Marriott has joined forces with a number of other hospitality companies to open a new concept called the Children's Inn in Atlanta. This twenty-four-hour-a-day, seven-days-a-week facility is slated to open in 1997 to provide childcare for lower-income employees. The inn will also have a "get-well" section and will serve as a family resources center. Marriott runs a mentoring program for women, and in 1995, it hosted a symposium on work and family issues for 300 female managers.

As we move forward into the next century, we must develop better models for the foodservice industry. The four companies just mentioned are outstanding examples of what can be done to accommodate women and families; however, realistically, those benefits may be more than a small company can provide. When companies begin making these family-oriented management decisions, they will find that their retention rate will increase. Just by making family a priority, companies will help women have a personal life as well as a fulfilling career.

Women's Perspectives on Goals for the Workplace

It is the goal of many women in the culinary arena to change the "work" model. As discussed earlier, all workers deserve a more balanced, happier, and healthier lifestyle. Benefits such as health insurance, flextime, job-sharing, and access to daycare aid in fostering a better lifestyle for all. While such accommodations may not be soon in coming, the fact that they are under consideration by more and more companies is a step in the right direction. In this section, we hear from those who feel that something needs to be done to help them balance their families and their work life.

Ferdinand Metz, president of The Culinary Institute of America, shares his thoughts on the future of our industry, and what he feels needs to be done in order for the industry as a whole to be more family-oriented. "The industry will face a continued shortage of skilled people that will come into the industry. Conditions today are infinitely better [than ever before]; that will continue, whether it's in the work environment, or the social benefits being offered, or the acceptance of women in the field—which also means that the cost of labor in our field will be higher. That will be a cost that continues to increase, because you cannot have a fairly attractive profession that people want to build their careers on, and at the same time not offer benefits that are commensurate with any operation or any other industry. Our industry has been notorious for providing just the basic benefits, but that's changing now. I think [the] bottom line is that there's going to be more competition for the dedicated, skilled people, and part of that competing is to make the work environment [and benefits] more commensurate with other professions."

As an employer, Judi Arnold struggles with the challenges of the expense of childcare and healthcare costs. "We hire women—we naturally gravitate to them—and so there have been a lot of childcare situations. We hire a lot of inner-city women, and a lot of them are single mothers; they have a big problem, and I would love it if we could have a large enough place to make a little childcare center. Unfortunately, we can't do that, so all we can do now is give them healthcare benefits and time off when they need it."

One of Nancy Oakes' priorities when she opened Boulevard was that she would be able to offer health insurance to all her employees. For Nancy, dealing with the finances of the business has been a challenge; she describes thinking about the numbers as they relate to healthcare costs. "This is the first time I've had to look at numbers and at least consider them as part of decision making. I've had to think about what is an appropriate amount of profit and how it is affected by the cost of supplying insurance to all the staff—a thing that I could never do in a small business." At Boulevard, Nancy provides insurance for all of her staff and has found a way to balance profitability with the needs of her employees.

What about benefits for those leaving the industry? In other industries, many companies offer pension plans, 401K plans, and other retirement options. According to the NRA study, *Business Culture's Impact on Restaurant Performance,* less than nine percent of foodservice venues offer pension plans for their salaried employees, and less than seventeen percent offer 401K plans. The problem is twofold; after devoting all of their time and energy to their positions within the industry, what are the fiscal and personal challenges employees face when it's time to retire?

"I know that we give our staff forty hours a week (to work), so they have a very nice life in terms of what goes on in the industry. Nobody here is working eighty hours a week. We're always putting in a tremendous amount of hours, but we're the owners. I don't want to kill my employees—what good does that do?"
—*Johanne Killeen*

1946: Walnut Acres Organic Farms has its beginnings in Pennsylvania.

Phyllis Flaherty feels that an industry goal needs to be that of helping the many women who are aging in the industry to find their next step, their next place in this ever-changing arena. "I think we're [women in this industry] going to go through an identity crisis, because we work so hard, our life is our job, and we've spent our whole life, the last 20, 25, 30 years, looking at: What's the next step? All of a sudden, there isn't going to be a next step! I think we're going to find another cause that gives us that fulfillment that we can put our time into, that's rewarding. It may not even be in foodservice."

Goals for Our Food

The previous chapters have explored the passions that many women share for food and the land. With all the genetic engineering that is being used to preserve foods, and the loss of seasonality of food through biotechnology, many chefs and cooks are committed to doing all they can to use natural, organically grown food. The next section discusses the goals and responsibilities necessary to preserve the land for the future.

Chefs Collaborative 2000

In 1993, Chefs Collaborative 2000 (CC2000) was created by a group of impassioned chefs concerned about the future of our world's food sources. The goals of these women and men were to help to promote sustainable food choices. CC2000 was established in conjunction with Oldways Preservation and Exchange Trust, an organization dedicated to the preservation of healthy, environmentally sustainable food and the agricultural traditions of many cultures. The CC2000 chefs combined forces to help promote an awareness of the impact of food choices on the public health, the vitality of cultures, and on the integrity of the global environment.

The individuals who created CC2000 established a charter (see Appendix G) that proclaimed their commitment to promoting learning environments for children, strengthening the farmer-chef connection, and providing safe and wholesome foods by emphasizing locally grown, seasonally fresh, and minimally processed food in their restaurants. Today, over 1,000 chefs are involved in this initiative, and it is strong and growing each year. The Chefs Collaborative includes some of the nation's most influential chefs and restaurateurs. Chefs, farmers, and teachers dedicated to the advancement of sustainable agriculture, educating for the future, and creating new "center of the plate" items that increase plant foods in our nation's diet—these are the ideas that are moving our industry positively into the twenty-first century.

Susan Regis, chef of BIBA in Boston, believes that as the world grows smaller and more accessible, there is more of a need to set goals that foster a respect for food and culture. "Our responsibility as chefs is about [helping] cooks to have respect for the cultures they try and emulate. It's about pro-

Native Americans in the agricultural fields, near Cornplanter, Pennsylvania, circa 1850–1880. Cornplanter is named after the noted Seneca Indian chief, Cornplanter (1736–1836). Courtesy of the Culinary Archives and Museum at Johnson and Wales University.

duce, organic farms, and the Chefs Collaborative—developing and appreciating what we have locally."

The Old Chatham Shepherding Company Inn, in upstate New York, raises much of their own products. Executive Chef Melissa Kelly, like Susan, feels strongly that we must have respect for our food supplies and sources. "My hope would be that we get back to a situation where people really are concerned with the products. When I first started cooking, I had no idea what went into the food. It was taking something out of a package, putting it on a grill, and putting it on a plate. There's so much that goes into it, and I think that cooking is a whole cycle, a whole chain. We decided [at the inn] to get pigs, because we wanted to recycle the food waste and then, on our pig compost pile, we grew these beautiful little heirloom tomatoes and pumpkins, and I said, 'We went total full-circle there!' To me, that's so amazing."

Melissa speaks of an issue that has many broad ramifications—that is, the need for immediate gratification, which has become so ingrained in the way Americans do everything today. By having these expectations, we go against the natural course of the food cycle, and we have lost much of the belief in the seasonality of products. Melissa says, "Tomatoes, strawberries, and raspberries in the winter have all too often become the norm. What I really appreciate in Europe is the small towns, with their bakery, butcher shop, patisserie, coffeeshop, bar, restaurant, and wine store. The wine comes from the region right

"I believe that we have to take care of this earth, we have to have sustainable agriculture, and we have to have sustainable communities. I think it's imperative, if you have a philosophy and knowledge, that you share that. What better way of sharing than being an instructor, being a teacher."

—Eve Felder

1949: General Mills and Pillsbury introduce prepared cake mixes.

"I tend to really get involved with my employees: I want to make sure that they are comfortable, that they have a good situation, are happy, motivated, and challenged, and that they're learning."
—*Melissa Kelly*

there, and the cheese is local—and you know, why do we have to have everything all the time? My hope is people will start to understand that."

Alice Waters has dedicated much of her career to promoting many of the same principles that are promoted by CC2000. Her goal: "By the year 2000, we will all buy from people who are taking care of the land. We will all buy organically grown produce!" As for her own practices, she says, "I'm going to shift [my buying] away from the anonymous people out there who are doing things that are destroying the natural resources—poisoning us, quite honestly. I think people have to learn how to farm, appreciate what it is to do that, what it is to have real food; I think the only way to do that is to put yourself in the farmer's shoes. That has to be part of educating children, [something] that they learn about, and maybe [then] we'll regain our palates as a nation!"

Many of the women in this book are involved with CC2000 and other community-based sustainable food projects. Alice Waters, Edna Lewis, Deborah Madison, Nora Pouillon, Odessa Piper, Mary Sue Milliken, Susan Feniger, Ana Sortun, Jamie Eisenberg, and many others believe that making sustainable food choices is one of the most important goals that we can set for our future, our children's future, and the future of the planet. Between these women and others involved with CC2000 who are working to promote local produce and natural resources, there is a better chance that by the year 2000, America will have developed a conscience and an appreciation for natural foods and work toward supporting sustainable agriculture. It is the goal to pass on this ideal to the young people entering the profession. It will then be up to them to help promote the changes necessary for a better future.

Many chefs have made it part of their life's work to save the land. Many of the chefs in this book are members of CC2000. In the Northeast, Jamie Eisenberg has become very active in using and teaching sustainable agriculture and sustainable food choices at NECI. "[I'm] networking like crazy in all different areas—the Northeast Organic Farming Association (NOFA), the Food Shed Coalition, and CC2000. It seems like every time I turn around, somebody's asking me to be on a committee, but I think that [this is] where I need to be, because I can make a difference. I think it's cutting edge because it's the trend of the future. It's where our industry needs to go in order to be responsible—it's totally turning back the clock! I think the best thing that I have to offer is that 120 students pass through my brain every year. I can affect each one of them, and their attitudes about buying and menu making. It [all] starts from the menu; if you don't put something on the menu, or you put on a regional product from outside of your region, it's like a snowball effect, and all the repercussions come to bear. Whether it's fuel consumption, food cost, or quality, those are the kinds of things I can tell my students in my own curriculum. I stress why it's important to stay within our region and to stay within our season. It supports the community and shows how we can have a relationship with the people that provide our food, like our grandparents used to. I think it's our job, as educators, to get students to a point where they start going out and making a difference in their own communities."

Deborah Madison is another woman who feels strongly about teaching people about food choices. For Deborah, the values perpetuated by the CC2000 are the values that have guided how she has been cooking and living for a long time. She told me, "[They] have always been a part of what I've taught, so I've never tried to formulate it any differently. I do farmer's market classes and often bring things with me that are from my own farmer's market. [I try] to help people see that there's something else besides limited choices and that if they keep their eyes open, they may find them in their own communities. I feel really strongly about eating foods in their season, and that means supporting your farmer's market. It means supporting agriculture in your community, or your state, your region, however you define it. I guess that's what I would call my philanthropy."

> *"For me, [being a mentor] just means that I try to be encouraging and an inspiration—not so much my personal method of how I do everything, but just the fact that you can get to where you want to go."*
> —Susan Spicer

What It Means to Be a Mentor

Many women welcome the opportunity to serve as a mentor or to help others find a mentor. As we saw in chapter three, mentors can influence someone's career and help young professionals find their strengths, overcome their weaknesses, and acquire vast amounts of knowledge. This section highlights women who are mentors, have been mentors, or who believe that mentoring is an invaluable experience for those entering the field.

Alison Awerbuch offers some advice about how to find a mentor, stressing how much women want to help other women who are entering the industry. "I would start by doing a little research as to who [the] female chefs are in the area. Call a local chef's association and find out if there are any women in the chapter; call a culinary school and find out if there are any alumna in the area. You'd be surprised how open and willing female chefs are to help other women in the industry. Most people I know, including myself, are more than happy [to help], and really enjoy it. That's something I *love* doing—[don't] be afraid to make the contact or the call."

While being a mentor can be a difficult and consuming task, it is one that many women feel is their responsibility; many of these women have been helped and/or mentored by others and see it as an opportunity to give something back. Jody Adams describes her role as mentor: "The responsibility [of

1950: Pillsbury inaugurates its first "Bake-Off" to develop recipes using its flour; both men and women are eligible to compete.

"I am proud of what I've done, and that pride has given me a sense of confidence and courage, a realization that I can make a difference. I owe that to my career more than to anything else; I didn't have that before."
—*Sarah Stegner*

being a mentor/role model] is the same responsibility I have being chef to my staff. It's integrity, being true to what I'm doing, and staying really close to the kitchen. At the same time, I have a responsibility as a woman. I have the responsibility to stand up for what's right—that continues to be my responsibility as a woman." Many other women share Jody's sense of responsibility.

Hilary DeMane has taught many of the young cooks that I have had the pleasure of working with professionally. She takes this responsibility seriously and says she wants to act as a role model to both women and men. "The important thing about teaching is to be a role model for the women who come in; that does mean a lot to me. I think they can see someone competent, someone successful, someone who is strong, focused, passionate—not just a woman. Maybe it's just as important, if not more important, to be that model for the men who come in, so they can see something they've possibly never seen before."

Anne Rosenzweig sees her position as role model as a duty that's truly important, and many women seek her out as a mentor. She explains: "I regard being a [mentor/role model] as a very big responsibility. One of the things I do is not only take all these students, [but also] people appearing at the doorstep. Some of my best employees have [been] people who have written letters and asked for advice, or appeared at the front door and said, 'I've got this burning passion; what do I do? Can I come and work for you? I'll do anything.' I've started a lot of people that way who have gone on to open their own places all over the country, and I think that's important. There's not a lot of places you can do that."

Kerry Heffernan has been both the recipient of mentoring and a mentor herself. Her advice is similar to Alison Awerbuch's: "Seek out women chefs, and ask them to mentor you. I mentor the women that work for me. I bring them to WCR [meetings]. I talk to people about what it's like [being a chef], and I think that is a requirement—it's giving back to your community; it's not an option. It's a requirement—you need to do it." Kerry goes on to add a little advice to women: "Balance your life; don't just be a cook, get out there. Read, eat, go to other restaurants, and volunteer to work in other people's kitchens so that you can see what they're doing. And pace yourself. ... It's a *really* long career—don't let yourself get too tired."

Sharon Waynes is an apprentice working and learning under the tutelage of Kerry Heffernan. Sharon presents the other side of the mentoring relationship. "I have met the most wonderful women throughout my life, very strong-willed women. I met Chef Kerry (Heffernan), and she's taken her time with me. She's so knowledgeable and so willing to share what she knows with me. I see that caring in her; she stops to talk to me, takes time out, and says, 'You're great; you're doing good, hang in there.' I've decided that I'm going to keep her around for a long time!"

Women in the Culinary Arena: Barbara Sanders

For most of us, lifelong learning is an aspiration—the means to fulfilling that goal is an individual pursuit. Barbara Sanders, chef and culinary educator, has made learning and teaching her mission.

Barbara grew up in New Hampshire and learned bread baking from her father, who ran a successful business first out of the back of a truck and then in Hanover, New Hampshire. She spent summers working at a resort across the lake from her childhood home and practiced her culinary skills in the kitchen before moving to the front of the house and managing the dining room. All the time, she was saving money for college at Keene State. She matriculated in 1952 and earned her degree in Home Economics by 1956.

After graduating from college, Barbara moved to Illinois and became involved in the social services. In this capacity, she was instrumental in changing the dietary habits of the children in a small corner of her new state. This motivated her to learn more about what she could do for her community. While raising two children with her husband, Barbara enrolled in the master's degree program at the Southern Illinois University at Carbondale. She participated in the program for dieticians and decided that she wanted to explore a practical application for her new degree: Nutrition with a minor in Rehabilitation. She started to work as an instructor for visually impaired individuals who lived independently. Her book, *A Cookbook Mate for the Blind and the Sighted,* was published in 1984, six years after her graduation.

Barbara and her family returned to the Granite State in 1976, and she began teaching at the White Mountains Regional High School. She progressed to Department Chairperson and taught culinary arts for twenty years, instilling knowledge, pride, responsibility, and passion in countless numbers of students. (Chef Sanders found time between teaching classes in 1988 to win a Gold Medal in the AAU Senior Women's National Luge Competition!) Barbara enrolled in many supplemental classes at Johnson and Wales University and earned her American Culinary Federation CCE accreditation in 1993. Honored with 'Chef of the Year' in 1993 by the New Hampshire Chapter of the ACF, she was chosen as the 'Premier Chef of the Year' by the American Dairy Council in 1994.

In 1993, Barbara was involved with the 'World's Cooks Tour,' for which she traveled to South Africa with thirty other chefs and cooked in Johannesburg for nine days. This was the beginning of her involvement with the ACF arm, the Chef and the Child Foundation, a philanthropic branch that aids in the education and nutrition of youth nationally.

Barbara retired from her position as chef-instructor in 1996, but that was not the end of her commitment to education and philanthropy. Barbara divides her time between writing, philanthropy, running her farm, and spending time with her family. Her advice to young people today? "Put your brain to work, and go for it!"

1950: General Mills introduces Minute Rice.

Toniann Beattie is new to the foodservice industry but has enough work experience to be able to discuss the values of mentoring. She explains why she feels women mentoring women is so important. "One of women's most valuable assets is their ability to help other women coming into this industry. There are enough men out there to tell us, 'This is where you belong and this is what you should do.' Women who sponsor and help and mentor other women—it's really just the most valuable tool. I find everywhere in life that if women work together, they can accomplish wonderful things."

Mentoring women of the next generation is one of the most important goals that we can have for the future. One of the easier ways to expedite this process is through organizations that give access to women chefs and cooks. The next section presents a number of these organizations and the work they do within the culinary community.

Using Organizations for Networking

Earlier in this book, we saw how mentors have propelled so many other women into the industry. Many women who spoke about their mentors are now mentors themselves. But how does someone go about finding a mentor? Where do we find them? How do we get access to the people we need to help us as peers and mentors?

There are many organizations that women chefs and cooks can join, but few are nationwide and geared toward culinarians. Two such groups are the Women Chefs and Restaurateurs (WCR) and the American Culinary Federation (ACF). Although these groups are very different from each other, they have one thing in common: a population of women who believe in supporting women in the culinary field. Appendix G lists many organizations that promote women in the industry; many offer mentoring programs and culinary school scholarships. We will hear about two of these organizations from their members' perspectives.

Women Chefs and Restaurateurs (WCR)

Women Chefs and Restaurateurs (WCR) was founded in 1993 in response to the need for an educational networking system for the increasing number of women in the restaurant industry. Eight women from across the United States—Lidia Bastianich, Elka Gilmore, Joyce Goldstein, Johanne Killeen, Barbara Lazaroff, Mary Sue Milliken, Anne Rosenzweig, and Barbara Tropp—were instrumental in coordinating the mission and goals of the fledgling association.

The WCR has grown into the largest professional advocacy group for women chefs and restaurateurs in the nation. As a catalyst for alternatives in the restaurant industry, WCR is dedicated to maintaining a safe and positive work environment, promoting workplace flexibility, and introducing the prospect of job-sharing. Additional goals of the group include facilitating the exchange of information between members both professionally and educationally, fostering environments that ensure professional equity, and promoting efforts to improve the global water and food supply. Because of the vision of these eight individuals, there is now a professional forum that enables and encourages women to excel in a rewarding career.

The Impetus for Starting the WCR Johanne Killeen is one of the eight founding members of the WCR. She offers her thoughts on the group's purpose and its role as a forum. "I think a lot of women are really excited to have a place to talk to veterans. A lot of women out there have reached a certain level of success coming from completely different backgrounds and completely different experiences. I think it's great to have a place where young women can feel comfortable asking questions about things that probably are pretty mysterious to them."

Anne Rosenzweig, another founding member of the WCR, relates why she feels this organization is important. "We can offer financial, legal, and public relations help to women who are going up in the industry. There are still so many people in the industry who want to break in, who are just starting, but who can't even get a foothold into it! [Some] communities are so closed—they're how it was twenty years ago! There's really a lot to be done in all aspects of helping women to break into the business and find jobs in different places, so that people can see that women are very capable—more than capable."

Barbara Tropp can truly be said to be one of the driving forces behind the founding of the WCR. Barbara had a vision and a mission, both of which help guide the group to this day. Barbara shares her memories of the group's inception. "For me, founding the WCR was a mission. I had been in the industry long enough to see [that] the larger family of women in the industry wasn't being given its due. There wasn't a proper structure for women to feel supported. In San Francisco there was this fabulous support network of women—[and I thought], 'We need to do something national!' Women in New Jersey and New York don't know each other the way women in California do. From this came an organization that will hopefully go on and on to support women in this industry, who oftentimes don't even *realize* that they need a voice!" The WCR continues to fulfill its founding mission of promoting the education and advancement of women in the restaurant industry and the betterment of the industry as a whole.

"I think [organizational skills] need to be inherent in a good chef ... women make good chefs because they're used to organizing homes, lives, kids, and husbands."
—*Clara Craig*

1950: Stouffer's test kitchens hire only women because they are found to follow instructions and recipes more carefully than their male counterparts.

"I think education and teaching the next generation of kids is something I need to do—nutrition for single parents and stuff like that! It's really important!"
—*Barbara Lynch*

The Benefits of Being a Member of WCR   Before WCR's inception, there was really no organized forum for women in the industry. Since it began, WCR has offered women the opportunity to share and benefit from the experiences of others. As Barbara Tropp states, "Women need a place where they feel supported. They need to find others with whom they share a common ground. They need a group with whom they can discuss the issues that are unique to women in the kitchen. They need what WCR is here to offer."

Frankie Whitman, the executive director of the WCR, addresses why she thinks it is imperative to have a group like WCR. "There's something important in the whole process of telling stories and raising the issues that exist within the industry. When people are isolated and dealing with all kinds of [issues] in their restaurants, whether it be sexual harassment, not getting recognition for their work, or not knowing when is the time to move onto a new place, there's a tremendous comfort and relief knowing that other people are going through this and learning skills for addressing [these] things."

Sarah Stegner talks about life before WCR, stressing how information is more accessible to those who are today in the position she was in six years ago. "I've found that I know enough chefs now that [when] I have questions about the industry and [when] issues come up, I know who to call and talk to. I learned this the hard way, because there weren't those groups [like WCR] available to me when I started as a chef six years ago. ... I think for some of the new chefs, organizations like the WCR allow you to get the answers to questions, and if they don't know, they can tell you who to talk to."

Traci Des Jardins also feels strongly that the WCR is important to all the women in this industry. She explains the struggle she and others have had rising through the ranks to chef. "I don't think any of us has come up through the ranks and really had the support that we've needed. It's been hard; most of us have gotten here because we are tenacious, have will, are smart, capable, and [have] had to push with all our might and force to get where we've gotten. It's only been through sheer will that it has happened, and it shouldn't be that way." Traci explains how WCR has made a difference. "[WCR] provides acceptability, role models, and contacts, so that young women coming into the business [can] talk to me about what I've done. I think it's giving us an opportunity to focus together, as a group, on goals for women in this business, to provide each other with information, and network, network, network. You get tired of hearing that, but it really does help."

Jody Adams also addresses using WCR as a forum for networking and as a comfortable place to ask questions and discuss problems. "I think that [WCR] has a serious place. I forget there [are] still young women out there who have no idea how to get involved, who don't think that there's really an avenue to find other women. I think the WCR is great for people who are entering the industry and need to find out what's going on and how to get there."

I personally believe that there is no greater voice for women chefs and cooks than the WCR. It is still a young organization, but in the four years since its inception, its membership has grown to over 2,000. I firmly believe that this organization can be a vehicle of change for the culinary community of the future.

The American Culinary Federation

Founded in 1929, the American Culinary Federation (ACF) is a melding of three major New York City chefs' organizations, with the primary goal of promoting the professional image of American chefs internationally. The Société Culinaire Philanthropique, the Vatel Club, and the Chefs Association of America all merged to form the first national not-for-profit, professional organization for chefs. This organization consolidated many smaller groups and clubs of chefs and was a national force by 1950.

The primary focus of the ACF is to educate and promote chefs internationally and on every level of expertise. There are currently 25,000 members with 300 individual ACF chapters in the United States and the Caribbean. Among its many achievements, the ACF was responsible for raising the level of executive chef from service status to the professional category in the U.S. Department of Labor's Dictionary of Official Titles in 1976.

One of the most important facets of the ACF is the accreditation of postsecondary education culinary programs that enable professionals to have a uniform and objective level of standards. The ACF, through its educational arm, the ACFEI, exclusively sanctions the only comprehensive certification program for chefs in the United States. This program bestows a certificate to cooks and chefs after a rigorous evaluation of their industry experience paired with their ACF activity participation (see Appendix B).

The philanthropic arm of the ACF is the Chef and the Child Foundation (CCF), a nonprofit organization. This aspect of the ACF is both community and nationally based, and provides nutrition education programs for children through ACF chefs and also provides disaster relief and aid for those in need.

The ACF is the largest chef and cooks organization in this country. Its current active voting membership is approximately forty percent women. Long held as a bastion of male hierarchy, the organization recently voted in the first female National Vice President, Kay Corning, which indicates that not only are women making headway in their representation within the organization, they are also playing increasingly important leadership roles within the organization. Many women with whom I spoke felt that they could use the ACF to meet other women, to garner education, and to find potential mentors.

"I want to have cooks that can season, taste, understand the flavors that work together, and can break down a fish. To have a cook on a line that can make an incredible sauce but doesn't know how to break down a salmon—that shouldn't happen; something went wrong."

—Sarah Stegner

1950: *Betty Crocker's Picture Cookbook* is a U.S. bestseller.

"We pretty much years and years ago decided that hunger and homelessness were going to be the two things that we would give to and really try to work with."

—*Maureen Pothier*

Kay Corning is running for President of ACF in the 1997 election. Kay shares her views of the organization: "I really don't remember how I heard of the ACF, but I really wanted to join. I just started attending meetings. I got elected first vice-president, second vice-president, treasurer of the chapter, and I was the first woman to get Chef of the Year from the Los Angeles chapter, which was quite an accomplishment. I can see where women in this organization will proceed and get recognized for what we do."

Phyllis Flaherty is Vice-President of Marketing for ComSource (a multinational food-purchasing group), a CIA graduate, a chef for many years, and a member of the ACF for over a decade. She thinks that women can find a connection in the ACF. She suggests using this organization as other women suggest using WCR—as a forum for getting advice from others in similar positions, or from others who have climbed up the ranks. "I think the role of women in the ACF should be mentoring. The ACF can be a [forum] to show your talents or to talk about [issues such as how to juggle a career and a family]." She also mentions time management, communication, and negotiating for better work conditions as other issues that can be discussed among ACF members.

Deborah Huntley describes how the ACF has helped with her career. "I decided that if I wanted to pursue further education, I could do it through the American Culinary Federation, with all the programs they have to offer. [I felt] having certification from the ACF would make a lot of difference, and I started focusing on achieving my certification—it played a big part in my development as a chef. I can see where people would say [it's tough on women], because the majority of the membership is composed of men! It's kind of odd sitting in a room with all men. You had to prove yourself, but I think it is changing. I think people are more accepting now than they were five years ago, and *much* more than ten years ago!"

I belong to both the WCR and the ACF and have found support, education, and networking opportunities in both. My relationship with the ACF started when I was a student at the CIA in 1979. This relationship fostered the pursuit and attainment of my current certification level as Certified Executive Chef, was a venue for culinary competitions, and has enabled me to network with other women chefs from around the country. The educational opportunities to participate in classes, demonstrations, seminars, and conferences have helped me grow professionally, even while living in rural areas without the benefit of a chefs' network.

The WCR has been a part of my culinary experience for the past two years. This organization, more than any other, has provided me with the support of, access to, and benefit from an association with other women chefs and restaurateurs. In the WCR I have found a group of caring, giving, supportive women who are passionate about the culinary arena and are willing to share their experience and knowledge. Every woman chef, cook, culinary educator, and restaurateur should join this group; in that way, all of the industry will benefit from this organization being a strong forum that helps to shape the future of the industry.

Women and Their Involvement in Socially Responsible Causes

Women in the culinary arena have found that their need to give of themselves goes beyond just their food and their careers. The need to nurture and care for people carries into a greater sphere of organizations devoted to food recovery projects, nutritional education, and hunger relief the world over. These are the areas in which many women chefs have committed their time and resources.

One of the wonderfully enlightening things that happened to me while I was writing this book was that I came to understand how much and in how many ways the women that I met were giving to others. This giving was not limited to contributing to the industry, but also giving to those who are not able to provide for themselves. It is awe-inspiring to be part of a community that places such a high value on giving to others.

The Desire to Give

In the past decade, there has been an unprecedented demand for chefs, their time and talent, by nonprofit organizations. Charitable organizations are increasingly realizing the profitability of marketing well-known chefs at fundraisers. The requests for time, energy, food, and financial commitment rise each year and can become overwhelming. In this section, women express both their desire to help and the difficulty they face finding the time for their charitable work in light of their many daily responsibilities. A recurring theme among these women is the importance of giving back to the community and staying connected in this way.

Amy Scherber loves being able to help out whenever she can; however, like many women, she finds that sometimes all the giving is hard, because it takes you out of your facility so often. "I love it! I do most every request: samples, donations, gift certificates, and time. The hardest is the time; there are functions when they ask you to come and cut up your samples and hand them out; I always go. I'm always there for the personal things. Food is part of every event! It's a tricky area to be in—you want to keep folks happy and stay connected to the neighborhood. It's very difficult to take time like that." While Amy does find the time to juggle both her own job and philanthropic commitments, she admits to often overextending herself.

"I think that the cooking community should be commended for what they have done in the way of giving, particularly in regards to their financial situation. You'll see a chef who makes $30,000 a year who will jump in and do a Meals-on-Wheels benefit working seventeen or eighteen hours a day without hesitation."
—Eve Felder

1950: *A Book of Mediterranean Food* by Elizabeth David is published.

Debra Ponzek sees many different benefits to participating in charity events. While she finds that participating in celebrity chef events can be chaotic, it helps to raise a lot of money for the charity and gives her restaurant positive exposure. "You're there because you hope that there's a thousand people who come. You want them to come to your restaurant. ... You want customers, and you want people to see what you're doing. The guest wants to see the chefs, the food—it's a great way to raise money." As Debra points out, these types of benefits can really work well for everyone; from a promotional standpoint, this is a way for restaurant owners to keep their restaurant's name in the public eye, and from a charitable standpoint, such events are profitable.

Cindy Salvato's need to give to others is in the form of a truly personal gift. Cindy has established a scholarship for women who would probably not have the opportunity to pursue a career in the culinary field. She has funded this scholarship with profits from her book, *The Dowry Cookbook*. She describes her intention for this scholarship: "I wanted to be able to give back, to help women, especially single women, single mothers. I have a scholarship set up with the profits from my book that will go to a single mom in college at Johnson and Wales. That's a big thing. It will be the first scholarship that goes out to a young woman who gets her college education! She can use the money for whatever she [needs], like books or daycare. I think it's important to offer opportunities to women from less advantaged segments of our population; it's very difficult for those women to be elevated; they have incredible responsibilities. I don't want to see women on welfare. We've got to get them into a position where they can feel good about themselves and be an example for their children. They can get off the system and start rolling. So, that's one way that I can [help] do that."

Among these amazing women who barely have the time to balance their own lives and their work, yet who find time to help others, is Siobhan Carew, chef-owner of Pomodoro in Boston. Siobhan, like her colleagues, wants to share her good fortune and passion for food with others. As she says: "If you're passionate about food, you have to be able to share it. I've been working in the foodservice industry for twenty years. As I learn more about food, my expectations and standards become higher and more sophisticated. The more I learn about food, the more I want to educate other people and pass it on to [them]. I always feel honored that I'm invited [to participate in a benefit] and I love to do everything—especially something involving women's issues, or with children. ... I always feel very fortunate that I have my own business, and I feel that if there are people I can help who are less fortunate, then I'm happy to give back. I think it's really important—you're kind of practicing what you're preaching."

Jody Adams, executive chef, wife, mother of two, and restaurant co-owner, still finds time to give in so many ways. Her actions speak even louder than her words. "The philanthropic stuff—I think it's really important to do. That's where I have found the balance of giving back. It's absolutely critical [for me] to maintain a connection to community at a really hands-on level. ... I'm much more interested in working with kids where I'm taken out of my other world. If you work in a restaurant as many hours as we all do, and you're working hours that most people are home, social hours are nonexistent—so you really have no connection with the community." Jody says that being a part of the community is immensely important to her and that working with high school students and "at-risk" youth have given her a sense of reciprocity. She has participated in a program called Workforce and another program at Cambridge Rindge and Latin school. Both programs seek to instill an understanding in the importance of food to teenagers.

Loretta Keller tells of the contribution she has made to a local health clinic over the past three years. "It's called the San Francisco Free Clinic, and once a year, about three restaurants get together and we have a lunch. They raise [almost] seventy percent of their annual budget at one lunch, and it's just a great thing. This is one of those rare, rewarding causes, where you know that it [goes] immediately to your community. I've had cooks who haven't qualified for health insurance, or chose not to pay for it, who have gone to this clinic. It's just exceedingly professional. All these doctors from the Palo Alto and the Stanford area donate a couple days a month. The thing has just become this wonderful project, and for three years now I've done that fundraiser. ... It is such a great cause."

Traci Des Jardins feels that catering to a privileged segment of the population can be disheartening at times. She wants to be doing more for those who don't have the means by which to treat or even feed themselves. "A large part of what I do in the restaurant doesn't really have to do with running the restaurant. It's the promotional and benefit work that is a very worthwhile thing. I feel like the work I do for different organizations [is] my way of contributing to society. ... I want to make a difference in the world and contribute to different causes and to society."

As much as chefs give, it seems at times to be not enough. Anne Rosenzweig has been a visible part of the industry for many years and barely a day goes by without someone calling and asking her to participate in a fundraiser. She raises the issue of finding balance between helping, giving, and maintaining your life and restaurant. "Every organization wants you to participate in some way, and you feel bad, or they make you feel bad if you don't. I think it's important to be involved in things that are related to food and hunger and anything else that you're interested in. But I think when Cerebral Palsy, Alzheimer's, Cancer Care, and everybody else [calls, it's a problem]. They've

"The people who get involved in the [Chef and the Child Foundation] have to come into it and decide whether this is something that's going to reinforce them. ... You can't dictate this kind of thing. But I do believe in the Chef and the Child."
—*Barbara Sanders*

1951: L'Ecole des Trois Gourmandes opens in Paris.

grabbed onto chefs as this conduit. Chefs are put in a very awkward position, I think, because you cannot do all the events, and yet you're made to feel that you're responsible. I think it has to push back onto all these organizations that chefs are not responsible for every organization—it's a very difficult position."

While many of these women wrestle with the problems of how to juggle their jobs, their families, and their personal time, they also find the time and energy to make contributions to the charity or cause of their choice. They do it willingly, selflessly, and with grace and generosity. This is all part of the evolution of women in the kitchen—part of the continuous evolution that fulfills their lives as well as the lives of those around them.

The Chef and the Child Foundation

Designed to address the nutritional and dietary needs of children, the American Culinary Federation (ACF) formed the Chef and the Child Foundation (CCF) in 1989. This nonprofit organization was initiated to foster, promote, encourage, and stimulate an awareness of proper nutrition in preschool and elementary school children. In addition, the foundation provides emergency food relief to victims of natural and other disasters.

The CCF pledges to address the dietary and nutrition education needs of the children in America. This philanthropic branch of the ACF provides grants to feed hungry children and aids in disaster relief. Under the auspices of the Chefs Educational Series, it also trains volunteers and personnel at soup kitchens and shelters to serve food that is safe, wholesome, and nutritious. In addition, CCF provides nutrition education through the Chef in the Classroom program. One of the primary assertions behind CCF is that all children need to learn how to cook and how to choose healthy foods. Their hope is that this can be accomplished while making an impact in the fight against childhood hunger.

I had the pleasure of meeting Audrey Lennon, chef-owner of Audrey's Catering in Orlando, Florida, during National Hunger Day in Washington, DC. For National Hunger Day, ACF chefs gather at the Capitol for a march on Congressional Hill in support of hunger relief programs. Audrey's ability to give seems endless; her philanthropic nature is as amazing as her story. She speaks of how CCF is growing and that people are anxious to get involved. "I've always had this thing since I was very, very little—of injustice. Didn't matter who. Didn't matter what. … Certain things just were not fair. Oh, I'd be on causes when I was little. I was the first one in my school to collect for the March of Dimes. I was determined to get everybody, and I *got* everybody."

The first National Childhood Hunger Day happened to be on the same day as the Million-Man March in 1995. The almost sixty chefs in white coats made a strong contrast in the midst of the million black men. Audrey continues her story as she describes being interviewed on her perspective of the march

Women in the Culinary Arena: Pat Thibodeau

Rare is the individual who is able to look beyond oneself consistently for the betterment of a situation. Pat Thibodeau saw the need for a solution and dedicated herself to improving the plight of hunger in the nation, embodying the adage 'Think globally, act locally.' Pat's dedication stems from a career in social welfare that prepared her for the politics of fundraising, budgeting, and setting priorities.

Pat's jobs include having worked for the Salvation Army and the State of Florida Food Stamp program; she was the first woman correctional counselor at a work release center in Florida. She joined the ACF chef apprentice program in 1989. While working at a large facility, she was amazed to realize the amount of food wasted daily in retail operations. This was a catalyst to develop one of the first food recovery programs in the nation. That in turn led to the development of a safe food-handling video and a training program for volunteers that taught them how to safely handle, store, and serve donated food.

Pat joined the executive committee of the Chef and the Child Foundation (CCF) in 1994 and has been director of the program since then. CCF acts as a not-for-profit hunger advocacy group that focuses on providing grants nationally to feed hungry children, train volunteers and personnel at non-profit feeding programs, and teach children nutrition and cooking. Pat's philosophy—"It only takes one person who isn't going to stand for it"—is one we can all try to learn from and incorporate into our daily practices.

while participating with the chefs in Childhood Hunger Day. "The United Press asked me, since I was black, and I was at a different cause with mostly white people, 'How did I feel?' I said, 'We are both marching for the same cause.' I said, 'Because if they can get those daddies to take care of their children, we wouldn't have to do this. So we'd solve the problem anyway, and that's what we're here for, to solve the problem with *children*.'" Trying to eradicate childhood hunger—what better cause for chefs?

Like Audrey, Pat Thibodeau has truly melded her passion for giving with her passion for food. I met Pat a few years ago at the first CCF National Hunger Day, also in Washington, DC. She impressed me with her energy and zeal dedicated to her belief of eradicating childhood hunger. It wasn't until the second chefs march on Washington that she told me how she first became involved with the fight against hunger. "When I got to Sea World, where I did my apprenticeship in 1989, I saw all the food they were throwing away. I was devastated. [They were] throwing away *a lot* of food. There [was] this day when we had 4,500 pieces of cold chicken served for lunch to some

1954: Frozen "TV" brand dinners are introduced by C. A. Swanson and Sons of Omaha, Nebraska.

"It's nice to be able to do as much as you can, not because of my profession, but if you're part of the community, you're part of the world!"
—*Susan Spicer*

cheerleaders. Well ... they didn't eat any of it. You know how any place is; you can't put the food back! So, the staff is all by the dumpster, and they've got all the [rolling racks] with the chicken. I'm in front of the dumpster and I'm saying, 'Don't throw [that] in the dumpster!' ... It's a weekend, and [a] manager walks by to see what's going on. 'She won't let us throw it in the dumpster,' said one of my co-workers. I said, 'Can we give it away?' The manager said, 'We can't keep it out here long; you have fifteen minutes to get somebody on the phone that'll come get it, and you have to get permission from the company, from somebody who's at home.'" Pat went on to tell me that she made those calls, got permission to give the food away, and it was picked up and taken to a shelter. "All it takes is that one person who isn't going to stand for it. I became a little internal hero at Sea World, and we started rescuing the food, which wasn't as simple as it sounds."

From that one standoff, Pat set up a food recovery system to feed the hungry. This involved renting a number of trucks for the recovery and redistribution of hundreds of thousands of pounds of food each year. That system eventually became part of Second Harvest, which is the largest charitable hunger relief organization in the United States. Through a nationwide network of food banks, Second Harvest distributes surplus food and grocery products to thousands of charitable agencies, which in turn serve millions of people each year. Pat explains that the Sea World food recovery program started out of the back of her truck. She tells of her quest for volunteers: "I tried to hook up with them [an anti-hunger group], so that they would provide the volunteers to come in, but they were socialites, and they were too busy on Saturday nights to come out. It was always me and my husband loading it into our van; we actually got a grant from the Chef and the Child Foundation to buy a van for $1,500, and we started hauling food." That was the beginning of the food rescue program. Pat's involvement in the Chef and the Child Foundation has been tireless.

Pat's initial focus was to impress upon food recovery centers the need to educate their staffs so that chefs would donate their food. She almost single-handedly produced a video that would provide this education; this remains a focus of the Chef and the Child Foundation. Pat tells this part of her story: "I went to the first Food Chain conference on my soapbox, telling them: 'The ACF will never donate food if you don't have some kind of safe food-handling training in place.' We created the video. A friend showed me how to use a computer, and I wrote the script myself. It was very hard. There were days when I said, 'If I can ever do this, God, I know I'm going to get into heaven!' ... I wrote the whole script, and we shot the video, and it was great! Two weeks after my surgery (for cancer) was my very first day-long Food Safety Handling seminar. They took me over in a wheelchair! We did the seminar; it was a great success." Pat believes that God puts us all here for a purpose, and she feels fortunate that she's found her purpose and has lived long enough to see it into fruition, because in her words, "I'm just too mean to die."

Share Our Strength (SOS) and Related Programs

Realizing that "it takes more than food to fight hunger," Billy Shore founded Share Our Strength (SOS) in 1984 in response to the Ethiopian famine and an increased awareness of hunger in the United States. This innovative Washington, DC-based anti-hunger nonprofit foundation addresses social problems by redefining traditional nonprofit ventures. Since its inception, SOS has raised more than $26 million to fight and prevent hunger in addition to awarding more than 800 grants to international anti-hunger organizations. SOS was instituted to alleviate and prevent hunger and poverty in the United States. SOS's goals are to offer food assistance and treatment for malnutrition as well as investing in long-term solutions to hunger.

Operation Frontline is the SOS nutrition education and food budgeting program that connects chefs with people who are at risk of poor nutrition and hunger. Spanning a broad base of economic backgrounds and education, chefs enable individuals at risk to make informed choices about nutrition and food options. By using this method, the interaction between chef and student over a six-week period is positive and rewarding for all involved. Kids Up Front, a partnership with Kraft Foods, is an extension of Operation Frontline and helps to teach children at risk of hunger to make healthier food choices. Share Our Strength has mobilized industries and individuals to contribute to a national anti-hunger effort. Individuals in the food service industry are in a unique position to make a difference in the battle against hunger because it does take more than food to solve hunger.

Susan McCreight Lindeborg has been working with SOS for a number of years. She explains her involvement in the program. "I signed up, went to the training classes, and ended up teaching the first Front Line class. I've been teaching for about three years. I think that teaching something to someone who really is interested ... gives them a new tool to make their life a little better. It's very very difficult to eat well on a low budget. Part of this class is giving each student a ten-dollar gift certificate, and we go to a store all together. We have a lesson about the store and what they can buy. We asked them to buy food to make a meal, or to make as many meals as they think they can make, and feed as many people as possible with the ten dollars."

Among Maureen Pothier's many contributions to her community, she has continuously been involved with SOS. Until recently, she and her husband owned a restaurant in Providence, Rhode Island, yet she still found the time to give both personally and financially. Maureen starts her story expressing many

"The nature of our business is that you give back a lot to society; we have such a fantastic opportunity to give through our work, it's a great way to be able to make good things happen."
—Susan Feniger

1957: The U.S. per capita margarine consumption overtakes butter for the first time.

of the same feelings that Susan expressed about getting involved. "I really feel like I'm doing something worthwhile when I spend time doing things for Share Our Strength or the [Anthony] Spinazzola Foundation (a Boston-based philanthropic organization). Maureen also describes her participation in Front Line. "We have classes of twelve students at a time, and sometimes there are as many as a dozen classes going on around the state of Rhode Island. We were one of the pilot cities for this program."

As another part of her SOS involvement, Maureen has taken part in teaching at-risk mothers and children to improve their eating habits. She explained how this program works: "We follow the food pyramid and start out with the grains and do the whole system. We keep the recipes pretty simple and try to keep them fairly low-fat and nutritious. We try to teach them to eat better themselves and to feed their children better—instead of cookies for a snack, give them popcorn or fruits and vegetables. It's been a really great program."

Maureen has been involved with two other projects: Women, Infants, and Children (WIC) and Sstarbirth. Maureen describes these: "The WIC program is a federal program for women, infants, and children that gives them extra food stamps for high-calcium products. We do a lot of classes with them. We've gone into the prison with the women who are a year from being paroled. Sstarbirth is a home for women (and their children) in need of drug and alcohol rehabilitation. The program helps these women to learn to take better care of their children and themselves."

Another organization, one to which Mary Sue Milliken and Susan Feniger give freely, is the Scleroderma Research Foundation. The disease is one that affects 500,000 women in the United States, and the foundation helps fund research to eradicate it. Seventy percent of the people diagnosed with this little publicized disease are women in their late thirties; they are generally forecasted a life expectancy of seven years. The increased production of collagen in one's body creates a breakdown of connective tissue and ultimately acts as an immobilizer; those afflicted with Scleroderma are unable to continue functioning independently due to chronic debilitation.

Susan Feniger has taken on this cause in part because her college roommate has been afflicted with Scleroderma for the past ten years. Cool Comedy/Hot Cuisine was founded by Susan in 1987 as a fundraiser and has drawn upon the skills of such comedians as Robin Williams, Ellen DeGeneres, Lily Tomlin, Dana Carvey, and Rosie O'Donnell. Not only is the food highlighted, but also it has been shown for years that comedy and laughing are very good for the soul and as digestifs!

Throughout this book we have met women who entered this industry because of their passion for food, their need to nurture, and their desire to give back to their communities. In this chapter, we have witnessed the ultimate in giving back. These women, whose lives are already filled to capacity, go one step beyond their everyday roles to make the lives of those in need a little less difficult. They help to feed the needy and to teach those who can help themselves. Their passion for the land has led many to work tirelessly to preserve the natural resources for food that we have available. This characteristic of giving of themselves is in keeping with how they live their lives, and thanks to them, many others are living better and healthier lives.

1958: A pound of chicken costs 46 cents, a pound of round steak costs 90 cents, and a Nathan's hot dog costs 25 cents.

Women and Their Future in the Culinary World

"A Natural Evolution"
—Dorothy Hamilton

"This is Florence during the Renaissance, truly. … I think it's an unbelievably wide-open field, from what the Department of Labor statistics say. It's the right field to be in … it's supposed to grow for the next twenty-five years. If you're there and you want to make it happen, you can."
—*Dorothy Hamilton*

The future of our industry is incredibly promising, and women will play an important role in helping to shape the profession in the twenty-first century. To quote Dorothy Hamilton, "I don't think it's a revolution in the kitchen, I think it's a natural evolution." That's where we are—going through another cycle of this evolution. Throughout this book, we have looked at women and food over the course of 10,000 years; we end our story close to where we started—in the kitchen. From the beginning of time, women have been food providers. Looking to the future, women will help to guide the industry and lead the way to a new, sustainable model for the kitchen and the culinary arena for the next 10,000 years. Based on the current trends and mode of thinking, this model will be one that values employees and their families, helps to dispel minority biases, and gives everyone with passion for food an equal chance to excel in the professional kitchen.

Future Trends

It's important to take a snapshot of where the industry is today and then move on to a discussion of the changes that need to be made. The depiction of the evolution of the industry should inspire all those within to keep reaching for the next level.

The culinary industry is full of potential as we gear up for tremendous growth in the next decade. The NRA *Foodservice Employee Profile* predicts that the demand for cooks and chefs will be up forty-eight percent in restaurants between 1992 and 2005, primarily due to the increasing popularity in dining out. The 1997 NRA booklet, *Inside Consumers' Heads,* states: "The typical person eight years old and older consumed an average of 4.1 commercially prepared meals per week in 1996." The report goes on to say that of the meals eaten at home, half had only one item that was prepared from scratch. Every indication is that we are seeing a trend toward a more sophisticated, value-oriented, demanding consumer, with more expendable income due to the increase in two-income families. The study ranks the "hallmarks of a great eating place" as one with the following attributes: "Great-tasting food made from fresh ingredients with unique and original flavors and served in a comfortable atmosphere."

Growing Market Segments

There are many trends emerging in the foodservice industry that are expected to produce new or enlarged market segments. Many of these will give rise to potential jobs for those who are looking to balance both career and family. The segments expected to see the largest increases are those in the home meal replacement market, including upscale to-go markets, commissary-style kitchens, and restaurants marketing upscale take-out food. The home meal replacement market is essentially a new version of the traditional "food to go." This market caters to the expanding population of households where both parents work and therefore have less time and desire to cook and clean yet want home-style and/or upscale food that can be eaten in the comfort of their own home.

Many grocery store chains, such as Fresh Fields, Bread and Circus, and Eatzi's are fast becoming a market segment offering premium prepared foods as an alternative to restaurant dining in order to accommodate the increasingly hectic lifestyles of families. This sector is expected to employ one out of every four chefs within the decade, and it is speculated that ninety percent of all fresh food products purchased in a grocery store will be able to be consumed within ten minutes of getting them home. With more and more emphasis on "fresh food departments," grocery store chains are seen by many restaurateurs as their largest source of competition for consumers in the next few decades.

Institutional food services offer increasing opportunities. These food services include colleges, hospitals, corporate dining rooms, and adult assisted living centers. They will have new growth opportunities, and will all have positions that might offer more attractive hours than traditional restaurant work.

1801 cookbook frontispiece. Courtesy of the Culinary Archives and Museum of Johnson and Wales University.

Another growing market segment in the United States is that of the small, casual, high-quality independent restaurant—especially those specializing in "home cooking" and "old-fashioned comfort food." These restaurants, offering quality, fresh ingredients, will be increasing in market share.

This trend should bode well for women, as documented by the Census Bureau's Economic Census Report, which reveals that women-owned small businesses have been on the rise in the past decade.

Lastly, cooking schools, which have increased from 100 to over 600 schools in the last ten years, will continue to see growth. More and more schools and the educators to run them will be needed in the coming decade.

The landscape of the foodservice industry will have a very different look in the decades to come. Small business will have a larger market share, meals

1959: Sweet 'n Low sugarless sweetener is introduced, using saccharin in place of sugar.

"If I was going to give my daughter a piece of advice and she wanted to be a chef, I'd tell her to go west. As far away from Europe as you can get. West-Northwest particularly seems to be an area where they're free of a lot of the tradition that's strangling the East coast in terms of women chefs."

—Pat Bartholomew

purchased in grocery stores and home meal establishments will replace many of the meals eaten out in restaurants, and the institutional foodservice market will continue to grow. All of these segments combined could allow for more women in foodservice and a more family-oriented workforce.

Consumers of the Future

The increased consumer desire for prepared foods can be explained by a number of trends. Two-parent working households are on the rise and have been accompanied by a new baby boom. In these same households, the parents are too busy to cook but want restaurant-quality meals. Nutritional awareness has been steadily highlighted with the realization that fully one-third of the population is overweight. "Healthy" eating habits have been elevated to a new height. Cooking has become a hobby and, in that capacity, has ignited curiosities about food and its preparation. This, in turn, has spurred a more sophisticated clientele, which feeds its "passion" through cookbook sales, TV cooking shows, and cooking classes.

The "cooking as hobby" trend has brought a new consumer awareness to the market focused on eating fresh, well-prepared, well-seasoned, and exotic foods. The more knowledgeable home cook is also developing a greater appreciation of the connections between a healthy environment and nourishing food. This translates into buying practices that value organics and sustainability. The increasing rarity of "family meal time," as well as an aging, more affluent population who miss the food of their childhood, has spurred the growth of "comfort food."

Growing Opportunities for the Future

As the market segments change and as the consumer evolves, so too do the opportunities that the industry has to offer to those entering the field. With the "traditional" foodservice labor pool of sixteen- to twenty-four-year-olds on the decline, as the overall population ages, the challenge of a labor shortage will initiate a number of changes in the way the industry operates. Three major studies and reports, *The 100 Best Companies for Working Women, Industry of Choice ... an Extensive Study of Employee Behavior and Attitudes in the Foodservice Industry,* and *Foodservice Employment 2000,* document evidence that the number one concern of foodservice employers is the lack of staff. Minorities, including women, will constitute the largest percentage of the new foodservice workers. To fulfill their needs, foodservice operators will have to become more employee-friendly, incorporating family concerns into compensation packages.

With the labor pool shrinking and the cost of providing benefits and wages increasing, a number of companies will be looking toward outsourcing products. To meet that demand, we will see a growth of small businesses focusing on manufacturing specialty products; the opportunity will be there for women to take advantage of these new growth industries.

It is my belief that shifting demographics and consumer preferences will spur these changes in the industry:[31]

- Demand for highly skilled and educated chefs and cooks will increase to over 500,000 in the coming decade.

- The need for more qualified employees will produce a rise in hotel, restaurant, and institutional degree programs.

- Turnover will be seen as something to be combated, foreshadowing a trend toward more staff-oriented programs.

- Minorities will fill a higher percentage of the kitchen staffs.

- More emphasis will be put on workers' family needs, such as flextime, daycare, healthcare, and job-sharing. Daycare facilities will become more common and more heavily subsidized.

- Restaurant operators will place more emphasis on efficiency and efficiency-enhancing equipment.

- Upscale convenience foods will have a larger market share and will account for a new growth segment of the industry, catering to value-added services and products.

- In-house staff training programs will be improved and emphasized to help produce higher productivity and to lower the turnover rate.

These changes won't be noticeable immediately, but they are bound to occur in the next decade. Visible changes in the twenty-first century will mean increased opportunities for all minorities in food services. Wage parity may become a reality, and benefits and compensation may become the rule instead of exception.

Industry Leaders Speak to the Trends

Research led my predictions for the future. What does the future look like to the industry leaders? This section looks at some of their thoughts and beliefs.

Fritz Sonnenschmidt of the CIA offers this prediction: "If I look across the board, I'd say the year 2000 is going to bring a lot of changes. One is [that] the upper ten percent [of foodservice operations], where everything is

"It seems safe to say that the new generation of great chefs will be American rather than French and will consist of a fifty-fifty ratio of women and men."
—*Madeleine Kamman*

1959: Some 22.5 million U.S. women work away from home, mostly on factory assembly lines or as office workers, retail clerks, schoolteachers, nurses, laundresses, and domestic servants.

"There are more women in the kitchen, or (there) will be—I see it as a positive thing. I see kitchens as being much more friendly, helpful, and creative. I hope it will be (that way) in the future."
—*Gloria Ciccarone-Nehls*

available—money, machinery, top salaries for chefs, clientele that can support it—is going to shrink to maybe five percent. The other factor is that [establishments] in between a family restaurant and a classical restaurant, [with] less money and more volume, [are going to flourish]." He attributes this to the need for companies to outsource in an effort to reduce payroll costs, or in some cases just the need to overcome the challenge of the shrinking labor pool. "We need to use more convenience foods; we can't [produce] from scratch anymore; there's going to be [more] outsourcing. I think the chef of the new millennium will become a chef who brings things together [at] the finish rather than from scratch. ... [There will be] a new profession where we will have some [companies] that just make stocks and vegetables. I am not a soothsayer! But I mean if I look around at what's happening right now, that is what I think."

Pam Parseghian, a food editor at *Nations Restaurant News* (NRN), sees many trends and offers her perspective on how they will affect women in the industry. "I'm seeing women going into corporate chef positions more, and with the rise of chain restaurants, women are going into consulting. ... That's a great place for women. ... It's so interesting, and you don't have the physical demands; but, at the same time, you're able to be creative and influence what millions of people will eat."

This challenge of staffing, benefits, and an orientation toward the family are issues that we have been discussing, yet these ideals are becoming more mainstream in corporations, than in small independently owned companies. In January 1997, the Coca-Cola Company sponsored a study that was presented by The Educational Foundation of the NRA called *Industry of Choice*. This study identified the most appropriate project for the Foundation to undertake in an effort to enhance the foodservice industry. The findings highlighted the foodservice industry's need to develop higher employee satisfaction to sustain financial viability and growth.

Attrition   According to *The NRA 1996 Restaurant Industry Operations Report,* the turnover rate in the foodservice industry is between seventy and eighty percent every year. When the cost of training is considered, the ramifications of these figures are staggering. The expense of training varies, depending upon position, but the low estimates are $1,000 per employee; the high is $1,700, with up to $5,000 for managers. To put this in perspective, if a restaurant has 100 employees and has a turnover rate of seventy-five percent, and if the training cost per employee is $1,500, then in a year, the property would spend $112,500 on training. Industry-wide, the money spent and the potential savings are staggering. Money saved could go toward funding programs that would help women and all those with families better balance work and life.

Clearly, employee attrition is costly to any establishment. Not only does it mean losing valuable workers, but it also means losing the time that was spent training, and losing the knowledge and skills that were acquired, and it also means having to go through the entire process again when replacing those who leave. Thus, by reducing turnover and the inherent training costs, there is great potential to save money. The shrinking labor pool is one of the greatest challenges facing the foodservice industry. Many culinary school graduates are looking for alternatives to the kitchen because they are convinced that one can't have a family and a career. If current professionals don't take aggressive action to reverse this perception, the industry will collapse from lack of skilled passionate culinarians. At a time when the industry is growing at such a rapid rate, resolving the labor problem is a pressing issue.

When I spoke with Anne Rosenzweig about the need to reverse the high rate of attrition in the food industry, she responded with some interesting insights. "Since we lose so many talented women, figuring out how to keep them in the industry is a priority. That's something I've tried to do, and I know my colleagues have tried too. Things have certainly changed that way. You now have men who want to have families. There are men who say, 'I want to be home a little bit too—how can we figure this out?' I certainly think that the workplace has become a lot less macho than it was, as we try to be inclusive. It's not just about women. It's about people who like to live a life that's not necessarily a macho life, whether they're men or women."

Janis Wertz, president of Housatonic Technical College and formerly a vice-president at the CIA says the food industry needs to catch up with the rest of the world. "It is a matter of changing the environment and looking at other ways to simply make it work better so that you can retain people. There's a foodservice work environment that needs the same kind of attention that some mavericks apply to other kinds of business environments, whether it's engineering, medicine, temp companies, or colleges. Who is going to cook in the future—who's going to want to do that? Without cooks, the rest of the industry collapses."

In the past decade, the challenge of staffing the foodservice industry has reached critical proportions. Clearly, the industry has to find and keep all of the best people it can and, in doing so, will have to make compensation, benefits, and family orientation a priority. When that has been accomplished, it will represent the industry of the future—taking care of its employees and their families and letting its employees take care of their customers.

Wages The restaurant industry is notorious for its low wages. Many believe that in comparison to other industries, chefs are paid less than business managers who are at equivalent levels within their organizations. To compound

"It comes down to reputation, investment—it's like a box; you keep putting things in it, and the more people who know you, and know what you've done, the more security you have. One thing I find women don't do very well is make sure people know what they do."
—*Phyllis Flaherty*

1960: Thirty-four percent of all women over the age of fourteen, and thirty-one percent of all married women, are in the work force.

"Society doesn't value the work that we do, the sacrifices that (are made). I know I'm at the low level (of pay); between $8 and $11 an hour; it's terrible. ... When I was an (accounting) consultant, I was earning ten or twelve times this much per hour. This feels like much more valuable work to me, yet I'm not paid for it; it's not viewed by the world as valuable."

—Elizabeth Germain

this problem, women are typically paid less than men in comparable positions. Fair pay for work performed would go a long way toward stabilizing the attrition rate.

The precedent for men being paid more than women for comparable work was highlighted in 1890, when women made forty-six cents compared to a dollar for men. In 1939, the pay for women had increased to fifty-eight cents for every dollar that men earned. By 1981, this discrepancy had changed by only a penny, with women earning fifty-nine cents per dollar; in 1992, it rose to sixty-four cents; and in 1994, it is said to have been seventy-one cents. An April 1997 Associated Press article reports, "The typical American working woman is paid 71 cents for each $1 earned by a man, the Census Bureau says."

Based on the figures in the table (opposite page), we can see that given the skill level, dedication, and hard work needed to become successful in the food and beverage industry, the wages of culinarians are below those available in other industries with similar levels of responsibilities. Disparity between the wages of the women surveyed for this book and industry averages can also be noted.

Pat Bartholomew discusses why she thinks a discrepancy in pay rates for women exists. "What [many] studies have in common is the assumption that women, because of their ability to bear children and subsequent childrearing responsibilities, pay a price in the workplace for this biological fact of life. The persistent economic inequality of women in the workplace was due not to [blatant] discrimination but rather had to do with the conflict experienced over families and careers—that women, to accommodate their desire for children, make choices that diminish their economic power."

Phyllis Flaherty discusses another aspect of the issue of equal pay. "You only get parity when the perceived value is there. But just getting the opportunity to show that you can do that same job means you initially have to end up doing it for less. I'm used to being so happy to have a job and grateful, that I don't know how to negotiate for executive pay." This has been an issue that we've seen before; women tend to be uncomfortable discussing or negotiating about money. Phyllis continues, "It's a self-worth issue—we feel guilty asking for more money. I don't even know what it is I should be negotiating for at this level! But I know I'm not at parity. Do you negotiate for a car allowance? Some people have a country-club membership—what are the things that I should be discussing? I don't even know that, because I haven't been trained in it. ... Men tend to teach each other."

Judy Rodgers knows that this disparity exists, so she tries to compensate her staff equitably. She feels that if you want quality food and good service, you get what you pay for. You can't get good people if you don't pay the price, and that price has to be passed on to the consumer. "Even at the wages you can

Salaries for Salaried Personnel and Hourly Managers

Position	Establishments with Revenues up to 500K	Establishments with Revenues from 500K to 2 M	Establishments with Revenues of 2M and up
Grocery Store Manager[3]			50,000-100,000
Department Manager[3]			50,000-75,000
Finance Manager[3]			59,274
Executive Chef-NRA[1]	25,000-36,000	35,0000-45,000	38,000-59,000
Hotel/Entertainment[3] Manager		40,753	
Women Executive Chef Survey[4]		27,000-41,000	
Chef-NRA[1]	18,000-28,000	22,000-37,000	30,000-41,700
Restaurant Managers[3]			39,388
Women Chef-Survey[4]		21,000-35,000	
Kitchen Managers[3]			29,845
Hotel Management[3] Trainee		26,368	
Sous Chef-NRA[1]	14,000-23,140	16,000-28,000	26,000-32,000
Women Sous Chef-Survey[4]		21,000-35,000	
Office Clerical Worker[3]		22,500	
Bank Teller[3]		19,500	
Receptionist[3]		18,500	
Pastry Chef-NRA[1]	15,000-17,000	16,000-30,000	23,000-35,000
Women Pastry Chef-Survey[4]		20,000-25,000	
Cook-NRA[2]	6.85-8.00/hour		
Assistant Cook[2]	6.25-7.00/hour		
Women Line Cook-Survey[4]	6.50-7.00/hour		
Grocery store check-out clerk[3]	6.75-7.25/hour		
Baker[2]	6.50-7.68/hour		
Prep Cook[2]	5.50-6.50/hour		

The figures are based on the NRA studies: *Compensation for Salaried Personnel in Foodservice* (1), the *Survey of Wage Rates for Hourly Employees* (2), The Coca-Cola-sponsored *Industry of Choice Study* (3), and the surveys of women in this book (4).

1961: *Mastering the Art of French Cooking* is published by Julia Child with Louisette Bertholle and Simone Beck.

Women in the Culinary Arena: Dr. Pat Bartholomew

There is an old saying: "From tiny acorns grow mighty oaks." Patricia Bartholomew is one of the mighty oaks of the culinary field. A woman who acknowledges that she grew up with 'normal fifties food,' Pat had a culinary epiphany in Belgium when she was young and food became a focus in her life.

In 1974, there were few women visible in the major kitchens of New York City. Pat enrolled in school and dedicated herself to both her culinary and academic education. Her primary skills remained administrative and organizational, and Pat was rejected from all forty-four kitchens she applied to until she was finally asked to open the first restaurant in the Guggenheim Museum in Manhattan. Ruskays', a small restaurant on the West Side, gave Pat her first job as a chef, and she pioneered the concept of job-sharing, running the establishment with two women classmates.

Pat earned her B.A. in communications and culinary arts from the City University of New York. After working at the Waldorf Astoria and in executive dining rooms in New York City, Pat accepted a position as food editor at *Restaurant Business* magazine, a unique opportunity to combine her writing skills with her culinary acumen. It was during this period that Pat began to teach various classes at the New School, New York University, and Westchester Community College. She found that education was her niche, and it allowed her to communicate with other culinarians and still have time to focus on her new family.

Pat continued to pursue academic goals, and she earned both her Masters and Ph.D. from New York University's Department of Nutrition and Food Studies. In 1986, Pat was offered a teaching job at New York City Technical College; she advanced to the position of chairwoman of the Department of Hospitality Management in 1990. Pat's doctoral dissertation, *The Elite Woman Chef: A Comparative Case Analysis of Women Chefs and Career Success*, was the principal comprehensive vision of contemporary women in the professional culinary field.

Pat demonstrates the importance of maintaining focus and persevering, regardless of the challenges that may be presented. She is a shining example to women of the goals that can be attained and philosophies that can be perpetuated with dedication and hard work. She has shown us that there is an Elite Woman Chef who is talented and driven and capable.

afford to pay your cooks, restaurants are already expensive! People come to work for me with horror stories of other restaurants. They're just shocked that we give them healthcare, paid vacation, sick pay, overtime, birthday bonuses, and staff discounts. If the restaurant needs a piece of equipment, we buy it, because we know that it's good business. They will be happy employees with the proper tools. Realize that a great restaurant is a long-haul restaurant. It's not a one-year restaurant, and you won't get a restaurant that'll last unless you have realistic parameters."

As Judy's treatment of her staff reflects, she understands that they are the life blood of her restaurant. "Your cooks are your right and left hands, your eyes and ears; understand that and treat them well. One of the things that pains me in a review of a restaurant is that they talk about prices—but a lot of the costs in the restaurant have to do with whether they're exploiting their employees or not! Paying employees fairly and providing healthcare doesn't get in a review. A lot of restaurants don't pay any benefits at all." Judy, however, believes in fair and just treatment. In fact, Judy's restaurant might serve as a model to those who have not yet found a way to keep their staff happy, their turnover low, and their consumers consistently satisfied.

"My budget [staging at Le Cirque] was $5 a day. Three dollars for subway fare to get to and from work, two dollars a day to have fun with, gee!"
—Nancy Stark

Changing the Arena

To stop the attrition, we must change the arena—change the model that for so long has been the standard in the industry. The NRA's booklet, *Women in Foodservice,* addresses one of the pretexts of the industry. "One common argument women encounter is that they must choose the area in which they want to succeed—either family or career, since attempted success in both is supposedly doomed to failure. An adjunct to this is the belief that women who do attempt to 'have it all' will raise children who are poorly adjusted." A study by Jon Ellis in 1991 and reported in the same NRA booklet found that "[there was] no difference to a child's behavioral development whether the mother worked part- or full-time or remained at home with the child. What our society has done is make women feel tremendously guilty if they attempt to have a career and have a family as well." The NRA study goes on to say: "Flexible schedules are one of the most important benefits an employer can provide, and it's one option the foodservice industry may be more capable of providing than many other industries."

Dell Hargis agrees that the industry should be accountable for its inequitable long-term management practices. "I would like to address … the responsibility the industry carries in making things right in the marketplace. I think the industry needs educating. They're happy to look at issues, but they need to carry the responsibility for them by setting the right atmosphere for hiring—if it's a job, the same pay. They need to set the example."

Anne Rosenzweig voices the same concerns and discusses some of the solutions that she believes the industry needs to implement. "We need to figure out ways in which women can still have families and do jobs. One of the things the WCR addresses is job-sharing. We also have to address how we

1962: *Silent Spring* by Rachel Carson is published and is one of the first books to warn of persistent pesticide use.

QUICK DINNERS COOK BOOK 122

QUICK DINNERS

FOR THE WOMAN
IN A HURRY
Cook Book

SHORT CUTS TO
COMPLETE AND
TASTY MEALS

25c

From the 1942 culinary
pamphlet, "Quick
Dinners," Chicago.
Courtesy of the Culinary
Archives and Museum of
Johnson and Wales
University.

handle healthcare in this industry. It's not an industry that traditionally provides healthcare; it's a lot of mom-and-pop-type businesses. Healthcare is expensive and getting more expensive—it's hard to figure out. I offer it at both of my restaurants, but sometimes I wonder—is this the thing that's going to put me out of business? We have to figure out a better way to do it. People want to feel that they come into an industry that's going to take care of them."

While most people in the industry agree that change is needed, Janis Wertz considers what it would take to initiate the process of change. "Change happens when someone just decides they're going to start changing it! They're just going to stop doing certain things, they're going to … 'just say no!' John Wesley said, 'I don't want to follow the Catholic model' and just started doing something different. Rosa Parks decided, 'I'm not going to sit at the back of the bus!' … It's going to take some people who are absolutely affected by the day-to-day nature of all of this to step forward and begin to make the difference happen."

Many other industries have already changed their model of the workplace to one that is more centered on the balance of work and life, career and family. This is what women chefs and cooks aspire to for the culinary industry. Janis continues: "There is a need to determine what pieces are the most important and what is it that needs to be initiated immediately. Who is it that needs to start working to make this happen? Pull the right people in the room, the human resources people from the major hotel chains—not to just sit on a panel—but to get some consensus that says, 'we want to change this environment so that it works better for all of us, so that we can affect retention and real job growth; so that there is sufficient training; and so that people will be loyal.' If one can put together that kind of a conversation, then I think that is really the beginning."

Felice Schwartz and Jean Zimmerman, in their book, *Breaking with Tradition: Women and Work, the New Facts of Life,* offer their interpretation of the current role of women in the workplace and what it's going to take to bring about change: "Now that working women have proven their smarts, their career commitment, and their indispensability to business, why are we asking them to sell their souls to stay in the game? Surely now women can ask that employers go halfway—that companies do whatever it takes to allow maternity and business to co-exist productively. The baby boomers and women bring new values and attitudes about work, family, life, and society to politics and

Women in the Culinary Arena: Tracy Cundiff

Some people are fortunate enough to know what they want from an early age; the benefit of this knowledge is the ability to concentrate on a pursuit unabashedly. Tracy Cundiff is one of those few individuals who targeted her passion and followed her heart. In 1997, Tracy Cundiff was a first-year student at the CIA. I first heard of her through a newspaper article that highlighted her passion and abilities.

Tracy's experiences began at the age of ten, when she bought a cookbook in her grade school bookstore. While in her heart she would like to be a pastry chef, Tracy has competed with great success in culinary competitions, earning over $8,000 in scholarship monies. She participated as the guest chef for a charity auction in Sarasota at the age of sixteen! Her rewards for time spent in front of the stove? Thus far, Tracy has won the Florida Restaurant Association's 'Student of the Year' twice. More importantly than that, she earns her satisfaction from attaining her goals and knowing that she can pursue what she truly loves to do.

Tracy embodies the spirit of the kitchen and the quest of knowledge. While Tracy comes from a family of visual artists, she affirms that her life's work is a type of artistry, too; though she is not drawing or painting, she calls cooking a 'beautiful, wonderful thing.' Her enthusiasm and passion at the age of eighteen are inspiring and encouraging. The industry needs to support women like Tracy to ensure ongoing success.

business. The new value shift centers around time, quality self-fulfillment, children, and general satisfaction with life." This is life as it should be within and outside of the culinary industry. This is our goal for the very near future.

Students: The Next Generation

ShawGuides' *The Guide to Cooking Schools,* published in 1997, lists 322 career and professional cooking schools, 474 nonprofessional schools, and 101 culinary apprenticeship programs. The percent of women versus men in culinary schools varies from school to school, with a low of twenty-four percent, a high of sixty-five percent, and an average of thirty-five percent. The total student enrollment of national cooking schools is over 60,000 and the apprenticeship programs have over 2,000 students. As stated in chapter six, the percentage of female instructors has not kept pace with the increase in female student enrollment from the 1970s, when less than ten percent of all culinary students were women, to the average of thirty-five percent in 1997. The majority (ninety-four percent) of the book's survey respondents said that they had three or fewer female instructors during their tenure at culinary school, which represents

"I think women will be the first to see that they'll have to have business skills. They'll see it en masse before men, because they have a greater need to see it, and therefore who(ever) sees it first gets the most opportunities. The next generation of chefs is going to be much more business-oriented."

—Phyllis Flaherty

1962: The *Joyce Chen Cookbook* is published. Chen taught cooking at home and at adult education centers.

"Don't cheat yourself—learn the business. You need to know dollar in, dollar out; if that can't be part of the joy of it for you ... then you're going to have a hard time. Be smart, focused, and learn the business."
—Rick O'Connell

approximately fifteen percent of all of their instructors. They indicated that of those instructors, half taught in nonculinary classes.

Professionals in the culinary field are responsible for training the next generation of chefs and cooks. Helping them in their careers is essential; they are the next workers, team members, and very possibly the next sous chefs. They may come from culinary schools, apprenticeship programs, or they may have come up through the ranks or from someone else's kitchen. But once they are in our kitchens, their continuing education becomes our responsibility. In this section, we hear some of the women discuss their goals in teaching students, their hopes and expectations in hiring students, and their feelings about formal education and apprenticeship programs.

Instructors' Perspectives on Students

In any discipline, individual instructors bring to their class their own philosophy and way of teaching students. The culinary instructors that I spoke with all share a passion for their role as teachers and mentors to their students. The next few stories detail what these culinary educators think about the next generation of culinarians and provide some advice for them.

Fritz Sonnenschmidt interacts with many future culinarians on an ongoing basis. Based on his experience with the students, I wondered if there were any particular obstacles that students face as they graduate from culinary programs. While he says that there are a lot of talented students, he acknowledges that times have changed and today's students are different than in the past. "The problem today is that we are all trained to see this television approach. ... We learn everything with the mind, like a demo. Our students come up and say, 'The chef didn't give me a demo—I didn't learn anything!' So I ask, 'What do you mean? Did the chef show it to you? Did he work with you; did you do it?' They say, 'Yep. He did. But he didn't give me a demo.' The demo to me is the television approach; they [just] see the picture and they think they can do it."

Cindy Salvato is an instructor at Johnson and Wales; she understands the frustration that some chefs feel when they deal with recent culinary school graduates. Cindy discusses how she deals with students' potential misconception. "Because I know my students think they're going to leave school and be a *chef,* I tell everyone the same thing: 'If you think for one minute you're going to leave here and be a chef, you're sadly mistaken!' If you go out there and you say to people that you're a chef, you're really harming the profession and yourself. You should be proud to be able to leave this school, to leave wherever you are, as an apprentice—you're a cook. Then, give yourself the goal that in ten years you will attain the level of a chef. If you go into the industry right now and somebody hires you as a chef, and you have *no* management skills, *no* business skills, no production skills, no line skills—or [if] you have no management training, you're going to fall down hard."

When students graduate from culinary schools and leave the instructors, they move on to become the pupils of the chefs in the industry. The next section contains some of the stories from the chefs' perspective.

Perspectives on Students from Cooks and Chefs in the Industry

While instructors like Cindy try to explain to students that they need to be patient and humble and climb the ranks, not all students heed that message and not all instructors enforce it. The attitude of some students who have graduated from culinary schools is a source of frustration for those in the industry who spent years of long, grueling hours learning and perfecting their craft. The sentiment echoed by many a frustrated chef is, "They come out of school thinking that they're chefs."

Anne Rosenzweig says she sees the tide changing. "People would graduate and think that they're fully grown chefs—now they're coming out with a little bit more humility. If you don't have the right attitude, it could be a very crushing experience and you can really miss having the rest of your education. The idea is that culinary school is only the beginning of your education. People go and come out, and feel, 'alright—I'm ready to be a sous chef.' Then when you get ready to own your own restaurant, you haven't seen fifty percent of what goes on." Anne talks about one of the first restaurants in which she worked, where the prep area was in the basement. She felt that she literally got to see the restaurant from the bottom up, from the deliveries to the final product, an invaluable experience. "I was down in the basement every day, seeing everything come through the door, how it was broken down and how it was accounted for. Just seeing every little nitty-gritty! When you go to culinary school, you're usually not starting in a basement. You miss that whole experience; it's very worthwhile."

Loretta Keller feels that there are two sides to the issue of whether or not culinary school training is preparing students for the workplace. "That's tough; I've had good experiences and bad experiences. It's up to them [the individual students]." She doesn't feel that students do enough reading and feels they should know more about foods in other countries. She explains, "It's completely available. I taught myself all about it when I was in college by reading books! I give out a list of books that I think everyone should read—I think at the schools there should be mandatory reading in different kinds of foods—Paula Wolfert, Patricia Wells, and Richard Olney, and just a whole bunch of people. I'm going to hire someone—if they have interest, some knowledge, an incentive, chutzpah, a palate! If they love food, let's start there!"

"I would advise [women coming into the field] to get good training. Professional schools are very useful. Start working with the best people in the best places you can. Suck up everything that they have to teach you and that they have to offer."
—Julia Child

1962: Frozen, dehydrated, and canned potatoes account for twenty-five percent of U.S. potato consumption.

View of a French kitchen, circa 1770s. Courtesy of the Culinary Archives and Museum of Johnson and Wales University.

"I like cooking schools. The one thing I dislike about them is the attitude of some of the students who feel that, 'OK, I'm a chef now that I've finished school.' It's like going to law school. You go to law school, you come out, and you find a job as a lawyer; you don't come out of school and be a judge."

—Debbie Gold

Johanne Killeen has seen many students fresh out of culinary schools over the years. In her estimation, the quality of those students has risen dramatically. "Years ago when we had a few applicants from culinary schools, they could barely hold a knife and they called themselves chefs—now they're coming out of school and saying: 'I want to learn—I'm a *cook*.' They don't throw that chef word around as much as they used to; they come out with a much better attitude. That's not across the board, but in general, we're getting just the cream of the crop applying here; the level really has gone up."

Students learn in a variety of settings, including restaurants, hotels, culinary schools, and apprenticeship programs. We have just heard from chefs and culinary educators about students and the prevailing attitudes in school and in the workplace right after they graduate. Next we look at the choice that students have to make when deciding whether to attend a formal culinary institution or to participate in an apprenticeship program.

Perspectives on Formal Education and Apprenticeship Programs

Teaching the next generation is one of the most important things that we as chefs can do. One of the questions prospective students often ask of me is: "Should I go to school, go through an apprenticeship program, or just start in a kitchen and work my way up?" I think the answer to that question depends upon the person. Following are the answers I received from the women I spoke with regarding formal education and apprenticeship programs. While some women believe that culinary schools are useful, others feel that a combination of culinary school with an opportunity to get some hands-on experience through an apprenticeship program is ideal.

Judy Rodgers thinks that a formal culinary education can be a plus in the industry, as long as you work hard to get as much out of it as you can. "I don't think there are any certain gains or losses from any paths. I'm pretty open-minded about cooking schools; I know a lot of people who think there's nothing worse than a formal culinary school education. Maybe because they're too rigid or whatever—I *love* rigid! If somebody else teaches them how to hold a knife and keep it sharp, I don't have to, and I think that's fabulous. A lot of times you get cooks that have come out of apprenticeships, but they've been working with people who aren't very good, and they don't know how to hold a knife and they can't slice an onion. I think it's possible to agree on what a sharp knife is and it's possible to learn the temperature at which egg yolks start to denature—it's possible to learn in an academic environment. My hope and belief is that the academies are just that—they're academies, and they should hand down received wisdom, and teach students to choose to question things."

Deborah Huntley also believes that people coming into the industry must have a formal education and a significant amount of time spent "hands-on" in the kitchen too. "I think the formal education that you can get through a culinary arts school is invaluable [but] getting your base groundwork in is [also] very important. You need to have the math; you have to have the balance in your academic classes along with your culinary classes and skills. The school of hard knocks—the four and a half years I was able to work in every position in the kitchen—really helped me become a chef. I've worked my way through the positions in the kitchen, and feel very comfortable in all of them, and understand what it takes to do them. An apprenticeship program is an ideal situation, where you can work the different departments, and have the hands-on experience, but it also has to be combined with academic studies."

Melissa Kelly is a graduate of the CIA but also apprenticed with some talented chefs. "I think it helps me when I know that someone went to the Culinary—I know what they know, because I've gone through the program. If I say, 'We're going to make this sauce, and the base is a *béchamel*,' a Culinary graduate has that foundation; you know exactly what they were taught. Whether they remember it or paid attention is another story. Coming up through the ranks, I think you can learn—it depends which ranks you come through. If you come up through really good kitchens, then you can learn all

"I think as far as education goes we need both apprenticeship and education. I think the French have it very well defined; they have theoretical schooling and apprenticeship combined—school during the day and work in the restaurant at night."
—Madeleine Kamman

1963: Julia Child's "The French Chef" cooking show debuts on WGBH, the Boston Public television station; Julia makes Boeuf Bourguignonne.

"My advice to young people going into (the field) is just work a little bit first, then decide whether you want to pay the money, and put in the time to go to school—because some people just go straight off to school, don't understand the dynamics of the restaurant or catering business, and then get into it and hate it!"
—*Ana Sortun*

those things along the way, but if you've come up in bad kitchens, you might have learned some bad habits. You might not understand things as well as someone who got all those basics laid down in stone."

Carol Levenherz returned to school at the age of 47 and earned her Associate of Occupational Studies (AOS) from the CIA in 1997. Carol has owned her catering company since 1981, but speaks from the vantage point of student when she talks about her culinary school influences. "I'd wanted to come to the CIA for years just to get formal training—to know more. I wanted to be cooking!" She goes on to say: "Even though I had fifteen years of field experience catering before attending the CIA, I still wanted the degree. It's like anything else; no matter how much you know, you realize how much more there is to learn. I think that you're a student all of your life, period."

Lidia Bastianich believes that there is a new cuisine, one being born of the melting pot of our country and one that will take a tremendous amount of learning to master. "Because the kids don't have these roots, this education, they need that time to learn, they need to formulate themselves. A cuisine's being born here [in America] that's being based on all the cultures that are here—I see it happening. I think they need to be really prepared; like artists, some of them are really artists, and some of them are just slapping it all together! But they need to be prepared; they need to know about the cultures they're using. They need a lot more exposure than four years at the Culinary to become great chefs."

Elizabeth Terry, chef-owner of Elizabeth on 37th, took a much different path than most; she is self-taught. Elizabeth talks about this nontraditional path: "I think that being self-trained is the long way to go; it took me fifteen years to learn. The fact that I wasn't school-trained has given the food a bit of an unusual edge here and the restaurant a bit of a flair that's very exciting to the customers. There are those who are well-trained, and then there are those who just have this magic spark that really sets them apart from others in the same business. That magic spark can't be taught; however, schooling is important. It's important to know how to make mashed potatoes smooth if that's how you want them and lumpy if that's how you want them—execution is important."

It always amazes me how many line cooks have minimal math skills. When I query them on costing a recipe, they invariably tell me they're bad at math and don't see why they need to know it, because all they want to do is cook. Barbara Sanders spent much of her career as a culinary educator. She discusses her philosophy on teaching her students. "My attitude was that you needed to do reading, writing, arithmetic—you do not just cook. If you're going to move upward in this profession, you *must* know all three. Take steaming green beans—if you don't understand the reasons why you don't put the lid on, then you'll put the lid on, and the beans are going to come out looking horrible! There are reasons why we need to have the basics 'down' first."

There's no one way to enter the culinary arena. One can attend a culinary school; others feel getting hands-on experience in a kitchen is the way to go; self-instruction is a third option. Clearly, there are many ways to gain the knowledge necessary to excel in the field. There is a consensus, however, about one aspect of this discussion—it takes time to become a chef. The fundamentals are important, whether they are learned in school, in the kitchen, or both. One needs to be prepared to take the time to learn to do everything the right way. The next section explores the differences between female and male students in the culinary arena.

Female versus Male Students

The culinary educators with whom I spoke unanimously agree that there are differences between female and male students. Among the generalizations that I heard are that the women tend to be in the minority of the student body but ultimately at the top of the graduating classes. Women also tend to achieve more honors and awards yet have fewer job possibilities than men upon graduation. Another difference appears to be that female students are generally less assertive, find themselves in supportive roles, and need to be pushed more than their male counterparts. The following stories highlight these points.

Hilary DeMane talks about how she has seen the male and female students interact in her classes. "The biggest frustration I have with the majority of women in the program is that they're very timid. They're very nonassertive. They'll be the ones who are prepping the carrots while the guy's over there cooking on the hot line. I say to the women, 'You are not somebody's handmaid or slave; *you* get up there and do the hollandaise! You get up there and sauté the fish! Don't allow yourself to be utilized as a handmaiden!' They need to assert themselves more—most of them, are very, very timid. I don't remember being that timid. In fact I know I was pretty aggressive. I can remember one of the first days at CIA. I was on the dish-station with two other guys. One guy hadn't been there the whole day, and I got really mad, and I said, 'Hey, you! Get your ass over here, and do some pots!' I said [to the other student], 'I'm not doing your pots for you! What do you think?' I said: 'I'm not your slave!' And the chef loved it! he said, 'That's it! You tell 'em!' So, it's not impossible, but I guess it's social. It's harder for [women] to be trained to be assertive."

Fritz Sonnenschmidt has this to say about some of the students he has interacted with: "Women students are much better than male students. They

> *"Don't expect to be treated differently; don't ask to be treated differently. You are professionals and you are doing a job. If you choose to be in a restaurant, you can ask for help; if you're not going to ask for help, and you're not going to hold (that 100-pound pot) up (by yourself), think about how you're going to do it."*
> —Noëlle Haddad

1963: The average meat consumption per capita reaches 170.6 pounds. Chicken consumption is 37.8 pounds, up from 23.5 pounds in 1945.

"If you're doing something that doesn't pay very much money, or doesn't pay you any money at all, if you can, think of it as work for yourself, work for your development, you're not working for somebody else—you're working for yourself!"
—*Jody Adams*

beat them on all levels: left, right, center. They're much more dedicated, and much stronger in many ways—it's a fact." Dell Hargis, the Director of Alumni Affairs at the CIA, shares a sentiment similar to Fritz's: "Women are the achievers. They are the outstanding students. And, more than that, I think the top [student in most classes] usually turns out to be female, mid-30s, career changer; [she] just has it all. She puts all the pieces together, knows beyond the shadow of a doubt what she's out there for and why, and she just accomplishes great, great things."

Why would it be that women are winning the awards and men are getting the jobs? Maybe part of it is that women are less assertive. Maybe it's just that women don't fit the preconceived image of certain positions. Whatever the reason is, this needs to be addressed. An industry goal must be to help support and promote these female students into professional roles that equate to the high level of which they are capable of attaining.

Advice for the Next Generation

One of the questions I asked all the women surveyed and interviewed is: "What advice would you give to women thinking of embarking on a culinary career?" Keep in mind that these women are doing what they're doing because it is their passion, and their career is a driving force in their lives. This passion penetrates their hearts and souls; that's the point of view from which they offer advice to future culinarians.

First and foremost, future culinarians are reminded that to make it in this industry you need to be prepared to work hard and put in the time. You will need to work with confidence, learn all that you can, understand the business, understand the potential attitudes of prospective employers toward women, and make yourself stand out from the crowd. Each piece of advice is based on the experience and observation over time, within the industry.

Sarah Stegner advocates a passion for the industry and acknowledges that this is a profession of long hours and little pay. "Working in the industry is never easy. It's not easy for anyone. It's a hard profession and it's demanding. If you don't love it, if you don't feel impassioned by it, then find an aspect of it that isn't so demanding. Maybe the restaurant side of it isn't the side you should be in—it's very important to love what you do. That is the key to success generally. To excel and to move ahead, keep your eye on your job, and if you do really well in your job; that's what supports the chef—that's what makes the difference in the kitchen."

Sarah also offers a bit of reality that is important for students to understand. "When you are a cook, you're not paid a great deal of money. But this is a trade profession; the skill is in your hands and in your palate, it takes time, often years, to develop. If you go to a culinary school, which right now costs twenty, thirty thousand dollars, you're paying a fortune—you're going to get out and make six, seven dollars an hour. To pay back a school loan, and to *live* off of an income like that, to handle that pressure, that financial pressure, instead of giving yourself the time you need to develop your skills, that's constant pressure. At the same time, we can't forget we're artisans—that the skill is in our hands and in our palate. And it takes time to develop, and you've got to slow down and give yourself a chance. Students coming out of the culinary schools expecting sous chef positions find that if they are smart enough and have the opportunity of getting into those positions, they don't have the skills it takes to back it up. It's an artist's profession; and although it's intensive, hard work, it's skill that you're developing, and it takes time; give yourself a chance. Plan for it."

Hilary DeMane says hard work is at the core of making it in this industry. "We're all guilty of saying, 'If you want to make it, you've got to work hard.' You always have to work hard—but how many *days* is enough? Is it too much to expect that you could have two days off in a week?" In some businesses, maybe not, but in this business, two days off isn't a reality (in many segments), especially when starting off. Hilary offers: "If you want to succeed in our business, you're going to have to put in some incredible sweat equity."

Guesdon del's "Cheminee a Morlaix," a circa-1880s view of a kitchen with large open hearth and two female cooks (western France). From *L'Art*.

Emily Luchetti offers a similar message as she describes her career: "I put my head down, started working, looked up, and ten years had passed. You just put your head to the grindstone, and you work and work and work." Even the long hours and hard work don't always guarantee success. For Emily, success was not the driving force. "I got into it because of my passion and my love for cooking. ... That's what drove me every day. It wasn't the notoriety or the fame or anything like that. A lot of the younger people don't realize how hard it is on a day-to-day basis. And unless you have that passion, it's not going to sustain you."

Suzanne Bussiere, executive sous chef of Boulevard in San Francisco, focuses on hard work and passion; however, one of the aspects of hard work that she discusses is working with others, getting along and thriving in the

1965: Kellogg's introduces Pop-Tart pastries.

*"For young women
... get real proficient
in meat and fish,
and you're going to
open a lot of doors for
yourself. Get profi-
cient in Spanish ...
bilingual chefs are
really important."*
—Gwen Kvavli Gulliksen

"heat." "It's hard work, not only physically, but mentally. You have to be in tune with what you are doing and always be aware—tasting and feeling, because everything is not going to stay the same. Things in the kitchen are constantly changing and the people that you work with are not going to be the same. Everybody has their moods; you can't let yourself get angry or beat yourself up for any little thing; you just have to move on and stay centered within yourself. ... If you don't like somebody, you have to grit your teeth. On a day when you're feeling good about yourself, just pull that person aside and talk to them one on one, with good eye contact and say *how you feel*, and if they respond, go from there. Don't ever assume anything; never assume. Each kitchen is different—keep smiling, keep hanging in there, don't cut yourself and don't burn your sauces! Enjoy being with people."

Susan Spicer agrees that hard work and stamina are critical, but so are attitude and ability. "You have to always try to do more, try to be exceptional. Average people are a dime a dozen; you have to stand out, have to go that extra mile to be noticed. It's about attitude and aptitude—those are the two things. You have to have some innate ability, some aptitude for it, and the other thing is, it's about tasting food constantly. Taste, taste, taste."

Both Shirley King and Edna Lewis come from decades of kitchen experience. Like Susan, they encourage tasting the food. However, they also feel that traveling and reading are very important for acquiring knowledge that will be useful in their careers. Shirley shared these thoughts. "My advice is to travel as much as possible, buy every magazine, read them all and taste everything that you can. Keep your nose and eyes totally involved. Use everything—it's knowledge." Edna shares the same priority of taste, travel, and knowledge. "I would tell them to not just go by a recipe; you have to think. Travel in the countryside and think about food! ... You have to have your own personal focus about food; investigate the seasonings. You have to taste, and taste, and taste. Everything is creating, you develop your own flair, your own taste, your own thoughts about it. The more you work in it, the more you become addicted to it!"

Eat, read, taste, cook, and travel—it's one of the mantras of the culinary world. To that Joyce Goldstein adds: "Work in the industry and make sure it's what you really want, because lots of times people get in the kitchen and discover, 'I've been cleaning shrimp for *four hours*—and I haven't cooked *anything!!*' It's production—there are these big stretches where you're doing nothing but peeling potatoes! I'd tell them to read, not just magazines, but books—find out the histories of these countries that they pretend to cook. I'm an old-fashioned person; I believe in starting with knowledge, and then doing the work! If you don't have any depth of knowledge going into the kitchen, you'll be eating off your own entrails. If you only have seven tricks, and now you've played them, where do you go? But if you start with knowledge, you learn a lot of tricks and then can make a living with those tricks."

Some offer practical advice about how to enter the culinary industry. At any given time, I may have as many as six or eight students working in my kitchen and I often find myself giving advice. One of the issues I always bring up with them is having a plan. Where are you now? What do you want to learn? Where do you want to be in three years or five? Ferdinand Metz also thinks having a plan is key. "There are some very standard things that still hold true, that still make sense. Map out a career plan. Don't agonize over, 'Is it right, or is it wrong?' Map it out and follow it. As you follow it and mature, you begin to realize … a plan is only a plan; it can be changed. Find out where you want to be ten years from now [and] determine what it would take to be in that position. What kind of qualifications will you need? What kind of experiences must you accumulate along the way? … It doesn't have to be a straight line; it can be a zig-zag! But along the way, gain the necessary experience and the necessary qualifications: the additional schooling, seminars, certifications, etc."

Phyllis Flaherty talks about preparing resumes and knowing how to use language, facts, and figures to sell yourself. She urges women to be more direct and use stronger, more active language than is typical of the women she has seen. "Women don't tend to write resumes correctly. Most likely it's a man reading the resume, and the things that you say need to be said differently then you would say them to a woman. The things that you highlight are different than what you might think they'd be. … One of the things I find in getting [women's] resumes: I call them too soft. When you get men's resumes, it says, 'I developed, I had sales of this total, I raised revenue by this much, I raised gross margin by this much.' Women's resumes don't tend to have that. Yet if you're a man running a business, looking to hire a chef, which would you pick? Someone who knew the numbers, or someone who didn't?" Of critical importance, says Phyllis, is the bottom line. "If someone's hiring you, bottom line, they're hiring you so they can make money. … Your role is not to be an artist—your role is to make somebody money."

Alison Awerbuch's thoughts turn to the importance of assessing your options. She feels it is important that when women apply for positions with different establishments, they should consider how women working in those operations have been treated in the past. "There are areas in the country where it is a lot tougher for a woman. Certain regions and also certain types of kitchens are more difficult for a woman. What I think is really important is that a woman seeking a position gains as much knowledge … about the kitchen she's putting herself into before accepting a position. Although all of us can probably survive anything, we should probably get more knowledge on the chef, the hierarchy, and how many females are in the kitchen. Are the women promoted as much

"You have to work very hard in this career … you also have to keep reading and traveling—to learn, to enrich yourself … you cannot think that you know everything."
—*Susanna Foo*

1967: The first compact microwave oven for national home use is introduced by Amana Refrigeration.

"It's a great field that's satisfying and challenging in many different ways; physically, mentally, and emotionally. It can be a really great career. It can also be a career in which you work as hard as you've ever known yourself to work and still go home feeling you did a lousy job—if it's been a bad night at the restaurant."

—Susan Spicer

as men? Are there women in significant positions? We should consider whether we want to be in a kitchen where there are no other females and where we feel like we may not get treated as fairly, or may not have the same opportunities for growth."

Once you know that you have the passion and love the work, and once you have explored your options and gained experience in the industry, you might decide that owning a restaurant is your life-long dream. If this is the case, Judy Rodgers offers some advice about the key responsibilities she feels are inherent in the job. "If you're going to open a restaurant someday, it should be a responsible restaurant. Don't just worry about getting your own name, because I can tell you, there are 150 hot new chefs every year, and nobody remembers their name next year! Do something bigger than your name in boldface! There are so many angles where you can make the restaurant business better. ... If you care about food a whole lot, you can seek out vendors and purveyors who are growing the best possible products in healthy, environmentally sound ways."

Judi Arnold also discusses the concerns that affect people who start their own businesses. She emphasizes the need to jump into the task with confidence. "I really passionately believe this—anybody, man or woman, can start a business but to do it, you have to take that little leap. You have to have an idea or a product, something that you believe firmly in and that you believe can be a success. It's taking everything you know, everything you are, everything you've learned, and making a leap with it—not intellectualizing it. I often use an analogy from Lee Strausburg, the method-acting teacher. He said to be a great actor you had to have talent, you had to go to school and learn every single technique and then throw it out and transcend yourself. That's what I think you have to do. It's *the leap* ... it's something indescribable, you have to be just willing to let go—[and have] blind faith."

People with a wide range of experiences, skills, and achievements offer advice to the next generation. Each of them has been in the industry for a number of years and speaks from those experiences. If you are entering the industry, their advice and observations should serve as, excuse the pun—"food for thought"—for your future. During the research stage of preparing this book, I came across a list of books that Jody Adams had written for her staff as a summer reading list. This gave me the idea to offer those who read this book a comprehensive list of the books that all the women interviewed recommended, which can be found in Appendix D. The purpose of this list is to allow readers the opportunity to garner more information in a number of different areas. This way, you can start heeding the advice offered in this section: read, taste, learn, and travel—develop a palate, be humble, and cook!

How Can We Effect Change?

There are a number of things that I feel need to happen to bring equality to the culinary industry. These include parity in wages and addressing the needs of families in order to keep the industry from imploding from lack of a culinary base. How will these changes occur? In this section, some of the options are discussed.

To promote change, the industry must work through the National Restaurant Association and the lobbying power it has with the government. We need to enact legislation that makes daycare, healthcare, flextime, and job-sharing not only more accessible, but more economically viable for business. We need to embark on an educational campaign that draws attention to the benefits of bringing women with families into the industry. We need to work through the NRA to have a *voice* that supports family life, raising children and having a career as equal goals, creating a better future for the industry and America.

The Women Chefs and Restaurateurs need support from everyone in this industry. The future depends on the end of all bias, the end of preconceived notions of value and worth, and the beginning of a national support system for women in the industry. We need to enact a nationwide networking and mentoring system that helps women in the industry find their place. We need job banks that bring talented women into the view of those looking for talented culinarians, wherever they might be. Scholarship programs need to be set up, not only for students, but for career changers as well, and these programs need to include support for family obligations.

An advocacy group established in 1997 that has the potential to bear influence on the foodservice industry is the MultiCultural Foodservice and Hospitality Alliance (MFHA), which is targeting equal opportunity for minorities. The group is being funded by several of the nation's most influential foodservice corporations to support and encourage diversity in hiring, career advancement, and vendor selection. Jerry Fernandez, national account manager for General Mills and president of the MFHA had this to say about the group. "Our objective is to promote diversity and economic benefits of a multicultural work force in the industry." Although not specifically targeting women, I applaud any group that is championing diversity and the end of bias and I think that the influence of the twenty-five major foodservice companies will have positive results. As an industry we need to make sure that the MFHA succeeds—it will help ensure the health of the industry for the future.

The American Culinary Federation has to take a leadership role in assuring position and pay equity for women in the culinary field. Although the ACF

"The biggest problem I see in the United States is we make such a big issue about male and women chefs. ... We are all chefs. We have to put this thing behind us ... it doesn't really matter ... if it's (a) woman, or (a) black chef, or whatever the case—we're chefs!"
—*Fritz Sonnenschmidt*

1968: Half of all U.S. mothers of school-age children are in the work force.

A Cordon Bleu female chef cooking. [Le Depot cher F. Gerret's "La Cuisiniere Bourgeoise (Cordon Bleu)," a hand-colored engraving, Paris No. 8, circa 1880. Engraver: De Melle Forsmeriter. Published by Charles Title, 86 Fleet Street, London.]

doesn't track membership by gender, it is believed that women make up twenty-five percent of the ranks. The challenge is that of those ACF members that are certified, only thirteen percent are women, and of those certified at the sous chef level or above, only eight percent are women. We need to support the advancement of women into the highest possible levels of the industry. Kay Corning, the first female national vice-president, is running for president in 1997; no matter the outcome, it is essential that the ACF support a place for women to network, mentor, and be mentored in all levels of the industry.

With the number of culinary schools growing exponentially, new and existing schools need to be the driving force in bringing talented women into the industry on an equal level with men. Their responsibility needs to include educating the students in all the skills that they will need to succeed in the workplace. These skills should incorporate dealing with bias, harassment, and inequities.

The foodservice industry has a responsibility to all its current and future employees. We hear the leaders of the country talking about the loss of family values and the deterioration of the family unit, yet our industry, which accounts for over four percent of the Gross Domestic Product and is the nation's largest employer, is one of the worst offenders. This must change. We have examined the NRA *Foodservice Employee Profile* at different points in this book. It reveals some very poignant facts on which we need to base our future decisions. It shows that women represent almost sixty percent of foodservice workers, and that forty percent are in their childbearing years, but only thirty-one percent are part of a two-parent household, which leaves a lot of single moms. This can be compared to the fact that fifty-eight percent of all working women with children are married with the spouse present. These facts lead me to believe, as so many have said, that the foodservice industry just isn't family-friendly and that the need for change is irrefutable.

While all members of the foodservice industry share the responsibility for effecting change, women especially have to support each other. We have to have the faith and trust to take the necessary risks, work hard, and find the right teachers and mentors. That being said, there are some paths that are easier than others. The NRA *Foodservice Employee Profile* gives us additional facts that can be used for guidance. For instance, the smaller the company, the less likely they are to have full-time employees, so if part-time work is a necessity, there may be more opportunities at smaller independent operations. The larger the company, the fewer women are employed on an hourly basis, and the more salaried women are employed. If we believe that corporate America understands business, then we can see that they believe in women as managers, and in their abilities in the marketplace.

If you love food, people, hard work, teamwork, and the world you've read about in this book, then go for it, just do it. Get up, jump up, stamp your feet, and find a way into this field. Find a way to follow your passions, dreams, your calling, and your heart. Make the best food and sustainable food choices that you can. Be the best cook you can be. Whether your passion is to cook in a restaurant, hotel or school; for your family or friends; or if you want to start a business then follow your heart and your dreams. If you need help, call me, call one of the women in this book, or one of the associations or institutions in the Appendix or anyone in the industry. Just make that call, get the help, and start working toward fulfilling your dream. You can make it happen. We can help.

"The most important thing is living a life that matters."
—*Madeleine Kamman*

1968: The average American eats eleven pounds of fish per year.

The Women Chefs' Biographies

Jody Adams, Executive Chef, RIALTO, Cambridge, MA
Jody is a New England native who studied Anthropology at Brown University.
In 1983, Jody's formal culinary career began while working under Lydia Shire
at the Four Seasons in Boston. From there, she went on to work at Michela's
in Cambridge, where she formed a partnership with owner Michela Larson.
That partnership aided in the development of the concept for Rialto, which
opened in 1994 in The Charles Hotel in Cambridge. In 1993, Chef Adams was
named "One of America's Ten Best Chefs" by *Food and Wine* magazine. Jody
is married with two children.

Dina Altieri, Executive Chef, MORE THAN A MOUTHFUL, Los Angeles, CA
Raised in a household that emphasized Italian food and cooking, Dina is a
1991 honors graduate of the CIA. After training under Marcel Desaulniers at
The Trellis in Williamsburg, Virginia, Dina traveled to Nantucket and finally
decided on Los Angeles as her locale of choice. Dina is executive chef of a busy
on-site and off-site catering facility and prides herself on combining a history
of great Italian food with a love of contemporary Mediterranean cuisine.

Judi Arnold, Co-Owner, DUFOUR PASTRY KITCHEN, New York, NY
Judi's multifaceted life includes having been a Journalism graduate from
Simmons College in Boston. She worked as a merchandizing editor for a dec-
orating magazine and spent fifteen years in the classical music industry. DuFour
Pastry Kitchen started in 1984, sharing a desk and kitchen space in the New
York equivalent of a garage! Today DuFour is housed in an extensive manu-
facturing complex and produces hors d'oeuvres, puff pastry dough, tart shells,
and other savories for some of the most exacting clientele in New York City.

1968: The Citizen's Board of Inquiry into Hunger and Malnutrition in the United States
observes that Federal Food Aid Programs reach only eighteen percent of the nation's poor.

Alison Awerbuch, Corporate Executive Chef, Co-Owner,
ABIGAIL KIRSCH CULINARY PRODUCTIONS, Tarrytown, NY
Alison began her career as a Business major at the University of Michigan-Ann Arbor. She graduated first in her class from the CIA in 1985 and immediately started working at Abigail Kirsch's as a catering cook. Within two years, Alison had earned the position of executive chef. She is now the corporate executive chef and co-owner of Abigail Kirsch Culinary Productions, with responsibility for overseeing three facilities. Alison lives in Westchester County, NY.

Monique Barbeau, Executive Chef, FULLER'S, The Sheraton Hotel,
Seattle, WA
Monique's career started as a caterer in her native Vancouver, British Columbia. She went onto the CIA and New York City, where she worked at The Quilted Giraffe, Le Bernardin, and Chanterelle. Monique took a hiatus from the kitchen to earn her B.S. in hospitality management from Florida International University in 1991. Back in the kitchen in 1994, Monique was honored as co-recipient of the James Beard 'Best Northwest Chef,' and she has appeared on the PBS program 'In Julia's Kitchen with Master Chefs.' Monique has been executive chef at Fuller's since 1992.

Loretta Barrett Oden, Co-owner, THE CORN DANCE CAFÉ, Santa Fe, NM
Originally from Oklahoma, Loretta found her culinary roots after a three-year 'walk-about.' A member of the Pottawattamie tribe, Loretta traveled the country talking and cooking with other women, comparing different regional cuisines. This experience helped her form her food philosophy of emphasizing healthy foods that are indigenous to the Americas, with a focus on foods with Native American origin. The Corn Dance Café opened in 1993.

Alison Barshak, Executive Chef, VENUS AND THE COWBOY,
Philadelphia, PA
A restaurant connoisseur by the time she graduated from high school, Alison attended Boston University and attempted a traditional education. Frequent trips to South America with her college roommate formed the basis of an early culinary education. After working in a number of Philadelphia establishments, Alison opened The Striped Bass in 1994 to rave reviews; *Esquire* named the restaurant "The Best New Restaurant in the Country." Alison stepped down from her position in 1996 and plans to open her new restaurant in 1997.

Dr. Pat Bartholomew, Chairwoman, Department of Hospitality
Management, City University of New York/New York Technical College
Pat graduated from the City University of New York with a degree in Communications and Culinary Arts, and she went on to earn a Masters and

Ph.D. from New York University's Department of Nutrition and Food Studies. Pat's doctoral dissertation, "The Elite Woman Chef: A Comparative Case Analysis of Women Chefs and Career Success," was one of the first looks at contemporary women in the professional culinary field. Pat has worked as a cook and a chef in restaurants, hotels, and executive dining rooms including The Waldorf Astoria and The Front Porch. She was food editor for *Restaurant Business* magazine. Pat is married with two children.

Lidia Bastianich, Co-owner, Executive Chef, FELIDIA, BECCO, and FRICO, New York, NY

After emigrating from Pula, Istria, in 1958, Lidia has earned the title of First Lady of Italian restaurants in the United States. Lidia shares the responsibilities of running three restaurants with her husband Felice and her son Joseph. Her daughter Tanya helps to organize *Esperienze Italiane,* a gastronomic and cultural travel company that specializes in regional trips to Italy. Lidia's passion for food and history are evident in her spare-time commitments to teaching, lecturing, and writing. Lidia is married with two children.

Toniann Beattie, Culinary Student, International Culinary Academy, Pittsburgh, PA

Toniann began her culinary career after having a marriage and two children. A daring move to sell her house and pursue her passion put this confident woman at the top of her culinary class. Toniann's philosophy that 'it's never too late' should prove exemplary to other women faced with similar decisions.

Catherine Brandell, Chef-Instructor, The Culinary Institute of America at Greystone, St. Helena, CA

Catherine's background spans the globe. After obtaining a B.A. in Anthropology from the University of California at Berkeley in 1967 and a teaching certificate in 1968, Catherine went to Australia to teach art to primary school students. She then returned to the United States and worked as a forager for Alice Waters at Chez Panisse. Part of Catherine's passion is to promote an understanding of sustainable agriculture and inspire the student chefs she works with at Greystone.

Sharon Brooks-Moses, Chef, Educator, Randallstown, MD

Sharon has a degree in Public Administration and was working for the Department of the Navy when she became aware of a culinary arts program that was being offered in the capitol district. A switch in careers placed Sharon

1969: Forty-three percent of all United States' women over the age of sixteen and forty-one percent of all married women are in the labor force; four percent of these women are farmhands or domestic servants.

in urban hotels for two years. She chose to attend the CIA and arrived in 1991 with a serendipitous twist; an anonymous scholarship entirely paid for her education. Sharon graduated and has subsequently become an educator herself. She and her husband live in Maryland.

Lyde Buchtenkirch-Biscardi, Chef-Instructor, The Culinary Institute of America, Hyde Park, NY

One of the first women to graduate from the CIA in 1972, Lyde has forged a professional path that opened doors for women in her wake. Following her commencement, Lyde taught at Johnson and Wales and returned to her alma mater as a chef-instructor in 1978. Consistently a pioneer, Lyde was the first woman to be selected for the ACF team that competed at the 1980 International Culinary Competition, where she earned two gold medals and a silver cup. Additionally, she was the first woman to qualify as a certified master chef (CMC) by fulfilling ACF requirements. Lyde is married and she and her husband live in the Hudson Valley region of New York.

Suzanne Bussiere, Executive Sous Chef, BOULEVARD, San Francisco, CA

After a career with the federal government, Suzanne decided to return to school at the California Culinary Academy and graduated in 1980. Her first job was at a French restaurant in San Rafael, California, and she advanced to Campton Place, where she helped Chef Bradley Ogden revamp his entire breakfast menu. She worked with Anne Gingrass, aiding in the opening of Postrio and additionally, she spent valuable time with Paul Bertolli in the Chez Panisse kitchen. Suzanne worked with Nancy Oakes at L'Avenue as sous chef from 1991 to 1993, then helped to open Boulevard in 1993.

Siobhan Carew, Co-owner POMODORO, Boston, MA, and MATT MURPHY'S, Brookline, MA

Siobhan grew up in County Tipperary, Ireland, and learned the value of fresh, quality foods throughout her childhood. Following a move to the United States, Siobhan worked at the Five Seasons, a natural health food café in Jamaica Plain, Massachusetts. She moved on to learn more about technique and composition at Michela's in Cambridge. Her first restaurant, a trattoria called Pomodoro, opened in 1991; the second restaurant, Matt Murphy's, opened in 1996. Siobhan is a graduate of Wheelock College and extends her culinary and management talents to helping her husband with their three daughters.

Mary Cech, Chef-Instructor, The Culinary Institute of America at Greystone, St. Helena, CA

A member of the 1991 World Cup Pastry team, Mary's pastry background and training are diverse. She began her education in 1984 at the CIA, taking advantage of their continuing education department, and apprenticed with Chef Albert Cumin, CMPC. Mary was selected as Pastry Chef of the Year in 1992 and was one of the Top Ten Pastry Chefs in 1994 and 1996. Before joining the faculty at Greystone in 1995, Mary was corporate pastry chef for the Chicago-based Lettuce Entertain You, Inc.

Deena Chafetz, Chef, FIREBIRD, New York, NY

Deena began her career and progressed quickly to the position of chef at the age of 21. She spent eight years in Vermont at small inns, then challenged herself to move to Santa Fe, New Mexico. A formative three years at the Hilton as executive sous chef prepared her to move back East and accept an executive chef position at a Connecticut inn, and soon afterward at a small Hudson Valley winery. Deena aided in the opening of Max on Main in Hartford, Connecticut before moving to New York City in 1996.

Julia Child, Author, Cook, Educator, TV Personality, and Pioneer, Cambridge, MA

A native Californian, Julia graduated from Smith College in 1934 and entered the public relations field. She met her future husband in Ceylon and after their marriage in 1946, they moved to Paris in 1948. This was to be the beginning of a lifelong dedication to teaching. After studying at the Cordon Bleu, Julia opened L'Ecole des Trois Gourmandes with the help of Simone Beck and Louisette Bertholle. *Mastering the Art of French Cooking* was published in 1961 and was the first comprehensible interpretation of French food for millions of American cooks. Julia began her television career in 1962 on the Boston public broadcasting channel. With more than five books and even more television shows to her credit, Julia has been awarded honorary degrees from Boston College, Bates College, Smith College, and Harvard University, in addition to the Peabody Award and an Emmy. Julia was instrumental in founding the American Institute of Wine and Food and The James Beard Foundation, Inc., two of the foremost showcases of young chefs today.

Gloria Ciccarone-Nehls, Executive Chef, THE BIG FOUR, The Huntington Hotel, San Francisco, CA

Gloria credits her background and strong Italian family for instilling a passion for food. She ran her first station in her grandparent's restaurant at the age of twelve and there, she trained the new staff members and oversaw the pantry! She studied at art school before supplementing her education with a degree from the CIA. Gloria has been with the Huntington Hotel since 1979; she was named executive chef in 1981. In 1995, the National Executive Chefs

1969: The National Women's Hall of Fame is founded in Seneca Falls, New York.

Association named Gloria Hotel Chef of the Year. Gloria and her husband live in the Bay area.

Kay Corning, Regional Vice-President ACF West, West Lake Village, CA
Kay's food career began at her mother's resort in upstate New York, where she swore that she would go and be a secretary or a model because cooking was such hard work! In 1964, she succumbed to cooking and learned bulk production under a baker in California; she opened her own pie shop in 1965, which blossomed into an extensive catering company. Kay still caters and divides her time between her company and her responsibilities with the ACF; she was the first woman to be named Chef of the Year by the Los Angeles chapter of the ACF.

Lucie Costa, CEC, Executive Chef and Owner, THE HISTORIC NORTH PLANK ROAD TAVERN 1851, Newburgh, NY
Lucie grew up in Montreal, Canada, graduating from Authunsic College in Montreal with a degree in Biochemistry. After spending time cooking in St. Martin, Lucie came to the United States in 1977. The Historic North Plank Road Tavern 1851 opened in 1979. Lucie was awarded the ACF mid-Hudson Valley Chef of the Year in 1995. Lucie is married and finds time to write, consult, and be a mom to two boys.

Clara Craig, Executive Chef, PROJECT OPEN HAND, San Francisco, CA
Clara began her career with a scholarship to the University of California, Berkeley, studying both math and English. After a short period of time, she found herself working first in the kitchen of a hospital and then working under two very different and positive mentors—one a French chef, and one a German chef. In 1982 she was the first female admitted into the Pacific Coast Chefs Association. Clara now is executive chef for Project Open Hand, an organization that provides 1,500 meals a day to housebound individuals in the San Francisco region diagnosed with AIDS. Clara is the mother of two children.

Tracy Cundiff, Student, The Culinary Institute of America, Hyde Park, NY
Tracy originally hails from Sarasota, Florida and is completing her AOS in baking and pastry prior to entering the Bachelor's degree program at the CIA. Tracy bought her first cookbook at the age of ten and practiced cooking meals for her family. In 1995 and 1996 the Florida Restaurant Association named Tracy Student of the Year. She was awarded a silver medal and $8,000 in scholarship monies in the Johnson and Wales Taste of Florida competition in 1996.

Ariane Daguin, Co-owner, D'ARTAGNAN, Jersey City, NJ
Ariane's traditional French background included growing up in her father's one-star Michelin restaurant and performing all of the duties of a 'goose-girl'. She moved to New York to attend Columbia University's School of Journalism; a summer job at The Three Little Pigs parlayed into a new career and a partnership with George Faison in 1985. This new venture, D'Artagnan, is the largest distributor of foie gras in the world, and Ariane has been listed in the James Beard Association's *Who's Who of Food and Wine*. Ariane is the mother of one daughter.

Hilary DeMane, CEPC, CCE, Chef-Instructor, Indiana University of Pennsylvania Academy of Culinary Arts, Punxsutawney, PA
Having graduated from the CIA in 1977, Hilary went on, at the age of twenty-four, to be the first woman and the first American to hold the position of pastry chef for Holland American Cruise Lines. From there, she proceeded to The Biltmore in Los Angeles, where she was executive pastry chef. Hilary has owned her own bakery with her husband; additionally, she was corporate pastry chef for Premier Cruise Lines. Now a chef-instructor, she was awarded the prestigious Senate Teaching Award in recognition of her teaching skills.

Kirsten Dixon, Chef-Owner, RIVERSONG ADVENTURES, Anchorage, AK
Originally educated in the field of nursing with a Master's degree from Syracuse University, Kirsten turned to cooking because nursing 'wasn't fun.' In 1983, she and her husband began to assemble the first of their three remote lodges, all built by hand from the ground up. Kirsten's training at the Cordon Bleu has been supplemented with stagière positions and continuing education classes. In 1992, *Esquire* magazine named Kirsten one of the Top Ten Best New Chefs. Kirsten has two daughters and is very active in home schooling.

Jamie Eisenberg, Director of Purchasing, Chef-Instructor, New England Culinary Institute, Essex, VT
Jamie's initial career pursuits were at the Rhode Island School of Design; she graduated with a B.F.A. in 1982. While attending RISD, she washed dishes at The Bluepoint Oyster Bar and her food career was born. She moved to Panache in Providence, where she started as sous chef in 1984, returning to become the executive chef in 1987. Her formal culinary training was at the New England Culinary Institute from 1985 to 1987. She returned to NECI as an instructor in 1991 and avidly promotes the benefits of sustainable agriculture and organic produce.

1969: Twenty-one million U.S. schoolchildren participate in the National School Lunch Program.

Eve Felder, Chef-Instructor, The Culinary Institute of America, Hyde Park, NY

Brought up as a traditional southern lady, Eve was not encouraged to enter the professional culinary world! She graduated from the College of Charleston in 1977 with a B.S. in Psychology. After experimenting with farming in Nebraska and Iowa, Eve attended the CIA and graduated with honors in 1988. For a seven-year period, she worked at Chez Panisse Café as a chef. In her position as chef-instructor, Eve is a dedicated proponent of the farm-restaurant connection and sustainable agriculture.

Susan Feniger and Mary Sue Milliken, Co-Chefs and Co-Owners, THE BORDER GRILL, Santa Monica, CA

Both of these dynamic women grew up in the Mid-west. For their primary culinary training, Susan went to the CIA and Mary Sue attended the Washburn Trade School in Chicago. The die was cast when they met in Chicago at Le Perroquet in 1978. They each traveled to France, and Susan was the first to return to California. They worked in the original City Café starting in 1981. This led to the opening of City Restaurant in 1985 and the Border Grill in 1990. Recognition was given by the California Restaurant Writer's Association for Chef of the Year 1987-1988, the first time the honor was ever shared. Their TV program, "Too Hot Tamales," premiered in 1995 on the TV Food Network to national acclaim. Mary Sue is the mother of one son.

Phyllis Flaherty, CEC, CCE, Vice-President of Marketing and Culinary Development, ComSource Independent Food Service Companies, Inc., Atlanta, GA

This Maine native had her culinary initiation as a baker's assistant at a busy downeast resort. Phyllis attended the CIA in 1974 and graduated with honors. She worked at the Breakers Hotel in Palm Beach, Florida and with the Sheraton Corporation before returning to the CIA as a chef-instructor in 1982. Phyllis worked with General Foods from 1987 to 1993, progressing to Executive Chef and working in National Account Development. She joined ComSource in 1994 and also serves on the Alumni Advisory Board of the CIA. In 1989 and 1995 she received a President's Award as a member of the National Nutrition Committee and Corporate Communications Chair. Phyllis is the mother of one son.

Susanna Foo, Executive Chef, Co-Owner, SUSANNA FOO'S CHINESE CUISINE, Philadelphia, PA

Susanna grew up in Inner Mongolia and spent her adolescence and college years in Taiwan. She moved to the United States in 1967 and earned a graduate degree in Library Science. Her entrance into the culinary world was as a front-of-the-house assistant at her in-law's restaurant in 1979, but that changed when Susanna entered the kitchen to help. In 1981, she enrolled in an eight-week course at the CIA to develop her base of cooking principles. Susanna and her husband bought the building that now houses their restaurant in 1987, and in 1989, *Food and Wine* magazine named Susanna one of America's Ten Best New Chefs. Susanna is married with two sons.

Diane Forley, Executive Chef, Owner, VERBENA, New York, NY

Growing up in the Long Island suburbs, Diane was ambitious enough to present herself in Michel Fitoussi's Palace Restaurant kitchen at the age of sixteen, wanting to learn. She went on to earn an honors degree in Comparative Literature from Brown University, writing her thesis on "The History of Gastronomy in Nineteenth-Century France, Examined through the Works of Balzac and Flaubert." After graduating, Diane attended Lanôtre School and studied under chefs in both France and New York City. In 1995, with her brother's design help, she opened Verbena to rave reviews; *Esquire* named Verbena One of the Top Restaurants of 1995.

Margaret Fox, Co-Owner, Chef, CAFÉ BEAUJOLAIS, Mendocino, CA

Margaret began cooking with her mother at a very young age. By the time she was a teenager, she was teaching the principles of bread baking at a local church and selling baked goods to small Berkeley stores. She pursued a degree in Psychology at the University of California at Santa Cruz and graduated in 1975. After traveling North, Margaret began cooking at The Mendocino Hotel before moving to Café Beaujolais. She spontaneously bought the restaurant in 1977 at the age of twenty-four. In 1984, she joined forces with Christopher Kump when he applied for the chef's position, and they were married in 1988. Margaret is busy developing a successful mail-order business, teaching, and writing.

Gale Gand, Co-Chef, Co-Owner, BRASSERIE T, Northfield, IL

Gale began her career as a silver and goldsmith. The tide turned when she took a job as a waitress and ended up in the kitchen in 1977. She has worked in a kitchen ever since, studying at LaVarenne before moving to New York City in 1984. In 1989, Gale was listed in *Food & Wine* as one of the People to Watch for in 1989. Gale traveled again to Europe and returned to Chicago to work at Charlie Trotter's in 1992. She opened her first restaurant, Trio, with her husband in 1993 and then opened Brasserie T in 1995, the Vanilla Bean Bakery opened in 1996. Gale and her husband are the parents of one child.

1970: Women are admitted to the CIA on a regular basis.

Laureen Gauthier, Chef-Instructor, New England Culinary Institute, Montpelier, VT

Laureen exemplifies the diversity presented by chefs. She earned her B.S. and M.S. in Forestry at Virginia Polytechnic Institute and State University, Blacksburg, Virginia; then she went to Holland and apprenticed in a baking and pastry program. She returned to the States and worked at the Grand Hotel in Washington, DC, where she was the executive pastry chef for seven years. Laureen decided to move to Vermont in 1993 to explore the challenge of being a baking and pastry instructor. In 1996 she was chosen to bake the Smithsonian Institute's 150th birthday cake, a 6' by 2.5' chocolate replica of the Smithsonian Castle.

Elizabeth Germain, Line Cook, THE EAST COAST GRILL, Consultant and Instructor, Cambridge, MA

After five years of working in New York City as a CPA, Elizabeth realized that food was her true passion. She enrolled in classes at Peter Kump's School of Culinary Arts and moved to Massachusetts in 1989. She acknowledged the farm-restaurant connection when working on an organic farm in Upton, Massachusetts, and went on to be the Program Director and retreat organizer for Chefs Collaborative 2000. Between hours of teaching, consulting, and recipe testing, Elizabeth has found time to get back into the restaurant world and is now cooking at The East Coast Grill.

Anne Gingrass, Co-Chef, Co-Owner, HAWTHORNE LANE, San Francisco, CA

Anne began her food life at the age of fifteen working for her mother's catering company in Connecticut. She formalized her education by attending the CIA, then moved to Los Angeles and began working at Spago for Wolfgang Puck. She and her husband David were married in 1986 and moved to San Francisco to aid in the opening of Postrio. They were named Chefs of the Year in 1989 by San Francisco's *Focus Magazine*. In 1995, Anne and David opened their own restaurant, Hawthorne Lane. They are the parents of one daughter.

Debbie Gold, Co-Executive Chef, THE AMERICAN RESTAURANT, Kansas City, MO

Debbie earned a degree in restaurant management from the University of Illinois at Urbana-Champaign. She began her culinary training in 1986 in France at L'Ecole Hôtelière de Tain L'Hermitage and then apprenticed at several Michelin-starred restaurants. Upon returning to Chicago in 1988, she worked at Charlie Trotter's and Everest, then in 1992 as executive chef at Mirador. Debbie and her husband Michael moved to Kansas City in 1994 to begin the job of co-executive chefs at The American Restaurant. In 1996, *Wine*

Spectator named Debbie and Michael Chefs to Watch in 1997. They are the parents of one child.

Rozanne Gold, Author, Consultant, Chef, Joseph Baum & Michael Whiteman Company, New York, NY

A native of Queens, New York, Rozanne earned a degree in Psychology from Tufts University, attended graduate classes at NYU, then turned to the kitchen. In 1978, at twenty-three, she was chef of Gracie Mansion and cooked for Mayor Ed Koch. She became the youngest female corporate executive chef in the country when she cooked for Lord & Taylor at the age of twenty-four. In 1994, Rozanne's cookbook *Little Meals* won the James Beard Award for Best General Cookbook. She is culinary counselor to Dunnewood Vineyards and the culinary director for the Joseph Baum & Michael Whiteman Co. Rozanne and her husband live in Brooklyn, New York.

Joyce Goldstein, Chef, Author, Consultant, Educator, San Francisco, CA

Joyce grew up in Brooklyn and earned a B.A. from Smith College and an M.E.A. from the School of Art and Architecture at Yale. A move to Rome in 1959 marked the beginning of her true culinary career; she relocated to San Francisco and opened the California Street Cooking School in 1965; she was director and an instructor there for eighteen years. In 1981, Joyce called Chez Panisse Café her kitchen for three years, and she became the chef-owner of Square One in 1984. *The Mediterranean Kitchen* was published in 1989, followed by *Back to Square One: Old World Food in a New World Kitchen* in 1992, which won both the Julia Child and the James Beard Award for Best General Cookbook. Square One closed in 1996, and Joyce spends her time writing, consulting, and teaching. Joyce is the mother of three children and grandmother to one; she lives in the Bay area.

Gwen Kvavli Gulliksen, Executive Chef, ROBERT MONDAVI WINE AND FOOD CENTER, Costa Mesa, CA

Gwen's original endeavors were in creative writing and art, fulfilled by a B.A. from Indiana University and an M.A. in Art History from the University of Virginia in 1989. She concluded her formal education by earning her culinary degree from the ACF in 1991. After training under such noted chefs as Madeleine Kamman, Jean-Louis Palladin, and Lulu Bertran, Gwen went on to be the executive chef of Foster's Restaurant and Wine Bar in Baltimore. She accepted the position of executive chef at the Robert Mondavi Wine and Food Center in 1996. Gwen is married and living in Southern California.

1970: The Women's Bureau of the U.S. Department of Labor reports that the median earnings for women ($5,323 per year) are 59.4 percent of the median for men ($8,966), down from 63.9 percent in 1955.

Noëlle Haddad, Private Chef, Director/Instructor, THE COOK SCHOOL, New York, NY

A native of Santiago, Chile, Noëlle graduated from the Universidad de Chile in 1994, Magna Cum Laude, with an M.S. in Textile Engineering. Noëlle moved to New York City to pursue a degree from The French Culinary Institute; she graduated with honors in 1995. She has apprenticed at Daniel's and Le Cirque and has cooked for the Swiss and Dutch embassies in addition to having been a private chef for numerous New York families. In 1996, Noëlle opened The Cook School to aid in demystifying the kitchen for frustrated homecooks.

Dorothy Cann Hamilton, President, Educator, The French Culinary Institute, New York, NY

Dorothy's career began with a B.A. honors degree from the University of Newcastle-upon-Tyne, England, followed by an M.B.A. from New York University. Dorothy's commitment to service and education was established early in her life when she served in the Peace Corps for two years in Thailand. Dorothy's impetus to start The French Culinary Institute was the desire to combine her love of teaching, food, and education to train future chefs and pastry chefs. She is a chairman emeritus of the AIWF, and is a board member of the WCR. Dorothy is married and the mother of one daughter.

Amy Handler, Freelance Pastry Chef and Artist, Cambridge, MA

Amy was a Visual Arts graduate of Bennington College in Vermont in 1972. After a brief stint as a screen printer, Amy followed her true passion, enrolled in courses at New York City Technical College, and got her first job at The Plaza Hotel in 1978. She advanced to pastry chef at the Yale Club and the New York Athletic Club. Her talents led her to open her own pastry shop in 1987 in upstate New York, and she created custom elaborate cakes for clients from three states. Amy has taught baking and pastry at New York City Technical School. She now resides in Cambridge, Massachusetts working on freelance projects, catering, teaching, and designing on-line classes and bulletin boards.

Dell Hargis, Director of Alumni Affairs, The Culinary Institute of America, Hyde Park, NY

Dell's multifaceted background made her a prime candidate for the position of placement coordinator at the CIA in 1981. She was promoted to Director of Alumni Affairs in 1986, and Dell is now responsible for contact with more than 23,000 graduates worldwide, maintaining an active database and overseeing the Alumni Board. Dell's 1986 study of 100 women graduates was the first acknowledgment in the industry to recognize a need for change to accommodate professional women chefs in the commercial kitchen. Dell and her husband live in the Hudson Valley.

Dr. Jessica Harris, Professor of English, Author, Brooklyn, NY

This New York native has spent a career involved with academics, her vocation and avocations so tightly intertwined, they are hard to separate. Jessica received her B.A. from Bryn Mawr College, her M.A. in French from Queens College, CUNY, her Licence es Lettres from the Université de Nancy in France, and her doctorate in Performance Studies from NYU. A tenured associate professor of English composition at Queens College, Jessica finds time to write restaurant reviews for the *Village Voice* and lecture at The Smithsonian Institute and The Museum of Natural History in New York City. In addition to her work as a culinary historian, Jessica is a national board member of the AIWF and an author of six cookbooks. Jessica lives in Brooklyn, New York.

Kerry Heffernan, Chef de Cuisine, PALACE HOTEL, San Francisco, CA

Kerry comes from a family rich with food heritage; both Kerry's maternal grandmother and her great-grandmother were professional cooks. Kerry pursued the traditional route of college, but in 1980, she was detoured by a passion for food and restaurant life. After apprenticing at the Beverly Hills Hilton, Kerry moved to Atlanta to work at the Ritz Carlton at Buckhead. She returned to San Francisco and worked at the Cyprus Club and the Paragon. Before joining the Palace as chef de cuisine, Kerry was Executive Sous Chef at Elka, in the Miyako Hotel.

Deborah Hughes, Chef/Co-Owner, UPSTAIRS AT THE PUDDING, Cambridge, MA

Deborah graduated from Cornell and found herself debating between whether to pump gas or wash dishes; she ended up taking a job at Peasant Stock in Cambridge in 1959 and that wrote the story of the rest of her life. She spent thirteen years at Peasant Stock and opened Upstairs at the Pudding in 1972 with both her former husband and her close friend Mary Catherine Deibel. A Cambridge mainstay, Upstairs at the Pudding is consistently noted as one of the town's favorite restaurants. Deborah is the mother of two children.

Deborah Huntley, Executive Chef, THE HARBORSIDE INN, Edgartown, MA

Deborah's first job was working in a hospital, washing dishes. She was put right on the hot line and her career began! By the age of twenty-three, she was a luncheon cook at a private club in the Keys. She met her first mentor, who gave

1970: Women earn on the average 57 cents for every dollar earned by a man for comparable labor.

her a copy of *Le Guide Culinaire* and said, "Read!" Deborah has cooked up and down the Eastern seaboard: Palm Beach, Nantucket, and Key West, while finding time to earn her ACF C.E.C. certification. Deborah has made Martha's Vineyard her home; she is the mother of one daughter.

Mika Iijima, Pastry Chef, NOBU, New York, NY

A native of Kanagawa, Japan and a 1992 graduate of the New York Restaurant School, Mika has pursued a determined route into the New York restaurant world. She enrolled at California State University, Northbridge in 1991 and moved to New York a year later. After interning at Michael's in New York City, she became the pastry chef at Basta Pasta in 1993. A move to Nobu in 1994 cemented this young woman's mark on the field of pastry arts. Nobu was the 1995 winner of the James Beard Foundation Best New Restaurant in America.

Raji Jallepalli, Chef-Owner, RESTAURANT RAJI, Memphis, TN

Raji came to the United States in 1971 for an extended honeymoon; this young Indian woman had just married a physician and had a degree in microbiology. After short stints of living in France and England, Raji realized the potential of Indian food combined with French techniques, and she sought out a location for her desired restaurant. She has consistently produced delightful and innovative dishes at Restaurant Raji since it opened in 1989; she cites Jean-Louis Palladin as one of her greatest mentors and supporters.

Traci Des Jardins, Executive Chef, San Francisco, CA

With an original intent to be a veterinarian, Traci attended the University of California at Santa Cruz at the age of sixteen. She realized she wanted to cook and at the age of seventeen, found work in a European kitchen in Los Angeles. Traci went to France for eight months, relocated to New York City and worked with Debra Ponzek at Montrachet in 1986. Traci opened her first restaurant, Patina, at the age of twenty-three in Los Angeles. In 1991, she moved to San Francisco, helped to open Aqua, and then worked with Elka Gilmore at Elka's. Traci and Drew Nieporent opened Rubicon together in 1994, the same year she was awarded *Focus* Rising Star Chef of the Year.

Madeleine Kamman, Educator, Chef, Author, Pioneer, St. Helena, CA

One of the foremost influences in the American culinary world, Madeleine came to the United States in 1961 after spending eight years in the airline industry. She and her husband settled first in Philadelphia, and she taught adult education culinary classes to combat homesickness for her native France. She moved to Boston in 1969, halfway through writing *The Making of a Cook*. France's loss was America's gain, and in 1970, The Modern Gourmet Cooking School opened in Newton Center, Massachusetts, soon to be followed by the restaurant Chez la Mère Madeleine as part of the school. Madeleine created the concept of The School for American Chefs in 1988, and the school opened in 1989 on the grounds of the Beringer Winery in St. Helena, California. Madeleine continues to teach and write and she makes time in her life for her husband, three children, and her grandchildren.

Katy Keck, Executive Chef, Co-Owner, NEW WORLD GRILL and SAVOIR FAIRE FOODS, New York, NY

Katy's kitchen beginnings on an Easy Bake oven were lost in pursuit of a University of Chicago M.B.A. and a seven-year career on Wall Street. However, food resurfaced in her life when she began to take cooking classes at the New School in Manhattan in 1980. She won the Marie Brizard Flavors of France contest and earned an apprenticeship at Le Grand Monarque in Chartres, France in 1986; after internships in three Michelin-starred restaurants, Katy never returned to Wall Street. Back in New York City in 1988, Katy worked on freelance food shoots and began to look for her own restaurant in 1990. Katy and business partner Richard Barber opened New World Grill in 1993 at the Worldwide Plaza in the theater district.

Loretta Keller, Executive Chef, Co-Owner, BIZOU, San Francisco, CA

Born in Vancouver, British Columbia and raised in Los Angeles, Loretta earned a degree in Literature from the University of California at Santa Cruz and traveled to New Orleans. Her food career began in 1983, when she got a restaurant job for minimum wage. She traveled to France with her husband in 1985, and worked as a stagière under Philippe Groult. Back in New Orleans, she worked as Susan Spicer's sous chef, opening Maison de Ville in 1986. Loretta and her husband moved to San Francisco, where she joined the staff of Star's in 1986 and worked there in various capacities—line cook, purchaser, and finally chef of Star's Café. Loretta and her husband opened Bizou in 1993.

Melissa Kelly, Executive Chef, OLD CHATHAM SHEEPHERDING COMPANY INN, Old Chatham, NY

Melissa's first experience in the kitchen was on Long Island as a waitress, and she begged to be allowed into the kitchen. A 1988 graduate of the CIA, Melissa's first job was under Hartman Handke at the Greenbriar. Melissa moved to New York City to join Larry Forgione's staff at the original American Place; her first executive chef position was in 1991, when Forgione took over the Beekman Arms. In 1993, Melissa moved to San Francisco and had the opportunity to work at Chez Panisse. Returning East in 1995, she opened the Old Chatham Sheepherding Company Inn in 1996 as executive chef.

1971: **Random House Dictionary defines** *chef* **as: a cook, esp. a male head cook.**

Kathleen Kennedy, Chef-Instructor, Caterer, Author, California Culinary Academy, San Francisco, CA

Kathleen's introduction to the culinary world was instruction at the cooking school Dumas Père, an Escoffier-based French cooking school in Glenview, Illinois. This led to a poissonnière position at the Ritz Carlton Chicago at the age of seventeen. Kathleen is a 1988 graduate of the CIA; she was an apprentice team member of the 1988 ACF/NRA Culinary Olympic Team and worked at Le Grenadin while in France. Kathleen cooked at Charlie Trotter's in 1989. A move to San Francisco in 1990 and she was cooking for the Perfect Palate Catering Company. Kathleen has been an instructor at CCA since 1994. Kathleen and her husband are the parents of one child.

Johanne Killeen, Co-Chef, Co-Owner, AL FORNO, Providence, RI

Johanne grew up in New Jersey and attended the Rhode Island School of Design in Providence, Rhode Island, where she studied photography. She met her husband at the same school in 1975. After deciding independently that they each loved Italian food, they opened the original Al Forno in 1980. Johanne and George were married in 1981. Al Forno moved to its current location in 1989 and in 1994 they were recognized by the James Beard Society as Rising Stars of America and by the *International Herald Tribune* as the Number One Casual Restaurant in the World. *USA Today* calls Johanne one of the top twenty chefs in the nation, and she is a founding member of the WCR.

Shirley King, Executive Chef, THE HARMONIE CLUB, Author, Instructor, New York, NY

A native of England and an alumna of Art Schools both in England and the United States, Shirley's penchant for food and cooking was evidenced when she began cooking for Lord Weinstock and his family in 1970. She became involved with catering in both England and France and published her first book, *Dining with Marcel Proust,* in 1979. After cooking at L'Escargot in London in 1982, she opened two summer restaurants on Long Island, New York. Cooking at Wilkinson's Seafood Café in New York City, she earned two stars and decided to stay in the U.S. She has been a chef-instructor at The New School, The French Culinary Institute, and Peter Kump's New York Cooking School. Shirley is currently the executive chef at a private club in Manhattan. She is the mother of one daughter.

Barbara Kuck, Chef, Educator, Curator, Culinary Archives and Museum at Johnson and Wales University, Providence RI

Barbara's culinary history is marked by her twenty years of working at the Chicago institution, The Bakery, with Chef Louis Szathmáry. Barbara attended the Washburne Trade School in Illinois, but she chose to eschew a formal education and participated in the apprentice program at The Bakery beginning in 1971. In 1991, she found a home for Chef Louis' extensive collection of culinary memorabilia at Johnson and Wales University, where she is the curator and museum director.

Pitita Lago, Executive Chef, New York, NY

Pitita spent her childhood in Ponce, Puerto Rico, and planned to study art as a young adult. After a trip through Spain and Italy, she traveled to the United States at the age of twenty-four and accepted a job as a dishwasher at a Washington, DC restaurant to supplement her income—she was hooked! Pitita moved to New York City and attended the New York Restaurant School; her career advanced to positions at Gotham Bar and Grill, Arizona 206, Remi, and The Rainbow Room. Pitita is currently writing and developing recipes; her last position was as Executive Chef at the Continental Club in Manhattan.

Sarah Langan, Chef-Instructor, New England Culinary Institute, Essex Junction, VT

From a large family in upstate New York, Sarah was always in the kitchen. Her initiation into the culinary world was working at a country club snack shop. After earning her Associates degree in 1979, Sarah attended the CIA and graduated with honors in 1982. She was the sauté cook at the Sheraton Royal Waikoloa in Hawaii until she chose to continue her education at the L'Ecole de Cuisine Française in England, where she received her Diploma Superior in 1988 and apprenticed at the Hostellerie Les Frenes in Montfavet-Avignon, France. A return to the States placed Sarah as lead saucier and banquet chef at the Westin La Paloma in Tucson, AZ. She joined NECI in 1991.

Audrey Lennon, Chef-Owner, Caterer, Philanthropist, Orlando, FL

Audrey's varied background runs the gamut from telecommunications to construction, but the mainstay has always been food and cooking. She learned authentic German and Jewish cooking as a child and young adult growing up in a diverse neighborhood in Long Island. She moved to Florida, reenrolled in school in 1989, and graduated from the Mid-Florida Technical Institute's two-year program in six months! Audrey started her own catering company and in 1993 founded the A. Lennon Foundation Inc., a nonprofit charitable organization dedicated to helping feed homeless and needy people, specifically children. Audrey has sponsored the distribution of the film, "One Mouth at a Time," which illuminates childhood hunger in this country.

1971: Annual U.S. beef consumption reaches 113 pounds per capita.

Carol Levenherz, Student, Chef-Owner, OVERTURES & FINALES, Wilton, CT

Carol returned to school at the age of 47 and earned her AOS with high honors from the CIA in 1997. Carol has owned her catering company since 1981; she specializes in catering to small corporate functions requiring quality products. She was a private catering contractor for the Juran Institute in Wilton, CT until 1995. Carol is married with two children.

Edna Lewis, Chef, Author, Pioneer, Atlanta, GA

Edna grew up in the small farm community of Freetown, Virginia and learned the value and flavors of freshly grown food. Her first job was cooking for the Brazilian embassy in Washington, DC at the age of fifteen. Edna was the chef at Café Nicholson in New York City in 1948 and went on to the Fearrington House and Middleton Place in Charleston. She returned to Manhattan and was the chef at Aschkenasy's U.S. Steak House before she moved to Gage and Tollner in Brooklyn. In 1984, she was inducted to the Who's Who of Food and Beverage in America. Edna has been instrumental in preserving the traditions of Southern food; she is an advocate of organic fresh produce and natural foods. Currently Edna is a consultant for a new restaurant in Atlanta. She is widowed and has raised a family of adopted Masai and Ethiopian children.

Jo Lynne Lockley, Owner, Chefs' Professional Agency, San Francisco, CA

Jo Lynne's background is as diverse as the chefs that she places in top restaurants around the world. She studied in Europe and worked her way through kitchens in Heidelberg, Berlin, and Stockholm before she returned to the United States and earned a Master's Degree in German at the University of California at Berkeley. Jo Lynne began working for the Swiss government in 1970 and was responsible for teaching and aiding in the establishment of a modernization system for the Swiss middle school system. Jo Lynne reestablished residence in the Bay area in 1985 to manage her family's culinary search firm. She has been a champion of women in the professional culinary field and advocates fair and equitable placement.

Emily Luchetti, Pastry Chef, Author, Sausalito, CA

Emily spent her childhood in New York State and went on to earn a B.A. in sociology from Denison University in 1979. She furthered her education by attending the New York Restaurant School in Manhattan and apprenticing under Gérard Pangeau. Emily moved to San Francisco, where she was on the opening team of Star's in 1984. After working through the stations in the kitchen, Emily chose to move into pastry and became Star's pastry chef from 1987 to 1995 and the co-owner of StarBake in 1994-1995. In 1994, *Chocolatier* magazine named her One of the Top Ten Pastry Chefs in the U.S.

Emily was nominated in 1994 and 1995 for the James Beard Best Pastry Chef in the U.S. Emily and her husband live in the Bay area.

Barbara Lynch, Executive Chef, Boston, MA

Raised in the housing projects of South Boston, Barbara began working at the age of eleven. An observant home economics teacher encouraged her passion for food and she read and traveled avidly to continue learning. She found further mentoring in the budding kitchens of Michela Larson and Todd English. Numerous trips to Italy focused Barbara's palate and aided in defining what would create the food style of a chef *Food & Wine* named one of the "Top Ten Rising Star Chefs" in 1996. This young chef and opera lover hopes to open her own restaurant in the fall of 1997.

Susan McCreight Lindeborg, Executive Chef, THE MORRISON-CLARK INN, Washington, DC

This native of Colorado went to New Mexico to learn to cook after attempts at graduate school proved unchallenging. Susan worked first at Bishop's Lodge and then at the La Fonda Hotel before she found her true mentors at The Periscope. She went on to work at L'Etoile in Madison, Wisconsin and was a visiting chef at Tapestries in Greenwich, Connecticut. Susan joined the staff of the Morrison-Clark Inn in Washington, DC in 1990. An advocate of community service, Susan was recognized by *McCall's* magazine as an 'Angel of Change' in 1995. She has been featured in *Cook's Illustrated, Fine Cooking* and the *Washington Post. Gourmet* recognized Susan as one of fourteen Chefs Across America and the Restaurant Association of Metropolitan Washington nominated her for 1996 Chef of the Year. Susan is married and living in the capitol district.

Deborah Madison, Chef, Author, Educator, Santa Fe, NM

A graduate of the University of California at Santa Cruz, Deborah received her culinary training at Chez Panisse in Berkeley, California in the early 1970s. She was the opening chef of Greens restaurant in San Francisco in 1979, and chose to leave in 1984 for a cooking position at the American Academy in Rome. Deborah relocated to Santa Fe and opened Café Escalera. She now focuses on teaching around the country, cooking and writing. She is the author of the IACP prize-winning book, *The Greens Cookbook;* she has also written *The Savory Way* and *The Vegetarian Table: America*. She is actively involved with the Santa Fe Area Farmers' Market as a way of expressing her commitment to seeing local, small-scale farming thrive in Northern New Mexico. Deborah is married and living in Santa Fe.

1972: The CIA moves to Hyde Park, New York; five percent of the students are women.

Zarela Martinez, Restaurateur, Chef-Owner, ZARELA, Author, New York, NY

Born in Northern Mexico, Zarela studied Mass Communication at the Instituto Technológico y de Estudios Superiores de Occident Guadalajara. She moved to El Paso, where she was a social worker, supplementing her family's income by catering. A trip to New Orleans introduced her to Paul Prudhomme, who championed her foods in the New York food world. She moved to New York in 1983 and started Signature Foods; she was executive chef at Café Marimba, and opened her own restaurant, Zarela, in 1987. *Food from My Heart* was published in 1992 and was a runner-up for the James Beard award for Best International Book. Zarela is the mother of three children.

Ferdinand Metz, CMC, Chef, President, The Culinary Institute of America, Hyde Park, NY

A native of Munich, Germany, Ferdinand was presented with a set of knives in 1955 by his parents and went on to participate in two culinary apprenticeships in cooking and baking. He traveled to the United States and was an experimental chef and senior manager with Heinz, USA for fifteen years. While working at Heinz, he earned his M.B.A. from the University of Pittsburgh at the age of thirty-five. Ferdinand joined the CIA in 1980 as President. In 1988, Chef Metz and his team won the gold medal in the Hot Foods Division of the International Culinary Competition. Julia Child has cited him as one of the people "who most enhanced the prestige of gastronomy and the foodservice industry."

Longteine de Monteiro, Chef-Owner, THE ELEPHANT WALK, Somerville, MA

A native of Cambodia, married to a diplomat in 1957 and living the life of a busy mother, Longteine never considered herself a chef or restaurateur. That all changed with the Khmer Rouge overthrow of the Cambodian government in 1975. Longteine and her family were able to find safe haven in France and opened Amrita, a Cambodian and Chinese restaurant in the south of France in 1980. After ten years in France, she and her husband sold the restaurant and came to Boston to join her youngest daughter; they opened The Elephant Walk in 1991 in Somerville. In 1992, the restaurant earned One of Boston's Best by *Esquire* magazine. Longteine's children made the decision to join the family business and a second restaurant was born in Boston in 1994. Longteine and her husband are the parents of two daughters.

Nadsa Perry, Chef, THE ELEPHANT WALK, Boston, MA

Nadsa, the daughter of a Cambodian ambassador and his wife, met her future husband in 1977 while attending the Taipei American School in Taiwan. They married in 1986 and moved to the United States, where Nadsa became a travel agent. In 1990, Nadsa worked as both a travel agent and a cook at the new Elephant Walk, opened when her parents moved from France. In 1992, she attended The Cambridge School of Culinary Arts and returned to the restaurant as sous chef. In 1994, Nadsa became chef of The Elephant Walk in Boston with the support of her older sister and brother-in-law. Nadsa and her husband live in the Boston area.

Sara Moulton, Executive Chef, *Gourmet* Magazine Cooking Arts Center, New York, NY

A native of New York City, Sara attended college in Michigan. She proceeded to Hyde Park, New York and graduated second in her class from the CIA in 1977. Her first job was working at The Harvest with Lydia Shire as her chef. Sara worked as chef at Cybele's in Boston and as associate chef for Julia Child on *"More Julia Child and Company."* After an apprenticeship in Chartres, France, Sara moved back to New York in 1981 and was sous chef at Café Amsterdam before accepting a position at Le Tulipe as tournant. In 1984, she became the food editor for *Gourmet* and in 1988, was appointed executive chef. Sara was instrumental in founding the Woman's Culinary Guild of New England and the New York Woman's Culinary Alliance. Sara and her husband are the parents of two children.

Corinna Mozo, Chef de Cuisine, Chez Henri, Cambridge, MA

Corinna grew up in Montreal and attended the University of Western Ontario, studying French Literature; she left in three years to go to the Stratford Chefs School. She sent out one resume in 1990 when she graduated from culinary school to Lydia Shire, at BIBA in Boston. Corinna was hired as a line cook and worked at BIBA for two years. In 1992, she moved to Providence as sauté cook and progressed quickly to sous chef. In 1994, she helped to open Chez Henri as chef de cuisine. Corinna and her husband live in the Boston area.

Leslie Myers, Chef-Instructor, New England Culinary Institute, Montpelier, VT

Leslie received her B.A. from James Madison University in 1989. She graduated from the CIA in 1991, where she was awarded the Scheifflen Award for outstanding achievement in wine studies and hospitality management. Leslie moved to Napa Valley and was the pastry chef at Mustards Grill for two years. Trying her hand in the front of the house, she was the General Manager of Bistro Don Giovanni and then aided in the opening of The Culinary Institute

1972: Leslie Revsin is the first female chef at the Waldorf Astoria.

of America's Greystone Restaurant as the Hospitality and Reservations Manager. Leslie returned East to accept a teaching position with NECI in 1996. Leslie and her husband live in the Montpelier area.

Alison Muir, Chef-Instructor, The French Culinary Institute, New York, NY

Alison grew up in Litchfield, Connecticut and started a catering company in high school. While other students were participating in after-school sports, Alison learned how to cook Asian cuisine at a small private cooking school. She continued her education at LaVarenne in Paris in 1985 and returned to Connecticut to work in a number of local restaurants. Alison began teaching in 1988 and joined the faculty at The French Culinary Institute in 1994.

Tamara Murphy, Executive Chef, Campagne, Seattle, WA

Tamara began her career studying art at Charlotte Community College. After various detours into the kitchen, she decided to change her career path and traveled to New York. Tamara was running the kitchen of the Cornelia Street Café within six months, cooking for customers like Robert DeNiro. Eight years later, she migrated to Seattle and started to work for Dominique Place, a mentor who encouraged Tamara to enter the 1990 Bocuse d'Or; she was one of twelve finalists. She has been executive chef at Campagne since 1990. In 1994, Tamara was honored with being named one of the Ten Best New Chefs by *Food & Wine* magazine.

Kristina Neely, Chef de Partie, The Peaks, Telluride, CO

Kristina's restaurant experience had been concentrated in the front of the house in her native Dutchess County, New York until she spent a day in the kitchen filling in for a sick staff member in 1989. Her true move to the kitchen came when she enrolled at the CIA in 1993. After graduation with honors from the CIA in 1995, Kristina apprenticed in Germany's Black Forest in Glottertal. She returned to the United States and has been cooking at The Peaks in Telluride, Colorado since 1996.

Nancy Oakes, Chef-Owner, Boulevard, San Francisco, CA

Nancy originally chose to go to art school at the San Francisco Art Institute to pursue printmaking and painting. However, after eight years of cooking at the venerable Alexis on Nob Hill, Nancy moved on in 1976 to a new culinary venture, Barnacle. In 1979, at the age of twenty-seven, Nancy opened her first restaurant, Pat O'Shea's Mad Hatter. Nine years later, Nancy opened L'Avenue next door and in 1993, she and her staff moved to the new Boulevard. Nancy was named *Focus* magazine's Best Newcomer in 1994, and her establishment was acknowledged by *Esquire* as One of the Nation's Ten Best Restaurants. Nancy and her husband live in the Bay area.

Rick O'Connell, Chef, Consultant, Caterer, San Francisco, CA
A native of Greenwich, Connecticut, Rick grew up in an Italian family who focused on food. Despite an early culinary influence, her first vocation was as an operating room nurse at Sloan Kettering Hospital. During the Vietnam War, she and her physician husband moved to Tokyo, and she started taking Chinese cooking classes; her passion for food was rekindled. Rick has been a restaurant chef in San Francisco kitchens for fifteen years, and she has also written a food column for the *San Francisco Chronicle*. An author of one cookbook, Rick currently consults and caters in the Bay area while finding time for her three children and four grandchildren.

Pam Parseghian, Writer, *Nation's Restaurant News*, Chef, New York, NY
Her grandmother initially fostered Pam's passion for food and Pam pursued her culinary education at the CIA. She cooked in hotels and resorts in New Jersey for four years before training in Europe for a year. Pam returned to New York and worked with Waldy Maloof and David Burke prior to choosing to express her love of food through writing.

Cindy Pawlcyn, Corporate Chef, Co-Owner, Real Restaurants, Sausalito, CA
A native of Minneapolis, Cindy has known since she was thirteen that cooking was her profession. After receiving a degree at Hennepin Technical Institute, Cindy went on to the University of Wisconsin-Stout and earned a B.S. with honors in hotel-restaurant management in 1977. A move to Chicago introduced her to her partners in what would be Real Restaurants. Cindy relocated to Napa Valley and was the chef at Meadowood Resort and cooked at Rose et Le Favour before she opened her first restaurant, Mustards Grill, in 1983. Now executive chef and owner of six restaurants, Cindy also writes and finds time to spend with her husband and two stepchildren.

Odessa Piper, Chef-Owner, L'Etoile, Madison, WI
Growing up in New England, Odessa learned to appreciate the value of local foods; she foraged for mushrooms with her family and baked breads at home. In 1970, she chose the nontraditional education of living within the first organic farm cooperative in Hanover, New Hampshire. She moved to Madison, Wisconsin in 1971 and started to bake breads for the Ovens of Brittany; she baked for three years before opening her restaurant, L'Etoile in 1976 at the age of twenty-three. Odessa has been honored by the James Beard Foundation and was featured in *Bon Appetit*; and she has written for *Fine Cooking, Eating Well*,

1973: An amendment to the School Lunch Act establishes a Women, Infants, and Children (WIC) program to improve diets in the nation's most nutritionally vulnerable population group.

and *Food and Wine.* Odessa is an advocate of sustainable agriculture and is passionate about using local, seasonal products.

Guida Ponte, Corporate Chef, LEGAL SEA FOODS, Allston, MA

Guida emigrated from the Azores in 1979. She moved to Boston where a friend of her former husband was a manager in the first Legal Sea Foods in Inman Square. Seventeen years later, Guida is still working for Legal Sea Foods, though her job title has changed considerably! While working full-time and raising three children, she earned an AOS from Newbury College in Food Service. Guida is married and the mother of four children.

Debra Ponzek, Chef-Owner, Caterer, AUX DÉLICES, Riverside, CT

Originally planning a career in engineering, Debra realized in her sophomore year at Boston University that cooking was her true calling. She enrolled in the CIA and graduated in 1984. After working at top restaurants in New Jersey, Debra began cooking at Montrachet in New York City; within ten months she was chef. She received three consecutive three-star ratings from the *New York Times,* the first woman ever to do so. Debra was selected as one of the Ten Best New American Chefs by *Food and Wine* magazine at the age of twenty-eight. She was named Chef of the Year in 1990 by the Chefs of America Association and in 1992, Debra was awarded Rising Star Chef of the Year by the James Beard Foundation. In 1994, Debra left Montrachet and wrote her first book; *Aux Délices* opened in 1995. Debra and her husband are the parents of one child and they live in Connecticut.

Maureen Pothier, Chef, Warwick, RI

Growing up in a large family influenced Maureen's love of cooking, and she pursued her culinary training at the Rhode Island School of Design in 1979, earning her degree in 1981. She worked at the Bluepoint Oyster Bar and Restaurant throughout her education and after graduating from Madeleine Kamman's school in 1984, Maureen returned to the Bluepoint as chef. The Bluepoint closed in 1996; Maureen now spends a majority of her time consulting, teaching, and volunteering with Share Our Strength programs and the Spinazzola Foundation. She and her husband live in Rhode Island.

Nora Pouillon, Chef-Owner, RESTAURANT NORA and ASIA NORA, Washington, DC

Nora's Austrian background was instrumental in laying the foundation of her beliefs regarding healthy, well prepared, and seasonal food. One of the foremost advocates of local, seasonal, sustainable food, Nora is a founding board member of Chefs Collaborative 2000 in addition to working with the

U.S. Department of Agriculture. Nora's two restaurants, Restaurant Nora (1979) and Asia Nora (1994), both showcase her trademark organic, local ingredients. In 1996, Nora published her first book, *Cooking with Nora,* and she was recognized as the 1996 U.S.A. Chef of the Year by the American Tasting Institute. Nora, her partner, and two of her children live in Washington, DC.

Stacy Radin, Chef-Instructor, The Culinary Institute of America, Hyde Park, NY

In 1974, at the age of seventeen, Stacey enrolled at the CIA. She graduated with honors and earned a scholarship that enabled her to continue her education for a semester studying pastry. After working in numerous hotels, Stacey returned to the CIA in 1994 as a Pastry Arts instructor; she resides in the Hudson Valley region of New York.

Susan Regis, Executive Chef, BIBA, Boston, MA

Susan grew up in New Hampshire and graduated from Skidmore College before moving to Steamboat Springs, Colorado. She returned to the East coast and got her first job at The Bostonian in 1983, where she worked with Executive Chef Lydia Shire. In 1986, Susan traveled to California and helped to open the Beverly Hills Four Seasons Hotel with Chef Shire. After working with Lettuce Entertain You in Chicago as a consultant, she returned to the East coast. Susan and Lydia collaborated and opened BIBA in Boston in 1989 and Pignoli two years later.

Leslie Revsin, Chef, Author, Pioneer, PAN PRODUCTIONS, Bronxville, NY

Cited as a pioneer by Madeleine Kamman, Leslie grew up in Chicago and graduated with a painting major from Macalester College in Minnesota, Magna cum Laude. She has a degree in Hotel and Restaurant Management from New York Technical College. Leslie was hired as a "kitchen man" at the Waldorf Astoria in 1971 and by 1973, she was the hotel's first woman chef. Restaurant Leslie opened in 1977 with Leslie as chef-owner until the early eighties; she went on to be executive chef at The Bridge Café, One Fifth Avenue, and Argenteuil. In 1992, Leslie moved to the Inn at Pound Ridge in Westchester and was executive chef for two years. She developed her own multifaceted culinary company, Pan Productions, in 1994. Leslie has just written her first book and has plans for a public television series. Leslie is the mother of one daughter.

1973: Nutritional labeling regulations mandated by the Food and Drug Administration standardize the type of information to be presented on U.S. food packages.

Judy Rodgers, Chef, ZUNI CAFÉ AND GRILL, San Francisco, CA

Judy's formative food experience was in 1973, when she lived with Jean and Pierre Troisgros and their families in Roanne, France. She returned to the States and earned her degree from Stanford University in 1978; that was her first year at Chez Panisse as lunch chef. Judy spent one more year in France, then combined forces to create the menu for the Union Hotel in Benicia, California in 1981. In 1984, she was one of the first fifty people named to Who's Who in Cooking in America. After a brief stint in New York City, Judy joined two partners as Chef of Zuni Café in San Francisco in 1987. Judy and her husband and two children live in the Bay area.

Anne Rosenzweig, Chef/Co-Owner, ARCADIA; Chef-Proprietor, THE LOBSTER CLUB, New York, NY

Anne grew up in New York City, where she is now chef-owner of Arcadia and The Lobster Club. She began her career graduating from Columbia University with a degree in Anthropology and was living in Nepal, Africa, and India when food became increasingly interesting to her. Returning to the United States, Anne apprenticed without pay in a number of New York restaurants. Anne cooked at Vanessa in Greenwich Village, starting in 1981 and moved up to the position of head chef. She also worked as a consultant before opening her first restaurant, Arcadia, in 1985. Arcadia has consistently earned three stars from *The New York Times;* The Lobster Club, Anne's second restaurant, opened in 1995 to a two-star review. Anne is active with public service in her community and serves on the "Kitchen Cabinet," a panel that advises the White House on menus and American food. Anne lives in New York City with her husband and daughter.

Alain Sailhac, Chef, Dean, The French Culinary Institute, New York, NY

Cooking as an apprentice at the age of fourteen, Alain learned his trade in the small town of Millau, France. He honed his skill at the Hotel Claridge and Normandie Hotel, and later at the Club Med and Relais Gastronomique. Alain moved to Chicago and worked at Le Perroquet and then moved to New York City in the early 1970s. He worked at Le Cygne, where he earned four stars from *The New York Times*. His next kitchens were Le Cirque, The "21" Club, and the Plaza Hotel. Alain joined The French Culinary Institute as Dean of Culinary Studies in 1991.

Cynthia Salvato, CEPC, Chef-Instructor, Johnson and Wales, Author, Entrepreneur, THE DOWRY COOKIE COMPANY, Providence, RI

A native New Englander, Cynthia grew up in Watertown, Massachusetts and apprenticed in the Formaggio Kitchen and the pastry-training program at Rudi's Bakery in Boston. In 1984, she aided in the opening of the Marriott

Copley Place in Boston. She progressed to pastry chef in 1987 and moved to L'Espalier as their pastry chef. Cynthia joined the staff at Michela's in Cambridge in 1989 and was pastry chef at Le Grenier Restaurant on Martha's Vineyard in 1991. She joined the staff at Johnson and Wales University's College of Culinary Arts in 1990. Cynthia also teaches in the Master Chef Series at Sakonnet Vineyards. Her first book, *The Dowry Cookbook*, was published in 1996 and she frequently writes for other publications.

Barbara Sanders, MS, CCE, AAC, Educator, Author, Chef, Monroe, NH
Barbara spent her childhood in the Granite State. In 1956, Barbara earned a Home Economics B.Ed. from Keene State College and she earned an M.S. in Nutrition with a minor in Rehabilitation from Southern Illinois University at Carbondale. She published *A Cookbook Mate for the Blind and the Sighted* in 1984. She was the consulting Nutritionist at the U.S. Olympic Training Center in 1986-1987. Barbara was the Department Chair and Culinary Arts instructor at the White Mountains Regional High School from 1977 until she retired in 1997. Barbara manages her family farm, raises Simmental beef cattle, and is an ABS certified technician. She is married with two children and two grandchildren.

Amy Scherber, Baker-Owner, AMY'S BREAD, Author, New York, NY
A double major in Economics and Psychology from St. Olaf College, in Minnesota, Amy decided not to enter her planned field of marketing when she moved to New York City in 1983. Instead she enrolled in the New York Restaurant School, got her first job at Bouley and progressed through every station in the kitchen, finally recognizing a passion for bread. Amy arranged four stages in France and spent three months in boulangeries. She returned to New York and was the pastry chef at Mondrian before opening Amy's Breads in 1992. In April of 1996, Amy published her first cookbook, *Amy's Bread*. A second bread-baking facility opened in the summer of 1996 and includes a small retail café.

RoxSand Scocos, Chef/Co-Owner, ROXSAND (RESTAURANT AND BAR), Phoenix, AZ
RoxSand attended art school in Detroit, Michigan and specialized in sculpture. She met Anne Willan and was encouraged to go to Paris to learn about food. RoxSand was hooked. She moved to Hawaii at the age of twenty-four and opened two restaurants before traveling again to Europe and finally settling in Arizona. RoxSand opened RoxSand in 1988 in Phoenix, Arizona, where she is a fierce advocate of local, sustainable organic agriculture. She uses her restau-

1974: Debbie Fields, age twenty-one, starts Mrs. Fields cookies.

rant as a platform to take a proactive role in the culinary world. She is an original member of the Chefs Collaborative 2000. In 1991, RoxSand was featured in the James Beard Rising Star Chef Series, and in 1995, she was inducted into the Scottsdale Culinary Hall of Fame. RoxSand is married with two daughters.

Lydia Shire, Chef-owner, BIBA; Owner, PIGNOLI, Boston, MA

A native of Brookline, Massachusetts, Lydia trained at the Cordon Bleu in London and graduated in 1970. She began cooking at Maison Robert in Boston and progressed to the position of restaurant chef at the Copley Plaza Hotel. While there, she received four stars from *The Boston Globe* and the restaurant was named Best Hotel Dining Room by *Boston Magazine*. In Beverly Hills in 1986, Lydia was the first woman chef to open a Four Seasons Hotel. Lydia returned to Boston and in 1989, she opened her premier restaurant, BIBA; Pignoli opened in 1994. Lydia has been listed in Who's Who of Food and Beverage in America and as America's Best Chef—Northeast by the James Beard Foundation; *Food and Wine* magazine called her one of America's Ten Best Chefs. Lydia is married and has four children.

André Soltner, Chef, Restaurateur, Educator, The French Culinary Institute, New York, NY

Born in Alsace, André began his culinary apprenticeship at the age of fifteen at the Hotel du Parc in Mulhouse. At the age of twenty-seven, he was executive chef at Chez Hansi in Paris. André moved to the United States in 1961 and opened Lutèce in New York City, consistently earning four-star ratings from *The New York Times*. Lutèce was open for thirty-four years and won more than twenty-five awards, including the French government's Chevalier du Mérite Agricole and the James Beard Lifetime Achievement Award. André joined the faculty of the FCI in 1995 and he completed his first book in 1996, *The Lutèce Cookbook*. He and his wife live in New York City.

Fritz Sonnenschmidt, CMC, Chef, Author, Culinary Dean, The Culinary Institute of America, Hyde Park, NY

Fritz began his career as an apprentice at culinary school in West Kermess, Germany in 1950. His career has led him through Europe, working in such hotels as the Piccadilly and the Grosvenor in London and at the Sommerville Hotel in Jersey, England. He came to the United States in 1962 and worked at the Eldorado Shore and Yacht Club in New Rochelle before moving on to the Sheraton in New York City. Fritz has been Culinary Dean at the CIA since 1968 and has participated in numerous Culinary Olympics in which he earned six medals in major competitions. He was honored as the ACF National Chef of the Year for 1995. Fritz and his wife live in the Hudson Valley region of New York.

Ana Sortun, Executive Chef, CASABLANCA, Cambridge, MA
A Seattle native, Ana moved to France to work as a stagière at L'Academie du Vin and as an interpreter and apprentice at LaVarenne Ecole de Cuisine, both in Paris. In 1990, Ana relocated to Massachusetts and joined A Mano Catering as executive chef. She became executive chef at Aigo Bistro in Concord, Massachusetts in 1992; two years later Ana opened 8 Holyoke in Cambridge as executive chef. After a brief apprenticeship in Spain at a Michelin two-star restaurant, Ana joined Casablanca as executive chef. She has been acknowledged by *Esquire* magazine, *The Boston Globe* and *The New York Times;* in 1993, Ana was named Boston's Best New Chef. Ana is a vocal advocate of local sustainable agriculture and an avid member of the Chefs Collaborative 2000.

Annie Somerville, Executive Chef, GREENS, Author, San Francisco, CA
Annie began her career as the head cook at Tassajara, in Marin County, California. She joined Greens in 1981 and worked with Deborah Madison. Annie became the Executive Chef in 1985. In 1993, she published her first cookbook, *Field of Greens: New Vegetarian Recipes from the Celebrated Greens Restaurant* and she has contributed to *The Open Hand Cookbook*. Annie is committed to using local resources and supporting local organic farmers.

Susan Spicer, Chef/Co-Owner, BAYONA, New Orleans, LA
Originally in the printing business, Susan made a change to the culinary world in 1979 when she apprenticed at Louis XVI Restaurant in New Orleans, Louisiana. She progressed to sous chef and chose to pursue an apprenticeship in France at the Hotel Sofitel in 1982. After extensive travel, Susan returned to New Orleans to open the Bistro at Maison de Ville as chef in 1986. 1990 marks the year that Bayona was born with Susan as co-owner and chef. She was honored with the James Beard Award for Best Chef—Southeast in 1993 and with the Robert Mondavi Culinary Award of Excellence in 1995.

Nancy Stark, Assistant Pastry Chef, OSTERIA DEL CIRCO, New York, NY
Nancy began her career as an artist, earning her B.F.A. from the Kansas City Art Institute in 1981. She opened her first restaurant, the West Side Café, in Kansas City, Missouri, in 1987 as chef/co-owner, followed by Blvd Café in 1990. She moved to New York City in 1995 and had a stagière under Chef Patissier Jacques Torres at Le Cirque. Nancy aided in the opening of Osteria del Circo in 1995 as assistant pastry chef; she divides her time between Circo and teaching pastry arts as a guest chef at the French Culinary Institute. In 1995, Nancy was awarded Godiva Dessert Competition's Best Tasting honor.

1974: The average price for a loaf of white bread is 34 cents, potatoes are 24 cents a pound, and coffee is $1.28 a pound.

Sarah Stegner, Executive Chef, The Dining Room, THE RITZ CARLTON, Chicago, IL

Training as a classical guitarist at Northwestern University, Sarah began her pilgrimage to the kitchen in 1983, when she decided to enroll at the cooking school Dumas Père in Evanston, Illinois. After graduation, Sarah's first job was at The Ritz Carlton, Chicago as poissonnière. Within six years, she was promoted to chef of the dining room, but not before she worked in France with Pierre Orsi at his two-star Michelin restaurant in Lyon. In 1994, Sarah was awarded the James Beard Rising Star Chef of the Year in America and in 1995 she was honored with the Robert Mondavi Culinary Award of Excellence.

Claire Stewart, Executive Chef, THE CONTINENTAL CLUB, New York, NY

Claire grew up in Sacramento, California in a family full of artists; after working in a number of restaurants and taking classes at a local college, Claire enrolled at the CIA in 1986. Claire graduated and worked at the Rainbow Room in New York City for four years before traveling to Europe with her husband and working in a restaurant in Oxford, England. Back in New York in 1995, she cooked at Gracie Mansion and was executive banquet chef at Highlawn Pavilion. Claire became Executive Chef at the Continental Club in 1996. Claire and her husband live in New Jersey.

Elizabeth Terry, Chef/Co-Owner, ELIZABETH ON 37TH, Savannah, GA

Elizabeth graduated from Lake Erie College for Women in 1966 with a degree in Psychology. While living in Atlanta, she opened a small sandwich shop in the back of a wine store in 1978. Following the birth of her second child, the family moved to Savannah and opened Elizabeth on 37th in 1981. In 1985, Elizabeth was acknowledged with being one of the 25 Hot New Chefs by *Food and Wine* magazine. Accolades continued; in 1993, *Nation's Restaurant News* inducted Elizabeth on 37th into their Fine Dining Hall of Fame; in 1995, the IVY award and the James Beard Best Chef: Southeast were both awarded. Her first book, *Savannah Seasons,* was published in 1996 with the help of her eldest daughter. Elizabeth is married and the mother of two daughters.

Pat Thibodeau, Chef, Philanthropist, Director, THE CHEF AND THE CHILD FOUNDATION, St. Augustine, FL

Pat's childhood was spent in the Bronx, New York. After studying Psychology in college, she focused on human interactions and began working for the Department of Corrections in Florida. Her background in social welfare placed her with The Salvation Army and the State of Florida Food Stamp program. In 1986, at the age of forty, Pat became chef-owner of the Runcible Spoon. In 1989, Pat's desire to learn was satiated by becoming an ACF chef apprentice at Sea World in Orlando. She graduated in 1991 and joined the staff of the Chef and the Child Foundation in 1994. Pat is married and the mother of two children.

Barbara Tropp, Chef, Restaurateur, Author, San Francisco, CA

Barbara spent her childhood in suburban New Jersey and is a graduate of Columbia and Princeton Universities. After spending time in Taiwan, China, and Japan, Barbara formed her culinary philosophy and merged her passion for Tung-Sung dynasty poetics with an equally consuming passion for food. In 1978, Barbara relocated to the West coast, settled in San Francisco, and began to write and teach cooking classes. She chose to learn the tenets of the restaurant business by working in a number of legendary restaurants: Chez Panisse, Spago, and Greens; Barbara opened China Moon Café in 1986. She is one of the founding members of the WCR. Barbara and her husband live in the Bay area.

Monica Velgos, Food Writer, Chef, Cambridge, MA

Monica's food love was born in England, where she was completing her master's degree in Language at the age of twenty-two. An Oklahoma native, she relocated to New York after her time in Europe to attend the French Culinary Institute. Following graduation, Monica combined her literary skills and her culinary education and joined *Food Arts* magazine as a writer. Monica currently lives in Cambridge, Massachusetts and is branching out into consulting and volunteer work.

Alice Waters, Chef-Owner, CHEZ PANISSE and CHEZ PANISSE CAFÉ, Pioneer, Berkeley, CA

A native of New Jersey, Alice graduated from the University of California at Berkeley in 1967 with a degree in French Cultural Studies. She trained at the Montessori School in London and traveled extensively through France. Returning to Berkeley, Alice opened Chez Panisse in 1971 to emulate the perfect dinner party at home. A single, fixed-price dinner was offered every evening based on what was fresh and seasonal at the market. Chez Panisse Café opened in 1980 and Café Fanny opened in 1984, a few miles away from the original restaurant. Acknowledgments of Alice's achievement began early and she was listed as *Cook's Magazine's* Top 50 Who's Who in 1982. In 1992, Alice and the restaurant were honored by the James Beard Foundation as Best Chef and Best Restaurant. Alice has written a number of books and staunchly advocates local, sustainable foods that are harvested in an ecologically sound manner. Alice is married and the mother of one daughter.

1976: The "21" Club hires their first waitress to settle a sex discrimination suit.

Sharon Waynes, Apprentice Chef, PALACE HOTEL, San Francisco, CA
Sharon is originally from the Washington, DC area and spent her first career as a vocational instructor, working with mentally and physically challenged adults. At the age of thirty-five, she felt that it was important to reexamine her goals and life plans. In 1992, she made the decision to leave the East coast and travel to San Francisco to pursue a culinary career. Sharon is an apprentice at The Sheraton Palace Hotel, working under Chef Kerry Heffernan. Her apprenticeship is certified through the American Culinary Federation program; she is enrolled in supplemental classes at the San Francisco Community College.

Susan Weaver, Executive Chef, 5757, The Four Seasons Hotel, New York, NY
After a backpacking trip through Europe, this Boston native discovered her passion for food on the small island of Corsica. Her first job in the States was at the Boston Park Plaza Hotel as a butcher under the guidance of Chef Fernand Gutierrez. Susan joined the staff of the Four Seasons in Houston in 1980 and returned to Europe in 1981 to participate in an apprenticeship at Le Lancaster Hotel in Paris. She reunited with Fernand in 1983 at the Four Seasons property in Chicago, The Ritz-Carlton. Susan went on to the Four Seasons in Toronto, where she was the first woman executive chef in a major Canadian hotel. In 1987, she earned a top ten finalist spot in the Bocuse d'Or competition. The National Executive Chefs Association named Susan USA Hotel Chef of the Year in 1994. Susan has been Executive Chef at 5757 in Manhattan since 1995 and consistently earns three stars from the *New York Times.*

Janis Wertz, BS, M.Ed. Ed.D. Educator, President, HOUSATONIC TECHNICAL COLLEGE, Bridgeport, CT
Janis has a long history of involvement with the academic world. She earned all three of her degrees from the University of Massachusetts at Amherst. She began her career as the coordinator of women's athletics at Williams College, then returned to her alma mater to fill the position of Assistant Dean of Students. After working as an adjunct professor, registrar, and assistant dean at other institutions of higher learning, Janis relocated to the CIA as Vice-President of Planning. Currently President at Housatonic Community-Technical College, she is actively involved in the National Association of Culinary Arts Professionals. Dr. Wertz is married.

Frankie Whitman, Executive Director, WOMEN CHEFS AND RESTAURATEURS, Chef, San Francisco, CA
Frankie earned her Master's degree in consumer economics and public policy from Cornell University in Ithaca, New York. She was involved with

Moosewood Restaurant as chef and kitchen manager prior to moving to Seattle, where she became involved with the Pike Place Market Preservation and Development Authority. Frankie married, moved to Washington, DC, and relocated to Anchorage, Alaska, where she opened a high-end confectionery shop and was instrumental in the revitalization of downtown Anchorage. Frankie joined the WCR as their Executive Director in 1995; she and her husband live in the Bay area.

Anne Willan, Director, President, LA VARENNE, Chef, Washington, DC, Burgundy, France

Anne began her education with a Master's degree in economics from Cambridge University and then went on to study at Le Cordon Bleu in London and Paris. She moved to New York in 1965 and began to write for *Gourmet* magazine. Anne married and moved to Washington, DC and became the food editor of *The Washington Star*. Anne moved back to Europe with her family and LaVarenne was born in 1975 in Paris. Anne has written numerous books and articles. In 1994, her twenty-six segment PBS show *Look & Cook* was produced based on her seventeen volume book series. She is a past President of the IACP and was awarded the *Food Arts* Silver Spoon Award in 1996. Anne and her husband are the parents of two children and they divide their time between Burgundy, France and Washington, DC.

Patricia Williams, Executive Chef, CITY WINE AND CIGAR COMPANY, New York, NY

The discipline of her first career of professional dance prepared this Texas native for the rigors of the professional kitchen, a second career that she has embraced with equal success. After falling in love with food on a trip to France, Patricia's first kitchen job was at the Quilted Giraffe in New York City, as a dessert plater. She moved to Arizona 206 and progressed through all of the luncheon cooking stations. Her next venue for learning was at Sarabeth's Kitchen and then at 150 Wooster. Patricia's first job as executive chef was at Restaurant Charlotte at the Hotel Macklowe in 1990, followed by the job as chef at The Supper Club in 1991. Returning to Restaurant Charlotte in 1993, she was executive chef until opening the City Wine and Cigar Co. in 1996.

1976: The U.S. Department of Labor officially acknowledges chefs as professionals.

Job Descriptions

Kitchen Descriptions

Baker: Responsible for preparing nonsweetened doughs for breads and rolls.

Chef (Chief): Responsible for all kitchen operations, including ordering, supervising all stations, and developing menu items. Also known as "Chef de Cuisine."

Chef de Partie (Line Cook): A person responsible for managing a designated station in a kitchen.

Chef Garde Manger: The person responsible for the preparation of cold items and the chef overseeing the garde manger and pantry stations.

Executive Chef: Responsible for all the duties ascribed to chef; additionally, may be responsible for multi-outlets and have fiscal responsibilities.

Line Cook: (*see* Chef de Partie)

Pantry Cook: Responsible for cold foods, including cold appetizers, salads, dressings, pâtés, and buffet items.

Pastry Chef: Responsible for planning dessert menus and preparation for all baked items, cakes, pies, pastries, and desserts.

Roundsman: Also known as the swing or relief cook. This individual works as needed throughout the kitchen and is knowledgeable about the management of all stations.

Saucier: Responsible for sauces, stews, stocks, hot appetizers, and all sautéed items. This position is often considered the most demanding and is responsible for all the line positions.

1977: Perrier water is introduced into the U.S. market, 113 years after its birth in Europe.

Sous Chef: *Sous* means "under." Second in command, answers to the chef. Fills in for the chef and assists the line cooks as needed. The sous chef is directly in charge of production.

Station: A designated area or section of production within a kitchen that is supervised by a Chef de Partie or a Line Cook.

American Culinary Federation Job Descriptions

Master Chef/Master Pastry Chef (CMC/CMPC): The master chef or master pastry chef is an individual who possesses the highest degree of professional knowledge and skill. These chefs teach and supervise their entire crew as well as provide leadership and serve as role models to the ACFEI apprentices.

Executive Chef (CEC): The executive chef is a full-time chef who is the department head responsible for all culinary units in a restaurant, hotel, club, hospital, or other foodservice establishment. He or she might also be the owner of a foodservice operation. The person in this position must supervise a minimum of five full-time persons in the production of food.

Executive Pastry Chef (CEPC): The executive pastry chef is a pastry chef who is a department head, usually responsible to the executive chef of a food operation or to the management of his/her employing research or pastry firm.

Culinary Educator (CCE): The culinary educator is a chef who is working as an educator at an accredited institution in a culinary or foodservice management program. Certification at this level requires extensive, postsecondary teacher education, in addition to having completed a minimum number of contact hours of teaching experience. The certification applicant must also possess culinary experience and expertise equivalent to that of the certified sous chef.

Chef de Cuisine (CCC): The chef de cuisine is a chef who is the supervisor in charge of food production in a foodservice operation. This could be a single unit of a multi-unit operation, or a freestanding operation. He or she is in essence the chef of this operation with final decision making power as it relates to culinary operations. The person in this position must supervise a minimum of three full-time people in the production of food.

Working Pastry Chef (CWPC): The working pastry chef is defined as a pastry chef responsible for a pastry section or shift within a foodservice operation.

Sous Chef (CSC): The sous chef is defined as a chef who is a supervisor of a shift, station, or stations in a foodservice operation. A sous chef must supervise a minimum of two full-time people in the preparation of food.

Cook/Pastry Cook: (1) A **cook** is defined as a person positioned in any one station in a foodservice operation, responsible for preparing and cooking sauces, cold foods, fish, soups and stocks, meats, vegetables, eggs, and other food items. (2) A **pastry cook** is defined as a person positioned in any one station in a foodservice operation, responsible for preparing and cooking pies, cookies, cakes, breads, rolls, or other baked goods and dessert items.

The ACF Certification Breakdown of Currently Active Certifications

	CMC	CMPC	CCE	CEC	CEPC	CCC	CWC	CWPC	CSC	CC	CPC
Women	1	0	82	92	33	11	154	34	10	400	31
Men	50	17	552	2134	139	128	1399	94	72	1833	66
	.02		.15	.04	.24	.09	.11	.36	.14	.22	.47

1977: Dr. Rosalyn S. Yalow, one of the first female Nobel Prize winners, noted in her acceptance speech, "The world cannot afford the loss of the talents of half its people if we are to solve the many problems which beset us."

Glossary

ACF (American Culinary Federation): A chef's advocacy group which has as its primary focus the education and promotion of chefs internationally and on every level of expertise. The group is also responsible for the sanctioning of all domestic culinary competitions and overseeing any international competitions that take place in the United States.

Brigade: A formal hierarchy in the professional kitchen based on the regimentation and organization of ranks within the military; the development of this system is often credited to Auguste Escoffier.

Cold Line: The area of a kitchen where foods are produced for meal periods without the immediate use of ovens or stoves. The food has been cooked prior to the service period and is kept at a cool temperature and plated.

Guild: A professional association of craftspeople and artisans usually joining together professionally for the financial and artistic benefit of all members.

Home Meal Replacement: A pre-prepared meal, purchased outside of the domicile for consumption within the home during a traditional family dining period.

Hot Line: The area of a kitchen where entrees are produced for meal periods using sautéing, frying, or poaching methods of cooking. The food is put onto plates and presented at a warm or hot temperature.

Inventory Sheets: The lists of goods that are counted daily, weekly, or monthly within a foodservice operation. These numbers are used to establish ordering and production lists for the chef and staff.

Menu Manual: A culinary reference book that includes, but is not limited to, the recipes and photographs of all food items produced within a specific

1978: Women now earn 65 cents for every dollar earned by their male counterparts for comparable jobs.

kitchen. The information can also include costing specifications, plating suggestions, and the chef's desired methods of preparation.

NRA (National Restaurant Association): The leading national trade association for the foodservice industry, founded in 1919. The NRA supports foodservice education and research in several educational institutions.

Outsourcing: The business practice of buying a component of a product from another source.

Stage: An apprenticeship position, traditionally in Europe, where an unpaid student works to learn a craft.

Stagière: Person in a stage position.

Toque: Tall white hat, traditionally worn only by the chef (chief) in the kitchen. The height of the hat made it possible to discern the head chef among a group.

The Women Chefs' Recommended Reading List

Books

Asterisks indicate the number of times a book was recommended.

Ackerman, Diane. *Natural History of the Senses*

Amendola, Joseph. *Baker's Manual*

Anderson, Jean. *The New Doubleday Cookbook*

Andrews, Coleman. *Catalan Cuisine, Europe's Last Great Culinary Secret*

Angelou, Maya. *I Know Why the Caged Bird Sings*

Baldwin, James. *Another Country, Go Tell it on the Mountain*

Barre, Nancy Verde, and Kathe Helander. *We Called it Macaroni: An American Heritage of Southern Italian Cooking*

Bastianich, Lidia. *La Cucina de Lidia: Distinctive Regional Cuisine from the North of Italy*

Bateson, Mary Catherine. *Composing a Life*

Bayless, Rick. *Authentic Mexican: Regional Cooking from the Heart of Mexico****

Beard, James. *Everything*

Bertolli, Paul. *Chez Panisse Cooking*

Blanc, George. *The Natural Cuisine of George Blanc*

Bolles, Richard Nelson. *What Color is My Parachute?*

Boni, Ada. *Italian Regional Cooking*

Bradbury, Ray. *Dandelion Wine*

Bugialli, Giuliano. *Fine Art of Italian Cooking, Bugialli on Pasta*

Child, Julia. *Mastering the Art of French Cooking(***); From Julia Child's Kitchen; Julia Child and Company; The Way to Cook*

Claiborne, Craig. *The New York Times International Cookbook; Craig Claiborne's Favorites from* The New York Times***

Clow, Barbara Hand. *Eye of the Centaur*

Cohen, Sherry Suit. *Secrets of a Very Good Marriage*

Duguid, Naomi, and Jeffrey Ford *Flatbreads and Flavors: A Baker's Atlas*

David, Elizabeth. *Elizabeth David Classics; An Omelet and a Glass of Wine; English Bread and Yeast Cookery****

DeGroot, Roy Andries. *The Auberge of the Flowering Hearth*

Dornenburg, Andrew, and Karen Page. *Becoming a Chef With Recipes and Reflections from America's Leading Chefs****

Ellis, Audrey. *Four Seasons Cookbook*

Escoffier, Auguste. *Le Guide Culinaire*

Farmer, Fannie. *Fannie Farmer Cookbook: 100th Anniversary Edition*

Field, Carol. *The Italian Baker*

Fisher, Mary Frances Kennedy. *The Art of Eating, The Gastronomical Me******

Freson, Robert. *Taste of France*

Foo, Susanna. *Susanna Foo's Chinese Cuisine*

Fox, Margaret. *Café Beaujolais, Morning Food*

Guerand, Michel. *Cuisine Gourmand*

Giovanni, Nikki. *Black Feeling, Black Talk*

Glassman, Bernard. *Instructions to the Cook*

Gold, Rozanne. *Recipes 1-2-3: More than 250 Recipes for Fabulous Food Using Only Three Ingredients*

Goldstein, Joyce. *The Mediterranean Kitchen; Mediterranean the Beautiful Cookbook*

Grigson, Jane. *The Fruit Book, The Vegetable Book*

Harris, Jessica. *The Welcome Table: African American Heritage Cooking*

Hazan, Marcella. *Essentials of Classic Italian Cooking***

Healy, Bruce. *Mastering the Art of French Pastry*

Herbst, Sharon Tyler. *The Food Lover's Companion*

Jackson, Wes. *Meeting the Expectations of the Land: Essays in Sustainable Agriculture and Stewards*

Jaffrey, Madhur. *The Taste of India*

Jones, Evan. *American Food*

Kamman, Madeleine. *When French Women Cook; The Making of a Cook, Savoie; In Madeleine Kamman's Kitchen; Dinner Against the Clock******

Killeen, Johanne, and George Germon. *Cucina Simpatica: Robust Trattoria Cooking*

King, Shirley. *Pampille's Table, Saucing the Fish, Dining with Marcel Proust*

Kuo, Irene. *Key to Chinese Cooking*

Montagne, Prosper. *Larousse Gastronomique*

Lewis, Edna, with Evangeline Peterson. *The Edna Lewis Cookbook; The Taste of Country Cooking*

Luchetti, Emily. *Four Star Desserts*

Lucas, Dione. *The Gourmet Cooking School Cookbook*

McClane, A. J. *The Encyclopedia of Fish Cookery*

Mc Gee, Harold. *On Food and Cooking; The Curious Cook******

McPhee, John. *Giving Good Weight, Oranges*

Madison, Deborah. *The Greens Cookbook, The Savory Way*

Martinez, Zarela. *Food From My Heart: Cuisines of Mexico Remembered*

Martz, Reimaginen, and Sandra Haldeman. *If I Had My Life to Live Over Again, I'd Pick More Daisies*

Mayle, Peter. *A Year in Provence*

McKeever, Mike P. *How to Write a Business Plan*

Milliken, Mary Sue, and Susan Feniger. *Cooking with Too Hot Tamales; City Cuisine*

Olney, Richard. *Simple French Food; The French Menu Cookbook****

O'Connell, Rick. *365 Easy Italian Recipes*

Pawlcyn, Cindy. *Fog City Diner Cookbook*

Peck, Scott. *The Road Less Traveled*

Pepin, Jacques. *La Technique, La Methode, Everyday Cooking with Jacques Pepin****

Peterson, James. *Sauces: Classical and Contemporary Saucemaking, Fish & Shellfish*

Ponzek, Debra, and Joan Schwartz. *French Food, American Accent: Debra*

1979: A U.S. federal law takes effect on April 29 that forbids employers to discriminate against pregnant employees or any other disabled workers.

Ponzek's Spirited Cuisine

Pouillon, Nora. *Cooking with Nora: Seasonal Menus from Restaurant Nora*

Redfield, James. *The Celestine Prophecy*

Revsin, Leslie. *Great Fish Quick*

Robinson, Janis. *The Oxford Companion to Wine*

Roden, Claudia. *A Book of Middle Eastern Food; Coffee: A Connoisseur's Companion; The Book of Jewish Food: An Odyssey from Samarkand to New York* **

Rombauer, Erma, and Marion Rombauer Becker. *The Joy of Cooking*

Root, Waverly Lewis. *The Food of Italy; The Food of France; Eating in America: A History; Food: An Authoritative Visual History and Dictionary*

Rosenzweig, Anne. *The Arcadia Seasonal Mural and Cookbook*

Rozin, Elisabeth. *Blue Corn and Chocolate; Ethnic Cuisine: How to Create the Authentic Flavors of 30 International Cuisines; Ethnic Cuisines: the Flavor Principle Cookbook*

Salvato, Cynthia. *The Dowry Cookbook*

Sands, Brinna B. *The King Arthur Flour Two-Hundredth Anniversary Cookbook*

Sanders, Barbara Rogers. *A Cookbook Mate for the Blind and the Sighted*

Scaravelli, Paola. *Cooking from an Italian Garden*

Scherber, Amy, with Toy Kim Dupree. *Amy's Bread*

Shere, Lindsay. *Chez Panisse Desserts*

Silverton, Nancy. *Desserts; Nancy Silverton's Breads from La Brea Bakery: Recipes for the Connoisseur*

Simeti, Mary Taylor. *Bitter Almonds: Recollections and Recipes from a Sicilian Girlhood* (with Maria Grammatico); *Pomp and Sustenance: Twenty-five Centuries of Sicilian Food; On Persephone's Island: A Sicilian Journal*

Simmons, Amelia. *American Cookery: 200th Anniversary Edition*

Sokolov, Raymond. *Saucier's Apprentice*

Soltner, André, with Seymour Britchky. *The Lutèce Cookbook*

Sonnenschmidt, Frederic H. *The Professional Chef's Art of Garde Manger*

Steinem, Gloria. *Revolution from Within: A Book of Self-Esteem*

Sullivan, Jim. *Service That Sells*

Suskind, Patrick. *Perfume: The Story of a Murderer*

Thibodeau, Karen, editor. *Dining During the Depression*

Thorne, John. *Outlaw Cook*

Tropp, Barbara. *Modern Art of Chinese Cooking; China Moon Cookbook*

Visser, Margaret. *Much Depends on Dinner*

Waters, Alice. *The Chez Panisse Menu Cookbook; Chez Panisse Pasta; Pizza & Calzone; Chez Panisse Vegetables****

Wells, Patricia. *Simply French: Patricia Wells Presents the Cuisine of Joel Robuchon; The Food Lover's Guide to Paris; Patricia Wells Trattoria: Healthy, Simple Robust Fare Inspired by the Small Family Restaurants of Italy*

Willan, Anne. *Great Cooks and Their Recipes: From Taillevent to Escoffier; LaVarenne Pratique: The Complete Illustrated Cooking Course; Techniques, Ingredients, and Tools of Classic Modern Cuisine****

Wolfert, Paula. *Paula Wolfert's World of Food; Mediterranean Cooking; The Cooking of Southwest France: A Collection of Traditional and New Recipes from France's Magnificent Rustic Cuisine; New Techniques to Lighten Hearty Dishes*******

Wolter, Annette. *The Best of Baking*

Magazines and Literary Publications

Art Culinaire

AIWF Annual Publication—*Wine, Food and the Arts*

The Wall Street Journal

U.S. News and World Reports

Get a library card! Read all the magazines you can get your hands on! Try to keep up with all current trends, news, and information, and keep your brain going!

1980: More than fifty-two percent of women aged fifteen to sixty-four in Western countries are in the work force.

A Sampling of Women Chefs and Their Restaurants Throughout History

Date	Restaurant Name - Place	Women and Their Positions
1840	Antoines - New Orleans	Julie Freyss helps Antoine develop the restaurant
1871	Antoines - New Orleans	Julie Freyss takes over the running of the operation from her husband
1922	Nut Tree - California	Helen Allsion Power opens Fig Stand
1922	La Mère Brazier - France	Eugenie Brazier, the one and only woman to be awarded three stars by the Guide Michelin; the restaurant will have three generations of women chefs
1927	Marriott's Hot Shoppe - Washington, DC	Alice, John Marriott's wife, heads the kitchen in this nine-seat root beer stand, the predecessor of the Marriott chain
1945	Russian Tea room - New York City	Faith Stewart Gordon takes over from her husband in 1967
1948	Café Nicholson - New York City	Edna Lewis, at age thirty-one, heads the kitchen staff
1955	Brennens - New Orleans	Ella Brennen (age thirty) the kitchen supervisor, takes over when her brother Owen dies
1958	Joyce Chen's	Joyce Chen opens her namesake restaurant
1961	Sylvia's - Harlem	Sylvia Woods, chef-owner
1962	Sign of the Dove - New York City	Henny Santo takes over from her husband
1969	Mandarin - San Francisco	Cecilia Chang, proprietress
1971	Chez Panisse	Alice Waters, chef-owner

1981: The U.S. Department of Agriculture responds to cuts in school lunch programs by announcing that ketchup can be counted as a vegetable.

Date	Restaurant Name - Place	Women and Their Positions
1972	Harvest Restaurant - Boston	Lydia Shire, chef
1972	Le Bernadin - New York City	Maguay le Coze, owner
1972	Waldorf Astoria - New York City	Leslie Revsin, first female chef
1973	The Swallow - California	Ruth Reichl, owner
1973	Chez la Mère Madeleine	Madeleine Kamman, chef-owner
1974	Commanders Palace - New Orleans	Ella Brennan, owner
1977	Silver Palate	Sheila Lukins and Julee Rosso, owners
1980	Al Forno - Providence	Johanne Killeen and George Germon, chef-owners
1981	Elizabeth on 37th	Elizabeth Terry, chef-owner
1982	City - Los Angeles	Mary Sue Milliken and Susan Feniger, chef-owners
1983	Mustards Grill - Napa Valley	Cindy Pawlcyn, chef-owner
1984	Square One - San Francisco	Joyce Goldstein, chef-owner
1984	Arcadia - New York City	Anne Rosenzweig, chef-owner
1986	Montrachet - New York City	Debra Ponzek, Executive Chef; first woman in New York to be awarded three stars
1986	China Moon Café - San Francisco	Barbara Tropp, chef-owner
1987	Susanna Foo's Chinese Cuisine - Philadelphia	Susanna Foo, chef-owner
1988	21 Club - New York City	Anne Rosenzweig hired to rejuvenate menu
1989	BIBA - Boston	Lydia Shire, chef-owner
1990	Border Grill - Los Angeles	Mary Sue Milliken and Susan Feniger, chef-owners
1990	Bayona - New Orleans	Susan Spicer, chef-owner
1991	Elephant Walk - Sommerville	Longteine de Monteiro and Nadsa Perry, chef-owners
1996	China Moon Café - San Francisco	Barbara Tropp sells China Moon Café
1996	Square One - San Francisco	Joyce Goldstein closes Square One

Survey Used in Research

• **CONTACT INFORMATION (optional)**

Name _____

Address _____

Phone _____

Fax _____

E-Mail _____

• **EMPLOYMENT INFORMATION**

Employer Name _____

Address _____

Phone _____

Fax _____

Position _____

      Type of facility _____

      Type of cuisine _____

      Number of seats _____

      Meal periods served _____

1986: Debra Ponzek, executive chef at Montrachet, is the first woman in New York City
to be awarded three stars.

Average guest check by meal period _____

What percent of your day is spent "hands-on versus management"?

□10% □20% □30% □40% □50% □60% □70% □80% or more

What were the three most predominant factors in choosing your current position? *(Please check only 3.)*

□Salary   □Creativity   □Challenge   □Family
□Location   □Education   □Advancement

Are you satisfied with your current position? Why or why not?

_____

_____

_____

_____

_____

_____

How many of your co-workers are female?

□None   □Less than 10%   □10-25%   □25-50%   □50-75%   □75% or higher

How many of your employees are female?

□None   □Less than 10%   □10-25%   □25-50%   □50-75%   □75% or higher

Is your direct supervisor a woman?   □Yes   □No

How many hours a day do you work?

□3-6   □7-10   □11-14   □15 or more

How many days a week do you work?   □1-3 □4-5 □6-7

Current salary (yearly)

□Less than $10,000   □$36,000-$50,000
□$10,000-$20,000   □$51,000-$65,000
□$21,000-$35,000   □More than $65,000

• PERSONAL DATA

Age:

☐18-23　　☐42-47
☐24-29　　☐48-53
☐30-35　　☐54-59
☐36-41　　☐60 and over

Marital Status:

☐Single　　☐Married　　☐Separated　　☐Divorced　　☐Widowed

Children:

☐None　　☐1　　☐2　　☐3　　☐4 or more

Race:

☐White　　　　☐Asian or Pacific Islander
☐Hispanic　　☐American Indian or Alaskan Native
☐Black

Is English your first language?　　☐Yes　　☐No

　If not, in which language do you have a strong written and spoken fluency?

☐French　　　　☐Korean
☐Spanish　　　☐Chinese
☐Italian　　　　☐Japanese
☐German　　　☐Other _____

• EMPLOYMENT HISTORY

Years in current position:　☐1-5　☐6-10　☐11-15　☐16-20　☐21 and over

Years in previous position:　☐1-5　☐6-10　☐11-15　☐16-20　☐21 and over

Years in industry:　☐1-5　☐6-10　☐11-15　☐16-20　☐21 and over

First foodservice job:　Title _____

　　　　　　　　　　Salary per hour:　☐$6 or less　　☐$15-$20
　　　　　　　　　　　　　　　　　　☐$7-10　　　　　☐$21-26
　　　　　　　　　　　　　　　　　　☐$11-$14　　　☐$27- and over

　　　　　　　　　　Year started _____

1986: U.S. women professionals outnumber men for the first time but still earn substantially less pay than their male counterparts.

• EDUCATIONAL HISTORY

☐Apprenticeship _____

☐Culinary School _____

    Specific reasons for choosing a culinary school versus apprenticeship or working in the field _____

    _____

    Specific reasons for choosing that school _____

    _____

    Percent of female students in your class

    ☐Less than 10%   ☐20-30%   ☐40-50%   ☐60-70%   ☐80% or more

    How do you feel your education was affected by this? _____

    _____

    _____

    How many female chef-instructors did you have direct contact with?

    ☐None   ☐1-3   ☐4-6   ☐7 or more

    What were the positions held or classes taught by those instructors?

    _____

    _____

    Comment on your preparedness derived from your education for work in the culinary field _____

    _____

☐College _____

☐Other Secondary Education _____

☐Continuing Education (Courses taken: what, where, when, how often)

1. _____

2. _____

3. _____

4. _____

5. _____

• PROFESSIONAL AFFILIATIONS

Organization Name _____

_____

_____

_____

Offices you hold, or have held, and dates _____

_____

Awards and honors _____

Certification level achieved _____

• COMPETITIONS

Have you participated in culinary competitions?   ☐Yes   ☐No

If yes, which ones, and what was the outcome? _____

_____

How many other women did you compete with? _____

What were your goals in entering the competitions? _____

_____

1988: Of all women aged twenty-five to twenty-nine, 87 percent have high school diplomas in comparison to 84.7 percent of men in the same age group.

• YOUR CAREER

Please give your description of the position of chef. _____

_____

_____

Why did you choose a culinary career? _____

_____

_____

What events in your life led toward that choice? _____

_____

_____

If you had not chosen the culinary path, what would you have chosen?

_____

What goals do you have both personally and professionally? _____

_____

_____

Where do you expect to be in five years? _____

_____

_____

What initiatives have you taken to advance your career? _____

_____

_____

Characterize the management style of your work environment and how you would change it. _____

_____

_____

What role does creativity play in your professional life? _____

_____

_____

_____

What are the sources of inspiration in your professional life? _____

_____

_____

Please comment on the challenges of being a woman in a historically male profession.

_____

_____

_____

_____

_____

Characterize the differences between female and male supervisors. _____

_____

_____

_____

Characterize your successes and failures as a culinarian and or businesswoman.

_____

_____

_____

How do you manage your successes? _____

_____

_____

1988: More than 56 million U.S. women are in the civilian work force.

Is your culinary career a second one?   ☐Yes   ☐No

   If yes, what was the first? _____

Who have been your mentors? _____

_____

_____

Who has most significantly impacted upon your culinary career?

_____

Are you currently a mentor to a student in the field?   ☐Yes   ☐No

What do you like most/least about our profession? _____

_____

_____

_____

What are the three major challenges you face today? _____

_____

_____

_____

What are the challenges you imagine facing in the next decade? _____

_____

_____

Have you experienced harassment on the job and did you report it? If so, what was the outcome? _____

_____

_____

Do you feel that you are paid on par with industry standards?   ☐Yes   ☐No

If you had a daughter, would you encourage her to enter our profession?
☐Yes   ☐No

Any additional comments on being a woman in the culinary profession?

_____

_____

_____

What advice would you give to the next generation of women chefs? _____

_____

_____

_____

_____

Please describe a typical day in your life, both personally and professionally. Please include the percent of time spent at work versus time spent both privately and with family. _____

_____

_____

_____

_____

_____

_____

_____

PLEASE SIGN BELOW BEFORE RETURNING THIS QUESTIONNAIRE

The undersigned hereby gives permission to Van Nostrand Reinhold to reprint all or part of the information included in this questionnaire:

_____

THANK YOU ONCE AGAIN FOR YOUR PARTICIPATION

1990: U.S. women earn on average 67 cents for every dollar earned by a man doing comparable work.

Professional Organizations

American Culinary Federation

Founded in 1929, the American Culinary Federation is a professional, not-for-profit, organization representing more than 25,000 U.S. cooks and chefs. The ACF was responsible for elevating the status of executive chef from a service status to the professional category in the U.S. Department of Labor's *Dictionary of Official Titles* in 1976.

The American Culinary Federation Educational Institute (ACFEI) was established in 1963 and is the national accrediting commission for culinary, baking, and pastry educational programs at postsecondary institutions. The ACF runs the only comprehensive certification program for chefs in the U.S.

American Culinary Federation
P.O. Box 3466
St Augustine, FL 32085
904-824-4468
800-624-9458
904-825-4758 (fax)

American Institute of Baking—AIB

The American Institute of baking is a nonprofit educational organization whose objective is to promote education and research in nutrition, the science and art of baking, bakery management, and the allied sciences. AIB was founded in 1919 and is supported by the contributions of more than 600 member companies.

American Institute of Baking (AIB)
1213 Bakers Way
Manhattan, KS 66502
913-537-4750
800-633-5137
913-537-1493 (fax)

1990: Lyde Buchtenkirch-Biscardi is the first and only female master chef.

AIWF—American Institute of Wine and Food

The AIWF was founded in 1981 to advance the understanding, appreciation, and quality of what we eat and drink. Founded on the premise that gastronomy is essential to the quality of human existence, the AIWF is a nonprofit educational organization with membership open to all. The institute is devoted to improving the understanding, appreciation, and accessibility of food and drink through a lively and comprehensive exchange of information and ideas in its conferences, publications, and chapter programs.

AIWF
1550 Bryant Street #700
San Francisco, CA 94103
415-255-3000
415-255-2874 (fax)

AWFW—Arizona Women in Food and Wine

Founded in 1987 to support and encourage women working in the food, beverage, and hospitality industries. Objectives of the AWFW are to promote high professional standards, to assist members in attaining public recognition, to offer practical educational programs, to provide professional and social opportunities, and to offer scholarships to women who have chosen to continue their education in culinary arts. Membership is open to any woman who either lives or works in the state of Arizona and who has an express interest in any segment of the food, beverage, or hospitality industries.

Helen Prier
Membership Chairman
1921 W. Culver Street
Phoenix, AZ 85007
602-256-7009
602-256-0353 (fax)

Chef and the Child Foundation

In 1988, the ACF designed a program addressing the nutritional and dietary needs of children, forming a nonprofit corporation, the Chef and the Child Foundation, Inc. The purpose of the foundation is to foster, promote, encourage, and stimulate an awareness of proper nutrition in preschool and elementary schoolchildren through education, community involvement, and fundraising.

Chef and the Child Foundation
c/o The American Culinary Federation
10 San Bartola Road
St. Augustine, FL 32086
904-824-4468

800-624-9458
904-825-4758 (fax)
E-mail: acf@aug.com

Chefs Collaborative 2000—CC2000

A nonprofit organization founded in conjunction with Oldways Preservation and Exchange Trust in 1993, CC2000 works to expand the links between chefs and farmers who are committed to producing food in an ecologically responsible way. Chef members are committed to advancing sustainable agriculture by designing their menus around seasonally fresh foods. While cooking with chef members in educational forums, children are taught to appreciate foods from different cultures; to make healthy, sustainable food choices; to understand and appreciate where their food comes from, and to understand the impact their eating habits have on their environment.

CC2000
25 First Street
Cambridge, MA 02141
617-621-3000
617-621-1230 (fax)

The Council on Hotel, Restaurant and Institutional Education—CHRIE

CHRIE, founded in 1946, is a leading international association for individuals and organizations involved in education and training for the hospitality and tourism industry (restaurants, foodservice, hotels, lodging, and travel-related businesses). CHRIE offers education programs in hotel and restaurant management, foodservice management, and culinary arts, in addition to providing networking opportunities and professional development to the broad spectrum of employees of the service industry.

CHRIE
1200 17th Street, NW
Washington, D.C. 20036
202-331-5990
202-785-2511 (fax)

Culinary Archives and Museum at Johnson and Wales University

Referred to as "The Smithsonian Institution of the Foodservice Industry," the Culinary Archives and Museum holds over 300,000 items related to the field of culinary arts and hospitality. The collection, valued at approximately $2 million, includes rare U.S. Presidential culinary notations; tools of the trade from the third millennium B.C.; Egyptian, Roman, and Oriental spoons dating back

1991: Chicken costs 89 cents a pound, and milk is $1.38 a half gallon.

1,000 years, original artwork; hotel and restaurant silver; and periodicals and documents relating to culinary arts and entertainment.

Culinary Archives and Museum at Johnson and Wales University
315 Harborside Boulevard
Providence, RI 02905
401-598-2805
401-598-2807

International Association of Culinary Professionals—IACP

Founded in 1978, the IACP is a not-for-profit professional society of individuals employed in, or providing services to, the culinary industry. IACP's mission is to be a resource and support system for food professionals, and to help its members achieve and sustain success at all levels of their careers through education, information, and peer contacts in an ethical, responsible, and professional climate. The association establishes professional and ethical standards through the Certified Culinary Professional program for Food and Beverage Departments.

IACP
304 Liberty Street, Suite 201
Louisville, KY 40202
502-581-9786
502-589-3602 (fax)
E-mail: iacp@aol.com
Web:http://www.iacp-online.org

International Food Service Executives Association—IFSEA

Founded in 1901 as the International Steward and Caterers; the IFSEA is a nonprofit educational and community service organization. It was the foodservice industry's first trade association with worldwide membership. The organization is dedicated to raising foodservice standards and to educating members and future leaders in the industry. Services include student scholarships and a certification program.

IFSEA
1100 S. State Road 7, Suite 103
Margate, FL 33068
954-977-0767
954-977-0874 (fax)

James Beard Foundation, Inc.

This charitable foundation was established in 1986 to keep alive the ideals and activities that made James Beard the acknowledged "Father of American

Cooking" and to maintain his home as the first historical culinary center in North America. A scholarship, apprenticeship program, and library have also been developed. In 1990, the foundation established The James Beard Awards, recognized as the Oscars of the fine food world.

The James Beard Foundation, Inc.
167 W. 12th Street
New York, NY 10011
212-675-4984
800-362-3273
212-645-1438 (fax)

Les Dames d'Escoffier International

Les Dames d'Escoffier is an international organization of women in the culinary field. The purpose of the organization is to support and promote the understanding, appreciation, and knowledge of this profession in the tradition of Auguste Escoffier. Members include professional women in the field with at least five years experience as chefs, cooking school owners and teachers, food writers and editors, caterers, hotel executives, purveyors, administrators, and public relations specialists.

Les Dames d'Escoffier
P.O. Box 2103
Reston, VA 20195-0982
703-716-5913

MultiCultural Foodservice and Hospitality Alliance—MFHA

The MultiCultural Foodservice and Hospitality Alliance is a Not for Profit Business League/Professional Association established in 1997. The Alliance is working for greater representation, development, and advancement of minorities within the foodservice and hospitality industries. Benefits of membership include networking opportunities, access to minority business development opportunities, and an extensive job bank.

P.O. Box 1113
Minneapolis, MN 55440-1113
612-540-4584
Fax-612-540-4794
E-mail: ferna001@mail.genmills.com

1992: Women in the United States own more than 128,000 food and beverage establishments, with revenues in excess of $28 million.

National Restaurant Association—NRA

Established in 1919, the NRA is the leading national trade association for the foodservice industry with a membership of over 30,000. The association provides education, research, communication, convention, and government services to its members. The NRA is open to anyone that operates facilities and/or supplies meal service to others on a regular basis.

National Restaurant Association
1200 17th Street, NW
Washington, DC 20036-3097
202-331-5900
800-424-5156
202-331-2429 (fax)
E-mail: isal@restaurant.org
Web. http://www.restaurant.org

Oldways Preservation and Exchange Trust

K. Dun Gifford founded Oldways in 1988. Oldways is a young and growing nonprofit organization with a single goal—to change the way the world eats. Objectives of the organization include slowing the worldwide epidemic of preventable chronic diseases by encouraging healthier eating, drinking, exercise, and lifestyle patterns; helping to reduce pollution from agriculture (the largest source of surface water pollution) by discouraging chemically intensive agriculture and promoting sustainable agriculture; and retarding the steady loss of cultural and biological diversity by preserving traditional ways of growing, cooking, and eating food. Oldways advances these objectives by developing educational programs that promote sensible diet and lifestyle behaviors.

Oldways Preservation and Exchange Trust
25 First Street
Cambridge, MA 02141
617-621-3000
617-621-1230 (fax)

Roundtable for Women in Foodservice—RWF

RWF is a national nonprofit organization of foodservice professionals devoted to providing educational, mentoring, and networking opportunities to enhance the development and visibility of women. Founded in 1983, the RWF's focus is on the development and enhancement of women's careers throughout all corporate and entrepreneurial operator, supplier, and service segments of the industry. RWF joins male and female restaurant operators, foodservice directors, and culinarians with suppliers, allied and associate professions, and students to form a single organization that focuses on a single mission of great benefit to every segment of the industry.

RWF, Inc.
National Headquarters
1372 La Colina Drive, Suite B
Tustin, CA 92780-2824
714-838-2749
800-898-2849
714-838-2750 (fax)

Second Harvest

Second Harvest, established in 1979, is a network of food banks that distributes millions of pounds of donated food and grocery products to the hungry through food pantries, soup kitchens, and homeless shelters.

Second Harvest
116 S. Michigan Avenue, Suite 4
Chicago, IL 60603
312-263-2305
800-532-3663
312-236-5626 (fax)

Anthony Spinazzola Foundation

The Anthony Spinazzola Foundation is a charitable corporation founded in memory of the Boston Globe's late food and wine critic, Anthony Spinazzola. The foundation provides grants and gifts to a variety of hunger-relief organizations and culinary schools throughout New England.

Anthony Spinazzola Foundation
5 Cabot Place
Stoughton, MA 02072
617-344-4413

Share Our Strength—SOS

SOS works to alleviate hunger and poverty in the United States and around the world. Since its founding in 1984, SOS has distributed more than $26 million in grants to over 800 anti-hunger organizations in the United States, Canada, and developing countries around the world. Operation Frontline is SOS's nutrition education and food budgeting program that connects chefs with people who are at risk of poor nutrition and hunger. Kids Up Front, a partnership with Kraft Foods, is the children's component of Operation Frontline, which helps children at risk of hunger to make better food choices and improve their diets over the long term.

1994: The National Restaurant Association reports that sixty percent of foodservice workers are women. The average woman in the industry is under thirty, working part-time, and living at home.

SOS
1511 K Street NW, Suite 940
Washington, DC 20005
202-393-2925
202-347-5868 (fax)

Wider Opportunities for Women—WOW

Founded in 1964, WOW was organized to expand employment opportunities for women through information, employment training, technical assistance, and advocacy. WOW sponsors Women's Work Force Network, a national network of 500 women's employment programs and advocates. This organization also offers technical assistance to educational institutions, government agencies, and private industry to increase women's participation in nontraditional employment and training.

WOW
1325 G St. NW, Lower Level
Washington, DC 20005
202-638-3143
202-638-4885 (fax)

Women Chefs and Restaurateurs—WCR

WCR was founded in 1993 to promote the education and advancement of women in the restaurant industry and the betterment of the industry as a whole. International members are industry professionals who range in experience from executive chefs to culinary students, from line cooks to restaurateurs. Members are dedicated to providing opportunities, encouragement, and support for women of all backgrounds who wish to enter or advance in the restaurant industry.

WCR
110 Sutter Street, Suite 305
San Francisco, CA 94104
415-362-7336
415-362-7335 (fax)
E-mail: iawcr@well.com

Source: Encyclopedia of Associations, 31st Editions.

Notes

[1] Dave Miller as quoted in a lecture on "Women, Food and Technology," April 9, 1990, to members of The Culinary Historians of Boston. Cited by Barbara Wheaton in *Culinary Historians of Boston Newsletter* Fall 1989-1990.

[2] Beverly Cox and Martin Jacobs, *Spirit of the Harvest*, New York: Stewart Tabor and Chang, 1991, p. 139.

[3] Ibid. p. 16.

[4] Kenneth Hester and Joseph McGowen, Jr., *Early Man in the New World*, Doubleday, Anchor Books, The National Library, 1962, pp. 38-39. As cited by June Stephenson, *Women's Roots, Status and Achievements in Western Civilization*, Napa, CA: Diemer, Smith Publishing Company. 1981, p. 15.

[5] Margaret Visser, *The Rituals of Dinner: The Origins, Evolution, Eccentricities and Meaning of Table Manners*, New York, Grove-Weidenfeld, 1991, p. 80. As cited by Margaret Mackenzie in *The Journal of Gastronomy*, AIWF, San Francisco, Vol 7, No 1, 1993, p. 37.

[6] Claude Levi-Strauss, *The Raw and the Cooked: An Introduction to a Science of Mythology*, Vol. 1, New York, Harper and Row, 1969. As cited by Margaret Mackenzie in *The Journal of Gastronomy*, AIWF, San Francisco, Vol. 7, No 1, 1993, pp. 36-37.

[7] Barbara Wheaton, *Savoring the Past: The French Kitchen and Table from 1300 to 1789*, Philadelphia, University of Pennsylvania Press, 1983, p. xviii.

[8] Reay Tannahill, *Food in History*, New York: Crown Trade Paperbacks, 1992, p. 63.

[9] Maguelonne Toussant-Samat, *History of Food*, Blackwell Publishers, Cambridge MA, 1992, p. 178.

1994: Only six to eight percent of the executive chefs in the United States are women.

[10]Tannahill, *op. cit.*, p. 63.

[11]Evelyn Reed, *Woman's Evolution: Matriarchal Clan to Patriarchal Family*, New York: Pathfinder Press, 1975.

[12]*Daily Hampshire Gazette*, Northhampton, MA, 7/26/96, Mickey Rathburn, *Chef's Best, Tasting History in Mystic—A Sailor's Fare from Lobcouse to Brambles*, p. 23.

[13]Barbara G. Carson, *Ambitious Appetites: Dining Behaviour and Patterns of Consumption in Federal Washington*. Exhibition Catalogue, the Octagon Museum, August 7, 1990–October 30, 1990.

[14]Better Homes and Gardens, *Heritage Cookbook*, Des Moines, IA, Meredith Corporation. 1979, p. 120.

[15]Issac Jefferson, "Memoirs . . ." as quoted in Bear, *Jefferson at Monticello*, p. 8.

[16]Jessica Harris quoted during a presentation at a Les Dames d'Escoffier conference in New York, at New York City Technical College, entitled, "You've Come Along Way Maybe," 1994.

[17]Linda Grant DePauw and Conover Hunt, *Remember the Ladies—1750 Women in America—1815*, New York: The Viking Press, 1976, p. 9.

[18]Charles Darwin, *The Descent of Man*, 1873, as cited by Glenna C. Matthews during a lecture on "Just a Housewife: The Rise and Fall of Domesticity in the United States," given to The Culinary Historians of Boston, March 1984.

[19]Robert Clarke, *Ellen Swallow: The Woman Who Founded Ecology*, Chicago: Follett Publishing Company, 1973, p. 215.

[20]*Dirt and Domesticity: Construction of the Feminine*, pp. 62-63.

[21]Miller, *op. cit.*, p. 10.

[22]Anna Dorn, as written in the Introduction of her cookbook, *The Newest or Great Universal Viennese Cookbook, A Guide to Cook for the Finest Tables in Ordinary Houses, Combing the Best Taste and the Greatest Elegance, Taking Advantage of the Economic Possibilities to make at Least Expense*, 1833. As cited by James Trager, *Food Chronology*, New York: Henry Holt and Company, 1995, p. 222.

[23]Better Homes and Gardens, *Heritage Cookbook*, Des Moines, IA, Meredith Corporation, 1979, p. 213.

[24]Isabella Beeton as written in *The Book of Household Management*, London, 1861. As cited by James Trager, *Food Chronology*, New York, Henry Holt and Company, 1995, p. 263.

[25]Quoted from a woman regarding Ellen Swallow Richards' New England Kitchen in Boston, MA 1890. As cited by James Trager *Food Chronology*, New York: Henry Holt and Company, 1995, p. 334.

[26]Barbara Wheaton, *Savoring the Past: The French Kitchen and Table from 1300 to 1789*, Philadelphia, University of Pennsylvania Press, 1983, p. xviii.

[27]The American Culinary Federation Web Site.

[28]Stephen Mennell, *All Manners of Food*, Basil Blackwell, New York, 1985, p. 201, as cited by Dr. Pat Bartholomew, "The Elite Women Chef: A Comparative Analysis of Career Success," UMI Dissertation Services, New York, 1996, p. 5.

[29]Art Siemering, *"A Woman's Place Is in the Restaurant Kitchen." The National Culinary Review*, 3/1997, p. 29.

[30]1997 Restaurant Industry Forecast Gets Inside Consumers' Heads, NRA, 9.7.

[31]*Industry of Choice . . . an Extensive Study of Employee Behavior and Attitudes in the Foodservice Industry, Foodservice Employment 2000*, and *1997 Restaurant Industry Forecast Gets Inside Consumers' Heads*.

1994: Women supervisors earned a median weekly wage of $294 in comparison to a male's wage of $372 for the same position.

Bibliography

"Women Making Inroads in Foodservice," News, July 16, 1996.
http://www.foodnet.com . . . ctions/news/women.htm,

Aburdene, Patricia, and Naisbitt, John, *Megatrends for Women,* Villard Books, New York, NY, 1992.

American Culinary Federation, Month by Month Certification Analysis, ACF, St. Augustine, FL, Feb. 29 1996.

American Culinary Federation Educational Institute, *Handbook for Certification and Certification Renewal,* The American Culinary Federation Educational Institute, St. Augustine, FL, 1990.

Anderson, Bonnie, and Zinsser, Judith, *A History of Their Own: Women in Europe from Prehistory to the Present,* Harper & Row, New York, NY, 1988.

Barber, Elizabeth Wayland, *Women's Work: The First 20,000 Years,* Norton, New York, NY, 1994.

Barnett, Rosalind, and Rivers, Caryl, *She Works/He Works: How Two-Income Families are Happier, Healthier & Better Off,* Harper Collins, New York, NY, 1996.

Bartholomew, Patricia, Ph.D., IAWCR Convention 1996 Opening Address, 1996.

Bartholomew, Patricia, Ph.D., "The Elite Woman Chef: A Comparative Analysis of Career Success," UMI Dissertation Information Service, Ann Arbor, MI, 1996.

Basbanes, Nicholas A., *A Gentle Madness: Bibliophiles, Bibliomanes, and the Eternal Passion for Books,* Henry Holt & Co., New York, NY, 1995.

1995: The average foodservice employee is female, single, under thirty years of age, and a high school graduate.

Bastianich, Lydia, and Jacobs, Jay, *La Cucina di Lidia,* Doubleday, New York, NY, 1990.

Batty, Jennifer, "Women in Food Service: Challenging Issues in a Changing Work Place," The National Restaurant Association, Washington, DC, 1993.

Berolzheimer, Ruth, *The American Woman's Cookbook,* Consolidated Book Publishers, Chicago, IL, 1946.

Bridges, Linda, "The Health Police," *The National Review Inc.,* Oct. 19, 1992, Vol. 44, no. 20, p. 64.

Brown, B. A., Burns, J., & Grigson, J., *Women Chefs: A Collection of Portraits and Recipes from California Culinary Pioneers—Women in Cuisine: Mere or Chef,* Aris Books, Berkeley, CA, 1987.

Bureau of Labor Statistics Current Population Survey, U.S. Bureau of Labor, Washington, DC, 1996.

Carlsen, Clifford, "The More the Merrier for the New Breed of Restaurateur," *San Francisco Business Times,* San Francisco, CA, Mar. 8, 1996, Vol. 10, no. 29, p. 8A.

Carlsen, Clifford, "Women Chefs Taking Back the Kitchen in the Bay Area," *San Francisco Business Times,* San Francisco, CA, June 9, 1995, Vol. 9, no. 41, p. 8A-2.

Chesser, Jerald W., CEC, CCE, *The Art and Science of Culinary Preparation,* The Educational Institute of the American Culinary Federation, Inc., St. Augustine, FL, 1992.

Classified Index of Industries and Occupations, U.S. Department of Commerce, Economics and Statistics Administration, Washington, DC, 1990.

Conan, Kerri, "A Kinder, Gentler Kitchen," *Restaurant Business Magazine,* Apr. 4, 1994, Vol. 93, no. 6, p. 52.

Costello, Cynthia, and Krimgold, Barbara, *The American Woman 1996-97: Women and Work,* W. W. Norton & Company, New York, NY, 1996.

Le Cordon Bleu History, Le Cordon Bleu Media, Jan. 1997.

Cox, Beverly, & Jacobs, Martin, *Spirit of the Harvest: North American Indian Cooking,* Stewart Tabori & Chang, New York, NY, 1991.

Crea, Joe, "California's Finest Chefs Bask in the Presence of Paul Bocuse, Culinary God," Knight-Ridder Tribune News Service, Oct. 31, 1994, p. 1031k1219.

Crystal, David, *The Cambridge Biographical Encyclopedia,* Cambridge University Press, New York, NY, 1994.

Cunningham, Marion, *The Fannie Farmer Cookbook,* Alfred A. Knopf, New York, NY, 1996.

DePauw, Linda Grant, and Hunt, Conover, with Schneir, Miriam, *Remember the Ladies: 1750 Women in America 1815,* Viking Press, New York, NY, 1976.

Donovan, Mary Deirdre (Ed.), *The New Professional Chef,* Van Nostrand Reinhold, New York, NY, 1996.

Dooley, Don (Editorial Director), *Heritage Cookbook,* Meredith Corp., Des Moines, IA, 1979.

Dorgan, Charity Anne, *Statistical Handbook of Working America,* Gale Research, Detroit, MI, 1995.

Dornenburg & Page, *Becoming a Chef,* Van Nostrand Reinhold, New York, NY, 1995.

Dornenburg & Page, *Culinary Artistry,* Van Nostrand Reinhold, New York, NY, 1996.

Dun & Bradstreet Corporation., Statistical Abstract of the United States 1996: The National Data Book, U.S. Department of Commerce, Washington, DC, 1996; p. 543.

Encyclopedia Americana, "Cooking," Encyclopedia Americana Corporation, 1995, p. 719.

Escoffier, Laurence, *Auguste Escoffier: Memories of My Life,* Van Nostrand Reinhold, New York, NY, 1997.

Executive Office of the President, *Standard Industrial Classification Manual,* U.S. Office of Management and Budget, 1987.

Farmer, Fannie, *The Boston Cooking School Cookbook,* Little, Brown, & Co., Boston, MA, 1929.

Figes, Eva, and Mead, Margaret, *Patriarchal Attitudes: Women in Society,* Persea Books, New York, NY, 1987.

Fine, Gary, *Kitchens: The Culture of Restaurant Work,* University of California Press, Berkeley, CA, 1996.

1995: Sixty-seven percent of all supervisors in foodservice occupations are female.

Folsom, LeRoi A. (Ed. and Text Author), The Professional Chef, *The Culinary Institute of America,* Cahners Books, Boston, MA, 1974.

Francke, Linda Bird, with Sullivan, Scott, "The King of the Kitchen," *Newsweek,* New York, NY, Aug. 11, 1975, Vol. 86, p. 53.

Fuenmayor, J., Haug, K., & Ward, F., *Dirt & Domesticity: Constructions of the Feminine,* The Whitney Museum of American Art, New York, NY, 1992.

Fussell, Betty (Ed.), *Wine, Food & the Arts: Works Gathered by The American Institute of Wine and Food,* Swan Island Books, Belvedere, CA, 1996.

Gfroerer, Joseph, "Preliminary Estimates from the 1995 National Household Survey on Drug Abuse," U.S. Department of Health and Human Services/Substance Abuse and Mental Health Services Admin. (SAMHSA), Rockville, MD, Feb. 1, 1997.

Gisslen, Wayne, *Professional Cooking,* John Wiley & Sons Inc., New York, NY, 1983.

Graham, Lawrence Otis, *The Best Companies for Minorities,* The Penguin Group, New York, NY, 1993.

The Guide to Cooking Schools, ShawGuides, New York, NY, 1997.

Hale, William, *The Horizon Cookbook,* American Heritage, New York, NY, 1968.

Handler, Amy, "Cassandra of the New Athens: Ellen Swallow Richards," student essay, The State University of New York at Albany, Oct. 1, 1992.

Hargis, Dell B., "Sampling of Problems Encountered by Female Graduates Working in Food Service," The Placement Department of The Culinary Institute of America, Hyde Park, NY, Sept. 1986.

Harris, Jessica, Les Dames d'Escoffier Conference: "You've Come a Long Way Maybe," New York City Technical College, Jan. 1994.

Hillstrom, Kevin (Ed.), *Encyclopedia of American Industries Volume Two: Service & Non-Manufacturing Industries,* Gale Research Inc., Detroit, MI, 1994; pp. 704-710.

Hoagland, Doug, "Called to Cook," *The Fresno Bee,* Fresno, CA, July 1996, p. F1-3.

"How Restaurants Fare on State's Economic Menu," *News & Observer,* The News and Observer Publishing Company, 1996.

International Association of Women Chefs and Restaurateurs, *IAWCR Membership Directory,* 1997.

Irwin, Janet, and Perrault, Michael, *Gender Differences at Work: Are Men and Women Really That Different? Analysis and Finding from a Study of Women and Men,* The Foundation for Future Leadership, Washington, DC, 1996.

Kramer, Louise, WCR Confab: "Despite Advances, Women Chefs Still Battling," *Nation's Restaurant News,* New York, NY, June 5, 1995, Vol. 29, no. 23, p. 26.

Kuck, Barbara, Culinary Archives and Museum at Johnson & Wales University, Information from the Archives, Providence, RI, Feb. 1997.

Lapiernik, Richard, "J. Willard & Alice Marriott," *Nation's Restaurant News,* New York, NY, Feb 1996, 50-Yr Anniv. Ed., pp. 106-108.

Lee, Mary Price, & Richard S., *Careers in the Restaurant Industry,* The Rosen Publishing Group, New York, NY, 1988.

Levenstein, Harvey A., *Paradox of Plenty: A Social History of Eating in Modern America,* Oxford University Press, New York, NY, 1993.

Levenstein, Harvey A., *Revolution at the Table,* Oxford University Press, New York, NY, 1988, pp. 192-193.

Locher, Frances C., (Ed.), *Contemporary Authors: A Bio-Bibliographical Guide to Current Writers in Fiction, General Non-Fiction, Poetry, Journalism, Drama, Motion Pictures, Television, and Other Fields,* Gale Research Company, Detroit, MI, 1982, Vol. 104.

Lowe, Kimberly, *The Supermarket Challenge,* Cahners Publishing, Newton, MA, March 1, 1997, Vol. 107, no. 6.

Mack, David, "Francis Roth & Katherine Angell," *Nation's Restaurant News,* New York, NY, Feb. 1996, 50-Yr. Anniv. Ed., p. 136.

Mackenzie, Margaret, *Journal of Gastronomy,* AIWF, San Francisco, CA, 1993, Vol. 7, no. 2.

Martin, Richard, "Top 100: Big-Get-Bigger Race Imperils Unit Margins," *Nation's Restaurant News,* New York, NY, Apr. 29, 1996, Vol. 30, no. 17, p. 3.

Martin, Richard, "Julia Child," *Nation's Restaurant News,* New York, NY, Feb. 1996, 50-Yr Anniv. Ed., pp. 60, 64.

McNamee, Harriet, National Museum of Women in the Arts, Washington, DC.

1995: Forty-three percent of all cooks in foodservice occupations are female.

Mendelson, Anne, *Stand Facing the Stove,* Henry Holt, New York, NY, 1996.

Microsoft Encarta Encyclopedia, "Industrial Revolution," Microsoft Corporation/ ©Funk & Wagnalls Corp., 1996.

Montague, Prosper, *Larousse Gastronomique: The Encyclopedia of Food, Wine & Cookery,* Crown Publishers, New York, NY, 1966.

Mooney, Joe, "Uniforms Unbound: The Classic Chefs Uniform Is Still Intact. Sometimes It's Just of a Different Color," *CHEF Magazine,* Talcott Communications Corporation, Chicago, IL, March 1997, pp. 48, 49.

Morton, Alexander Clark, *The Official Guide to Food Service and Hospitality Management Careers,* International Publishing Company of America, 1982.

Moskowitz, Milton, and Townsend, Carol, "100 Best Companies for Working Mothers," Woman's Wire website http://www.women.com/work/best/#summary, Jan. 1997.

National Opinion Research Center: Brittingham/Hoffman/Larison, "Drug Use Among U.S. Workers: Prevalence and Trends by Occupation and Industry Categories," U.S. Department of Health and Human Services/Substance Abuse and Mental Health Services Admin. (SAMHSA), Rockville, MD, May 1996.

National Restaurant Association, "Business Culture's Impact on Restaurant Performance," NRA, Washington, DC, Jan. 1995.

National Restaurant Association, "Current Issues Report: Foodservice Industry 2000," NRA, Washington, DC, 1988.

National Restaurant Association, "Foodservice Employee Profile," NRA, Washington, DC, 1995.

National Restaurant Association, "Foodservice: Employment 2000," NRA, Washington, DC, Jan. 10, 1989.

National Restaurant Association, "Restaurant Industry Forecast Gets Inside Consumers' Heads," NRA, Washington, DC, 1997.

National Restaurant Association, "Restaurant Industry Operations Report," NRA, Washington, DC, 1996.

National Restaurant Association, "Survey of Wage Rates for Hourly Employees," NRA, Washington, DC, 1994.

Neuborne, Ellen, "Debate Rages on Swapping Overtime for Comp Time," *USA Today, Gannett,* March 3, 1997, p. 4b.

NRA & Deloitte & Touche LLP, "Restaurant Industry Operations Report," NRA, Washington, DC, Sept. 1996.

NRA & Hay Group, "Compensation for Salaried Personnel in Foodservice," NRA, Washington, DC, 1996.

Oliver, Sandra L., *Saltwater Foodways,* Mystic Seaport Museum, Mystic, CT, 1995.

Perry, Charles, "As American as Slapjacks: Two Historic Cookbooks Celebrate Anniversaries," *The Palm Beach Post,* West Palm Beach, FL, July 4, 1996, pp. 1FN-2FN.

Poris, Jim, "Stirs and Stripes Forever," Food Arts Publishing, New York, NY, Dec. 1996, Vol. 9, no. 10, pp. 71-73.

Bartlett, Michael; Bernstein, Charles; Lorenzini, Beth; McDowell, Bill; Stephenson, Susie; Rousseau, Rita; & Scanlan, James, *Restaurants & Institutions 1996 Annual Forecast,* Cahners Publishing, Newton, MA, Jan. 1, 1996, Vol. 106, no. 1, p. 18.

Random House Dictionary of the English Language, Random House Publishing, New York, NY, 1971, p. 133.

Rathbun, Mickey, "Tasting History in Mystic—A Sailor's Fare from Lobscouse to Brambles," *Daily Hampshire Gazette,* Northhampton, MA, July 26, 1996, pp. 23-24.

Reed, Evelyn, *Woman's Evolution: Matriarchal Clan to Patriarchal Family,* Pathfinder Press, New York, NY, 1975.

Reskin, Barbara, and Steiger, Thomas, *Baking & Baking Off: Deskilling & the Changing Sex Makeup of Bakers,* Temple University Press, Philadelphia, PA, 1990.

Reskin, Barbara, *Job Queues, Gender Queues: Explaining Women's Inroads into Male Occupations,* Temple University Press, Philadelphia, PA, 1990.

Revel, Jean-François, *Culture & Cuisine,* Doubleday, New York, NY, 1982.

Rix, Sara E., ed. for The Women's Research & Education Institute, *The American Woman 1990-1991: A Status Report,* W. W. Norton & Company, New York, NY, 1990.

1996: *The Fannie Farmer Cookbook* has its 100-year anniversary.

Rorty, Amelie Oksenberg (Edited by Sara Ruddick and Pamela Daniels), *Working It Out: 23 Women Writers, Artists, Scientists, and Scholars Talk About Their Lives and Work,* Pantheon Books, New York, NY, 1977.

Rousseau, Rita (Senior Ed.), "Employing the New America," *Restaurants & Institutions,* Cahners Publishing, Newton, MA, March 15, 1997, Vol. 107, no. 7, pp. 40, 41, 46, 48, 50, 52.

Rozin, Elisabeth, *Blue Corn and Chocolate,* Alfred A. Knopf, New York, NY, 1992.

Ruggless, Ron, "Ella Brennan—Martin & Dick Brennan," *Nation's Restaurant News,* New York, NY, Feb. 1996, 50-Yr Anniv. Ed., p. 37.

Sawinski, Diane, "U.S. Industry Profiles: The Leading 100," Gale Research, Detroit, MI, 1995.

Schremp, Geraldine, *Kitchen Culture: Fifty Years of Food Fads,* Pharos Books, New York, NY, 1991, p. 133.

Schwaar, Carol, "Kitchens: Women Chefs' Perspectives," *Chef* magazine, Chicago, IL, May 1995, Vol. 5, no. 4, pp. 38-41.

Schwartz, Felice, and Zimmerman, Jean, *Breaking with Tradition—Women & Work: The New Facts of Life,* Warner Books Inc., New York, NY, 1992.

Sheraton, Mimi, "The Top 10 Women Cooks—1996," *New Woman,* New York, NY, Jan. 1996, pp. 100-107.

Siemering, Art, "A Woman's Place is in the Restaurant Kitchen," *The National Culinary Review,* American Culinary Federation, St. Augustine, FL, Mar. 1997, Vol. 21, no. 3.

Sims-Bell, Barbara, "Career Opportunities in the Food and Beverage Industry," Facts on File Inc., New York, NY, 1994.

Standard & Poor's Industry Surveys, "Leisure Time: Basic Analysis," Standard & Poor's, New York, NY, April 18, 1996, Vol. 164, no. 16, sec. 3, pp. L51-54.

Statistical Abstract of the United States, U.S. Bureau of the Census, Washington, DC, 1996.

Stead, Jennifer, *Food and Cooking 18th Century Britain—History and Recipes,* The Historic Buildings and Monuments Commission for England, 1985.

Stephens, Beverly, *Women Chefs: Role Models for the 90's (Take That!),* Food Arts Publishing, New York, NY, Sept. 1992, Vol. 5, no. 7, pp. 34, 38, 76, 77.

Stephenson, June, *Women's Roots: Status & Achievements in Western Civilization*, Diemer, Smith, Napa, CA, 1981.

Stillman, Julie, *Great Women Chefs*, Turner Publishing, Atlanta, GA, 1996.

Storck, William, "Women Score Higher as Managers in New Study," *C & E News*, Easton, PA, Oct. 7, 1996, Vol. 74, no. 41.

Tannahill, Reay, *Food in History*, Crown Trade Paperbacks, New York, NY, 1988.

The Educational Foundation of the National Restaurant Association, "Industry of Choice: An Extensive Study of Employee Behavior and Attitudes in the Food Service Industry," Coca-Cola Company, Foodservice Research Forum, Jan. 1997.

The Los Angeles Times Book Review, The Los Angeles Times, Los Angeles, CA, Nov. 20, 1983, p. 3.

The New York Times Book Review, The New York Times, New York, NY, June 6, 1982, p. 19.

The New York Times, Classified Advertisements, New York, NY, September 4, 1966, page W17, 4W.

Toussaint-Samat, Maguelonne, *History of Food*, Blackwell Publishers, Cambridge, MA, 1992.

Trager, James, *Food Chronology*, Henry Holt & Co. Inc., New York, NY, 1995.

Trager, James, *The Women's Chronology*, Henry Holt & Co. Inc., New York, NY, 1994.

Van Warner, Rick., Editorial, *Nation's Restaurant News*, New York, NY, Mar. 11, 1996, p. 27.

Victory, Dick, "Excellent Adventures," *Washingtonian*, Washington, DC, Feb. 1996, pp. 127-132.

Walkup, Carolyn, "IAWCR Panel Discusses Career Opportunities, Compromises," *Nation's Restaurant News*, New York, NY, Aug. 19, 1996, Vol. 30, no. 32, p. 68.

Walkup, Carolyn, "Myron Green," *Nation's Restaurant News*, New York, NY, Feb. 1996, 50-Yr Anniv. Ed., p. 72.

1998: *"A Woman's Place Is in the Kitchen,"* on the evolution of women chefs, is published.

Wheaton, Barbara, *Culinary Historians of Boston Newsletter,* Fall 1989-90.

Wheaton, Barbara, *Savoring the Past: The French Kitchen and Table from 1300 to 1789,* University of Pennsylvania Press, Philadelphia, PA, 1983.

Willan, Anne, *Great Cooks and Their Recipes—From Tallevent to Escoffier,* Pavilion Books Ltd., London, England, 1995.

Williamson, Paul, *Chef Louis' Inspiring Career, The National Culinary Review,* American Culinary Federation, St. Augustine, FL, Feb. 1997, Vol. 21, no. 2.

Zuber, Amy, "Women in Foodservice Converge in Annual IAWCR Convention in NYC," *Nation's Restaurant News,* New York, NY, June 10, 1996, Vol. 30, no. 23, p. 43.

Index

A. Lennon Foundation, Inc., 239
Abel, Mary, 22
Abigail Kirsch Culinary Productions, 122, 224
Aburdene, Patricia, 138
Adams, Jody, 35, 41, 48, 50, 60, 63, 74–75, 94, 116, 120, 134, 135, 157, 160, 177–178, 182, 186–187, 214, 218
  biographical information, 223
African-Americans, as cooks and chefs, 29
African slave trade, culinary history of, 8–9
Afro-American culture, influence of, 55–56
Age issues, 103–106
Agrarian lifestyle, emergence of, 3–5
Agricultural community, women's cultivation of, 3–5
Agriculture, sustainable, 34, 47, 176
Alcohol abuse, 96
Alexis on Nob Hill, 244
Al Forno, 117, 238, 238
Altieri, Dina, 106, 160
  biographical information, 223
American Cookery, or the Art of Dressing Viands, Fish, Poultry, and Vegetables, and the Best Modes of Making Pastes, Puffs, Pies, Tarts, Puddings, Custards, and Preserves, and All Kinds of Cakes from the Imperial Plumb to Plain Cake

Adapted to This Country and All Grades of Life (Simmons), 14, 25
American Culinary Federation (ACF), 25, 28, 183–185, 188, 219–220, 281
  apprenticeship program of, 63, 64–65, 68
  job descriptions by, 258–259
American Culinary Federation Educational Institute (ACFEI), 117
American Home Economics Association, 119
American influence, on women and food, 54–56
American Institute of Wine and Food (AIWF), 67, 227, 282
American Restaurant, 41, 232
American Woman 1990–91, A Status Report, 103
Amrita, 242
Amy's Bread, 40, 249
Anastasio, Karyn, 105
Angelica, Cheribino, 81
Angell, Katherine, 21, 22
Anthony Spinazzola Foundation, 192, 287
"Apprentice houses," 68
Apprenticeship experience. *See also* Training
  American influence on, 68
  French influence on, 65–67
Apprenticeship programs
  influence of, 64–69

perspectives on, 210–213
Arcadia, 30, 132, 164, 248
Arnold, Judi, 112, 153–154, 164, 173, 218
  biographical information, 223
Art Culinaire, 40
Art of Cookery Made Plain and Easy (Glasse), 14
Asian culture, influence of, 56–57
Asia Nora, 33, 246, 247
Assertiveness, 89
  importance of, 151
Associate of Occupational Studies (AOS) programs, 68
Astor House, 49
Attitudes, mentors' influence on, 59–61
Audrey's Catering, 188
Aux Délices, 73, 246
Awerbuch, Alison, 122, 149, 167–168, 177, 217–218
  biographical information, 224

Back to Square One: Old World Food in a New World Kitchen (Goldstein), 233
Bain-marie, 11
Baird, Ninnie Lilla, 24
Baker, job description for, 257
Bakeries, women in, 23–24
Bakery, The, 42, 238
Baking & Baking Off: Deskilling & the Changing Sex Makeup of Bakers, 11
Baking powder, introduction of, 67

Balance
  failure to achieve, 166–168
  maintaining, 112–113
  between personal and professional lives,
    149
  success and, 152
  between success and family, 159–162
  between success and job priorities,
    165–168
  between success and personal life,
    162–165
  in the workplace model, 206
Barbeau, Monique, 70, 72, 167
  biographical information, 224
Barber, Richard, 237
Barshak, Alison, 99
  biographical information, 224
Bartholomew, Pat, 28, 68, 72, 86,
    87–88, 108–109, 146, 151, 165,
    198, 202, 204
  biographical information, 224–225
Basta Pasta, 236
Bastianich, Lidia, 34–35, 75–76, 95,
    127–128, 143, 159, 212
  biographical information, 225
Bayona, 251
Bean, Cathy, 138
Beard, James, 61
Beattie, Toniann, 35, 70, 76–77,
    103–104, 152, 160, 180
  biographical information, 225
Becco, 35, 225, 127
Beck, Simone, 67, 203
Becoming a Chef (Kamman), 108
Becoming a Chef (Page and
    Dornenburg), 77
Beecher, Catherine, 15
Beekman Arms, 106
Beeton, Isabella, 16
Benefit work, 187
Ben & Jerry's, 171
Bertholle, Louisette, 67, 203
Bertolli, Paul, 226
Bertran, Lulu, 233
Betty Crocker Cookbooks, 17, 183
Betty Crocker's Cooking School of the Air,
    17
BIBA, 62, 63, 174, 247, 250
Big Four, 227
Birdseye Frosted Foods, 137
Birthing cycles, agricultural society and, 4
Bizou, 32, 165, 237
Black, Lizzie, 17, 111
Bluepoint Oyster Bar and Restaurant,
    133, 229
Blvd Café, 251
Bocuse, Paul, 95

Book of Household Management
    (Beeton), 16
Book of Mediterranean Food (David),
    185
Border Grill, 39, 132, 230
Boston Cooking School, 21, 91
Boston Cooking-School Cookbook
    (Farmer), 15, 16
Boulanger, 23
Boulevard, 44, 102, 119, 173, 215,
    226, 244
Bouley, 40
Brandell, Catherine, 225
Brassard, Elisabeth, 165
Brasserie T, 49, 83, 231
Brazier, Eugenie, 129
Bread and Circus, 197
*Breaking with Tradition: Women and
    Work, the New Facts of Life*
    (Schwartz and Zimmerman), 87,
    90, 206–207
Brigade system, 13, 107
Brittany Hollow Farm, 47
Brooks-Moses, Sharon, 69, 71, 78,
    112, 162
  biographical information, 225–226
Buchtenkirch-Biscardi, Lyde, 22, 25,
    71–72, 92, 93–94, 281
  biographical information, 226
Buonavia, 128
Burnout, 113, 163
*Business Culture's Impact on Restaurant
    Performance* (NRA), 100, 170,
    171, 173
Businesses
  family orientation of, 170–172
  financing, 100
  women-owned, 25
Business ownership, 73, 79–80, 218.
    See also Food business; Restaurant
    ownership
  challenges of, 163
Business startup, advice for, 129
Bussiere, Suzanne, 27, 51, 101–102,
    119, 163, 215–216
  biographical information, 226

Café Beaujolais, 231
Café Escalera, 241
Café Fanny, 253
Café Nicholson, 29, 34, 240
California Culinary Academy (CCA),
    38, 73, 238
California Restaurant Writers
    Association, 132
California Street Cooking School, 233
Cambridge School of Culinary Arts, 68

Campagne, 139, 244
Campbell Soup Company, 75
Campton Place, 102
Career choices, 79–81. *See also* Culinary
    careers
Carême, Antonin, 39
Carew, Siobhan, 56, 169, 186
  biographical information, 226
Carson, Rachel, 205
Casablanca, 47, 251
Catering, 122
Cech, Mary, 125–126, 163
  biographical information, 226–227
Chafetz, Deena, 119
  biographical information, 227
Champagne, "riddling," 35
Charitable organizations, 185
Charitable work, women's role in, 16,
    185–188. *See also* "Giving back"
    concept; Socially responsible causes
Charlie Trotter's, 49, 161, 232, 238
Chef and the Child Foundation (CCF),
    64, 102, 103, 183, 188–191, 189,
    252, 282
Chef de cuisine, job description for, 258
Chef de partie, job description for, 257
Chef/farmer connection, 47
Chef garde manger, job description for,
    257
Chef-instructor position, 125–127
Chef in the Classroom program, 188
Chef-owner position, 117
Chef position, 118–119
Chef profession. *See also* Culinary pro-
    fession
  age issues in, 103–106
  passion for, 48–51
  substance abuse in, 96–97
  women's exclusion from, 86–90
Chefs. *See also* Women chefs
  African-American, 29
  certification of, 183
  defined, 24–25, 28–32
  experience of, 41–51
  genderless definition of, 28
  high-profile, 107–110
  job description for, 257
  as managers, 135, 136
  process of becoming, 39–41
  promotion of, 183
  standards of excellence for, 39
  versus business owners, 132–133
  versus cooks, 31–32, 105
Chefs' Professional Agency, 240
Chefs Collaborative 2000 (CC2000), 47,
    132, 174–177, 283
Chefs Educational Series, 188

Chef's work, as art versus craft, 30–31
Chen, Joyce, 207
Chez Henri, 62, 243
Chez la Mère Madeleine, 43, 237
Chez Panisse, 25, 31, 59, 60, 225, 226, 253
Chez Panisse Café, 230, 233, 253
Chez Panisse Menu Book (Waters), 60
Chez Panisse Vegetable Book (Waters), 60
Child, Julia, 21, 22, 29, 67, 124, 151, 157, 203, 209, 211
  biographical information, 227
Childcare issues, 74–75
Children's Inn, 172
China Moon Café, 31, 50, 99–100, 129, 158, 253
China Moon Cookbook (Tropp), 158
Chinese culture, influence of, 58
Ciccarone-Nehls, Gloria, 148, 200
  biographical information, 227–228
CITY, 132
City Café, 132, 230
City Wine and Cigar Co., 36, 255
Classroom teaching position, 125–127
Clicquot, Nicole-Barbe, 35
Cloister on Sea Island, apprenticeship at, 68
Cochrane, Joseph, 93
Colonial women, as food providers, 8
"Comfort food," 9
Communication, with staff, 141
Community involvement, 187. *See also* Socially responsible causes
Compensation for Salaried Personnel in Foodservice (NRA), 170
Competition, politics of, 88
Compleat Housewife, or Accomplish'd Gentlewoman's Companion (Smith), 14, 21
ComSource Independent Food Service Companies, 184, 230
Consulting, women in, 200
Consumer trends, future, 198
Continental Club, 30, 252
Convenience foods, 200
Cook, School, The, 234
Cookbook Mate for the Blind and the Sighted (Sanders), 179, 249
Cookbooks
  to help support charitable causes, 15–16
  women and, 13–19
"Cooking as hobby" trend, 198
Cooking schools, 207–208. *See also* Culinary schools
  growth of, 197
  women and, 20–22

Cooking techniques, early, 3
Cooking tools, 2
Cooking with Nora (Pouillon), 247
Cooking with the Seasons (Palladin), 61
Cook/pastry cook, job description for, 259
Cooks
  key difficulties for, 105
  versus chefs, 31–32, 105
Cool Comedy/Hot Cuisine, 192
Cordon Bleu Cooking School, 63, 83. *See also* Le Cordon Bleu
Corn Dance Café, 45, 48, 224
Cornelia Street Café, 244
Corning, Kay, 183, 184, 220
  biographical information, 228
Corporate chef positions, 200
Costa, Lucie, 101, 130, 140, 156
  biographical information, 228
"Court cuisine," 86
Craig, Clara, 75, 80–81, 146, 152, 181, 188
  biographical information, 228
Crocker, Betty, 17, 18–19, 127
Cruise ship experience, 141
Cuisinière, 28
Culinary careers. *See also* Culinary industry
  advice concerning, 214–218, 214–218
  challenges of, 86–90
  decision making about, 70–81
  effect on family and children, 71–77
  job descriptions for, 257–259
  personal sacrifice and, 81–83
  relationships and, 77–79
Culinary education. *See also* Apprenticeship programs; Culinary schools
  French, 65–67
  perspectives on, 210–213.
Culinary educator
  career as, 212–213
  job description for, 258
Culinary industry. *See also* Foodservice industry
  alternative roles in, 122–127
  bias against women in, 24
  demographics of, 33
  effecting change in, 219–221
  future trends in, 196–205
  macho influence in, 95
  mass appeal of, 155
  next generation in, 207–208
  role of the press in, 107–110
  women's choices in, 170–172
  women's roles in, 116–122
Culinary Institute of America at Greystone, 125, 225

Culinary Institute of America (CIA), 21–22, 28, 59, 167, 171, 172, 230, 231, 234, 241, 242, 247, 250
Culinary Olympics, 68
Culinary Olympic Team (ACF/NRA), 38
Culinary profession. *See also* Chef profession; Culinary careers
  celebrity aspects of, 155–157
  changes for women in, 25
  substance abuse in, 96–97
Culinary programs, accreditation of, 183
Culinary schools, 22, 68–69. *See also* Apprenticeship programs
  women instructors in, 123–124
  women's enrollment in, 116
Culinary students, 207–208
  chefs' and cooks' perspectives on, 209–210
  female versus male, 213–214
  instructor's perspectives on, 208–209
Cultural influences, in the United States, 54–56
Cultural taboos, 58
Culture, agriculture-based, 4
Culture and Cuisine (Revel), 142
Cumin, Albert, 227
Cundiff, Tracy, 82, 149–150, 207
  biographical information, 228
Customers
  communicating with, 136–137, 153
  focus on, 129
Czak, Richard, 62

Daguin, Ariane, 141
  biographical information, 229
Daniel's, 51
Darwin, Charles, 10
David, Elizabeth, 60, 185
de Cleofa, Maria, 11
DeMane, Hilary, 72, 93, 99, 101, 115, 121, 126, 141, 154, 178, 213, 215
  biographical information, 229
Demographics, effect on culinary industry, 199
de Monteiro, Longteine, 49, 68, 82–83, 111
  biographical information, 242
DePauw, Linda Grant, 9
Desaulniers, Marcel, 223
Descent of Man, The (Darwin), 10
Des Jardins, Traci, 36, 40–41, 50, 51, 61, 65, 72, 134–135, 139, 141, 154–155, 156, 166, 182, 187
  biographical information, 236
Dining room staff, communication with kitchen staff, 134–135
Dining with Marcel Proust (King), 238

Dion, Holly, 92
Directions for Cookery (Leslie), 14, 43
Dirt and Domesticity: Construction of the Feminine, 11
Discrimination, 88–89, 265. *See also* Gender bias; Sexism
  women's experiences with, 90–96
Disney World, apprenticeship at, 68
Distel, Marthe, 20, 83
Dixon, Kirsten, 38, 80, 106–107
  biographical information, 229
Doganiero, Gilda Ann, 104
Dorn, Anna, 14
Dornenburg, Andrew, 77
Dowry Cookbook (Salvato), 186, 249
Dowry Cookie Company, 129, 248
Drug abuse, 96–97
Drug Use Among U.S. Workers: Prevalence and Trends by Occupation and Industry Categories, 96
D'Artagnan, 229
DuFour Pastry Kitchen, 112, 153, 223
Dumas Pere, 238, 252
Durrenberger, Sandra, 93

East Coast Grill, 232
Eatzi's, 197
Ecology movement, 10
Educational influences, on women chefs, 68–69
Education programs, influence of, 64–69. *See also* Apprenticeship programs; Training
Eisenberg, Jamie, 49, 96–97, 114, 126, 136, 157–158, 167, 176–177
  biographical information, 229
Elandt, Coral, 24
Elephant Walk, 49, 68, 111, 242
Elite Woman Chef: A Comparative Case Analysis of Women Chefs and Career Success (Bartholomew), 204, 225
Elizabeth on 37th, 131, 212, 252
Elka, 40, 50, 235, 236
Ellis, Jon, 205
Employee attrition, 200–201
Employee benefits, 170–172
Employees, as mentors, 59–60
Equal pay issues, 201–205
Escoffier, Auguste, 13, 23, 103, 107
Esperienze Italiane, 128, 225
Ethnic cuisine, 58
Executive chef, 117–118
  job description for, 257, 258
  women as, 26
Executive pastry chef, job description for, 258
Exercise, importance of, 162

Extended family, culinary traditions of, 8–9

Faison, George, 229
Family
  balancing with success, 159–162
  culinary careers and, 71–77
  influence on women chefs, 33–35
  relationship to cooking, 35
  women as cultivators of, 5–6
Fanny at Chez Panisse (Waters), 60
Farmer, Fannie, 1, 4, 15, 16, 21, 124, 299
Farming methods, Native American, 48
Felder, Eve, 31, 45, 47–48, 48, 50, 59, 112, 142, 175, 185
  biographical information, 230
Felidia, 35, 76, 127, 225
"Female support roles," 89
Feniger, Susan, 39, 66–67, 81, 98–99, 114, 132, 163, 176, 191, 192
  biographical information, 230
Fenzl, Barbara, 140
Fernandez, Jerry, 219
Fettiplaces, Elinor, 13
Field of Greens: New Vegetarian Recipes from the Celebrated Greens Restaurant (Somerville), 251
Fields, Debbie, 249
5757, 254
Figes, Eva, 86
Fine, Gary, 30, 31, 33
Fire
  role in transforming food, 5
  women's discovery of, 3
Firebird, 227
First jobs, influence on women chefs, 36–37
Fisher, Abby, 87
Fisher, M. F. K., 151, 161
Fitoussi, Michel, 231
Five Seasons Café, 226
Flaherty, Phyllis, 62, 78, 91–92, 174, 184, 201, 202, 207, 217
  biographical information, 230
Flavor, passion for, 45–46
Foo, Susanna, 58, 93, 113, 118, 130, 149, 217
  biographical information, 230–231
Food
  goals for, 174
  influence on women chefs, 33–35
  love for, 155
  passion for, 42–45
  role of fire in transforming, 2
  women's connection with, 13

women's contribution to the development of, 6
Food and Wine magazine, 156, 223
Food Arts, 80
Food attitudes, mentors' influence on, 59–61
Food business, owning and operating, 127–137. *See also* Business ownership
Food Chain conference, 190
Food choices, sustainable, 176
Food creations, women's versus men's, 142–144
Food from My Heart (Martinez), 242
Food in History (Tannahill), 6
Food products, adulteration testing of, 23
Food publishing, 80
Food recovery systems, 190
Food relief, 188
Food Safety Handling seminar, 190
Foodservice companies, training programs of, 64
Foodservice Employee Profile (NRA), 33, 36, 116, 138, 196, 220
Foodservice industry. *See also* Culinary industry
  attrition in, 200–201
  changing the environment of, 201, 205–214
  discrimination in, 89
  employee benefits in, 170–171
  growing market segments of, 196–198
  growing opportunities in, 198–199
  needed change in, 170–172
  responsibility of, 220
  study of women's challenges in, 88–90
  trends in, 47
  turnover in, 200–201
Foodservice Industry 2000, 47
Foodservice managers, profile of, 138
Foodservice operations, woman-owned, 116
Foodservice positions, women in, 26, 33
Food Shed Coalition, 176
Food writers, 122
Food writing careers, 80
Forgione, Larry, 106, 237
Forley, Diane, 58, 129, 144
  biographical information, 231
Foundation for Future Leadership, 137
Four Seasons Hotels, 62
  Beverly Hills, 63
  New York City, 36
Fox, Margaret, 231
France, apprenticeship in, 65–67
Frank-Johnson, Tudie, 30

Frank Leslie's Illustrated Newspaper, 121
Frauenhofer, Elaine Deal, 65
French Chef cooking show (Child), 211
French Chef Cookbook, The (Child), 67
French chefs, 21–22
French Culinary Institute (FCI), 69, 80, 162, 234, 244, 248, 250
Fresh Fields, 197
Freshly grown food, value of, 33
Fresh Sheet, 47
Fresh Start Program, 164
Frico, 35, 225, 127
Fuller's, 70, 224
Fundraising, 187
Fusion cooking, 61

Gand, Gale, 49, 61, 65–66, 73, 78, 83
  biographical information, 231
Gastronomical Me, The (Fisher), 161
Gaudreau, Darlene, 86
Gauthier, Laureen, 114, 121–122, 135, 161, 174
  biographical information, 232
Gender-based discrimination, 89. *See also* Discrimination
Gender bias, 87. *See also* Discrimination; Sexism
  in the culinary profession, 90–93
General Federation of Women's Clubs, 11
General Foods Corporation, 123, 137
Germain, Elizabeth, 83, 202
  biographical information, 232
Gilmore, Elka, 40, 50, 61, 156, 236
Gingrass, Anne, 76, 92–93, 102, 114, 133–134, 226
  biographical information, 232
Gingrass, David, 102
"Giving back" concept, 147–148, 183, 187, 193. *See also* Socially responsible causes
Glasse, Hannah, 13, 14
Goals. *See also* Workplace goals
  for food, 174
  future, 170–172
  reaching, 148–150
  setting, 149
Goddess worship, 7
Gold, Debbie, 41–42, 77, 124–125, 153, 210
  biographical information, 232–233
Gold, Rozanne, 50, 75, 78, 110, 150
  biographical information, 233
Goldstein, Joyce, 46, 109, 117, 129, 147, 149, 167, 216
  biographical information, 233

Good Housekeeping, 16
Good Samaritan Hospital, 128
Gourmet Magazine Cooking Arts Center, 243
Grand Diplome credential, 20
Grausman, Richard, 102
Green, Nancy, 101
Greene, Gael, 108
Green Gulch Farm, 59
Greens, 49, 150, 241, 251
Greens Cookbook (Madison), 241
Groult, Philippe, 237
Guilds, formation of, 12
Gulliksen, Gwen Kvavli, 78–79, 216
  biographical information, 233
Gutierrez, Fernand, 62, 254

Haddad, Noëlle, 51, 69, 92, 162, 168, 213
  biographical information, 234
Hain, Lillian, 62
Hamilton, Dorothy Cann, 73, 94, 118, 162, 195, 196, 234
Handke, Hartman, 237
Handler, Amy, 127
  biographical information, 234
"Hands-on" experience, 211
Harassment, dealing with, 93–94. *See also* Gender bias; Discrimination; Sexism
Harborside Inn, 235
Harborview Inn, 46
Hargis, Dell, 88, 172, 205, 214
  biographical information, 234–235
Harmonie Club, 238
Harris, Jessica, 5, 8, 55, 123
  biographical information, 235
Hawthorne Lane, 133, 232
Hazing, dealing with, 94–96
Healthcare, 206
Health insurance, 173
Health issues, dealing with, 100–103
Hearing impairment, dealing with, 101–102
Heffernan, Kerry, 40, 41, 50, 78, 94, 96, 134, 136, 154, 178
  biographical information, 235
Hennings, James, 8
Historic North Plank Road Tavern, 130, 228
History of Food (Toussaint-Samat), 6
Hix, Marlo, 68
Home economics, 23
Home Economics Association, 23
Home Economics Society, 10
Home meal replacement market, 196–197

Hotels, apprenticeship at, 68
Houghton, Michele A., 69
How to Cook a Wolf (Fisher), 151
Hughes, Deborah, 78
  biographical information, 235
Hume, Rosemary, 21, 149
Hunt, Conover, 9
Hunter-gatherer societies, 3
Hunting, decline in importance of, 5
Huntington Hotel, 148
Huntley, Deborah, 42, 46, 141, 154, 160, 184, 211
  biographical information, 235–236
Husband–wife partnerships, 77–78

Iijima, Mika, 46
  biographical information, 236
Il Cibo Di Lidia, 128
Indian culture, influence of, 58
Industrial Revolution, women's roles in, 9–12
Industry leaders, predictions by, 199–205
Industry of Choice, 200
Ingredients. *See also* Sustainable agriculture
  ecologically sound, 60
  seasonal local, 34
Initiation rites, 95
Inside Consumers' Heads (NRA), 196
Institutional food services, 197
International Culinary Competition, 226
International influences, on women and food, 56–58
Irish culture, influence of, 56
Irwin, Janet, 137–138
Italian culture, influence of, 56
Italian food, visibility for, 128

Jallepalli, Raji, 44, 57–58, 61–62, 79–80, 82, 83–84, 127, 131, 154, 165–166
  biographical information, 236
James Beard Awards, 25
James Beard Foundation, 67, 156, 227, 284–285
Jarmon, Major, 63
Jefferson White House, slave cooks in, 8
Job choices, 79–81. *See also* Culinary careers
Job descriptions, 257–259
Job priorities, balancing with success, 165–168
Job-sharing, 205–206
Johnson, Mary, 6, 21

Johnson, Nancy, 51
Johnson and Wales College of Culinary
    Arts, 248, 249
Johnson and Wales Culinary Archives
    and Museum, 42, 238
Jones, Amanda, 77, 97
Joseph Baum & Michael Whiteman
    Company, 233
Joyce Chen Cookbook, 207
Joy of Cooking (Rombauer), 17, 133
Julia Child Award, 158

Kamman, Madeleine, 22, 35, 43, 57,
    76, 85, 104, 108, 124, 126–127,
    147, 199, 211, 221
  biographical information, 236–237
Keck, Katy, 6, 38, 66, 130–131,
    147–148, 152
  biographical information, 237
Keller, Loretta, 32, 93, 118, 143, 165,
    171, 187, 209
  biographical information, 237
Kelly, Melissa, 69–70, 106, 117–118,
    159, 175–176, 211–212
  biographical information, 237
Kennedy, Kathleen, 38, 67, 68, 72–73,
    149, 161–162
  biographical information, 238
Kids Up Front program, 191
Kiernan, Mary Pat, 67
Killeen, Johanne, 59, 77–78, 117, 137,
    173, 181, 210
  biographical information, 238
King, Shirley, 216
  biographical information, 238
Kitchen, reentry of women into, 7–9.
    See also Professional kitchen
"Kitchen Cabinet," 164, 248
*Kitchens: The Culture of Restaurant
    Work* (Fine), 30, 31
Kitchen staff, communication with din-
    ing room staff, 134–135
"Kitchen talk," 93
Knives, man's use of, 2
Kuck, Barbara, 42
  biographical information, 238–239
Kump, Christopher, 231
Kump, Peter, 232, 238

La Chapelle, Vincent, 22
La Cuisine Creole, 9
La Cuisiniere Cordon Bleu, 20
Ladies Home Journal, 16
La Fonda Hotel, 51
Lago, Pitita, 96
  biographical information, 239
Land. *See also* Sustainable agriculture

connecting to, 48
passion for, 46–48
protection of, 47
Langan, Sarah, 42, 91, 148
  biographical information, 239
Larson, Michela, 223
La Varenne, 231, 255
L'Order des Chevaliers du Saint Espris,
    20
Leavened bread, discovery of, 6
Le Cirque, 44, 51, 110
L'Ecole de Cordon Bleu, 163. *See also*
    Cordon Bleu Cooking School
L'Ecole de Cuisine Française, 239
L'Ecole des Trois Gourmandes, 67, 185,
    227
Le Cordon Bleu, 20, 107. *See also*
    Cordon Bleu Cooking School
Lee, Mother Ann, 8
Leffler, Janet, 24
Legal Sea Foods, 246, 246
Le Grand Monarque, 237
Le Guide Culinaire, 236
Lennon, Audrey, 37, 186, 188–189
  biographical information, 239
L'Avenue, 42, 51, 102
Le Perroquet, 39, 132, 230
Le Petit Cordon Bleu, 21, 149
Leslie, Eliza, 14, 43
L'Etoile, 51, 99, 245
Lettuce Entertain You, Inc., 227, 247
Levenherz, Carol, 79, 157, 212
  biographical information, 240
Levi-Strauss, Claude, 2, 5
Lewis, Edna, 29, 33, 34, 46, 56, 216
  biographical information, 240
Lewis, Rosa, 23, 113, 176
Limit setting, in the work world,
    112–114
Lindeborg, Susan McCreight, 51, 60,
    114, 140, 150–151, 151–152, 191
  biographical information, 241
Line cook, 119–121
  job description for, 257
Literacy, for women, 13
Little Meals (Gold), 233
Lobster Club, The, 30, 132, 164
Lockley, Jo Lynne, 240
London Worshipful Company of Bakers,
    11
Look & Cook, 255
L'Oasis, 132
Lucas, Dione, 21, 149
Luchetti, Emily, 32, 37, 46, 67, 80, 136,
    143, 162–163, 192, 215
  biographical information, 240–241
Lutèce, 250

Lutèce Cookbook (Soltner), 250
Lynch, Barbara, 59, 122, 156
  biographical information, 241
Lynch, Loretta, 182

Madeleine Kamman's School of
    Traditional French Cuisine, 43
Madison, Deborah, 50, 55, 59, 79,
    150, 176, 177
  biographical information, 241
Maison de Ville, 237
Maison Robert, 63
Making of a Cook (Kamman), 236
Male chefs, prestige associated with, 86
"Male" management model, 139
Management
  inequitable practices in, 205
  male versus female styles of, 137–142
  women's exclusion from, 89
  Zen philosophy of, 142
Marie Brizard recipe contest, 66
Marriott International, 172
Martinez, Zarela, 49, 62, 64
  biographical information, 242
Master chef, 31
  job description for, 258
Mastering the Art of French Cooking
    (Child), 67, 203, 227
Master pastry chef, 258
Matriarchal society, transition from, 7
Matt Murphy's, 226
Maurice et Charles Bistro, 102
Max on Main, 227
Mead, Margaret, 86
Media
  handling, 156
  role of, 107–110
  using to advantage, 157
Mediterranean Kitchen, The
    (Goldstein), 233
Megatrends for Women (Aburdene and
    Naisbitt), 138
Mennell, Stephen, 86
Mentoring, 148
  art of, 58–64
  meaning of, 177–180
Mentors
  influence on food attitudes, 59–61
  selecting, 126
  as teachers and professional advisors,
    61–64
Menu manuals, 134
Metz, Ferdinand, 47, 172–173, 217
  biographical information, 242
Metzler, H. J., 101
Miccosuke Indians, 5
Miller, Dave, 4

Milliken, Mary Sue, 39–40, 66–67, 72, 76, 95, 98–99, 114, 132, 159–160, 176, 192
biographical information, 230
Million-Man March, 188
Minor's Base Company, 63
Minorities, 198
equal opportunity for, 219
Miss Beecher's Domestic Receipt-Book (Beecher), 14–15
Miss Farmer's School of Cookery, 15, 21
Mitterer, Franz, 40
Modern Art of Chinese Cooking (Tropp), 158
Modern Gourmet Cooking School, 43, 236
Mondrian, 40
Montrachet, 40, 73, 156, 271
More Than a Mouthful, 223
Morrison-Clark Inn, 51, 241
Mortellaro, Kate, 79, 107
Moskowitz, Milton, 171
Mother/daughter food connection, 35
Moulton, Sara, 63, 159
biographical information, 243
Mozo, Corinna, 62, 63, 119, 139, 160–161
biographical information, 243
Mrs. McLintock's Receipts for Cookery and Pastry-Work, 17
Muir, Alison, 244
MultiCultural Foodservice and Hospitality Alliance, 219, 285
Murphy, Tamara, 32, 60, 80, 113, 139–140, 180
biographical information, 244
Mustards Grill, 45, 243
Myers, Leslie, 76, 125–126
biographical information, 243–244
Mythology, about nurture technology, 4–5

Nahmias, Dominique, 66
Naisbitt, John, 138
Natale, Chef, 69
National Childhood Hunger Day, 188–189
National Household Economics Association, 11
National Hunger Day, 188, 189
National Restaurant Association (NRA), 25, 219, 286
Business Culture's Impact on Restaurant Performance, 170, 171, 173
Compensation for Salaried Personnel in Foodservice, 170

Foodservice Employee Profile, 33, 36, 116, 138, 196, 220
Inside Consumers' Heads, 196
1996 Restaurant Industry Operations Report, 200
Restaurant Operations Report, 58
Women in Foodservice, 138, 205
Nations Restaurant News (NRN), 80, 200, 245
Native American foods, 45
Native American influences, 54–55
Natural foods, 176
Neely, Kristina, 44, 51, 125, 137
biographical information, 244
Negotiating skills, 89
Networking, using organizations for, 180–185
New England Culinary Institute, 42, 49, 125, 135, 229, 232, 239, 243
New England Kitchen, 22, 23
Newest or Great Universal Viennese Cookbook, a Guide to Cook for the Finest Tables in Ordinary Houses, Combining the Best of Taste and the Greatest Elegance, Taking Advantage of the Economic Possibilities to Make it Least Expense (Dorn), 14
New Professional Chef, 28
New World Grill, 6, 66, 130, 237
New York Restaurant School, 40, 236
New York Woman's Culinary Alliance, 243
Nieporent, Drew, 36, 40, 61, 236
1997 Guide to Cooking Schools, 22
1996 Restaurant Industry Operations Report (NRA), 200
Nobu, 236
Northeast Organic Farming Association (NOFA), 176
North Plank Road Tavern, 101
Nurturer role, 13
Nurture technology, 4–5
Nurturing instinct, food and, 38
Nutrition, advocacy for, 23. *See also* Chef and the Child Foundation (CCF)
Nutritional awareness, 198

Oakes, Nancy, 42–44, 51, 102, 109, 133, 145, 153, 155, 173
biographical information, 244
Oden, Loretta Barrett, 44–45, 48, 54–55
biographical information, 224

Oekologie, 23
Ogden, Bradley, 102, 226
Old Chatham Shepherding Company Inn, 106, 118, 175, 237
Oldways Preservation and Exchange Trust, 174, 286
Olney, Richard, 60
100 Best Companies for Working Mothers (Moskowitz and Townsend), 171, 198
"One Mouth at a Time," 239
O'Connell, Pat, 139
O'Connell, Rick, 56, 104, 167, 208
biographical information, 245
On-the-job teaching, 124–125
Open Hand Cookbook, 251
Operation Frontline, 191
Opryland, apprenticeship at, 68
Organic Gardening and Farming (Rodale), 155
Organic produce, 176
Organics movement, 48
Organizational skills, 118
Organizations, using for networking, 180–185
Orsi, Pierre, 252
Osteria del Circo, 44, 120, 251
Outsourcing, 198–199, 200
Overdorf, Jill, 120
Overtures & Finales, 240

Pacific Coast Chefs Association, 228
Page, Karen, 77
Palace, The, 40, 231
Palace Hotel, 235, 254
Palate, 46
Palladin, Jean-Louis, 61, 233, 236
Palmer House, 146
Panache, 229
Pan-American Olympics, 94
Pangeau, Gérard, 240
Pan Productions, 247
Pantry cook, job description for, 257
Parker House restaurant, 65
Park Hotel, 45
Parseghian, Pam, 80, 200
biographical information, 245
Partners, working with, 159
Passion
finding, 51
importance of, 214
Pastry chef, 121–122
job description for, 257
Pastry cook
job description for, 259
Patina, 40, 236
Pat O'Shea's Mad Hatter, 42, 244

Patriarchal Attitudes: Women in Society
    (Figes), 86
Patriarchal society, transition to, 7
Pawlcyn, Cindy, 45–46, 113
    biographical information, 245
Pay, discrepancies in, 89, 90
Peacock, Scott, 34
Peaks, The, 244
Peasant Stock, 235
Peer recognition, 149, 153–155
Pension plans, 173
People skills, 153
Pepperidge Farm (Bread), 24, 147
Perfection, desire for, 114
Periscope, 51, 60
Perrault, Michael, 137–138
Perry, Nadsa, 68
    biographical information, 242–243
Personal chefs, 122
Personal life, balancing with success,
    162–165
Personal sacrifices, 81–83
    relationships and, 83–84
Personnel, salaries for, 203
Peter Principle, 105–106
Pignoli, 63, 250
Pillsbury "Bake-Off," 175
Piper, Odessa, 48, 51, 71, 99, 153, 176
    biographical information, 245–246
Place, Dominique, 244
Planning, importance of, 217
Pleasant, Mammy, 55
Pomodoro, 186, 226
Ponte, Guida, 55
    biographical information, 246
Ponzek, Debra, 25, 29, 36, 40, 73, 131,
    156–157, 186, 271
    biographical information, 246
Portrait of a Chef: The Life of Alexis Soyer,
    11
Post, Marjorie Merriweather, 123
Postrio, 92, 102, 226, 232
Pothier, Maureen, 133, 184, 191–192
    biographical information, 246
Pouillon, Nora, 33–34, 45, 48, 74, 100,
    139, 161
    biographical information, 246–247
Prehistoric peoples, eating habits of, 2
Press, role of, 107–110. *See also* Media
Price, Pam, 160
Products
    first nutritional investigation of, 12
    outsourcing, 198–199, 200
Professional Chef, The, 68
Professional cooking, beginnings of,
    12–13
Professionalism, in management style, 142

Professional kitchen
    women's entry into, 22–25
    women in the upper echelons of,
        116–122
Professional persona, forming, 62
Programs, education and apprenticeship,
    64–69
Project Open Hand, 75, 81, 228, 228
Prudhomme, Paul, 242
Puck, Wolfgang, 92, 102, 232

Quilted Giraffe, 36

Radin, Stacy, 92
    biographical information, 247
Rainbow Room, 30
Randolph, Mary, 14, 41
Rappaport, Amelia, 143
Rathbun, Mickey, 3
Reading, importance of, 218
Real Restaurants, 45, 113, 245
Receipt Book (Fettiplaces), 13
Recipe development, 122
Recognition, importance of, 153–155
Redoubt Bay Lodge, 38
Regis, Susan, 63, 109, 117, 143,
    163–164, 174
    biographical information, 247
Reid, Evelyn, 7
Relationships
    culinary careers and, 77–79
    effect of sacrifices on, 83–84
*Remember the Ladies—Women in America
    1750–1835* (DePauw and Hunt), 9,
    15
Remote locations, working in, 106–107
Resorts, apprenticeship at, 68
Respect, gaining, 92
Responsibility, delegating, 135–136
Restaurant business, women in, 25–26.
    See also Business ownership
Restaurant Business magazine, 204
Restaurant Charlotte, 255
Restaurant industry, wages in, 201–205
*Restaurant Industry Forecast Gets Inside
    Consumers' Heads*, 47
Restaurant Leslie, 108, 247
Restaurant L'Olympe, 132
Restaurant Nora, 33, 100, 246, 247
Restaurant openings, 117–118
Restaurant ownership, 97–100, 127–137.
    See also Business ownership
Restaurant Raji, 44, 79–80, 236
Restaurants
    financing, 100
    independent, 197

Resume writing, 217
Reuter, Laurene R., 90
Revel, Jean-François, 7, 12, 142–143
Revsin, Leslie, 107–108, 118,
    152–153, 154, 155, 243
    biographical information, 247
Rialto, 35, 223
Richards, Ellen Swallow, 10, 22, 23,
    119, 124
Rising High Dough Rollers, 37
Rising Star Chef award, 61, 156
Risk taking, 110–112
Ritz Carlton (Atlanta), apprenticeship
    at, 68
Ritz Carlton (Chicago), 252
Riversong Adventures, 229
Riversong Lodge, 38, 106
Robert Mondavi Wine and Food
    Center, 233
Rodale, J. I., 155
Rodgers, Judy, 40, 135, 165,
    202–205, 211, 218
    biographical information, 248
Role models, for women chefs, 58–64.
    See also Mentors
Rombauer, Irma, 17, 133
Rosenzweig, Anne, 30, 37, 54, 57, 95,
    109, 130, 132, 138, 143, 164,
    178, 181, 187–188, 201,
    205–206, 209
    biographical information, 248
Roth, Frances, 21, 22
Roundsman, job description for, 257
RoxSand, 59–60, 249–250
Rubicon, 40, 61, 236
Rudkin, Margaret, 24, 147
Runcible Spoon, 252
Ruskays', 204

Sailhac, Alain, 2, 54, 116
    biographical information, 248
Salary, negotiating, 89
Salcido, Silvana, 41
Salvato, Cindy, 83, 91, 125, 128–129,
    148, 163, 186, 208
    biographical information, 248–249
Sanders, Barbara, 104, 179, 187,
    212–213
    biographical information, 249
San Francisco Free Clinic, 187
Sanitation in Daily Life (Richards), 10
Sara Lee Corporation, 171–172
Saucier, job description for, 257
Savannah Seasons (Terry), 252
Savoir Faire Foods, 6, 237
Savoring the Past (Wheaton), 5–6
Savory Way, The (Madison), 241

Scherber, Amy, 40, 81, 98, 150, 185
  biographical information, 249
Schloo-Yazujian, Linda A., 111
Schmidt, Arno, 108
Scholarships, 186
School lunch programs, 23
Schroeder, Lisa, 28
Schwartz, Felice, 87, 90, 206–207
Scleroderma Research Foundation, 132, 192
Scocos, RoxSand, 59–60, 69, 73–74, 150
  biographical information, 249–250
Seasonal buying, 48
Seasons Restaurant, 63
Sea World food recovery program, 190
Second Harvest, 190, 287
Self-instruction, 212, 213
Senate Award for Educator of the Year, 154
Settlement Cookbook (Black), 17, 111
Settlement House, 17
Sexism, 90–93
Sexual harassment, 89
  dealing with, 93–94
Shaker sect, 8
Share Our Strength (SOS) program, 191–192, 287
Shaw Guides' *The Guide to Cooking Schools*, 22, 207
Shine, Lindsey, 59
Shire, Lydia, 36, 62, 63, 70, 139
  biographical information, 250
Shore, Billy, 191
Signature Foods, 62
Silent Spring (Carson), 205
Silverton, Nancy, 72
Simmons, Amelia, 14, 25
Slave women, in culinary history, 8–9
Small businesses, woman-owned, 197.
  See also Business ownership
Smith, Eliza, 14, 21
Smith, Karen, 72, 100
Socially responsible causes, women's role in, 185–192
Society for the Revival and Preservation of Southern Food, 34
Sohn, Joung, 110
Soltner, André, 22, 30, 31, 39, 97
  biographical information, 250
Somerville, Annie, 142, 251
Sonnenschmidt, Fritz, 92, 93–94, 199–200, 208, 213–214, 219
  biographical information, 250
Sortun, Ana, 26, 47, 62, 66, 113, 176, 212

biographical information, 251
Sous chef, 119
  job description for, 258, 259
Southern cooking, 34
Spago, 232
Specialty products, 198–199
Spicer, Susan, 105, 139, 177, 190, 216, 218
  biographical information, 251
Splichal, Joachim, 40
Square One, 129, 233
Sstarbirth, 192
Staff
  communication with, 141
  hiring, 130
  working with, 133–135
Staffing, challenges of, 201
Stagière, 40, 65, 105, 110
StarBake, 32, 240
Stark, Nancy, 44, 79, 81–82, 110, 205
  biographical information, 251
Stars, 32, 118
Station, defined, 258
Stegner, Sarah, 62–63, 105, 126, 135–136, 142, 165, 166, 178, 182, 214–215
  biographical information, 252
Stephenson, June, 5
Stewart, Claire, 30–31, 38, 69, 82, 95, 111
  biographical information, 252
Storch, Anita L., 73
Stouffer's, 24, 181
Stratford Chefs School, 62
Stress, handling, 116, 120
Striped Bass, 99, 224
"Student of the Year" award, 207
Substance abuse, in the chef profession, 96–97
Success
  achieving, 151–153
  balancing with family, 159–162
  balancing with job priorities, 165–168
  balancing with other life factors, 157–158
  balancing with personal life, 162–165
  challenges accompanying, 155–157
  defining, 146–158
  elusiveness of, 150–151
  peer recognition and, 153–155
Successful Poultry Journal, The, 12
Susanna Foo's Chinese Restaurant, 130, 230
Sustainable agriculture, 34, 47, 176
Sustainable food choices, 176
Szathmáry, Louis, 25, 42, 238

Tannahill, Reay, 6
Teaching, on-the-job, 124–125

Team players, women as, 140
Teams, fostering, 133–135
Terry, Elizabeth, 131, 152, 212
  biographical information, 252
Thibodeau, Pat, 63–64, 102–103, 189–191
  biographical information, 252–253
Tocque, 29
Toll House Inn, 141
"Too Hot Tamales," 40, 132, 230
Tools, women's, 2
Torres, Jacques, 44, 110, 251
Toussaint-Samat, Maguelonne, 6
Tower, Jeremiah, 32
Towey, Maureen, 98
Townsend, Carol, 171
Training. *See also* Apprenticeship experience
  French, 65–67
  importance of, 209
  responsibility for, 208
  of staff, 136
  in the United States, 68
Tramonto, Rick, 49
Trends, predicting, 199–205
Trio, 49, 231
Troisgros, 65
Tropp, Barbara, 31–32, 44, 49–50, 56–57, 99–100, 103, 113, 129–130, 156, 158, 161, 181, 182
  biographical information, 253
Trotter, Charlie, 161
TV Food Network, 40, 230
"21" Club, 164, 253
Twohy, Cherie, 110

U.S. Women's Pure Food Vacuum Preserving Co., 97
United States
  apprenticeship in, 68
  culinary influences on, 54
  history of women and food in, 7–9
Upstairs at the Pudding, 235

Vanessa, 164
Vanilla Bean Bakery, 231
Vegetarian food, 55
Vegetarian Table: America (Madison), 241
Velgos, Monica, 80
  biographical information, 253
Venus and the Cowboy, 99, 224
Verbena, 231
Victory gardens, 157, 159
Virginia Housewife, The (Randolph), 14, 41
Visibility, importance of, 153

Visser, Margaret, 5
von Rumford, Count, 8

Wages, trends in, 201–205
Wakefield, Ruth, 141
Walnut Acres Organic Farms, 173
Washburne Trade School, 132
Waters, Alice, 25, 31, 47, 48, 59–60,
    108, 170, 176
    biographical information, 253
Waynes, Sharon, 144, 178
    biographical information, 254
Way to Cook, The (Child), 67
Weaver, Susan, 36, 62–63, 83,
    110–111
    biographical information, 254
Wegman's Food Markets, 172
Wertz, Janis, 154, 201, 206
    biographical information, 254
West Side Café, 251
*What Mrs. Fisher Knows About Old
    Southern Cooking* (Fisher), 87
Wheaton, Barbara, 5
White, Jasper, 63
Whitman, Frankie, 182
    biographical information, 254–255
Who's Who of Food and Wine, 229
Wiederhold, Brittany, 91
Willan, Anne, 22, 124
    biographical information, 255
Williams, Patricia, 36, 120
    biographical information, 255
Wine, Barry, 36
Wine making, women and, 6
Winterlake Lodge, 38
Wittenmyer, Annie, 71
Woman's Congress, 11
Woman's Culinary Guild of New
    England, 243

*Woman's Evolution: Matriarchal Clan to
    Patriarchal Family* (Reid), 7
Woman's Home Companion, 16
Woman's magazines, 16
Women. *See also* Women chefs
    colonial, 13, 15
    cookbooks and, 13–19
    cooking schools and, 20–22
    early roles of, 2–7
    exclusion from the chef profession, 2,
        86–90
    experiences with discrimination, 90–96
    in the labor force, 59
    nonassertiveness among, 213
    perspectives on workplace goals,
        172–177
    as providers, 5
    in the restaurant business, 25–26
    socialized roles of, 138–139
    support for women by, 220
    workplace role of, 206–207
"Women, Food, and Technology"
    (Miller), 4
Women, Infants, and Children (WIC)
    program, 192, 245
Women chefs
    American influences on, 54–56
    changes concerning, 25
    cultural influences on, 54–58
    educational influences on, 68–69
    influences on, 33–38
    international influences on, 56–58
    role models of, 58–64
    studies on, 86
    as teachers, 123–124
Women Chefs and Restaurateurs (WCR),
    70, 116, 132, 158, 164, 205–206,
    180–183, 219, 254, 288
Women Chefs for Peace, 164

Women foodservice employees, statistics
    on, 33
Women in Foodservice (NRA), 138, 205
"Women's Laboratory" (MIT), 23
"Women's Leadership Style," 138
Women's roles
    in the culinary industry, 116–122
    Industrial era through early 1900s,
        9–13
    in socially responsible causes, 185–192
*Women's Roots, Status and Achievements
    in Western Civilization*
    (Stephenson), 5
Women's work styles, 137–142
Work, obsession with, 166–168
Workaholism, 160, 167–168
Working pastry chef, job description for,
    259
Work methods, women's, 140
Workplace, role of women in, 206–207
Workplace goals, women's perspectives
    on, 172–177
Workplace model, change in, 172–173,
    206
Work styles, women's versus men's,
    137–142
World's Colombian Exposition, 11
World's Cooks Tour, 179
World Cup Pastry team, 226

Yalow, Dr. Rosalyn S., 259

Zagat Survey, 128
Zarela, 62, 242
Zen Center, 49
Zen management philosophy, 141–142
Zimmerman, Jean, 87, 90, 206–207
Zuni Café and Grill, 135, 248
Zuni Indians, 4–5

Identification of Women Chefs in Cover and Chapter-Opener Photographs

Front Cover Chef List (left to right)

Patricia Williams
Elizabeth Terry
Madeleine Kamman
Annie Somerville
Ann Cooper
Cindy Pawlcyn
Diane Forley
Mika Iijima
Roxsand Scocos
Ariane Daguin
Loretta Barrett Oden
Clara F. Craig
Catherine Brandell
Longteine de Monteiro and
    Madsa de Monteiro-Perry
Joyce Goldstein
Monique Barbeau
Sara Moulton
Lidia Bastianich
Odessa Piper
Gwen Kvavli Gulliksen
Susanna Foo
Kerry Heffernan
Nancy Oakes

Back Cover Chef List (left to right)

Gale Gand
Anne Willan
Guida Ponte
Gloria Ciccarone-Nehls
Deborah Hughes
Emily Luchetti
Margaret Fox
Pitita Lago
Siobhan Carew
Sarah Stegner
Claire Stewart
Susan Weaver
Alison Muir
Nora Pouillon
Leslie Revsin
Amy Scherber
Raji Jallepalli
Katy Keck

Chapter Two Opener List
(left to right) Page 27

Loretta Barrett Oden
Eve Felder
Susan McCreight Lindeborg
Nora Pouillon
Madeleine Kamman
Kerry Heffernan
Loretta Keller
Edna Lewis
Traci Des Jardins
Ana Sortun

Chapter Three Opener List
(left to right) Page 53

Deborah Madison
Raji Jallepalli
Kirsten Dixon
Jody Adams
Roxsand Scocos
Corinna Mozo
Nancy Stark
Alice Waters
Julia Child
Lydia Shire

Chapter Four Opener List
(left to right) Page 85

Dell Hargis
Sarah Langan
Claire Stewart
Jamie Eisenberg
Alison Barshak
Lucie Costa
Judi Arnold
Leslie Revsin
Suzanne Bussiere
Lyde Buchtenkirch-Biscardi

Chapter Five Opener List
(left to right) Page 115

Hilary DeMane
Johanne Killeen
Lidia Bastianich
Alison Awerbuch

Katy Keck
Susan Feniger and Mary Sue Milliken
Deena Chafetz
Leslie Myers
Laureen Gauthier
Cindy Salvato
Joyce Goldstein

Chapter Six Opener List
(left to right) Page 145

Nancy Oakes
Sarah Stegner
Gloria Ciccarone-Nehls
Debra Ponzek
Rozanne Gold
Dina Altieri
Barbara Lynch
Noëlle Haddad
Annes Rosenzweig
Barbara Tropp

Chapter Seven Opener List
(left to right) Page 169

Siobhan Carew
Melissa Kelly
Frankie Whitman
Susan Spicer
Phyllis Flaherty
Amy Scherber
Audrey Lennon
Maureen Pothier
Odessa Piper
Barbara Sanders

Chapter Eight Opener List
(left to right) Page 195

Emily Luchetti
Gwen Kvavli Gulliksen
Carol Levenherz
Shirley King
Pam Parseghian
Dorothy Cann Hamilton
Janis Wertz
Debbie Gold
Tracy Cundiff
Pat Bartholomew